Outlines of Journalism

Outlines of Journalism

Sanoj Singh

RANDOM PUBLICATIONS
NEW DELHI (INDIA)

Outlines of Journalism

ISBN 978-93-5111-633-2

Published in 2015 in India by

RANDOM PUBLICATIONS

4376-A/4B, Gali Murari Lal, Ansari Road
New Delhi-110 002
Phone : +9111-43580356, 011-23289044, 011-43142548
e-mail: sales@randompublications.com,
info@randompublications.com, randomexports@gmail.com

Reprinted 2024

Type Setting by : Friends Media, Delhi-110089
Digitally Printed at : Replika Press Pvt. Ltd.

Preface

Journalism is gathering, processing, and dissemination of news and information related to the news to an audience. The word applies to both the method of inquiring for news and the literary style which is used to disseminate it.

The role and status of journalism, along with that of the mass media, has undergone profound changes over the last two decades with the advent of digital technology and publication of news on the Internet. This has created a shift in the consumption of print media channels, as people increasingly consume news through e-readers, smartphones, and other electronic devices, challenging news organizations to fully monetize their digital wing, as well as improvise on the context in which they publish news in print.

Journalism is a discipline of collecting, analyzing, verifying, and presenting news regarding currentevents, trends, issues and people. Those who practice journalism are known as journalists. News-oriented journalism is sometimes described as the "first rough draft of history", because journalists often record important events, producing news articles on short deadlines.

While under pressure to be first with their stories, news media organizations usually edit and proofread their reports prior to publication, adhering to each organization's standards of accuracy, quality and style. Many news organizations claim proud traditions of holding government officials and institutions accountable to the public, while media critics have raised questions about holding the press itself accountable.

The history of journalism, or the gathering and transmitting of news, spans the growth of technology and trade, marked by the advent of specialized techniques for gathering and disseminating information on a regular basis that has caused, as one history of journalism surmises, the steady increase of "the scope of news available to us and the speed with which it is transmitted."

This book is essential reading for practising journalists, students and scholars of journalism and mass communication and also the informed/ interested general reader.

I would like to thank my team for standing beside me throughout my career and writing this book. My special thanks go to "Random Publications" who have published the book.

– Sanoj Singh

Contents

1

Introduction

New Journalism was a style of 1960s and 1970s news writing and journalism which used literary techniques deemed unconventional at the time. The term was codified with its current meaning by Tom Wolfe in a 1973 collection of journalism articles he published as *The New Journalism*, which included works by himself, Truman Capote, Hunter S. Thompson, Norman Mailer, Joan Didion, Robert Christgau, and others.

Articles in the New Journalism style tended not to be found in newspapers, but rather in magazines such as *The Atlantic Monthly*, *CoEvolution Quarterly*, *Esquire Magazine*, *New York*, *The New Yorker*, *Rolling Stone*, and for a short while in the early 1970s, *Scanlan's Monthly*.

Various trends and tendencies throughout the history of American Journalism have been labeled "new journalism." Robert E. Park, for instance, in his *Natural History of the Newspaper,* referred to the advent of the penny press in the 1830s as "new journalism."

Likewise, the appearance of the yellow press, papers such as Joseph Pulitzer's *New York World* in the 1880s, led journalists and historians to proclaim that a "New Journalism" had been created. Ault and Emery, for instance, said "Industrialization and urbanization changed the face of American during the latter half of the Nineteenth century, and its newspapers entered an era known as that of the 'New Journalism.'

"In 1960 John Hohenberg, in *The Professional Journalist,* called the interpretive reporting which developed after World War II a "new journalism which not only seeks to explain as well as to inform; it even dares to teach, to measure, to evaluate."

During the sixties and seventies the term enjoyed widespread popularity, often with meanings bearing manifestly little or no connection with one another. Although James E. Murphy noted that '"...most user of the term seem to refer to something more specific than vague new directions in journalism" Curtis D. MacDougal devoted the Preface of the Sixth Edition of his *Interpretative Reporting* to New Journalism and cataloged many of the contemporary definitions: "Activist, advocacy, participatory, tell-it-as-you-see-it, sensitivity, investigative, saturation, humanistic, reformist and a few more." *The Magic Writing Machine—Student Probes of the New Journalism,* a collection edited and introduced by Everette E. Dennis, came up with six categories, labelled new non-fiction (reportage), alternative journalism ("modern muckraking"), advocacy journalism, underground journalism and precision journalism. Michael Johnson's *The New Journalism* addresses itself to three phenomena: the underground press, the artists of Non-fiction, and changes in the established media.

Journalists recognized as using the style include Norman Mailer, Joan Didion, Truman Capote, P. J. O'Rourke, George Plimpton, Terry Southern, and Gay Talese. Hunter S. Thompson was a major practitioner of new journalism and gonzo journalism, his own particular style.

Thompson's first book, *Hell's Angels: The Strange and Terrible Saga of the Outlaw Motorcycle Gangs*, is a more conventional piece, and shows the beginnings of a more memoir-based approach to reportage. Gay Talese's 1966 article for Esquire, *Frank Sinatra Has a Cold*, was an influential piece of new journalism that gave a detailed portrait of Frank Sinatra without ever interviewing him.

New journalism writers brought new approaches to areas already covered by the mainstream press. The psychedelic movement was something that many of the writers of the period covered, such as in Tom Wolfe's *The Electric Kool-Aid Acid Test.* The Vietnam War was another common topic, as was the political turmoil on the homefront. Terry Southern's Grooving in Chi documented the 1968 Chicago National Democratic Convention for Esquire Magazine in new journalism manner.

New journalism's techniques were also applied to less obvious subjects, such as financial markets (by George Goodman under the pseudonym Adam Smith, in essays originally published in New York Magazine and later collected in a book called *The Money Game*.)

Some authors of conventional fiction switched to writing in the style of new journalism, such as Truman Capote's *In Cold Blood*, and Norman Mailer's *Armies of the Night*. However, neither author ever agreed to their style's comparison to Wolfe's school of narration, nor did many others who have been retrospectively promoted as being members and therein associated. Much to the contrary, many of these writers would deny that their work was generically relevant to other new journalists at the time.

EARLY DEVELOPMENT

THE SIXTIES

How and when the term New Journalism began to refer to a genre has not been clear. Tom Wolfe, a practitioner and principal advocate of the form, wrote in at least two articles in 1972 that he had no idea of where it began.

Trying to shed light on the matter, literary critic Seymour Krim, offered his explanation in 1973. I'm certain that [Pete] Hamill first used the expression. In about April of 1965 he called me at *Nugget* Magazine, where I was editorial director, and told me he wanted to write an article about new New Journalism.

It was to be about about the exciting things being done in the old reporting genre by Talese, Wolfe and Breslin. He never wrote the piece, so far as I know, but I began using the expression in conversation and writing. It was picked up and stuck. But wherever and whenever the term arose, there is evidence of some literary experimentation in the early 1960s, as when Norman Mailer broke away from fiction to write *Superman Comes to the Supermarket* A report of John F. Kennedy's nomination that year, the piece established a precedent which Mailer would later build on in his 1968 convention coverage (*Miami and the Siege of Chicago*) and in other Non-fiction as well.

Wolfe wrote that his first acquaintance with a new style of reporting came in a 1962 *Esquire* article about Joe Louis by Gay Talese. "'Joe Louis at Fifty' wasn't like a magazine article at all. It was like a short story. It began with a scene, an intimate confrontation between Loius and his third wife..." Wolfe said Talese was the first to apply fiction techniques to reporting.

Esquire claimed credit as the seedbed for these new techniques. *Esquire* editor Harold Hayes later wrote that "in the Sixties, events seemed to move too swiftly to allow the osmotic process of art to keep abreast, and when we found a good novelist we immediately sought to seduce him with the sweet mysteries of current events." Soon others, notably *New York,* followed *Esquire's* lead, and the style eventually infected other magazines and then books.

THE SEVENTIES

Much of the criticism favorable to this New Journalism came from the writers themselves. Talese and Wolfe, in a panel discussion cited earlier, asserted that, although what they wrote may look like fiction, it was indeed reporting: "Fact reporting, leg work." Talese called it.

Wolfe, in *Esquire* for December, 1972, hailed the replacement of the novel by the New Journalism as literature's "main event" and detailed the points of similarity and contrast between the New Journalism and the novel. The four techniques of realism that he and the other New Journalists employed, he wrote, had been the sole province of novelists and other *literati.*

They are scene-by-scene construction, full record of dialogue, third-person point of view and the manifold incidental details to round out character (*i.e.*, descriptive incidentals). the result... is a form that is not merely like a *novel.* It consumes devices that happen to have originated with the novel and mixes them with every other device known to prose. And all the while, quite beyond matters of technique, it enjoys an advantage so obvious, so built-in, one almost forgets what power it has': the simple fact that the reader knows *all this actually happened.* The disclaimers have been erased. The screen is gone. The writer is one step closer to the absolute involvement of the reader that Henry James and James Joyce dreamed of but never achieved.

The essential difference between the new Non-fiction and conventional reporting is, he said, that the basic unit of reporting was no longer the datum or piece of information but the scene. Scene is what underlies "the sophisticated strategies of prose." The first of the new breed of Non-fiction writers to receive wide notoriety was Truman Capote, whose 1965 best-seller, *In Cold Blood,* was a detailed narrative of the murder of a Kansas farm family. Capote culled material from some 6000 pages of notes.

The book brought its author instant celebrity. Capote announced that he had created a new art form which he labelled the "Non-fiction novel." I've always had the theory that reportage is the great unexplored art form... I've had this theory that a factual piece of work could explore whole new dimensions in writing that would have a double effect fiction does not have—the every fact of its being true, every word of its true, would add a double contribution of strength and impact. Capote continued to stress that he was a literary artist, not a journalist, but critics hailed the book as a classic example of New Journalism.

Wolfe's *The Kandy-Kolored Tangerine-Flake Streamline Baby,* whose introduction and title story, according to James E. Murphy, "emerged as a manifest of sorts for the Non-fiction genre," was published the same year. In his introduction Wolfe wrote that he encountered trouble fashioning an *Esquire* article out of material on a custom car extravaganza in Los Angeles, in 1963. Finding he could not do justice to the subject in magazine article format, he wrote a letter to his editor, Byron Dobell, which grew into a 49-page report detailing the custom car world, complete with scene construction, dialogue and flamboyant description. *Esquire* ran the letter, striking out "Dear Byron." and it became Wolfe's maiden effort as a New Journalist. In an article entitled "The Personal Voice and the Impersonal Eye," Dan Wakefield acclaimed the Non-fiction of Capote and Wolfe as elevating reporting to the level of literature, terming that work and some of Norman Mailer's Non-fiction a journalistic breakthrough: reporting "charged with the energy of art"

A review by Jack Newfield of Dick Schaap's *Turned On* saw the book as a good example of budding tradition in American journalism which rejected many of the constraints of conventional reporting: This new genre defines itself by claiming many of the techniques that were once the unchalanged terrain of the novelist: tension, symbol, cadence, irony, prosody, imagination. A 1968 review of Wolfe's *The Pump House Gang* and *The Electric Kool-Aid Acid Test* said Wolfe and Mailer were applying "the imaginative resources of fiction" to the world around them and termed such creative journalism "hystory" to connote their involvement in what they reported. Talese in 1970, in his Author's Note to *Fame and Obscurity,* a collection of his pieces from the 1960s, wrote:

The new journalism, though often reading like fiction, is not fiction. It is, or should be, more reliable as the most reliable reportage although it seeks a larger truth than is possible through the mere compilation of verifiable facts, the use of direct quotations, and adherence to the rigid organizational style of the older form.

Seymour Krim's *Shake It for the World, Smartass* which appeared in 1970, contained "An Open Letter to Norman Mailer" which defined New Journalism as "a free Non-fictional prose that uses every resource of the best fiction." And in "The Newspaper As Literature/Literature As Leadership" he called journalism the *de facto* literature of the majority, a synthesis of journalism and literature that the book's postscript called "journalit."

In 1972, in "An Enemy of the Novel" Krim identified his own fictional roots and declared that the needs of the time compelled him to move beyond fiction to a more "direct" communication to which he promised to bring all of fiction's resources.

David McHam, in an article titled "The Authentic New Journalists," distinguished the Non-fiction reportage of Capote, Wolfe and others from other, more generic interpretations of New Journalism. Also in 1971, William L. Rivers disparaged the former and embraced the latter, concluding, "In some hands, they add a flavour and a humanity to journalistic writing that push it into the realm of art."

Charles Brown in 1972 reviewed much that had been written as New Journalism and about New Journalism by Capote, Wolfe, Mailer and others and labelled the genre "New Art Journalism," which allowed him to test it both as art and as journalism. He concluded that the new literary form was useful only in the hands of literary artists of great talent.

In the first of two pieces by Wolfe in *New York* detailing the growth of the new Non-fiction and its techniques. Wolfe returned to the fortuitous circumstances surrounding the construction of *Kandy-Kolored* and added:

Its virtue was precisely in showing me the possibility of there being something "new" in journalism. What interested me was not simply the discovery that it was possible to write accurate Non-fiction with techniques usually associated with novels and short stories.

It was that—plus. It was the discovery that it was possible in Non-fiction, in journalism, to use any literary device, from the traditional dialogisms of the essay to stream-of-consciousness...

THE EIGHTIES

In the Eighties the use of New Journalism saw a decline, several of the old trailblazers still used fiction techniques in their Non-fiction books. But younger writers in *Esquire* and *Rolling Stone,* where the style had flourished in the two earlier decades, shifted away from the New Journalism. Fiction techniques had not been abandoned by these writers, but they were used sparingly and less flamboyantly. "Whatever happened to the New Journalism?" wondered Thomas Powers in a 1975 issue of *Commonweal*. In 1981, Joe Nocera published a postmortem in the *Washington Monthly* blaming its demise on the journalistic liberties taken by Hunter S. Thompson. Regardless of the culprit, less than a decade after Tom Wolfe's 1973 New Journalism anthology, the consensus was that New Journalism was dead.

HISTORY AND GROWTH OF JOURNALISM

Journalism is a discipline of collecting, analyzing, verifying, and presenting news regarding currentevents, trends, issues and people. Those who practice journalism are known as journalists. News-oriented journalism is sometimes described as the "first rough draft of history", because journalists often record important events, producing news articles on short deadlines. While under pressure to be first with their stories, news media organizations usually edit and proofread their reports prior to publication, adhering to each organization's standards of accuracy, quality and style. Many news organizations claim proud traditions of holding government officials and institutions accountable to the public, while media critics have raised questions about holding the press itself accountable.

The history of journalism, or the gathering and transmitting of news, spans the growth of technology and trade, marked by the advent of specialized techniques for gathering and disseminating information on a regular basis that has caused, as one history of journalism surmises, the steady increase of "the scope of news available to us and the speed with which it is transmitted."

PREHISTORIC, ANCIENT AND MIDIEVAL PERIODS

Early methods of transmitting news began with word of mouth, which limited its content to what people saw and relayed to others; accuracy in new depended on the scope of the event being described and its relevance to the listener. Ancient monarchial governments developed ways of relaying written reports, includinng the Roman Empire from Julius Caeser onward, which recorded and distributed a daily record of political news and acts to Roman colonies. After the empire collapsed, news dissemination depended on travelers' tails, songs and ballads, letters, and governmental dispatches.

The Renaissance Period

The invention of the movable type printing press, attributed to Johannes Gutenberg in 1456, led to the wide dissemination of the Bible and other printed books. The first newspapers appeared in Europe in the 17th Century. The first printed periodical was the Mercurius Gallobelgicus, first appearing in Cologne, now Germany, in 1592; it consisted of Latin text, was printed semiannually and distributed in book fairs. The first regularly published newspaper was the Oxford Gazette, first appearing in 1665, which began while the British royal court was in Oxford to avoid the plague in London and was published twice a week. When the court moved back to London, the publication moved with it. An earlier newsbook, the Continuation of Our Weekly News, had been published regularly in London since 1623.

The first daily newspaper, the Daily Courant, appeared in 1702 and continued publication for more than 30 years. Its first editor was also the first woman in journalism, although she was replaced after only a couple of weeks. By this time, the British had adopted the Press Restriction Act, which required that the printer's name and place of publication be included on each printed document.

The first printer in Britian's American colonies was Stephen Day in Cambridge, Massachusetts, who began in 1638. The British regulation of printing extended to the Colonies. The first newspaper in the colonies, Benjamnin Harris's Publick Occurences both Foreighn and Domestick, was supressed in 1690 after only one issue under a 1662 Massachusetts law that forbade printing without a licence. The publication of a story suggesting that the King of France shared a bed with his son's wife probably also contributed to the suppression.

A second newspaper, the Boston News-Letter, appeared in 1704. It was not suppressed, but it was late reporting local and European news and survived until 1722. The first newspaper published outside New England was Andrew Bradford's American Weekly Mercury, which published between 1719 and 1746.

The first real colonial newspaper was the New England Courant, published as a sideline by printer James Franklin, brother of Benjamin Franklin. Like many other Colonial newspapers, it was aligned with party interests and did not publish balanced content. Ben Franklin was first published in his brother's newspaper, under the pseudonym Silence Dogood, in 1722, and even his brother did not know. Ben Franklin's pseudonymous publishing represented a common practice of newspapers of that time of protecting writers from retribution from those they criticized, often to the point of what would be considered libel today.

After James Franklin suspended publication of the Courant, Ben Franklin moved to Philadelphia in 1728 and took over the Pennsylvania Gazette the following year. Ben Franklin expanded his business by essentially franchising other printers in other cities, who published their own newspapers. By 1750, 14 weekly newspapers were published in the six largest colonies. The largest and most successful of these could be published up to three times per week.

By the 1770s, 89 newspapers were published in 35 cities. "Most papers at the time of the American Revolution were anti-royalist, chiefly because of opposition to the Stamp Act taxing newsprint." Though the tax was imposed on newsprint, not publication itself, Colonial governments could supress newspapers "by denying the stamp or refusing to sell approved paper to the offending publihser."

Newspapers flourished in the new republic — by 1800, there were about 234 being published — and tended to be very partisan about the form of the new federal government, which was shaped by successive Federalist or Republican presidencies. Newspapers directed much abuse Towards various polticians, and the eventual dual between Alexander Hamilton and Aaron Burr was fueled by controversy in newspaper pages.

As the 19th Century progressed in America, newspapers began functioning more as private businesses with real editors rather than partisan organs, though standards for truth and responsibillity were still low. "Other than local news, much of the reporting was simply copied from other newspapers, sometimes verbatim. In addition to news stories, there might be poetry or fiction, or (especially late in the century) humorous columns.Newspapers in general remained political with strong bias Towards the government; Andrew Jackson started his own newspaper, funnelled government printing work to it, and forced his Washington competition out of business. As American cities like New York, Philadelphia, Boston and Washington grew with the growth of the Industrial Revolution, so did newspapers. Larger printing presses, the telegraph and other technological innovations allowed newspapers to print thousands of copies, boost circulation and increase revenue.The first newspaper to fit the modern definition as a newspaper was the New York Herald, founded in 1835 and published by James Gordon Bennett.

It was the first newspaper to have city staff covering regular beats and spot news, along with regular business and Wall Street coverage. In 1838 Bennett also organized the first foreign correspondent staff of six men in Europe and assigned domestic correspondents to key cities, including the first reporter to regularly cover Congress.Not to be outdone was the New York Tribune, which began publishing in 1841 and was edited by Horace Greeley. It was the first newspaper to gain national prominence; by 1861, it shipped thousands of copies daily to other large cities, including 6,000 to Chicago, while other Eastern newspapers published weekly editions for shipment to other cities. Greeley also organized a professional news staff and embarked on frequent publishing crusades for causes he believed in.

The Tribune was the first newspaper, in 1886, to use the linotype machine, invented by Ottmar Mergenthaler, which "rapidly increased the speed and accuracy with which type could be set."The New York Times, now considered one of the best newspapers in the world, was founded in 1851 by George Jones and Henry Raymond. It established the principle of balanced reporting in high-quality writing. At the time, it did not acheive the circulation and success it now enjoys.The influence of these large newspapers in New York and other Eastern cities slowly spread to smaller cities and towns, Weekly newspapers gave way to dailies, and competition between newspapers even in small towns became fierce.In the Midwest and beyond, there was a boom for local newspapers, which remained more focused on local news and services than the larger urban newspapers. Many newspapers flourished during the conquest of the West, as homesteaders were required to publish notices of their land claims in local newspapers. Many of these papers died out after the land rushes ended.

The Rise of the Wire Services

The American Civil War had a profound effect on American journalism. Large newspapers hired war correspondents to cover the battlefields, with more freedom than correspondents today enjoy. These reporters used the new telegraph and expanding railways to move news reports faster to their newspapers. The cost of sending telegraphs helped create a new concise or "tight" style of writing which has became a standard for journalism through the next century. The ever-growing demand for urban newspapers to provide more news led to the organization of the first of the wire services, a cooperative between six large New York City-based newspapers led by David Hale, the publisher of the Journal of Commerce, and James Gordon Bennett, to provide coverage of Europe for all of the papers together. What became the Associated Press received the first cable transmission ever of European news through the trans-Atlantic cable in 1858.

New Forms of Journalism

The New York dailies continued to redefine journalism. James Bennet's Herald, for example, didn't just write about the disapperance of David Livingstone in Africa; they sent Henry Stanley to find whim, which he did, in Uganda. The succes of Stanley's stories prompted Bennett to hire more of what would turn out to be investigative journalists. He also was the first American publisher to bring an American newspaper to Eurpoe by founding the Paris Herald, which was the precursor of the International Herald Tribune.Charles Anderson Dana of the New York Sun developed the idea of the human interest story and a bette defintion of news value, including uniqueness of a story.William Randolph Hearst and Joseph Pulitzer both owned newspaper chains in the American West, and both established papers in New York City: Hearst's New York World in 1883 and Pulitzer's New York Journal in 1896.

Their stated missions to defend the public interest, their circulation wars and their embrace of sensational reporting, which spread to many other newspapers, led to the coinage of the phrase "yellow journalism." While the public may have benefitted from the beginnings of "muckraking" journalism, their often excessive coverage of juicy stories with sensational reporting turned many readers against them.Muckraking journalism continued into the 20th Century, led by well-known investigative journalists Lincoln Steffens, Ida Tarbell and Upton Sinclair. Their work exposed the dismal conditions of the Chicago slums and meatpacking industry, the monopolistic practices of the Standard Oil Co. and more.

Smaller newspapers and magazines published more investigative stories than the larger dailies, and took more of the risk. These would be the fouding publications of the alternative press movement, which today is typified by alternative weekly newspapers like The Village Voice in New York City and the Phoenix in Boston, as well as political magazines like Mother Jones and the Nation.The rampant and flagrant segregation of and discrimination against African-Americans did not prevent them from founding their own daily and weekly newspapers, especially in urban areas. These newspapers and other publications flourished because of the loyalty their readers had to them.

As immigration rose dramatically during the last half of the 19th Century, many immigrants published newspapers in their native languages to cater to their fellow expatriots. One good example were many newspapers published in Yiddish for the thousands of Jews who left Eastern Europe.

Birth of Broadcasting in the 20th Century

Gugliemo Marconi and colleagues in 1901 used a wireless radio transmitter to send a signal from the United States to Europe. By 1907, his invention was in wide use for transatlantic communications.

Reporting

Journalism has as its main activity the reporting of events — stating who, what, when, where, why and how, and explaining the significance and effect of events or trends. Journalism exists in a number of media: newspapers, television, radio, magazines and, most recently, the World Wide Web through the Internet.

The subject matter of journalism can be anything and everything, and journalists report and write on a wide variety of subjects: politics on the international, national, provincial and local levels, economics and business on the same four levels, health and medicine, education, sports, hobbies and recreation, lifestyles, clothing, food, pets, sex and relationships.... Journalists can report for general interest news outlets like newspapers, news magazines and broadcast sources; general circulation specialty publications like trade and hobby magazines, or for news publications and outlets with a select group of subscribers. Journalists are usually expected and required to go out to the scene of a story to gather information for their reports, and often may compose their reports in the field. They also use the telephone, the computer and the internet to gather information. However, more often those reports are written, and are almost always edited, in the newsroom, the office space where journalists and editors work together to prepare news content.

Journalists, especially if they cover a specific subject or area (a "beat") are expected to cultivate sources, people in the subject or area, that they can communicate with, either to explain the details of a story, or to provide leads to other subjects of stories yet to be reported. They are also expected to develop their investigative skills to better research and report stories.

Print Journalism

Print journalism can be split into several categories: newspapers, news magazines, general interest magazines, trade magazines, hobby magazines, newsletters, private publications, online news pages and others. Each genre can have its own requirements for researching and writing reports.

For example, newspaper journalists in the United States have traditionally written reports using the inverted pyramid style, although this style is used more for straight or hard news reports rather than features. Written hard news reports are expected to be spare in the use of words, and to list the most important information first, so that, if the story must be cut because there is not enough space for it, the least important facts will be automatically cut from the bottom. Editors usually ensure that reports are written with as few words as possible. Feature stories are usually written in a looser style that usually depends on the subject matter of the report, and in general granted more space.

News magazine and general interest magazine articles are usually written in a different style, with less emphasis on the inverted pyramid. Trade publications can be more news-oriented, while hobby publications can be more feature-oriented.

Broadcast Journalism

Radio journalists must gather facts and present them fairly and accurately, but also must find and record relevant and interesting sounds to add to their reports, both interviews with people involved in the story and background sounds that help characterize the story. Radio reporters may also write the introduction to the story read by a radio news anchor, and may also answers questions live from the anchor.

Television journalists rely on visual information to illustrate and characterize their reporting, including on-camera interviews with people involved in the story, shots of the scene where the story took place, and graphics usually produced at the station to help frame the story. Like radio reporters, television reporters also may write the introductory script that a television news anchor would read to set up their story. Both radio and television journalists usually do not have as much "space" to present information in their reports as print journalists.

On-line Journalism

The fast and vast growth of the Internet and World Wide Web has spawned the newest medium for journalism, on-line journalism. The speed at which news can be disseminated on the web, and the profound penetration to anyone with a computer and web browser, have greatly increased the quantity and variety of news reports available to the average web user.

The bulk of on-line journalis has been the extension of existing print and broadcast media into the web via web versions of their primary products. New reports that were set to be released at expected times now can be published as soon as they are written and edited, increasing the deadline pressure and fear of being scooped many journalists must deal with.

Most news Web sites are free to their users — one notable exception being the Wall Street Journal Web site, for which a subscripton is required to view its contents — but some outlets, such as the New York Times Web site, offer current news for free but archived reports and access to opinion columnists and other non-news sections for a periodic fee. Attempts to start unique web publications, such as Slate and Salon, have met with limited success, in part because they do or did charge subscription fees.

However, the growth of blogs as a source of news and especially opinion on the news has forever changed journalism. Blogs now can create news as well as report it, and blur the dividing line between news and opinion. The debate about whether blogging is really journalism rages on.

VARIATIONS OF JOURNALISM

Feature Journalism

Newspapers and periodicals often contain features written by journalists, many of whom specialize in this form of in-depth journalism. Feature articles usually are longer than straight news articles, and are combined with photographs, drawings or other "art." They may also be highlighted by typographic effects or colours.

Writing features can be more demanding than writing straight news stories, because while a journalist must apply the same amount of effort to accurately gather and report the facts of the story, the reporter must also find a creative and interesting way to write the article, especially the lead, or the first one or two paragraphs of the story. The lead must grab the reader's attention yet accurately embody the ideas of the article. Often the lead of a feature article is dictated by its subject matter. Journalists must work even harder to avoid clichéd images and words when writing the lead and the rest of the article.In the last half of the 20th Century the line between straight news reporting and feature writing blurred as more and more journalists and publications experimented with different approaches to writing an article. Tom Wolf, Gay Talese, Hunter S. Thompson and other journalists used many different approaches to writing news articles. Urban and alternative weekly newspapers went even further blurring the distinction, and many magazines fan more features than straight news.

Some television news shows experimented with alternative formats, and many TV shows that claimed to be news shows were not considered as such by many critics, because their content and methods did not adhere to accepted journalistic standards. National Public Radio, on the other hand, is considered a good example of a good mixture of straight news reporting, features, and combinations of the two, usually meeting standards of high quality. Other U.S. public radio news organizations have achieved similar results.

However, a majority of newspapers still maintain a clear distinction between news and features, as do most television and radio news organizations.

Sports Journalism

Sports journalism covers many aspects of human athletic competition, and is an integral part of most journalism products, including newspapers, magazines, and radio and television news broadcasts. While some critics don't consider sports journalism to be true journalism, the prominence of sports in Western culture has justified the attention of journalists to not just the competitive events of sports, but also to athletes and the business of sports. Sports journalism in the United States has traditionally been written in a looser, more creative and more opinionated tone than traditional journalistic writing; however, the emphases on accuracy and underlying fairness is still a part of sports journalism. An emphasis on the accurate description of statistical performances of athletes is also an important part of sports journalism.

Science Journalism

Science journalism is a relatively new branch of journalism, in which journalists' reporting conveys information on science topics to the public. Science journalists must understand and interpret very detailed, technical and sometimes jargon-laden information and render it into interesting reports that are comprehensible to consumers of news media.

Scientific journalists also must choose which developments in science merit news coverage, as well as cover disputes within the scientific community with a balance of fairness to both sides but also with a devotion to the facts. Many, but not all, journalists covering science have training in the sciences they cover, including several medical doctors who cover medicine.

Investigative Journalism

Investigative journalism, in which journalists investigate and expose unethical, immoral and illegal Behaviour by individuals, businesses and government agencies, can be complicated, time-consuming and expensive — requiring teams of journalists, months of research, interviews (sometimes repeated interviews) with numerous people, long-distance travel, computers to analyze public-record databases, or use of the company's legal staff to secure documents under freedom of information laws.

Because of its inherently confrontational nature, this kind of reporting is often the first to suffer from budget cutbacks or interference from outside the news department. Investigative reporting done poorly can also expose journalists and media organizations to negative reaction from subjects of investigations and the public, and accusations of gotcha journalism. However, done well, it can bring the attention of the public and government problems and conditions that the public deem need to be addressed, and can win awards and recognition to the journalists involved and the media outlet that did the reporting.

Investigative journalism is a kind of journalism in which reporters deeply investigate a topic of interest, often involving crime, political corruption, or some other scandal.

An investigative journalist may spend a considerable period researching and preparing a report, sometimes months or years, whereas a typical daily or weekly news reporter writes items concerning immediately available news. Most investigative journalism is done by newspapers, wire services and freelance journalists. An investigative journalist's final report may take the form of an expose.

The investigation will often require an extensive number of interviews and travel; other instances might call for the reporter to make use of activities such as surveillance techniques, tedious analysis of documents, investigations of the performance of any kind of equipment involved in an accident, patent medicine, scientific analysis, social and legal issues, and the like. In short, investigative journalism requires a lot of scrutiny of details, fact-finding, and physical effort. An investigative journalist must have an analytical and incisive mind with strong self-motivation to carry on when all doors are closed, when facts are being covered up or falsified and so on.

People Journalism

Another, less reputable, area of journalism that grew in stature in the 20th Century is 'celebrity' or 'people' journalism, which focuses on the personal lives of people, primarily celebrities, including movie and stage actors, musical artists, models and photographers, other notable people in the entertainment industry, as well as people who seek attention, such as politicians, and people thrust into the attention of the public, such as people who do something newsworthy. Once the province of newspaper gossip columnists and gossip magazines, celebrity journalism has become the focus of national tabloid newspapers like the National Enquirer, magazines like People and Us Weekly, syndicated television shows like Entertainment Tonight, Inside Edition, The Insider, Access Hollywood, and Extra, cable networks like E!, AandE Network and The Biography Channel, and numerous other television productions and thouasands of Web sites. Most other news media provide some coverage of celebrities and people.

Celebrity journalism differs from feature writing in that it focuses on people who are either already famous or are especially attractive, and in that it often covers celebrities obssessively, to the point of these journalists behaving unethically in order to provide coverage. Paparazzi, photographers who would follow celebrities incessantly to obtain potentially embarrassing photographs, have come to characterize celebrity journalism.

Professional and Ethical Standards

Journalists are expected to follow a stringent code of journalistic conduct that requires them to, among other things:Use original sources of information, including interviews with people directly involved in a story, original documents and other direct sources of information, whenever possible, and cite the sources of this information in reports; Fully attribute information gathered from other published sources, should original sources not be available (to not do so is considered plagiarism; some newspapers also note when an article uses information from previous reports);

Use multiple original sources of information, especially if the subject of the report is controversial;

- Check every fact reported;
- Find and report every side of a story possible;
- Report without bias, illustrating many aspects of a conflict rather than siding with one;
- Approach researching and reporting a story with a balance between objectivity and skepticism.
- Use careful Judgement when organizing and reporting information.
- Be careful about granting confidentiality to sources (news organizations usually have specific rules that journalists must follow concerning grants of confidentiality);
- Decline gifts or favors from any subject of a report, and avoid even the appearance of being influenced;
- Abstain from reporting or otherwise participating in the research and writing about a subject in which the journalist has a personal stake or bias that cannot be set aside.

Recognition of Excellence in Journalism

There are several professional organizations, universities and foundations that recognize excellence in journalism. The Pulitzer Prize, administered by Columbia University in New York City, is awarded to newspapers, magazines and broadcast media for excellence in various kinds of journalism. The Columbia University Graduate School of Journalism gives the Alfred I. duPont-Columbia University Awards for excellence in radio and television journalism, and the Scripps Howard Foundation gives the National Journalism Awards in 17 categories. The Society of Professional Journalists gives the Sigma Delta Chi Award for journalism excellence. In the television industry, the National Academy of Television Arts and Sciences gives awards for excellence in television journalism.

Failing to Uphold Standards

Such a code of conduct can, in the real world, be difficult to uphold consistently. Journalists who believe they are being fair or objective may give biased accounts — by reporting selectively, trusting too much to anecdote, or giving a partial explanation of actions. Even in routine reporting, bias can creep into a story through a reporter's choice of facts to summarize, or through failure to check enough sources, hear and report dissenting voices, or seek fresh perspectives.

As much as reporters try to set aside their prejudices, they may simply be unaware of them. Young reporters may be blind to issues affecting the elderly. A 20-year veteran of the "police beat" may be deaf to rumors of departmental corruption. Publications marketed to affluent suburbanites may ignore urban problems. And, of course, naive or unwary reporters and editors alike may fall prey to public relations, propaganda or disinformation.

News organizations provide editors, producers or news directors whose job is to check reporters' work at various stages. But editors can get tired, lazy, complacent or biased. An editor may be blind to a favorite reporter's omissions, prejudices or fabrications. Provincial editors also may be ill-equipped to weigh the perspective (or check the facts of) a correspondent reporting from a distant city or foreign country. A news organization's budget inevitably reflects decision-making about what news to cover, for what audience, and in what depth. Those decisions may reflect conscious or unconscious bias. When budgets are cut, editors may sacrifice reporters in distant news bureaus, reduce the number of staff assigned to low-income areas, or wipe entire communities from the publication's zone of interest. Publishers, owners and other corporate executives, especially advertising sales executives, can try to use their powers over journalists to influence how news is reported and published. Journalists usually rely on top management to create and maintain a "firewall" between the news and other departments in a news organization to prevent undue influence on the news department. One journalism magazine, Columbia Journalism Review, has made it a practice to reveal examples of executives who try to influence news coverage, of executives who do not abuse their powers over journalists, and of journalists who resist such pressures.

Reporting Versus Editorializing

Generally, publishers and consumers of journalism draw a distinction between reporting — "just the facts" — and opinion writing, often by restricting opinion columns to the editorial page and its facing or "op-ed" (opposite the editorials) page. Unsigned editorials are traditionally the official opinions of the paper's editorial board, while op-ed pages may be a mixture of syndicated columns and other contributions, frequently with some attempt to balance the voices across some political or social spectrum.

However, the distinction between reporting and opinion can break down. Complex stories often require summarizing and interpretation of facts, especially if there is limited time or space for a story. Stories involving great amounts of interpretation are often labelled "news analysis," but still run in a paper's news columns. The limited time for each story in a broadcast report rarely allows for such distinctions.

Ambush Journalism

Refers to aggressive tactics practiced by journalists to suddenly confront with questions people who otherwise do not wish to speak to a journalist. The practice has particularly been applied by television journalists, such as those on the CBS-TV news show 60 Minutes and by Geraldo Rivera, currently on the Fox News cable channel, and by hundreds of American local television reporters conducting investigations. The practice has been sharply criticized by journalists and others as being highly unethical and sensational, while others defend it as thc only way to attempt to provide those subject to it an opportunity to comment for a report. Ambush journalism has not been ruled illegal in the United States, although doing it on private property could open a journalist to being charged with trespassing.

Gotcha Journalism

Refers to the deliberate manipulation of the presentation of facts in a report in order to portray a person or organization in a particular way that varies from an accurate portrayal based on balanced review of the facts available. It particular is applied to broadcast journalism, where the story, images and interviews are tailored to create a particular impression of the subject matter.It is considered highly unethical to engage in gotcha journalism. Many subjects of reporting have claimed to have been subjected to it, and some media outlets are guilty of deliberately biased reporting.

Rights of Journalists Versus those of Private Citizens and Organizations

Journalists enjoy similar powers and privileges as private citizens and organizations. The power of journalists over private citizens is limited by the citizen's rights to privacy. However, many who seek favorable representation in the press (celebrities, for example) grant journalists greater access than others enjoy. The right to privacy of a private citizen may be reduced or lost if the citizen is thrust into the public eye, either by their own actions or because they are involved in a public event or incident.

Citizens and private organizations can refuse to deal with some or all journalists; however, the powers the press enjoy in many nations often make this tactic ineffective or counter-productive.

Citizens in most nations also enjoy the right against being libeled or defamed by journalists, and citizens can bring suit against journalists who they claim have published damaging untruths about them with malicious disregard for the truth. Libel or defamation lawsuits can also become conflicts between the journalists' rights to publish versus the private citizen's right to privacy. Some journalists have claimed lawsuits brought against them and news organizations — or even the threat of such a lawsuit — were intended to stifle their voices with the threat of expensive legal procedings, even if plaintiffs cannot prove their cases. This is referred to as the Chilling effect.

In many nations, journalists and news organizations must function under similar threat of retaliation from private individuals or organizations as from governments. Criminals and criminal organizations, political parties, some zealous religious organizations, and even mobs of people have been known to punish journalists who speak or write about them in ways they do not like. Punishments can include threats, physical damage to property, assault, torture and murder.

Right to Protect Confidentiality of Sources

Journalists' interaction with sources sometimes involves confidentiality, an extension of freedom of the press giving journalists a legal protection to keep the identity of a source private even when demanded by police or prosecutors; withholding sources can land journalists in contempt of court, or jailtime.

The scope of rights granted journalists varies from nation to nation; in the United Kingdom, for example, the government has had more legal rights to protect what it considers sensitive information, and to force journalists to reveal the sources of leaked information, than the United States. Other nations, particularly Zimbabwe and the People's Republic of China, have a reputation of persecuting journalists, both domestic and foreign.

In the present decade in the U.S., despite a long tradition of a journalist's ability to protect sources from government inquiry, the Supreme Court has upheld lower federal court rulings that restrict to varying degrees the rights of journalists to withhold information, and prosecutors on the state and federal levels have sought to jail journalists who refuse demands for information and sources they seek to protect.

Right of Access to Government Information

Like sources, journalists depend on the rights granted by government to the public and, by extension, to the press, for access to information held by the government. These rights also vary from nation to nation and, in the United States, from state to state. Some states have more open policies for making information available, and some states have acted in the last decade to broaden those rights. New Jersey, for example, has updated and broadened its Sunshine Law to better define what kinds of government documents can be withheld from public inquiry.

In the United States, the Freedom of Information Act (FOIA) guarantees journalists the right to obtain copies of government documents, although the government has the right to redact, or black out, information from documents in those copies that FOIA allows them to withhold. Other federal legislation also controls access to information. The Bush Administration, however, has been much more aggressive in asserting its right to restrict information from the press, which has led to claims that the government is attempting to circumvent FOIA, and to more ligitation between press organizations and the federal government. The federal courts have acted in different ways in different cases, but often have sided with the government against press access.

Bloggers enjoy Rights of Journalists

The growth of Internet do-it-yourself publishing in the late 1990s, especially the weblog or blog style of personal publication, gave rise to debates of "are bloggers journalists?" At issues are not only role-definitions, egos and relative status, but practical questions of access, as well as legal questions in jurisdictions where journalists have special privileges — such as protection against being forced to disclose confidential sources or information.

Bloggers are on the watch for cases that might set legal precedent concerning their rights as journalists. For example, in a 2005-2006 California case brought by Apple Computer, an Appeals Court judge said online writers who published information from anonymous sources were entitled to the same protection as other journalists. There was "no workable test or principle that would distinguish 'legitimate' from 'illegitimate' news," the court said.

Freedom of the Press

Freedom of the press is the guarantee by a government of free public press for its citizens and their associations, extended to members of news gathering organizations, and their published reporting. It also extends to news gathering, and processes involved in obtaining information for public distribution. In the U.S. this right is guaranteed by the First Amendment to the United States Constitution. Not all countries are protected by a bill of rights or the constitution pertaining to Freedom of the Press. For example, Australians have nothing in their constitution nor a bill or rights that suggests anything to do with Freedom of the Press.

With respect to governmental information, a government distinguishes which materials are public or protected from disclosure to the public based on classification of information as sensitive, classified or secret and being otherwise protected from disclosure due to relevance of the information to protecting the national interest. Many governments are also subject to sunshine laws or freedom of information legislation that are used to define the ambit of national interest.

In developed countries, freedom of the press implies that all people should have the right to express themselves in writing or in any other way of expression of personal opinion or creativity. The Universal Declaration of Human Rights indicates: *"Everyone has the right to freedom of opinion and expression; this right includes freedom to hold opinions without interference and to seek, receive, and impart information and ideas through any media regardless of frontiers"*

This philosophy is usually accompanied by legislation ensuring various degrees of freedom of scientific research (known as scientific freedom), publishing, press and printing the depth to which these laws are entrenched in a country's legal system can go as far down as its constitution. The concept of freedom of speech is often covered by the same laws as freedom of the press, thereby giving equal treatment to media and individuals.

Besides said legal environment, some non-governmental organizations use more criteria to judge the level of press freedom around the world. Reporters Without Borders considers the number of journalists murdered, expelled or harassed, and the existence of a state monopoly on TV and radio, as well as the existence of censorship and self-censorship in the media, and the overall independence of media as well as the difficulties that foreign reporters may face. Freedom House likewise studies the more general political and economic environments of each nation in order to determine whether there exist relationships of dependence that limit in practice the level of press freedom that might exist in theory. So the concept of independence of the press is one closely linked with the concept of press freedom.

The Media as the Branch of Government

The notion of the press as the fourth branch of government is sometimes used to compare the press (or media) with Montesquieu's three branches of government, namely an addition to the legislative, the executive and the judiciary branches. Edmund Burke is quoted to have said: "Three Estates in Parliament; but in the Reportpooopers' Gallery yonder, there sat a Fourth estate more important far than they all".

The development of the Western media tradition is rather parallel to the development of democracy in Europe and the United States. On the ideological level, the first advocates of freedom of the press were the liberal thinkers of the 18th and 19th centuries.They developed their ideas in opposition to the monarchist tradition in general and the divine right of kings in particular. These liberal theorists argued that freedom of expression was a right claimed by the individual and grounded in natural law. Thus, freedom of the press was an integral part of the individual rights promoted by liberal ideology.

Freedom of the press was (and still is) assumed by many to be a necessity to any democratic society. Other lines of thought later argued in favor of freedom of the press without relying on the controversial issue of natural law; for instance, freedom of expression began to be regarded as an essential component of the social contract (the agreement between a state and its people regarding the rights and duties that each should have to the other).

CHARACTERISTICS OF JOURNALISM

As a literary genre, New Journalism has certain technical characteristics. It is an artistic, creative, literary reporting form with three basic traits: dramatic literary techniques; intensive reporting; and reporting of generally acknowledged subjectivity.

AS SUBJECTIVE JOURNALISM

Pervading many of the specific interpretations of New Journalism is a posture of subjectivity. Subjectivism is thus a common element among many (though not all) of its definitions. In contrast to a conventional journalistic striving for an objectivity, subjective journalism allows for the writer's opinion, ideas or involvement to creep into his story.

Much of the critical literature concerns itself with a strain of subjectivism which may be called activism in news reporting. In 1970 Gerald Grant wrote disparagingly in *Columbia Journalism Review* of a "New Journalism of passion and advocacy" and in the *Saturday Review* Hohenberg discussed "The Journalist As Missionary" For Masterson in 1971, "The New Journalism" provided a forum for discussion of journalistic and social activism. In another 1971 article under the same title Ridgeway called the counter-culture magazines such as *The New Republic* and *Ramparts* and the American underground press New Journalism.

Another version of subjectivism in reporting is what is sometimes called participatory reporting. Robert Stein, in *Media Power,* defines New Journalism as "A form of participatory reporting that evolved in parallel with participatory politics..."

AS FORM AND TECHNIQUE

The above interpretations of New Journalism view it as an attitude Towards the practice of journalism. But a significant portion of the critical literature deals with form and technique.

Critical comment dealing with New Journalism as a literary-journalistic genre (a distinct type of category of literary work grouped according to similar and technical characteristics) treats it as the *new Non-fiction*. Its traits are extracted from the criticism written by those who claim to practice it and by others. Admittedly it is hard to isolate from a number of the more generic meanings The new Non-fiction where sometimes taken for advocacy of subjective journalism. A 1972 article by Dennis Chase defines New Journalism as a subjective journalism emphasizing "truth" over "facts" but uses major Non-fiction stylists as its example.

AS INTENSIVE REPORTAGE

Although much of the critical literature discussed the use of literary or fictional techniques as the basis for a New Journalism, critics also referred to the form as stemming from intensive reporting. Stein, for instance, found the key to New Journalism not its fictionlike form but the "saturation reporting" which precedes it, the result of the writer's immersion in his subject. Consequently, Stein concluded, the writer is as much part of his story as is the subject and he thus linked saturation reporting with subjectivity. For him New Journalism is inconsistent with objectivity or accuracy. But other have argued that total immersion enhances accuracy.

As Wolfe put the case: I am the first to agree that the New Journalism should be as accurate as traditional journalism. In fact my claims for the New Journalism, and my demands upon it, go far beyond that. I contend that it has already proven itself *more* accurate than traditional journalism—which unfortunately i saying but so much... Wolfe coined "saturation reporting" in his *Bulletin of the American Society of Newspaper Editors* article. After citing the opening paragraphs of Talese's Joe Louis piece, he confessed believing that Talese had "piped" or faked the story, only later to be convinced, after learning that Talese so deeply delved into the subject, that he could report entire scenes and dialogues.

The basic units of reporting are no longer who-what-when-where-how and why but whole scenes and stretches of dialogue. The New Journalism involves a depth of reporting and an attention to the most minute facts and details that most newspapermen, even the most experienced, have never dreamed of.

In his "Birth of the New Journalism" in *New York,* Wolfe returned to the subject, which he here described as a depth of information never before demanded in newspaper work. The New Journalist, he said, must stay with his subject for days and weeks at a stretch.

In Wolfe's *Esquire* piece saturation became the "Locker Room Genre" of intensive digging into the lives and personalities of one's subject, in contrast to the aloof and genteel tradition of the essayists and "The Literary Gentlemen in the Grandstand." For Talese, intensive reportage took the form of interior monologue to discover from his subjects what they were thinking, not, he said in a panel discussion reported in *Writer's Digest,* merely reporting what people did and said.

Wolfe identified the four main devices New Journalists borrowed from literary fiction:

- Telling the story using scenes rather than historical narrative as much as possible
- Dialogue in full (Conversational speech rather than quotations and statements)
- Point-of-view (present every scene through the eyes of a particular character)
- Recording everyday details such as behaviour, possessions, friends and family (which indicate the "status life" of the character)

Despite these elements, New Journalism is not fiction. It maintains elements of reporting including strict adherence to factual accuracy and the writer being the primary source. To get "inside the head" of a character, the journalist asks the subject what they were thinking or how they felt.

WRITERS

Which writer who are New Journalists is hard to define. In *The New Journalism: A Critical Perspective* Murphy writes, "A a literary genre, New Journalism [...] involves a more or less well defined group of writers [...].

Each is stylistically unique, but all sharing common formal elements." Among the most prominenet writers of New Journalism, Murphy lists: Jimmy Breslin, Truman Capote, Joan Didion, David Halberstam, Pete Hamill, Larry King, Norman Mailer, Joe McGinniss, Rex Reed, Mike Royko, John Sack, Dick Schaap, Terry Southern, Gail Sheehy, Gay Talese, Hunter S.

Thompson, Dan Wakefield, and Tom Wolfe. In *The New Journalism,* Johnson and Wolfe, also includes George Plimpton for his *Paper Lion*, *Life* writer James Mills, Robert Christgau and a few others. Christgau, however, stated in an 2001 interview that he did not see himself as a New Journalist.

CRITICISM

While many praised the New Journalist's style of writing, Wolfe et al., also received severe criticism from contemporary journalists and writers. Essentially two different charges were leveled against New Journalism: criticism against it as a *distinct genre* and criticism against it as a *new* form. Robert Stein believed that "In the New Journalism the eye of the beholder is all—or almost all," and in 1971 Philip M. Howard, wrote that the new Non-fiction writers rejected objectivity in favour of a more personal, subjective reportage. This parallels much of what Wakefield said in his 1966 *Atlantic* article.

The important and interesting and hopeful trend to me in the new journalism is its personal nature—not in the sense of personal attacks, but in the presence of the reporter himself and the significance of his own involvement.

This is sometimes felt to be egotistical, and the frank identification of the author, especially as the "I" instead of merely the impersonal "eye" is often frowned upon and taken as proof of "subjectivity," which is the opposite of the usual journalistic pretense.

And in spite of the fact that Capote believed in the objective accuracy of *In Cold Blood* and strove to keep himself totally out of the narrative, one reviewer founf in the book the "tendency among writers to resort to subjective sociology, on the other hand, or to super-creative reportage, on the other." Charles Self termed this characteristic of New Journalism as "admitted" subjectivity, whether first-person or third-person, and acknowledged the subjectivity inherent in his account.

Lester Markel polemically criticized New Journalism in the *Bulletin of the American Society of Newspaper Editors,* he rejected the claim to greater in-depth reporting and labelled the writers "factual fictionists" and "deep-see reporters." He feared they were performing as sociologists and psychoanalysts rather than as journalists.More reasoned, though still essentially negative, Arlen in his 1972 "Notes on the New Journalism," put the New Journalism into a larger socio-historical perspective by tracing the techniques from earlier writers and from the constraints and opportunities of the current age.

But much of the more routine New Journalism "consists in exercises by writer... in gripping and controlling and confronting a subject within the journalist's own temperament. Presumably, " he wrote, "this is the 'novelistic technique.' " But he conceded that the best of this work had "considerably expanded the possibilities of journalism."

Much negative criticism of New Journalism were directed at individual writers For example, Cynthia Ozick asserted in *The New Republic,* that Capote in *In Cold Blood* was doing little more than trying to devise a form: "One more esthetic manipulation." Sheed offered, in "A Fun-House Mirror," a witty refutation of Wolfe's claim that he takes on the expression and the guise of whomever he is writing about. "The Truman Capotes may hold up a tolerably clear glass to nature," he wrote, "but Wolfe holds up a fun-house mirror, and I for one don't give a hoot whether he calls the reflection fact or fiction."

"PARAJOURNALISM" AND THE NEW YORKER AFFAIR

Among the hostile critics of the New Journalism were Dwight MacDonald, whose most vocal criticism compromised a chapter in what became known as "the *New Yorker* affair" of 1965. Wolfe had written a two-part semi-fictional parody in *New York* of the *New Yorker* and its editor, William Shawn.

Reaction notably from *New Yorker* writers, was loud and prolonged, but the most significant reaction came from MacDonald, who counterattacked in two articles in the *New York Review of Books* In the first, MacDonald termed Wolfe's approach "parajournalism" and applied it to all similar styles. "Parajournalism," MacDonald wrote... seems to be journalism—"the collection and dissemination of current news"—but the appearance is deceptive. It is a bastard form, having it both ways, exploiting the factual authority of journalism and the atmospheric license of fiction.

The *New Yorker* parody, he added, "... revealed the ugly side of Parajournalism when it tries to be serious."

In his second article, MacDonald addressed himself to the accuracy of Wolfe's report. He charged that Wolfe "takes a middle course, shifting gears between fact and fantasy, spoof and reportage, until nobody knows which end is, at the moment, up" *New Yorker* writers Renata Adler and Gerald Jonas joined the fray in the Winter 1966 issue of *Columbia Journalism Review.* Wolfe himself returned to the affair a full seven years later., devoting the second of his two February *New York* articles (1972) to his detractors but not to dispute their attack on his factual accuracy. He argued that most of the contentions arose because for traditional *literati* Non-fiction should not succeed—which his Non-fiction obviously had.

Gail Sheehy and "Redpants"

In *The New Journalism: A Critical Perspective* Murphy writes, "Partly because Wolfe took liberties with the facts in his *New Yorker* parody, New Journalism began to get a reputation for juggling the facts in the search for truth, fictionalizing some details to get a larger 'reality.'

"Widely criticized was the technique of the composite character, the most notorious example of which was "Redpants," a presumed prostitute whom Gail Sheehy wrote about in *New York* in a series on that city's sexual subculture.

When it later became known that the character was distilled from a number of prostitutes, there was an outcry against Sheehy's method and, by extension, to the credibility of all of New Journalism. In the *Wall Street Journal,* one critic wrote: It's all part of the New Journalism, or the Now Journalism, and it's practiced widely these days. Some editors and reporters vigorously defend it. Others just as vigorously attack it. No one has polled the reader, but whether he approves or disapproves, it's getting harder and harder for him to know what he can believe. *Newsweek* reported that critics felt Sheehy's energies were better suited to fiction than fact John Tebbel in an article in *Saturday Review*, although treating New Journalism in its more generic sense as new a trend, chided it for the fictional technique of narrative leads which the new Non-fiction writers had introduced into journalism and deplored its use in newspapers.

CRITICISM AGAINST NEW JOURNALISM AS A DISTINCT GENRE

Newfield, in 1972, changed his attitude since his earlier, 1967, review of Wolfe. "New Journalism does not exist," the later article titled "Is there a 'new journalism'?" says. "It is a false category. There is only good writing and bad writing, smart ideas and dumb ideas, hard work and laziness." While the practice of journalism had improved during the past fifteen years, he argued, it was because of an influx of good writers notable for unique styles, not because they belonged to any school or movement.

DIFFERENCES IN JOURNALISTIC PRACTICE

In order to make some generalized comparisons of journalists and journalistic practice in the United States, in English-speaking Canada, and in French-speaking Canada, it is necessary to indulge in some oversimplifications about groups which, in themselves, tend to be rather complex and diverse. Lysiane Gagnon, in her discussion of "Journalism and Ideologies in Quebec," offers a useful starting point in her review of the classic work by Siebert, Peterson, and Schramm on The Four Theories of the Press, which provides a framework for generalizing about differences between these three groups of journalists and for beginning to identify the French, English, and American influences on the practice of journalism in North America.

While the so-called "social responsibility" theory of the press grew out of the 1947 report of the Hutchins Commission on Freedom of the Press in the United States, American journalists have tended not to accept its basic premise, which calls for government intervention when and if the media fail to act responsibly.

For the most part, they continue to subscribe to the more libertarian view and its imperative that the press be free from government control and influence. However, the most recent national survey of journalists in the United States reveals a shift in the perceived functions of journalism favoring some of the original recommendations of the Hutchins Commission. As Weaver and Wilhoit explain, "most journalists in 1992 appeared to have a `belief system' that reflected the Commission's goal of investigating `the truth about the facts' and providing `a context which gives them meaning.'"

Concerning the appropriate role for government, journalists in English Canada, who share British traditions allowing for more government secrecy and control of information and the reporting of information, are more tolerant than their American counterparts of government intervention and control. And by further comparison, journalists on French-language media in Quebec subscribe even more to the tenets of the social-responsibility theory and are willing to accept an even greater role for government involvement in media matters to assure the public's right to information. According to Fulford, English-Canadian journalists have inherited most of their techniques from Britain and the United States, except for the extensive foreign correspondence of British journalism and the investigative reporting in the United States. Further, and perhaps more important, is his observation that English-Canadian newspapers tend to mix elements of British and American heritage and share the ideal which involves truth, completeness, and justice. Explaining that English-Canadian journalists seek "to report the truth," Fulford quotes publisher Stuart Keate who wrote that "Any publisher, editor or reporter worth his salt recognizes that he has only one basic duty to perform: to dig for the truth; to write it in language people can understand; and to resist all impediments to its publication."

While changes in English-Canadian journalism during this century have paralleled similar changes in the United States, journalism in Quebec has been more influenced by French models that include government distribution agencies, newspapers with more readily identifiable political leanings, and greater acceptance of government intervention in media affairs. The latter is linked to the basic tenet of the social-responsibility theory of the press which, according to Gagnon, has become more accepted by journalists in the province of Quebec than anywhere else in North America. One of the recent presidents of Quebec's federation of professional journalists, Real Barnabe, supported this observation by writing: "Now that they have acquired the conditions under which they may practice their profession with dignity, never have they Quebec journalists been so preoccupied by their responsibilities."

Gagnon further explains that the notion of freedom of the press, which was widely accepted by Quebec journalists in the 1940s and 1950s, has given way to a more complex concept of the public's "right to know," and that this has enjoyed considerable success in Quebec, certainly more than it has in English Canada and, with even more reason, the United States. Part of the explanation for this has to do with the French traditions and perspectives which place a greater value on collectivism over individualism.

As Siebert, Peterson, and Schramm explain in their classic work, the social responsibility theory is "in closer harmony with a collectivist theory of society than with the individualistic theory from which the libertarian system sprang."

Other ways in which the French tradition has contributed to differences between French and English journalism and journalists in Canada include: the emphasis on analysis over simple reporting of facts; the tendency to treat matters conceptually rather than in terms of people and events; the need to rationalize; and a greater personalization of articles and editorials. This is not to say that Quebec journalists are less committed to the facts and to being factual. A recent study by Pritchard and Sauvageau, for example, found that Quebec journalists are more likely than other Canadian journalists to think that it is important to accurately report comments from news sources. Similarly, an earlier study by Langlois and Sauvageau, which also documented this commitment to the facts, found there to be considerable variation among newspaper journalists in Quebec.

Concerning the greater personalization of articles and editorials, mentioned above, Siegel found in his study of the coverage of the FLQ crisis in 1970 that the French-language papers tended to project an image of self-importance in a variety of ways including "frequent reference to media and journalists; personalized coverage which, at times, included the raising of rhetorical questions which they then proceeded to answer; and editorials written in the first person."

Another conclusion he reached point to still another important difference between journalism in English and French Canada. Following a comparison of coverage of several major issues or events, as well as a comparison of French and English broadcasting, Siegel found a homogeneity of outlook in the French press system.

"Of particular interest is the leadership role in French-Canadian society in which French-language journalists see them-selves. The articulation of a clearly defined value system is evident in French-language journalism, a practice that goes back a long time."

He found no such uniformity of outlook on the part of the English press, which he termed "fragmented." His conclusion is reinforced by David Thomas, an English-speaking journalist from Quebec: "Unity of thought was, and remains, infinitely more obvious in Quebec's French-language media—a phenomenon implicitly recognized by politicians and journalists who repeatedly point to the harsher treatment accorded the government by the English media."

Dominque Clift, a Montreal author and free-lance journalist who worked for major Canadian newspapers in both French and English Canada, characterized this uniformity of French-language journalists in a different way: the way in which they viewed themselves and their role in Quebec society.

In his article, "Solidarity on a Pedestal: French Journalism in Quebec," he charged that "French journalists see for themselves a much more exalted role in society than do their English-speaking counterparts," adding that: "It is in the actual practice of journalism that French and English writers differ in the most pronounced manner. It has to do with the way in which journalists look upon themselves, their profession, their public, as well as on their employers."

But Florian Sauvageau, in his more systematic study of journalists on French-language dailies in Quebec, could find no such homogeneity in Quebec's journalistic circles. Instead, he found changes in Quebec media to parallel those in the modern corporate media of North America. Those include: the tendency to view newspapers as, first and foremost, businesses and journalists as "news workers"; journalists talking not so much in terms of "news" but of the "product"; and business and marketing functions gradually replacing the news function.

Journalists are far from all being those radicals trying to control the news, as depicted a few years ago with some help from the pronouncements of the most militant of them. There are some, of course, who still turn for inspiration to the theses of the news as a driving force, and journalism as a tool for development, seeing themselves as agents of change and keeping up with the rhetoric of the 1960s and 1970s.

However, a good number are content simply to report the remarks of the dignitaries they meet, or to get the news out as quickly as possible.

The result, he said, is that the work of journalists is becoming more and more routine and fairly unfulfilling, and that this is partly due to the rigid application of certain clauses in collective agreements between journalists and management.

In summary, this brief review of research and commentary on journalists and journalism in the United States, English Canada, and Quebec provides some insight into how the practice of journalism in these different settings has been influenced in a variety of ways by English, French, and American traditions.

Our concern, however, is in how these different traditions or perspectives may have resulted in journalistic practices that vary in their tendencies to promote individualism or to serve the community or broader societal interests.

ANECDOTAL EVIDENCE

Despite the growing body of literature from systematic studies of journalists in Canada and the United States, most of the "evidence" about how journalists and journalistic practices differ between the two countries tends to be anecdotal rather than the result of formal research. There are some exceptions, of course. For example, we already reported how the most recent national survey of journalists in the United States shows a shift Towards some of the values articulated by the Hutchins Commission, which advanced the "social-responsibility" theory of the press. Also, French-language journalists in Canada tend to be more willing than their English-Canadian and especially their American counterparts to perceive the press as a public service that can be regulated by the government. As evidence, Langois and Sauvageau found that nearly two-thirds of the French-speaking journalists in their study agreed that the state should intervene in the field of information. Even before the Kent Commission issued its report and recommendations in 1981, Sauvageau argued that the government might intervene to assure the citizen's right to information, similar to the way it has done in education and health care.

More often, though, evidence is used to explain how the traditions and perspectives of journalists in Canada and the United States vary considerably in terms of tolerance for intervention by government and the courts in ways that limit the media and the practice of journalism. This chapter began with a good example of this variety by comparing reactions to the decision in the United States to publish the Unibomber's manifesto with reaction to CBC cooperation with the RCMP in meeting broadcast demands of a group of renegades in British Columbia. Another example is reaction to certain recommendations of the Kent Commission on Newspapers. Following the simultaneous sale of newspapers in Winnipeg and Ottawa by two major Canadian newspaper groups, the federal government established the Kent Commission in 1980 and authorized it to study the new newspaper industry and make recommendations to the government. One of the more controversial recommendations called for the establishment of a Press Rights Panel within the Canadian Human Rights Commission.

Response came mainly from representatives and publishers of newspapers owned by large newspaper groups in Canada. The reaction was tempered and mild compared to what one would expect in the United States if similar recommendations were to come out of a government committee that spent more than $3 million to investigate the daily newspaper industry. Reactions in the United States to any threat of government intervention or control in media affairs tend to be immediate and predictable. Media owners and spokespersons for associations of journalists, particularly in the print media, are quick to call "infringement" and issue charges of improper violations of cherished First Amendment guarantees of freedom of the press.

Still another example has to do with media coverage of criminal trials. During the months of exhaustive coverage and commentary related to the O.J. Simpson trial in the United States, a trial court judge in Ontario issued a restraining order on the media in the Paul Bernardo murder trial that included, as well, a ban on publication of most information from his wife's trial several months earlier. Canadian journalists complained but complied with the court order, while American journalists in neighboring border cities did not, continuing what one U.S. newspaper editor had earlier referred to as a "border battle with Canadian law."

These examples help illustrate the differences between Canada and the United States in terms of their legal systems, judicial traditions, and accepted journalistic practice and show a stronger commitment in Canada to the values of community over the individual rights of journalists and the news media.

Discussion

Important differences in the traditions of law and in the practice of journalism in Canada and the United States result in different approaches to how the rights of the news media are appropriately balanced against the needs of the community and the broader interests of society. To begin with, while the two legal systems share a similar tradition in English Common Law, their judicial and political approaches are different in important ways.

As Lipset and Pool explain, while both nations seek to protect the rights of the individual while promoting and protecting the general welfare of the community, they do "strike different balances, with Canada tipping Towards the interests of the community, and the United States Towards the individual."

This review of the development of media law in the two countries shows that the courts on both sides of the border have expressed a strong commitment to the principle of a free press. However, Canadian courts have been less likely than those in the United States to provide strict protections for the media to publish without government restraint or interference. This is most obvious in matters related to coverage of the courts, where judicial restraints are more allowable in Canada. Also, Canadian courts have permitted government bans on the publication of truthful information, lawfully obtained, while American courts have held that such bans on the press or punishment for publishing such information is uncon-stitutional. Also, media in the United States are allowed greater latitude to criticize public officials than are media in Canada, where the courts have been reluctant to adopt the American approach to civil libel. In other areas, however, involving newsgathering, the duty to testify, and access to information, the courts in both countries have attempted to balance the rights of the news media against the broader interests of society.

Apart from differences in the law are differences in the practice of journalism in Canada and the United States. Journalists in Canada are more inclined Towards a "social responsibility" view of the role of the media in society. While this particular perspective was proposed by the prestigious Hutchins Commission on Freedom of the Press in the United States, American journalists have tended not accept its basic premise, which calls for government intervention when and if the media fail to act responsibly. For the most part, they continue to subscribe to the more libertarian view and its imperative that the media be free from government influence and control. Canadian journalists, however, whether sharing British traditions that allow for more government secrecy and control of information or French traditions that are more accepting of government intervention in media affairs, tend to be more tolerant of government intervention in ways that directly affect the media while serving the broader needs and interests of society. The most recent national survey of American journalists suggests that there may be some shift Towards some of the goals of the Hutchins Commission, which originally proposed the social responsibility model.

Some Future Considerations

There is, and has been, considerable discussion about the Constitution in

Canada since the Charter of Rights and Freedoms was adopted in 1982. However, little if any of the controversy centers around concerns over government control of the media or court limitations of Charter guarantees of press freedom. This is not to say that journalists and media owners in Canada do not have concerns about these issues or that they would not prefer greater freedom and less government control. It is just that these are not major concerns, at least not compared to the larger constitutional issues being discussed.

This is not the case in the United States, where journalists and media owners have long been eager and vocal critics of any attempts by government or the courts to limit press freedoms and violate their First Amendment guarantees. However, the growing criticism and concerns about court interpretations of the speech-press clause in the United States are coming from Non-media sources who are concerned about too much freedom at the expense of other interests, particularly the rights and interests of disadvantaged groups like women and minorities. In particular, concerns being raised by feminists, critical scholars and, especially, critical legal theorists are that the court's continuing emphasis on protecting press freedoms serves only to advance the status quo and favors the special interests of corporate-owned media conglomerates.

These are variations of the same kinds of criticism and concerns expressed by Jerome Barron, who argued nearly thirty years ago that "Our constitutional theory is in the grip of a romantic conception of free expression, a belief that the `marketplace of ideas' is freely accessible. But if ever there were a self operating marketplace of ideas, it has long ceased to exist." He went on to argue for a legal right of access to the media to provide citizens with the kind of marketplace originally intended by the Founding Fathers.

Barron, an American, raises these same concerns over recent developments in media law in Canada, and a growing number of critical theorists and legal scholars in Canada are expressing concerns of their own about constitutional developments related to court interpretations of the Canadian Charter of Rights and Freedoms. Michael Mandel, for example, frames his criticisms in terms of what he calls "The legalization of politics in Canada," and argues that the representative institutions like Parliament, the legislatures, and municipal councils "are now being pushed from centre stage and told what they can and cannot do by judges elected by and accountable to nobody."

David Schneiderman, in his edited volume on Freedom of Expression and the Charter, explains that critics are not optimistic about the consequences of the constitutionalization of freedom of expression in Canada and are concerned that the Charter favors the value system of liberal individualism over the collectivist aims of the modern welfare state. In the United States, concerns are also being raised in journalistic circles about the status of American journalism, about public criticism of the press, and about the appropriate roles and responsibilities of the media in a free democratic society.

One of the best recent books on this subject is by Anderson, Dardenne, and Killenberg, who argue for a more ecumenical, constructive, participative, and democratically responsive role for journalism's institutional future. Other recent authors like Davis Merritt, Jay Rosen, and James Fallows have called for a revision in journalistic practices in order to promote community through civic or public journalism. This approach has challenged the way responsible media report on and relate to the communities they serve.

As Dennis and Merrill put it, "The new communitarians are waging a rhetorical war against Enlightenment liberalism—against individualism and libertarianism." More specifically, Christians argues that journalists should discard the liberal politics of rights, which "rests on unsupportable foundations," and that such rights should be "given up for a politics of the common good."

In response, critics of this approach argue that it "confuses journalism with community organization, a social work concept" and are concerned that if journalists became activists and took positions on community issues, they would lose "any claim to impartiality and would sacrifice credibility."

In summary, what emerges from a review of issues like these is the fact that some of the basic foundations of law and journalistic practice are being challenged in very significant ways by credible practitioners and scholars in Canada and the United States alike.

This is all part of the important ongoing discussions about how to appropriately balance the freedoms of the press and other media of communication against the larger interests of society, and about how to frame the practice of journalism in the best way possible to serve the democratic process. The quality of these discussions on both sides of the border can be enhanced by examining the experiences in both countries and, indeed, in other societies, to see how these issues are being played out against the backdrop of different traditions, practices, values, and beliefs.

2

The Authority and Self-definition of Journalism

The institution of American journalism has earned a mantle of authority in American society. The mere fact that many historians rely on newspaper and magazine accounts as primary source material indicates in a small way how journalism and the work of journalists become authoritative. As purveyors of facts and interpretation, journalists use this authority to describe events and everyday life to the public. Gieryn and Figert describe this kind of authority as social power: "'Cognitive authority' is the legitimate power (in designated contexts) to define, describe or explain bounded realms of reality".

The public entrusts journalists with this cognitive authority to the extent that they believe in journalists and their work. When the authority is threatened, journalists respond to consolidate their power. Paul Starr, in his studies of the medical profession, calls this power *cultural authority*. He says "cultural authority entails the construction of reality through definitions of fact and value".

Starr distinguishes cultural authority from social authority, which he says "involves the control of action through the giving of commands." Cultural authority, on the other hand, is derived from performing a service and from the ability to determine the *needs* of clients. If journalists perform the service of informing public debates, then they determine which cultural conversations people need to be aware of and engaged in.The cultural authority of journalists, therefore. is based on the dependence of the public on the ability of journalists to present important information in a coherent and reliable fashion, or at least make it seem that way. This authority is reproduced in and through the everyday practices of journalists as well as later through boundarywork rhetoric. Starr says the cultural authority of medical doctors rests on three aspects of legitimacy: collegial, cognitive, and moral. For journalistic cultural authority, these same aspects of legitimacy are appropriate:

- The collegial legitimacy of the journalist—the acceptance by others in their profession;

- The cognitive legitimacy of the journalistic product—it is perceived to be based on rational, objective methods; and
- The moral legitimacy of the journalist—journalists' judgments are expected to be oriented Towards altruism and public service.

Threats to cultural authority of an institution or profession do not always come from outside the institution or profession. A well-publicized case of fraud or fakery is perhaps the prime example of an internal threat to the cultural authority of a social institution or profession. Such turmoil is publicly discussed and thereby constructed as an issue or problem.

The discussion of the issue occurs as discourse within journalistic media by journalists who control the content and topics of the medium. For example, in 1980, *Washington* Post reporter Janet Cooke fabricated a news story about an imaginary eight-year-old heroin addict and was on the verge of accepting a Pulitzer Prize for it when the deception was revealed.

The *Post*'s subsequent analysis of the deception argued that the problem was not organizational, the problem was that Cooke was an aberration—a compulsive liar. As Dahlgren notes, one of the distinctive aspects of turmoil within the institution of journalism is that those within the institution "strive to maintain discursive control over such turmoil. Among other things, this helps to consolidate and legitimate professional practices and identity (by). retain(ing) definitional control of the field, its problems and potential solutions".

Definitional control of the boundaries of journalism is also accomplished by journalists when they do things like formulate definitions of news and news work. It is also accomplished through the selection of news topics.

Defining news is not a simple task. A 1965 textbook for journalists admits, "To recognize news is easier than to define it". Yet the primary role of journalists is to determine what is newsworthy, that is, to define news. In defining news, journalists also define what it is they do. This study shows how journalists often define journalism in rclation to its neighboring professions.

SOME BACKGROUND ABOUT "THE PROBLEM"

Many journalism critics have recently argued that American journalism is undergoing a profound change because it now regularly mixes entertainment with the news. Critics typically argue that this entertainment is in the form of sensationalistic celebrity-scandal. In fact, there is a long history of sensationalism in American journalism, a fact documented by several journalism historians.

But the main point of contemporary critics is that sensationalism and tabloid-style techniques, which were always present on the fringes of journalism, are now becoming the norm in American journalism, and are being adopted by so-called "mainstream" media as part of economic survival strategies in the cutthroat business climate of American mass media.

These contemporary critics typically argue that there should be a rigid boundary between mainstream journalism and other kinds of mass communication such as tabloid journalism. The critics imply that one kind of communication is more legitimate in certain contexts than the other, and even that tabloid journalism is not journalism at all but is instead entertainment. As noted above, one of the claims made by mass media critics is that journalism just recently got worse.

But this may be a perennial complaint. A quick review of journalism criticism reveals that the argument that journalism used to be better but just recently got worse is common throughout the history of journalism. The critiques usually say that journalism used to make bold distinctions between news and entertainment but now combines the two.

These critiques construct the logical conclusion that journalism has steadily decreased in quality over many years. Taken together, the criticisms add up to the conclusions that the people who used to do journalism were better and had higher standards than those of today and that the distinctions between news and entertainment used to be greater. Examples of this critique can be found in even the earliest discussions of American journalism.

For instance, critics panned Benjamin Day New York Sun of the early 1830s because it often contained humour and sensational news of suicides. Similarly, some critics hated James Gordon Bennett New York Herald of the mid- to late-1830s because it contained entertaining, satirically written police court reports, as well as in-depth crime stories.

Bennett pioneered the "human-interest story" or feature story, when he wrote in vivid detail in 1836 about the grisly murder of the prostitute Helen Jewett, quoting her madam and describing Jewett's apartment in minute detail. Bennett's day-by-day narrative of the ensuing sensational trial reminds us of how journalism and entertaining literature have been combined for many years to make newsworthy stories "more palatable for consumption."

Bennett was soundly criticized by his competitors and others for blurring the boundary between journalism and entertainment. His detractors, many of them his competitors, waged what they called a "Moral War" in the late 1830s against Bennett and his enjoyable but sensationalistic newspaper. They maintained that Bennett was a "deviant" journalist because he blurred the boundaries of journalism by making his newspaper entertaining and popular.

Those running the "Moral War" against Bennett were unsuccessful at running him out of the journalism business, but they did seriously wound his business. In the 1920s, many journalists were labeled "yellow journalists" because they sensationalized and twisted the news by appealing to prurient interests and base instincts.

In 1962, philosopher Jürgen Habermas argued that the boundaries between news and entertainment are blurring because people prefer "entertaining" news and its immediate rewards: Public affairs, social problems, economic matters, education and health. 'delayed reward news'—are not only pushed into the background by 'immediate reward news' (comics, corruption, accidents, disasters, sports, recreation, social events, and human interest) but, as the characteristic label already indicates, are already read less and more rarely.

In the end the news generally assumes some sort of guise and is made to resemble a narrative from its form down to stylistic detail (news stories); the rigorous distinction between fact and fiction is ever more frequently abandoned.

News and reports and even editorial opinions are dressed up with all the accouterments of entertainment literature, whereas on the other hand the belletrist contributions aim for the strictly 'realistic' reduplication of reality "as it is" on the level of clichès and thus, in turn, erase the line between fiction and report.

The integration of the once separate domains of journalism and literature. Brings about a peculiar shifting of reality—even a conflation of different levels of reality. Under the common denominator of so-called human interest emerges the mixtum compositum of a pleasant and at the same time convenient subject for entertainment that, instead of doing justice to reality, has a tendency to present a substitute more palatable for consumption and more likely to give rise to an impersonal indulgence in stimulating relaxation than to a public use by reason.

Habermas, in making the observation that literature and news were "once separate domains," is doing, in 1962, journalism/entertainment boundary work. An example of a similar critique of journalism boundary-degradation—but attributed to a different root cause—is the melodramatic opening paragraphs of Ron Powers' 1977 book *The Newscasters*, which says the sea-change in journalism happened in the 1970s:

The biggest heist of the 1970s never made it on the five o'clock news. The biggest heist of the 1970s *was* the five o'clock news.The salesmen took it. They took it away from the journalists, slowly, patiently, gradually, and with such finesse that nobody noticed until it was too late. By the 1970s, an extravagant proportion of television news—local news in particular—answered less to the description of "journalism" than to that of "show business."

This transformation, carried out by the sales-oriented station managers in an unbounded quest for profits, bore the profoundest implications in the way Americans were to receive information and perceive political choices. Many local newscasts ceased serving the public (at best, they served the public only incidentally) and bequeathed their primary allegiance to the advertisers.

Powers blames the quest for profits, instead of journalistic values, for the swing Towards show business techniques and content. Similarly, Edwin Diamond, in 1975, notes that the potential for profits associated with high ratings points for news Programmes led to the downfall of journalistic control in local television newsrooms around the country. The responsibility of controlling the news process was relinquished to news consultants who had no knowledge of journalism but who were well-versed in audience survey techniques and behavioural psychology.

In other words, they knew how to design a local news programme that would attract a mass audience but not one that would inform it: Up until a few years ago, television news was in the hands of professional news directors and producers, traditionally trained in newspaper or magazine work or broadcast journalism.

It still is at the networks. But local station management has not had the same professional approach, especially since the local stations began discovering that their news times could be highly salable, often cheaper to run than straight entertainment shows, and attractive to many advertisers. Not only has television news become longer. It has become too important to be left to the newspeople.

Audience research has been perceived as the key to ratings success. For Diamond, "professionals" are those trained in journalism, especially in newspaper and magazine journalism, areas where audience research has not been pursued as thoroughly as in television.

In taking control away from the professionals, journalism has taken a back seat to superficiality, and news judgments are now made by managers skilled in audience research. Powers' and Diamond's critiques of television journalism are quite similar to the critiques that were raised throughout the early history of the television medium.

They seem to argue for a monopolization of authority and protection of autonomy for journalists. In other words, Powers and Diamond would like to see journalists maintain control over all aspects of journalism and keep others from controlling any aspects of it. Recently, Steven Stark, a commentator on popular culture for National Public Radio, wrote that the root cause of increased sensationalism in radio and television news is the advent of all-news channels in the 1980s, such as CNN.

He says the increased demand for news around the clock has caused journalists to become irresponsible: Unlike the old days, when there were, at most, two news cycles a day, there is now a 24-hour demand for information. That means the network news and newspapers have to provide a different product than they once did, because they assume people get their headlines elsewhere.

The result has been a considerable broadening of what is considered reportable news and analysis—much of it far less objectively verifiable than in the past. We now have fields of news that didn't exist 15 years ago, such as entertainment reporting. News from the tabloids is considered fair game.

Call-in shows can put forward any "expert" they can drum up, while encouraging callers to speculate and gossip. Some TV commentary itself is close to staged: Crossfire and The McLaughlin Group are to James Reston and Edward R. Murrow what pro wrestling is to sports. Because of the incessant demand, news is also presented more quickly to the public, with the inevitable result that there's a far thinner line between fact and rumor—one reason why personal details about celebrities get reported more quickly, if not falsely—than before.

This is all part of a far larger cultural pattern—the babble of a postmodern age that has seen feeling gain pre-eminence over thought, while elites collapse. Stark's theory that journalists responded to the increased frequency of news "cycles" and an increased demand for news by lowering their standards for newsworthiness implies that journalists are not doing their jobs, and are, in fact, remiss in their responsibility to decide what counts as news.

This is not a new critique, though the root cause selected by Stark may be a new idea. Many other examples could be cited of journalists and others arguing that journalism is changing, moving Towards more entertainment and less information. The critique is indeed perennial.

As shown above, examples of it can be shown from the very beginnings of American journalism right up to the present. Journalism professor and historian Mitchell Stephens (1988) puts this kind of criticism in context:

Some of the criticism television journalism inspires is. shortsighted. News and entertainment [did not] meet and mate for the first time on often giggly, often frivolous, local television newscasts in the United States; their affair dates back at least as far as criers and minstrels.

Television news, in other words, did not inject a foreign substance—playfulness—into the news; news has been enjoyed for as long as it has been exchanged.

Like the penny papers of the 1830s, the yellow journals of the 1880s and 1890s and the tabloids of the 1920s, television has succeeded in attracting a new audience to the news. Once television sets became affordable, news became available to audiences of many millions, including even those lacking the energy, skill or maturity to read a newspaper or concentrate on a radio narrative. If the critique is perennial, then there must be a reason for it being so persistent. Perhaps these critiques serve an important purpose. Instead of evaluating the legitimacy of these claims and critiques, the constructivist approach to this debate focuses on how self-interested stakeholders (relevant actors) construct a conception of journalism that makes sense to them and that helps to consolidate their power and prestige.

These stakeholders believe that the cultural authority of their institution depends on distinct boundaries, which, in turn, rest on concepts such as the perceived credibility and objectivity of their work. This constructivist approach to the issue helps us understand how the boundaries of journalism are constructed, negotiated, and maintained, giving us insights into what journalism means to people. To say that these boundaries are *constructed* implies that they have no firm, absolute contours. Instead, they are contextually contingent, local, and episodic, with the *potential* to become stable and widespread. To give a brief example of boundary-work analysis, let us examine the words of the authors cited earlier in their arguments about the blurring of the news/entertainment boundary. They all imply that "real" journalism is something different from what we have now.

The characteristics of "real" journalism that the various authors mentioned earlier in this section cite include distinctions such as: News is meant to inform, not entertain; it presents facts, not fiction; it does not include speculation or gossip; and it is controlled by professionals who serve the public, not by advertisers who seek only profits.

These are demarcation criteria that help journalists "construct" their role in society—and help them understand the shape and contours of the *cultural space* in which journalism resides. Looking at the claims more closely, it appears that the authors mentioned earlier in this section cite the *functional* differences between news and entertainment: One informs, the other entertains.

They also note *epistemological* differences: One is a factual kind of knowledge, the other contains fiction. They also cite *methodological* and *organizational* differences: One uses gossip and speculation, the other does not; and one is controlled by professionals who serve the public, the other serves less-altruistic goals.

As an analyst, I am not in a position to "solve" the debates about these issues. Instead, I look at how others solve them. In particular, I examine the apparent goals of boundary debates; how interested parties pick out the essential elements of the boundaries; and whether and how their work achieves any results.

The goal of this project is to analyse how the boundaries between news and entertainment are "constructed" by relevant actors. To accomplish that goal, I look at several examples of constructions of monopoly, deviance, and autonomy as "social issues" with stakeholders in journalism. The constructivist approach to questions about what is journalism and what is not replaces the answer with the question as the thing to be studied.

In other words, I do not try to find a definitive-necessarily essentialist—answer to the question "What are the boundaries of journalism?" Instead, I analyse and examine how journalists and others have attempted to answer this perplexing question, particularly when they claim that certain acts and practices are not journalism but are entertainment.

In these kinds of claims, we gain valuable in sight into the ways journalists make sense of what they do, and about the role of journalism in society. Journalism, like all social institutions, is socially constructed. Questions about where journalism ends and entertainment begins are a viable field of study that up to this point, has been largely ignored. This project should begin to remedy this situation by examining what many call journalism ethics issues from a constructivist point of view.

The way journalists make distinctions about acceptable behaviours, intentions, and content says a lot about culture production and how society creates and defines itself. Throughout this study, cartographic metaphors—mapping images-are used as a way of thinking about the relationships between different institutions in American culture. Journalists map out the cultural space of journalism by specifying where the boundaries are located.

As Gieryn notes, cartographic metaphors are useful when discussing the idea of a cultural space—territorial markers that people use to make sense of the world around them. He says, "cartographic metaphors offer a robust language for thinking about relations among cultural phenomena," particularly the relations between adjacent phenomena.

In the cultural space of mass media, news and entertainment appear to be adjacent phenomena. Gieryn suggests thatwe consider using cartographic terms such as "contours, landmarks, scale, orientation, coordinates, points of interest, and legend". These terms compel us to examine how this cultural space was slowly carved out of the cultural landscape rather than privilege journalism-as-it-is as the only logical outcome.

Some of the boundaries of journalism may be moving and flexible or perhaps blurry and indistinct. In other places they may be uncontested and easy to see. In any case, it is the players on either side of the alleged boundary (or in the middle of it) who are the primary stakeholders in constitutive rhetoric that attempts to delineate borders.

That is why the primary site of this study is in the rhetoric of journalists: They have the most to gain or lose by such rhetoric about the boundaries of journalism.

Newspapers and periodicals often contain features written by journalists, many of whom specialize in this form of in-depth journalistic writing. Feature articles are usually longer forms of writing; more attention is paid to style than in straight news reports. They are often combined with photographs, drawings or other "art." They may also be highlighted by typographic effects or colors.

Writing features can be more demanding than writing straight news stories, because while a journalist must apply the same amount of effort to accurately gather and report the facts of the story, he or she must also find a creative and interesting way to *write* it. The *lead* must grab the reader's attention and yet accurately embody the ideas of the article.

In the last half of the 20th Century the line between straight news reporting and feature writing has blurred. Journalists and publications today experiment with different approaches to writing. Tom Wolfe, Gay Talese, Hunter S. Thompson are some of these examples. Urban and alternative weekly newspapers go even further in blurring the distinction, and many magazines include more features than straight news. Some television news shows experimented with alternative formats, and many TV shows that claimed to be news shows were not considered as such by traditional critics, because their content and methods do not adhere to accepted journalistic standards.

National Public Radio, on the other hand, is considered a good example of mixing straight news reporting, features, and combinations of the two, usually meeting standards of high quality. Other US public radio news organizations have achieved similar results. A majority of newspapers still maintain a clear distinction between news and features, as do most television and radio news organizations.

Professional journalism is a form of news reporting which developed in the United States at the beginning of the 20th century, along with formal schools of journalism which arose at major universities. As documented by Robert McChesney, "[n]one of these schools existed in 1900; by 1915, all the major schools such as Columbia, Northwestern, Missouri, and Indiana were in full swing."

According to McChesney, professional journalism arose in the response to the capitalist imperative of consolidation. As the many independent newspapers which existed at the turn of the century, often with a radical agenda and with no presumption of balance or objectivity, were acquired and consolidated, the large resulting newspapers understood they needed to appear balanced and objective to their audience and advertisers. Thus, professional codes developed, as well as the academic Programmes to fill these positions.

Sports journalism covers many aspects of human athletic competition, and is an integral part of most journalism products, including newspapers, magazines, and radio and television news broadcasts.

While some critics don't consider sports journalism to be true journalism, the prominence of sports in Western culture has justified the attention of journalists to not just the competitive events in sports, but also to athletes and the business of sports.

Sports journalism in the United States has traditionally been written in a looser, more creative and more opinionated tone than traditional journalistic writing; the emphasis on accuracy and underlying fairness is still a part of sports journalism. An emphasis on the accurate description of the statistical performances of athletes is also an important part of sports journalism.

Science journalism is a relatively new branch of journalism, in which journalists' reporting conveys information on science topics to the public. Science journalists must understand and interpret very detailed, technical and sometimes jargon-laden information and render it into interesting reports that are comprehensible to consumers of news media. Scientific journalists also must choose which developments in science merit news coverage, as well as cover disputes within the scientific community with a balance of fairness to both sides but also with a devotion to the facts. Science journalism has frequently been criticized for exaggerating the degree of dissent within the scientific community on topics such as global warming, and for conveying speculation as fact.

Investigative journalism, in which journalists investigate and expose unethical, immoral, and illegal behaviour by individuals, businesses and government agencies, can be complicated, time-consuming and expensive — requiring teams of journalists, months of research, interviews (sometimes repeated interviews) with numerous people, long-distance travel, computers to analyse public-record databases, or use of the company's legal staff to secure documents under freedom of information laws.

Because of its high costs and inherently confrontational nature, this kind of reporting is often the first to suffer from budget cutbacks or interference from outside the news department. Investigative reporting done poorly can also expose journalists and media organizations to negative reaction from the subjects of investigations and the public, and accusations of gotcha journalism.

When conducted correctly it can bring the attention of the public and government to problems and conditions that the public deem need to be addressed, and can win awards and recognition to the journalists involved and the media outlet that did the reporting.

New Journalism was the name given to a style of 1960s and 1970s news writing and journalism which used literary techniques deemed unconventional at the time. The term was codified with its current meaning by Tom Wolfe in a 1973 collection of journalism articles.

It is typified by using certain devices of literary fiction, such as conversational speech, first-person point of view, recording everyday details and telling the story using scenes. Though it seems undisciplined at first, new journalism maintains elements of reporting including strict adherence to factual accuracy and the writer being the primary source. To get "inside the head" of a character, the journalist asks the subject what they were thinking or how they felt.

Because of its unorthodox style, new journalism is typically employed in feature writing or book-length reporting projects. Many new journalists are also writers of fiction and prose. In addition to Wolfe, writers whose work has fallen under the title "new journalism" include Norman Mailer, Hunter S. Thompson, Joan Didion, Truman Capote, George Plimpton and Gay Talese.

Gonzo journalism is a type of journalism popularized by the American writer Hunter S. Thompson, author of *Fear and Loathing in Las Vegas*, *Fear and Loathing on the Campaign Trail '72* and *The Kentucky Derby is Decadent and Depraved*, among other stories and books. Gonzo journalism is characterized by its punchy style, rough language, and ostensible disregard for conventional journalistic writing forms and customs.

More importantly, the traditional objectivity of the journalist is given up through immersion into the story itself, as in New Journalism, and the reportage is taken from a first-hand, participatory perspective, sometimes using an author surrogate such as Thompson's Raoul Duke. Gonzo journalism attempts to present a multi-disciplinary perspective on a particular story, drawing from popular culture, sports, political, philosophical and literary sources. Gonzo journalism has been styled eclectic or untraditional.

It remains a feature of popular magazines such as *Rolling Stone* magazine. It has a good deal in common with new journalism and on-line journalism (see above). A modern example of gonzo journalism would be Robert Young Pelton in his "The World's Most Dangerous Places" series for ABCNews.com or Kevin Sites in the Yahoo sponsored series on war zones called "In The Hot Zone"

Another area of journalism that grew in stature in the 20th Century is 'celebrity' or 'people' journalism, which focuses on the personal lives of people, primarily celebrities, including movie and stage actors, musical artists, models and photographers, other notable people in the entertainment industry, as well as people who seek attention, such as politicians, and people thrust into the attention of the public, such as people who do something newsworthy.

Once the province of newspaper gossip columnists and gossip magazines, celebrity journalism has become the focus of national tabloid newspapers like the *National Enquirer*, magazines like *People* and *Us Weekly*, syndicated television shows like *Entertainment Tonight*, *Inside Edition*, *The Insider*, *Access Hollywood*, and *Extra*, cable networks like E!, AandE Network and The Biography Channel, and numerous other television productions and thousands of Web sites. Most other news media provide some coverage of celebrities and people.

Celebrity journalism differs from feature writing in that it focuses on people who are either already famous or are especially attractive, and in that it often covers celebrities obsessively, to the point of these journalists behaving unethically in order to provide coverage. Paparazzi, photographers who would follow celebrities incessantly to obtain potentially embarrassing photographs, have come to characterize celebrity journalism.

An emerging form of journalism, which combines different forms of journalism, such as print, photographic and video, into one piece or group of pieces. Convergence journalism can be found in the likes of CNN and many other news sites.

Ambush journalism refers to aggressive tactics practiced by journalists to suddenly confront and question people who otherwise do not wish to speak to a journalist. The practice has particularly been applied by television journalists, on news shows like The O'Reilly Factor and 60 Minutes and by Geraldo Rivera and other local television reporters conducting investigations. The practice has been sharply criticized by journalists and others as being highly unethical and sensational, while others defend it as the only way to attempt to provide those subject to it an opportunity to comment for a report. This can usually be discerned by the level of physical aggression the journalist displays and in the time allowed for an uninterrupted answer.

In the 1920s, as modern journalism was just taking form, writer Walter Lippmann and American philosopher John Dewey debated over the role of journalism in a democracy. Their differing philosophies still characterize a debate about the role of journalism in society and the nation-state.

Lippmann understood that journalism's role at the time was to act as a mediator or translator between the public and policy making elites. The journalist became the middleman. When elites spoke, journalists listened and recorded the information, distilled it, and passed it on to the public for their consumption. His reasoning behind this was that the public was not in a position to deconstruct the growing and complex flurry of information present in modern society, and so an intermediary was needed to filter news for the masses.

Lippman put it this way: The public is not smart enough to understand complicated, political issues. Furthermore, the public was too consumed with their daily lives to care about complex public policy. Therefore the public needed someone to interpret the decisions or concerns of the elite to make the information plain and simple.

That was the role of journalists. Lippmann believed that the public would affect the decision-making of the elite with their vote. In the meantime, the elite (*i.e.* politicians, policy makers, bureaucrats, scientists, etc.) would keep the business of power running. In Lippman's world, the journalist's role was to inform the public of what the elites were doing. It was also to act as a watchdog over the elites, as the public had the final say with their votes.

Effectively that kept the public at the bottom of the power chain, catching the flow of information that is handed down from experts/elites.

Dewey, on the other hand, believed the public was not only capable of understanding the issues created or responded to by the elite, it was in the public forum that decisions should be made after discussion and debate. When issues were thoroughly vetted, then the best ideas would bubble to the surface.

Dewey believed journalists should do more than simply pass on information. He believed they should weigh the consequences of the policies being enacted. Over time, his idea has been implemented in various degrees, and is more commonly known as "community journalism."

This concept of *community journalism* is at the centre of new developments in journalism. In this new paradigm, journalists are able to engage citizens and the experts/elites in the proposition and generation of content. It's important to note that while there is an assumption of equality, Dewey still celebrates expertise. Dewey believes the shared knowledge of many is far superior to a single individual's knowledge. Experts and scholars are welcome in Dewey's framework, but there is not the hierarchical structure present in Lippman's understanding of journalism and society. According to Dewey, conversation, debate, and dialogue lie at the heart of a democracy.

While Lippman's journalistic philosophy might be more acceptable to government leaders, Dewey's approach is a better description of how many journalists see their role in society, and, in turn, how much of society expects journalists to function. Americans, for example, may criticize some of the excesses committed by journalists, but they tend to expect journalists to serve as watchdogs on government, businesses and other actors, enabling people to make informed decisions on the issues of the time.

According to *The Elements of Journalism*, a book by Bill Kovach and Tom Rosenstiel, there are nine elements of journalism. In order for a journalist to fulfill their duty of providing the people with the information they need to be free and self-governing. They must follow these guidelines:

- Journalism's first obligation is to the truth.
- Its first loyalty is to the citizens.
- Its essence is discipline of verification.
- Its practitioners must maintain an independence from those they cover.
- It must serve as an independent monitor of power.
- It must provide a forum for public criticism and compromise.
- It must strive to make the significant interesting, and relevant.
- It must keep the news comprehensive and proportional.
- Its practitioners must be allowed to exercise their personal conscience.

In the April 2007 edition of the book, they have added one additional element, *the rights and responsibilities of citizens* to make it a total of ten elements of journalism.

In the UK, all newspapers are bound by the Code of Practice of the Press Complaints Commission. This includes points like respecting people's privacy and ensuring accuracy. However, the Media Standards Trust has criticised the PCC, claiming it needs to be radically changed to secure public trust of newspapers. This is in stark contrast to the media climate prior to the 20th Century, where the media market was dominated by smaller newspapers and pamphleteers who usually had an overt and often radical agenda, with no presumption of balance or objectivity.

There are several professional organizations, universities and foundations that recognize excellence in journalism in the USA. The Pulitzer Prize, administered by Columbia University in New York City, is awarded to newspapers, magazines and broadcast media for excellence in various kinds of journalism. The Columbia University Graduate School of Journalism gives the Alfred I. duPont-Columbia University Awards for excellence in radio and television journalism, and the Scripps Howard Foundation gives the National Journalism Awards in 17 categories. The Society of Professional Journalists gives the Sigma Delta Chi Award for journalism excellence. In the television industry, the National Academy of Television Arts and Sciences gives awards for excellence in television journalism.

Such a code of conduct can, in the real world, be difficult to uphold consistently. Journalists who believe they are being fair or objective may give biased accounts—by reporting selectively, trusting too much to anecdote, or giving a partial explanation of actions. Even in routine reporting, bias can creep into a story through a reporter's choice of facts to summarize, or through failure to check enough sources, hear and report dissenting voices, or seek fresh perspectives.

A news organization's budget inevitably reflects decision-making about what news to cover, for what audience, and in what depth. Those decisions may reflect conscious or unconscious bias. When budgets are cut, editors may sacrifice reporters in distant news bureaus, reduce the number of staff assigned to low-income areas, or wipe entire communities from the publication's zone of interest.

Publishers, owners and other corporate executives, especially advertising sales executives, can try to use their powers over journalists to influence how news is reported and published. Journalists usually rely on top management to create and maintain a "firewall" between the news and other departments in a news organization to prevent undue influence on the news department.

One journalism magazine, Columbia Journalism Review, has made it a practice to reveal examples of executives who try to influence news coverage, of executives who do not abuse their powers over journalists, and of journalists who resist such pressures.

Self-censorship is a growing problem in journalism, particularly in covering countries that sharply restrict press freedom. As commercial pressure in the media marketplace grows, media organizations are loath to lose access to high-profile countries by producing unflattering stories. For example, CNN admitted that it had practiced self-censorship in covering the Saddam Hussein regime in Iraq in order to ensure continued access after the regime had thrown out other media.

PREPARING THE NEXT GENERATION OF JOURNALISTS

The news industry has been undergoing a fundamental paradigm shift since the end of last century. An increasing number of media companies around the United States, such as the Washington Post in Washington, DC, Media General in Virginia, the Tribune Company in Chicago, and New England Cable News, have taken solid steps to merge different media such as newspapers, television stations, radio stations, and online journalism companies to disseminate news content on multiple media platforms. As a result, in a metropolitan area, one company would own print, TV, and online venues. Media call this industrial trend "media convergence," though the concept means much more than media mergers. Media convergence muddies the lines among broadcast journalism, print journalism, and online journalism, leaving college journalism educators to wonder whether traditional journalism Programmes have become dinosaurs.

After surveying 200 newspaper publishers worldwide, the World Association of Newspapers (WAN) found, "Despite a somewhat gloomy outlook for wholesale convergence in media companies worldwide in the near term, convergence is already being implemented with varying degrees of enthusiasm and speed among the world's media companies".

The Innovation International Media Consulting Group estimates that at least 100 of the world's multiple media companies are planning and implementing integration strategies. South and Nicholson drew a sketch of a converged media company:

Daily journalists need to embrace the 24-hour news cycle, with continuous deadlines. And the story needs to be reported and produced for a multi-platform audience. That may mean delivering content first to the Web and cell phones, a streaming video broadcast later in the day, a TV talk-back interview still later, and a "second day" interpretive story for the next morning's newspaper.

Dominic Gates (2002) pointed out, "Convergence with broadcast and online media is the shape of things to come for newspapers." The trend remains controversial. Critics complain that such cross-ownership of both a television station and a newspaper in the same market is a threat to democracy because it limits the number of voices1.

Delegates of the Communication Workers of America, a 60,000-member guild, passed a resolution in June of 2002 at the group's annual convention in Las Vegas, pledging to increase public awareness about the risks of ongoing media convergence. The delegates complained that shrinking media markets are a threat to editorial diversity and job security.

In 1975, the Federal Communications Commission (FCC) ruled that no new broadcast licenses would be granted to companies that own a major daily newspaper and a local television station in the same city. Fairness and Accuracy In Reporting (FAIR) calls on the FCC to roll back limits on media consolidation. The Newspaper Association of America (NAA), on the other hand, has asked the FCC to appeal the rule. On June 2, 2003, the FCC voted 3 to 2 to relax or eliminate some ownership restrictions, such as a rule barring media companies from owning television stations in markets where they publish daily newspapers.

Although some lawmakers and advocacy groups are still fighting in the courts and on Capitol Hill to overturn the FCC's new media ownership rules, these rules will be likely to encourage cross-media ownership in the years to come. The mergers have raised questions about whether they are good for the craft of journalism itself. Critics complain that by requiring journalists to be jacks of both trades, print and broadcast, the journalists will be masters of none. Robert J. Haiman, president emeritus of The Poynter Institute, compared the media convergence trend to an Amphicar, a cross between a boat and a car. The Amphicar, hawked in Florida during the 1950s, flopped. "It flopped because people quickly discovered that while it really was an ingenious combination of a car and a boat, it was a lousy car (because it also had to be a boat), and it was a lousy boat (because it also had to be a car)".

Willingly or unwillingly, many news practitioners' functions are gradually changing or are expected to change as media convergence rolls on. For a reporter in a converged media environment, knowing how to write is probably no longer enough. S/he could be expected to write the same story for different media in a timely manner.

Ideally, s/he can readily talk in front of a video camera. As a photographer, knowing how to tell a story both in video and in still images is more and more in demand. A designer should know how to prepare still graphics for print, moving graphics for television and dynamic graphics for the Web. At the online version of the Chicago Tribune, for instance, staffers are supposed to cover stories, take pictures, operate video cameras, and create digital pages.

The editors, too, need a wider variety of skills than the traditional paper editors. Along with infrastructure changes and the attempt to create synergy among the various media outlets, a new breed of journalists-digital or multimedia journalists-is expected.As media jobs become more demanding, some news practitioners are beginning to team up to complete projects. At the same time, fear, confusion, and frustration from news practitioners are creeping into newsrooms. Carr wrote: "Convergence frightens many people who wonder whether their current skill sets have prepared them for-or will even be needed in-that great undiscovered country, the future.

This is probably the primary reason why I still find such great hostility to convergence among certain journalists." Killebrew (2001), a mass communications professor from the University of South Florida, suggested that "journalists must be prepared to either crosstrain themselves or seek training from other sources while management must be prepared to give them the opportunities and time to do so."

The 1999-2000 president of the Association for Schools of Journalism and Mass Communication (ASJMC), Shirley Staples Carter, questioned whether, in the midst of the "Internet revolution," Programmes are prepared to educate journalists of the future. When specifically talking about writing, Keith Hartenberger, manager of news and programming for Tribune Regional Programming, said that journalism schools should make their students aware of the many ways to present the news. "It's a multimedia world out there," he said. "If you're just being prepared to write newspaper stories, you won't be prepared". "At some point, this [cross-media training] is something we're going to expect from everyone".Media convergence, as a trend that is gradually shaping the landscape of the media industry in the new century, has called into question the conventional journalism school practice of having separate tracks-print, broadcast, etc. Journalism educators around the country also are trying to figure out what they should do, if anything, to better prepare students for the converged media.

For instance, should journalism educators consider merging different sequences such as magazine, newspaper, broadcast, and photojournalism, or still teach all such courses as if they were unrelated media? "Traditionally defined segments of the communications industry are less and less distinguishable for technological and market convergence," observed Moon.

Are college journalism educators themselves both theoretically equipped and technologically prepared to teach their students for converged media? What do media companies expect from future news practitioners? What do current news practitioners in converged media feel is lacking? For both news practitioners and professors, the two most urgent questions cry for answers: Should journalism schools train specialists or fit for-all generalists? And how should college journalism education balance the teaching of critical thinking and technical skills?

Apart from all these education-related questions, we are also interested in finding out what are the driving forces behind the media mergers, who are regarded as the beneficiaries of this trend, and how people's political beliefs are related to their attitude Towards teaching media convergence in colleges? These questions pertain closely to college journalism education, which has been the subject of debate and criticism for two decades.

A national survey was conducted among colleges, daily newspapers, and commercial television stations to explore the issue of how journalism schools should prepare students for the trend of media convergence from the perspectives of news editors, news professionals, and journalism professors. The study measured the level of general support for convergence education and determined if a new model of journalism education was called for.

If so, it examined whether consensus existed among the three groups on the direction educators should take when revisiting Progamme designs. Where consensus was not apparent, divisions among the sample of educators, editors, and reporters were defined. The goal of the study is to provide evidence that will help journalism educators make informed decisions about how to respond to media convergence in their curricula and courses and lay an empirical foundation for further discussions and conversations about media convergence.

The search results show that media convergence is a comparatively new topic in media research, though articles about it have inundated the Internet, magazines, and newspapers. Most research writings appeared no earlier than

1998. Many writings have addressed one of the toughest questions: What is media convergence? How to define "media convergence" had a direct bearing on how we conducted this study. Out of these writings, we identified four categories of media convergence that directly affect how journalism will be taught in colleges.

CONTENT CONVERGENCE

As Tremayne noted, decades ago, the term media convergence referred to the content convergence between competing newspapers and even among newspapers, magazines, and television. Today, pure content convergence continues on the Internet. For instance, the St. Petersburg Times has incorporated local Channel 10's TV news into its online newspaper though they are independent business entities. In other words, media convergence may not necessarily be tied to media merger.

Form convergence (or technological convergence). Around the mid-1990s, as Tremayne and Wurtz noted, computer technology and Internet technology made possible the convergence of all forms of mediated communications including video, audio, data, text, still photo, and graphic art for "on-demand" audiences.

Using these different forms to tell news stories on the World Wide Web has been widely regarded as the future of mass communication regardless of the fact that most online news sites have had a hard time making ends meet, let alone making a profit. Form convergence, often called technological convergence, has been a fundamental force to guide and lead convergence in the market, industry, and regulation.

CORPORATE CONVERGENCE

Since the late 1990s, media convergence has been escalated to the level of media mergers. The News Centre located in Tampa, Florida, owned by Media General, and the Tribune Interactive, owned by the Tribune Company, for instance, are the products of media mergers.

In The News Centre, WFLA-TV, The Tampa Tribune, and Tampa Bay Online operate out of the same building. They share daily tips and information, spot news, photography, enterprise reporting, franchises, events, and public service. Each of the three entities in The News Centre has its own independent newsroom, but they issued a joint statement of coverage principles, titled "News Centre Pledge".

The Tribune Interactive has brought together the interactive functions of the company's four newspapers and more than a score of television stations including WGN-TV and CLTV. The individual media outlets have their own newsgathering staff, but their coverage is enhanced by their multimedia desks in the Chicago Tribune newsroom and the Tribune Media Centre in Washington.

"A synergy-team of print editors and TV news veterans at the Chicago Tribune work together to manage resource sharing and the relationship". Media merger has made both content convergence and form convergence handy. Corporate convergence via vertical and horizontal integration, mergers, alliances, and acquisitions will make traditionally defined segments of the communications industry less and less distinguishable.

Role convergence. Russial identified several examples of role convergence in newsrooms. For instance, the roles of reporter and librarian, the roles of copyeditor and compositor, the roles of graphic artist and Web designer, and the roles of photo editor, darkroom technician, and photographer are all converging in different media.

In more recent years, content convergence, form convergence, and especially corporate convergence have sparked more in-depth role convergence among news practitioners.

For instance, Victoria Lim from The News Centre in Tampa revealed at a February 2002 conference on media convergence at the University of Florida that she primarily works as a television reporter for WFLA-TV, but she also has to write for the company's newspaper, The Tampa Tribune, as a senior consumer investigative reporter and for the Web company TBO.com on a daily basis; at the time of the conference, she was working on 31 stories.

A newspaper reporter may also produce a newspaper in QuarkXPress or serve as a TV news anchor, while a newspaper photographer may shoot video stories or produce interactive online stories in Flash. Role convergence requires that both reporters and editors re-equip themselves both journalistically and technologically.

Of the four types of convergence, role convergence has the most direct effect on future journalism education. Within the media industry, there are serious doubts about whether training cross-media journalists is possible or desirable. When asked whether reporters of the future must be equally skilled in print, TV, and online, Forrest Carr, news director of WFLA-TV at The News Centre in Tampa, said no.

He said he believed that there would always be areas of specialization and students may still choose specialties, but said that it no longer makes any sense to pretend print journalists and electronic journalists are in different professions. On the other hand, he said that journalists who have skills in TV, print, and online media certainly will be more valuable to their employers; and he emphasized that prospective employees must be willing to work in an environment where reporters cooperate across platforms.

In most cases currently, he said, cooperating across platforms simply comes down to the sharing of tips and information. Charles Kravetz, the vice president for news and station manager of New England Cable News (NECN), the largest regional news network in America, concurs with Forrest Carr.

When asked "Do you see a time when all journalists will have to be able to file stories on all platforms (print, TV, radio, online)?" Kravetz said: "I am not sure that is the way it is going to work out. This notion we had that one-journalist-fits-all-media is perhaps not that realistic. There are very few people we will talk about in the future that are TV/newspaper/internet reporters".

Gates agreed, "The 'backpack journalist'-a superhack master of multimedia who can do it all and who routinely packs a laptop and a video camera along with the tape recorder and steno notebook-may be the subject of avant-garde j-school courses, but it's not likely to become the norm."

Some other media executives have tried to define the extent to which role convergence is expected. Gil Thelen, executive editor and senior vice president of The Tampa Tribune, for instance, gave suggestions to journalism educators based on his two years of experience in The News Centre.

"The fully formed, all-purpose, multiplatform, gadget-laden journalism grad is NOT what we're looking to hire. Journalism schools must continue to produce graduates who are competent in one craft area: reporting, design, producing, directing, editing." However, Thelen encouraged journalism schools to train writers to write for print, online, and broadcast and train print photographers to learn how to shoot and produce TV packages.

Thelen said that cultural resistance is the biggest hurdle for converging newsrooms, and that employees or current journalism students need to learn to cooperate and collaborate across newsrooms.

What is unclear is whether these media administrators' predictions are limited by the status quo of the current generation of news practitioners who might not be very well prepared for convergence or who might even resist the notion of media convergence.

At Brigham Young University, students with multiple skills are more valued and feel more comfortable in the converged media environment. In addition, sharing tips and information does not entail convergence. Reporters have been doing this for decades. It seems that keeping convergence only on the level of sharing tips and information can hardly justify the high cost of rebuilding infrastructures like The News Centre.

We are interested in finding out what expectations media companies have for future journalists. From news professionals' self-evaluations of their preparedness for media convergence, we should also be able to infer what is most desirable in the media industry nowadays.

In the face of increasing demand for technically skilled journalists-conversant with QuarkXPress, Photoshop, Avid, and Dreamweaver and able to crunch statistics using spreadsheets and other statistical methods in order to uncover the hidden story-should longstanding staples such as ethics, law, and theory remain at the heart of journalism curricula? Or should such materials, commonly grouped together as "critical thinking", share equal hilling with technology or "skills" training? In other words, how should journalism schools balance the teaching of professional skills and that of critical thinking in an era when technology penetrates every facet of news gathering, preparation, editing, production, and delivery?

Convergence further complicates this age-old battle in journalism education. Abraham noticed that the goal of most restructuring in journalism institutions is to provide an integrated skills environment where students would get the chance to practice the skills of multimedia production. Abraham argued: "The role of journalism academy should be very different from that of the industry.

Its role should not simply be to inculcate skills that will help students to flag down jobs. They should aim to provide a scholarly background for a deeper intellectual understanding of our lives, media forms and of communication in general".

The dean of the University of Nevada at Reno thinks the ability to use multiple media skills is essential. Brigham Young University, which has built a working converged newsroom into its curriculum, expects students to graduate with multiple skills. University News Director, Dean Paynter, said, "We expect our students to more than anchor, more than report, and more than produce.

The best ones can do it all, including write for the newspaper". Mitchell Stephens (2000), professor of journalism and mass communications at New York University, holds up the other end. "In a world where corporate pressures on 'content providers' seem to be increasing and civic affairs decreasing, the argument for emphasizing the basics does have much to recommend it."

Thomas Kunkel (2002), dean of the Philip Merrill College of Journalism at the University of Maryland, sums it up: "Today's journalists, first and foremost, must be strong critical thinkers who know enough about geography, history and the human condition to understand why events play out as they do. They must be intellectually curious. They should speak a second language. They should read something other than Jim Romenesko's MediaNews site. They ought to have a world view."

A controversy in late 2002 at Columbia University demonstrates how volatile the argument is currently. The debate arose when the graduate school of journalism at Columbia University halted its search for a dean. The new university president, Lee Bollinger, wanted to re-evaluate the school's mix of craft versus theory (Babcock), and the move created a flurry of opinion about the journalism school's existing curriculum.

This critical curriculum question is often reflected in the questions of whether and how new technology classes should be included in the existing curriculum and how they should be taught. Some journalism schools are preparing to embrace the wave of media convergence in their new curricula by converging print and electronic media sequences to adapt to the industrial trends and the new technological environment. Blanchard and Christ warn that universities with limited resources will no longer tolerate duplicating specializations with separate courses such as writing for television, writing for newspapers, writing for public relations, and writing for advertising. Blanchard and Christ add that the communications revolution (the media's convergence and related trends) is making journalism and mass communication's traditional sequences obsolete.

Actually, Blanchard and Christ's opinion is not something new. Early in 1972, the University of Iowa School of Journalism already eliminated its sequences but at the expense of being denied reaccreditation by ACEJMC. About thirty years later, their decision seemed to be finding more sympathy.

Many schools are still exploring where to go. In October 2001, seventeen professors and leaders of new media from thirteen journalism Programmes across the country gathered in Berkeley, California, and had a discussion about new media in journalism education.

The University of Nevada, Reno, offered several different elective courses in new media, but it did not have a special sequence. It was struggling with how to incorporate them in other classes. The University of Florida had a concentration in online media, which was equivalent to other concentrations such as reporting and editing and photojournalism.

Students who were not in that concentration couldn't always squeeze in the online media courses because they did not have any leftover électives they could take in the school. American University had three divisions, journalism, public communication, and visual media, but they did not work together very well most of the time.

The University of South Carolina was restructuring its graduate masters Progamme in newspaper leadership and was focusing it on convergence. The University of Maryland had an online curriculum, but it was not formally structured as such. Northwestern University had an introductory New Media course at the undergraduate and graduate level, which was offered as an elective.

It was packed with everything from new skills training to wrestling with the business issues of new media to actual production. After three admission cycles, enrollment declined. The University of Minnesota established the Institute for New Media Studies, which merged broadcast journalism and print journalism Programmes to make them a concentration with the idea that future journalists would work in a multi-channel environment and should know how to operate within all those channels.

Although editors and academics sometimes agree on the qualifications a journalism student needs, an ideal curriculum doesn't always include convergence preparedness courses. In a 2000 poll, editors and educators agreed "on the same five of 14 types of knowledge considered most necessary for journalism graduates and listed them in the same order of importance".

Technical skills were not mentioned in the top five, surpassed instead by "understanding of a journalist's responsibility to the public, understanding of the ethics of journalism, knowledge of current events, broad general knowledge, and knowledge of government".

With so much variance across universities, we are interested in finding out how many journalism schools have revamped their curricula to prepare students for the trend of media convergence, what professors' attitudes are Towards teaching critical thinking vs. teaching technical skills and training generalists vs. training specialists, and what editors' and news professionals' attitudes are Towards the same issues. In this regard, several scholars and news practitioners have tried to give advice to journalism professors and students in the context of media convergence.

In 2002, David Bulla from the University of Florida presented his "Media convergence: Industry practices and implications for education" to the AEJMC annual conference in Miami. This is the first research writing of its kind. The theme of the paper is the closest to that of this study. Bulla's study looked at the changing nature of contemporary mass communications practices, focusing on multimedia or converged journalism.

It described what scholastic journalism scholars are doing to prepare their students for these changes and provided recommendations to educators about how to update curricula to account for convergence.

The research questions for that study were: (1) what are journalism educators currently doing to incorporate convergence into their curricula; and (2) what abilities, skills, and attitudes do professional journalists expect from their newest employees? Media convergence in Bulla's study was defined as multimedia journalism, which means reporting, writing, and disseminating content in two or more media platforms.

Because of the controversy about media mergers, Bulla tried to find answers to some hot issues concerning democracy including: Does corporate media merging reduce public discourse and hinder democracy? Will it ultimately mean the need for fewer and fewer reporters, as the development of other technology has meant a decline in the number of employees in other areas of the production process? All these questions pertain to our study.

Bulla obtained a sample of 114 news practitioners working at newspapers, television stations, wire services, magazines, radio stations, and online publications in the United States. The sample was randomly selected from Editor and Publisher and Yahoo lists of media companies in the U.S. Media Web sites. With a response rate of 36 percent, Bulla interviewed 41 news practitioners. Bulla also interviewed college educators, but he did not state how he sampled them.

What is unclear is the extent to which the Yahoo list and Editor and Publisher list overlap each other and if a sample from two potentially overlapping lists is any longer a random sample. In addition, since Bulla's questions were almost all unstructured, that is, he conducted interviews,10 he did not really need a random sample.

Researchers strive for depth rather than breadth and don't mean to claim external validity in the statistical sense by conducting interviews. Finally, if he did need a random sample, a sample of 114 people with a 36 percent response rate could be statistically defective because of big statistical errors. Bulla needed a better research design to make his study valid and reliable.

Some scholars doubt whether journalism school professors are theoretically and especially technologically prepared to teach media convergence. In an article written for Journalism Education magazine, John Irby, a professor from Washington State University and a veteran newspaper editor and publisher, for instance, was concerned about the disconnection between the newsroom and the classroom.

Irby (2000) asked: Are universities and educators effectively preparing students for the Workforce? Do educators understand what newspapers are looking for in future reporters and editors? Does the newspaper industry have a responsibility in the division between educators and professionals? Are journalism educators "discounted" by professionals who believe those who teach couldn't succeed in newspapers?

Irby said older generations of newspaper reporters also appeared on radio and television periodically though they had no training; they never even felt like it was part of their job and thus did not take it very seriously. But now, he continued, print journalists do need to take it seriously; journalism educators need to re-evaluate, and probably modify, the separatetrack approach in training print and broadcast journalists.

Irby believed that there is still a need for specialization, but he told students to take both broadcast and print courses and told them that computer literacy is as crucial as the old-fashioned kind. A study about the impact of media convergence on journalism education without consulting Robert J. Haiman's article "Can convergence float?" (2001) should be considered incomplete.

Haiman's fervent talk against media convergence raised some challenging questions that educators must face. Haiman, president emeritus of The Poynter Institute, argued that the converged media world is one from which good journalism, and good journalists, are going to be in great need of defence.

He stuck to his notion of the mission of good journalism he stated 40 years ago: "To inform the public about the public's business, creating a society that is equipped with the knowledge it needs to make the right civic decisions more often than it makes the wrong civic decisions, and thus helping to perpetuate self-government and democracy."

Expressing his deep concern for journalism, Haiman said: "I think that convergence may end up being good, maybe even very good, for media companies. I fear, however, that it is going to be bad, and maybe even very bad, for journalism." He continued to explain: I think it is going to be bad for journalism because, even if it goes as well as it possibly can, I believe that it is going to distract journalists, journalism teachers, and journalism students away from that single most important imperative of the craft - to create an informed society capable of intelligently governing itself. And if it does not go well, I fear it is going to subject journalists to time, resource, craft, and ethical pressures, all of which will be bad for journalists, bad for journalism, and bad for the country.

In his talk, Haiman mentioned a top education reporter who had done a "superb job" for more than 18 years. Now, he had to do short reports for the TV station with which that newspaper was converged. However, "he's not exactly ready for prime time." After this reporter retires, Haiman is afraid that that he will be replaced by "someone who may not report like a buzz saw and write like a dream, but who probably will report and write education okay and who will also look good and sound good on television."

"When that happens," he continued, "the journalism quality of all of the education reporting coming out of that converged news operation is going to go down." We believe that few people would disagree with Haiman's point that quality content is the king, to use his own words, but Haiman's above comment could be limited, again, by the performance of the current generation of reporters who are not prepared for media convergence.

Haiman was suggesting that a future reporter who has been trained to work for different media platforms and who has learned more about reporting would produce reporting of less quality. In our study, we would like to find out to what extent Haiman's concern is shared by editors, news professionals, and professors.

While convergence is still in its infancy, Haiman suggested that journalists, journalism students, and journalism teachers do three "terribly important things":

- For journalists who want to keep good journalism alive in the converged world to take a blood oath to fight, scrap, kick and scream whenever any attempt is made to dilute good journalism values.
- For journalism schools and journalism teachers to offer students the right curriculum to function best in that converged world, and this does not mean offering new courses in convergence.
- For journalism students to emphasize the right areas of study and take the right courses so they will be able to defend themselves against the evils of convergence, prosper in that new world, and contribute to the effort to sustain informed self-government.

Haiman said, "If we decide to teach anything about convergence at Poynter, that is the lesson I hope we'll teach." To students, Haiman said that the journalists who will be the most successful in the converged world are the same ones who are the most successful today, and they are the ones who are best trained in six areas: reporting, writing, editing, ethics, and media law, research techniques and specialized knowledge such as business, finance, law, science, health, aging, and the environment.

Since the top reporter in education Haiman mentioned can hardly survive the converged media world, our question is whether gaining knowledge in these six areas is sufficient and what else, if any, students need to learn. Do students need to learn any new skills? What new skills do news practitioners need?

Also, we would like to see how the attitudes of the respondents from these three groups Towards media merger affect their views of how to train future journalists. As South and Nicholson (2002) commented, "If the industry doesn't agree on what new skills journalists need, it will be hard for journalism schools to know what to teach."

LARGER CONTEXT OF THE STUDY

The questions concerning teaching skills vs. critical thinking and training specialists vs. generalists are not new. They have been contextualized in ongoing conversations across disciplines over decades on many campuses in the United States.

But such conversations take on new meanings in journalism schools when many reporting jobs today are becoming high-tech-oriented and many news companies are demanding high-tech skills from new hires upon their graduation. The impact of such industrial demands on universities brings us back to the core issue-the role of the university in the shaping of the young souls in its charge.

In other words, how should a university achieve the desired product-a truly educated human being for newsrooms. The question of teaching skills vs. critical thinking winds down to a perennial competition between acquiescing pervasive vocationalism with its emphasis on skills training in an attempt to enable college students to survive outside academic institutions and establishing the relevance of the broad spectrum of knowledge to the career goals and lives of individuals.

E. D. Hirsch argues: "Narrow vocational education, adjusted to the needs of the moment, is made ever more obsolete by changing technology What is required is education for change, not for static job competencies". Probably no one has better expressed than Joanne G. Kurfiss the importance of imparting critical thinking as skills of analyzing and constructing arguments, as construction of meaning, and as the manifestation of a contextual theory of knowledge."Critical thinking can result in a new way of approaching significant issues in one's life or a deeper understanding of the basis for one's actions. Or it might result in political activity". Along the similar line as Kurfiss's critical thinking theory and unlike Allan Bloom, who condemns the introduction of non-

Western materials into the university curricula so as to protect the curriculum from the contamination of ideological conflict, Jerry Herron also highly promotes the teaching of critical thinking by calling on faculty to bring their conflicting ideologies into open engagement so that students can discover what is at stake in different ideas and can see their representational meaning.

The questions are whether universities should totally give up the teaching of skills today and how the needs of the job market and the goal of college education can be in harmony. In other words, can the teaching of common traditional content and the teaching of higher order skills join forces? Patracia Graham, ex-dean of the Harvard Graduate School of Education, argues that we need both commonality and flexibility in American education and there is no reason we cannot have both at once.

The question of training specialists vs. generalists is an extension of a larger conversation about reforming the fragmented curricula in higher education. Often classified as "cultural right," Ernest Boyer, Allan Bloom, and E. D. Hirsch share similar views about the problems in higher education. They point out that the university now is anarchistic.

There is no vision of what an educated human being is. The curriculum is disjointed and disciplines are fragmented into smaller pieces. Undergraduates find it hard to see patterns in their courses and relate what they learn to life. Careerism conflicts with the liberal arts.

And finally, schools have failed to thoroughly carry out the educational goal of promoting mature literacy for all our citizens. They all agree that an educational reform is needed to teach more common traditional content apart from the higher-order skills that are commonly emphasized.

Boyer calls for a balance between individual interests and shared concerns while the actual priority is given to the latter. To promote a liberal education, Boyer advocates the "integrated core" or "enriched major"-a Progamme of general education that introduces students not only to essential knowledge, but also to connections across the disciplines, and, in the end, to the application of knowledge to life beyond the campus.

Boyer points out, knowledge becomes important only when we use it and apply it to humane ends; therefore, the undergraduate experience should not only generate new knowledge, but channel that knowledge to the service of the society.

It is a matter of invigorating "the claims of community while protecting with full vigour the dignity and origins of each individual," to use Boyer and Kaplan's words. In a similar vein, Bloom calls on teachers to look Towards the goal of human completeness and to provide students a liberal education, in which learning is both synoptic and precise.

To Bloom, liberal education feeds the student's love of truth and passion to live a good life. It also requires that a student's whole life be radically changed by it. Bloom offers an ivory tower vision of the university-"the good old Great Book approach"-undergraduate students spend four years reading certain generally recognized classic texts for answers to philosophical questions of personal and human identity and aspirations.

Bloom thinks that man may live more truly and fully in reading Plato and Shakespeare than at any other time because then they are participating in essential being and are forgetting their accidental lives.

In accordance with Boyer's and Bloom's points of view, Hirsch argues that "the greatest human individuality is developed in response to a tradition, not in response to disorderly, uncertain, and fragmented education" and "only by accumulating shared symbols, and the shared information the symbols represent can we learn to communicate effectively with one another in our national community".

However, Hirsch places emphasis more on the content of education, ensuring that students acquire all the "right" elements of knowledge that will enable them to get along in the Real World. He believes that neither the content-neutral curriculum of Rousseau and Dewey nor the narrowly specified curriculum of Plato is adequate to the needs of a modern nation.

Hirsch calls for a curriculum, including extensive curriculum and intensive curriculum with an emphasis on the former, which is traditional in content and provides students with a common core of cultural information. "The conception of a two-part curriculum avoids the idea that all children should study identical materials" Hirsch says.Based on our literature review, media convergence in our study is defined as the assimilation of media content for multiple media platforms. Media convergence may involve any combination of the convergences of media contents, media forms, media companies, and roles of news practitioners.

Our general research question is how college professors should prepare students to cope with media convergence. To be specific, should college professors prepare generalists who can competently work in multiple media platforms or prepare specialists who know inside out how to work for one particular medium platform?And how should journalism schools balance the teaching of critical thinking and technical skills? Corresponding to these two questions, we also would like to find out if college journalism educators themselves are both theoretically equipped and technologically prepared to teach their students about media convergence.

The study serves both as an attitude finder and a fact finder.We believe that professors, editors, and news professionals are the best candidates to answer these questions. Editors represent the media companies to hire news staffers with news reporting abilities desired by the company. News professionals work in the forefront of news reporting and know best about what news reporting abilities they need.The attitudes of the editors and the current generation of news professionals Towards media convergence will have a great implication on future journalism education. Professors run journalism schools, and they have the final say about where their schools are going. Their attitudes Towards journalism education in terms of media convergence will have the most direct influence on the kind of education journalism students will receive and how the students will perform in tomorrow's media.

Editors include daily newspaper editors in charge of newsroom operations or online news operations and news directors in charge of newsroom operations in a commercial TV station with news content, both in the United States. News professionals refer to non-management news staff, such as reporters, anchors, photographers, designers, producers, Web staff, etc., working in American media companies. Journalism professors are defined as full-time instructors with any academic rankings who teach journalism courses in a U.S. journalism school, department, Progamme, or division, which could be administratively affiliated with an institution with a name like College of Communications or Department of Communications Studies.

To obtain opinions about media convergence, we could have targeted our survey only at those editors and news professionals in a converged media environment. The opinions obtained from those editors and news professionals, however, could be biased. Those media companies that have not gone through convergence must have a reason for not doing so. We also wanted to find out what they are doing about convergence. Balanced views both from the converged and un-converged media companies will better assist colleges in their strategic planning.

We conducted a national survey among editors, news professionals, and journalism professors with three different versions of online survey questionnaires posted on a school Web site. Respondents were asked to fill out the questionnaire online and submit answers online as well. The answers went through a commercial form handler and reached the primary investigator's e-mail address.

By doing so, the primary investigator had no way to detect who answered the questionnaire unless the respondent voluntarily revealed his/her e-mail address to request the findings from the study.

There were twenty-two questions in each of these three questionnaires. Almost all questions were close-ended. About half of the questions used a 5-point Likert Scale from "Strongly Agree" to "Strongly Disagree." Some questions across the three questionnaires shared similarity, so that comparisons could be made when analyzing data.

A text field was created for respondents to provide feedback to the survey freely. The textual answers in the text field will be reported along with the statistics to illustrate and explain the quantitative findings. All questionnaires went through pilot tests. The unit of analysis was each participant. In order to conduct a systematic random sampling of editors and news professionals, we needed a list of newspaper editors and TV news directors in the United States and a list of newspaper and TV news staffers. We found that such lists did not exist, though lists of newspapers and lists of TV stations did exist in multiple places online like Editor and Publisher Yearbook and Broadcasting Sr Cable Yearbook. Therefore, we decided to construct our own.

To do so, we went through two steps. First, we constructed a combined list of daily newspapers and TV stations so that we could sample these news institutions. Second, we visited the Web sites of all sampled news institutions to find the e-mail of the editor/news director and the e-mail of one news professional randomly chosen.

Then, we visited each of those Web sites to find the e-mail address of the managing editor, chief editor, online editor, or equivalent in each of those dailies and sent out a survey invitation e-mail to him/her.

In total, we extracted 674 TV stations with a valid URL. Since this population is smaller than that of the newspapers, we over-sampled it. Instead of sampling every other four, we sampled every other station. Then, we visited each of those Web sites to find the e-mail address of the news director or equivalent in each of those TV stations and sent out a survey invitation e-mail to him/her.

We also sampled one news professional out of each of the sampled U.S. dailies and TV stations for the survey. Since there was always more than one professional in a company, we simply randomly clicked on one name and picked him/her and made sure that s/he was on the news staff.

Then, we sent him/her a survey invitation e-mail. If an individual e-mail address was not available, we replaced it with a generic e-mail address and specified whom the e-mail was for. S/he was asked to fill out a questionnaire that was worded in a slightly different manner. In total, we successfully sent out invitation e-mails to 398 news professionals.

We also needed to conduct a systematic random sampling of college journalism professors, but we were disappointed that all lists we found had many J-schools, even major ones, missing.

In total, the new list contains 205 alphabetically ordered U.S. J-schools that contain 2,194 journalism professors. We sampled one out of every four professors from the virtually running list of all journalism professors across the schools. For instance, if a school had six journalism professors, we picked the fourth one; then, the second journalism professor from next school was picked.

We sent an invitation e-mail to every professor in the sample. In total, we successfully sent out 500 e-mails. The three samples of editors, news professionals, and professors included 1,421 cases. We understood that nonresponse had been a serious problem with online surveys in recent years.

In order to counter possible low response rates in our survey, we created three samples for editors, news professionals, and professors containing roughly 500 people for each group, which were much larger than the sample sizes for populations recommended by Mildred Patten (2000) in her book Understanding Research Methods: An Overview of the Essentials so that, if low response rates occurred, we could base our confidence limits on the actual number of responses themselves. We also sent out one reminder e-mail to the samples, which drastically boosted the response rates, especially for professors and news professionals.

FINDINGS AND DISCUSSION

After two weeks of online data collecting in November 2002, we received 223 responses from professors (a 44per cent response rate), 151 responses from editors (a 29per cent response rate), and 142 responses from news professionals (a 35per cent response rate). The overall response rate is 36per cent. As Singletary (1994) notes, returns of 30per cent to 40per cent are common in mail surveys.

The response rates of this online survey seem typical. However, the response rates are still comparatively low. A response bias is potentially present. Many respondents (41per cent) left textual answers to explain and illustrate their answers to the close-ended questions and/or made comments on the topic.

By the end of 2002, 19per cent of the newspapers and commercial television stations with news content in the United States had gone through media mergers. Being merged or not has to do with the size of a company. Larger companies tend to have been merged while smaller ones have not. Roughly half of the news professionals surveyed (48per cent) reported that they produced news content for multiple media platforms on a routine basis; that was true both in merged media (50per cent) and non-merged media (48per cent).

In other words, media merger is not the precondition for practicing news for multiple media platforms. The pressure on news professionals to learn to produce multimedia content is also felt in many non-merged media companies. This finding confirms that media convergence is not necessarily related to media merger.

A typical editor or news director was a man (71per cent) between 36-45 years old (42per cent) with a bachelor's degree (76per cent) who had worked for at least two media (57per cent) for more than 20 years (53per cent). A typical news professional was either a man (52per cent) or woman (48per cent) between 26-35 years old (43per cent) with a bachelor's degree (84per cent) who had worked for at least two media (60per cent) less than ten years (62per cent).

Editors had generally worked for more years than news professionals, but they did not have more multiplatform experience than news professionals. As more news companies are practicing cross-media reporting with or without their companies being merged, it is important that editors with multiplatforrn experiences are chosen to direct newsroom businesses. Many editors need cross-media training more urgently than news professionals do if the news company they work for produces news contents for multiple media platforms on a daily basis.

Should J-schools Train Specialists or Generalists?

Gil Thelen (2002) said that writers should learn how to write for multimedia and still photographers should learn how to shoot videos, but he was not interested in hiring people with multiple sets of skills. We designed four questions to test how popular Thelen's opinion was.

The majority of the respondents (84per cent) agreed or strongly agreed with Thelen that journalism students should learn how to write for multiple media platforms. One-way ANOVA shows significant difference among the means for professors (4.35), professionals (4.05), and editors (3.99). Tukey HSD post hoc tests show that professors were more positive on this statement than editors and professionals, while no significant difference existed between editors and professionals.

A similar number of respondents (85per cent) agreed or strongly agreed with Thelen that journalism students with a visual emphasis should learn how to produce and edit photos, videos, and online interactive images. One-way ANOVA shows significant difference among the means for professors (4.55), professionals (4.22), and editors (3.91).

Tukey HSD post hoc tests show that professors were more positive on this statement than professionals, while professionals were more positive than editors. Most respondents (78per cent) agreed or strongly agreed that all journalism majors should learn multiple sets of skills, such as writing, editing, TV production, digital photography, newspaper design, and Web publishing.

Oneway ANOVA shows significant differences among the means for professionals (4.28), editors (3.99), and professors (3.86). Tukey HSD post hoc tests show that news professionals who worked in the forefront of news production felt this need more deeply than other respondents. Editors also had such an expectation for them.

There is no significant difference between editors and professors. These findings support the growing evidence that news professionals are being asked to wear multiple hats. The findings also indicate that Thelen's view has its market at this moment when news professionals with multiple sets of skills are highly desirable but not easy to find.

Such a view may change as more journalism graduates equipped with multiple sets of skills cntcr thc job market. The professors' textual answers show that some of the difficulties J-schools have come across include the lack of a friendly curriculum, lack of credit hours to include the components of convergence content, lack of willing cooperation among faculty from different sequences, and lack of expertise, interest, or even time for some professors to develop new courses on convergence.

When asked whether journalism students should still have a specialization, such as writing, photojournalism, broadcasting, and new media, over half (63per cent) of the respondents agreed or strongly agreed. Over a quarter of the respondents (28per cent) were negative and 9per cent were not sure. One-way ANOVA mean comparisons show no significant difference of attitude among professionals (3.42), editors (3.51), and professors (3.72).

Comparing the support rate for this question to those for the first three questions, it is fair to argue that editors, news professionals, and professors emphasized the importance of cross-media training more than that of specialization, though they believed that specialization should not be neglected either.

Currently, students in many J-schools specialize in one area by subscribing to a sequence such as news-editorial, magazine, photojournalism, and broadcast. When asked whether sequences should be reorganized considering the trend of media-platforms merging in the industry, 56per cent of the professors agreed or strongly agreed, 22per cent were not sure, and another 22per cent disagreed or strongly disagreed.

The concept of sequences is being shaken among professors though it is still being accepted as a legitimate means of training students in various specialization areas in some J-schools. Speaking on behalf of herself and her colleagues, Professor offered some special insight on this issue:

We can't teach for the "now." We have to prepare students for when they graduatewhich in most instances is now five years out. And, we feel a commitment to expose them to all types of writing in all platforms so they can be flexible about their career choice at the front end of their academics. Then, they can apply the skills to a specialty area where they are totally proficient.

"Flexible" is a key term repeatedly seen in editors' and news professionals' textual answers as a suggestion for future journalists. Editor 's statement is typical: Our job descriptions are open ended and new hires understand that they are being hired for their skills. They may be hired today to cover the city beat. In six months or in two weeks, if necessary, a person with Quark skills may be asked to fill in or shift duties to include pagination of a particular section. It is important that hires stay flexible.

The new hires, wrote Editor, "need to understand that the information they gather and process can have many different uses, audiences and shelf lives. They need to understand the complexities of the audience mix and be able to respond." "Those unwilling to be flexible may find themselves in a difficult scenario later in their careers". From a different perspective, Professional concurred: "Students must be flexible, have a vigorous skill set and be prepared to get laid off and move around in the changing media arena." In short, "young journalists must be prepared to fill a variety of roles if they hope to succeed". "The most successful journalists are those that take on assignments willingly, can learn and want to learn".

Specialization in journalistic jobs is still honored, but is losing its favour to cross-media capability in converged media. Today, professionals with different specializations team together to work on multiple media projects. Tomorrow, it is likely that one-man bands will be more and more desired in newsrooms.

Most respondents (93per cent), especially professors, agreed or strongly agreed that journalism students should both learn technical skills, such as online information search and Web design, while learning critical thinking skills in media law, ethics, etc. One-way ANOVA shows significant difference among the means for professionals, editors, and professors. Tukey HSD post hoc tests show that professors were more positive on this point than editors and professionals, while no significant difference existed between editors and professionals.

But, should journalism students spend more time on learning critical thinking skills than on technical skills? Opinions were divided. More than half of the respondents (62per cent) believed that should be the case, but 19per cent of the respondents were not sure and another 19per cent of them did not agree. Oneway ANOVA shows significant difference among the means for professors (3.21), professionals, and editors. Tukey HSD post hoc tests show that editors were more positive on this point than professionals, and professionals were more positive than professors.

Throughout all the answers from the three groups of respondents, critical thinking was highly regarded as being more important than technical skills. Editors, news professionals, and professors all liked to see good stories, and good stories come from good thinking ability. An editor said: "Journalism graduates need to have a broad, well-rounded education; be critical thinkers; have the ability to write clearly; have a serious work ethic; and know computer basics - in that order"."You can teach a monkey to type," echoes a writer. Therefore, he strongly suggested that J-schools "get more critical thinking skills pounded into the skulls of the students". While highly emphasizing the importance of critical thinking ability, editors did not mean to neglect the importance of teaching technical skills in schools. We will develop this point when we discuss the next question.

Comparing the professors' highest mean for the first question and their lowest mean for the second question, it is clear that professors saw critical thinking as highly important, but preferred a comparatively balanced approach for the teaching of the two sets of knowledge. One professor's comment illustrated this observation: Knowing technical skill alone will not make you a "good" journalist. Critical thinking is vital not just to a career but to life itself.

Without developing your ability to discern and evaluate, you will become "the prey" of society. Next, a technical skill is critical to a career in journalism today.

Even print Journalism is very high tech these days and all electronic media require extensive computer knowledge as well as other technical skills. I would place critical thinking skills first on your list of things to do because a developed mind will make it that much easier to develop a creative and technically sound understanding of the technical side of the business.

From a holistic view, there was no substantial disagreement between classrooms and newsrooms when we examine the issue of teaching critical thinking vs. teaching technical skills. Compared to Terry's 2000 poll, this study shows that professors gave a higher status to technical skills in journalism curricula in 2002 than they did in 2000. This is a period during which media convergence garnered its momentum. In short, all respondents generally agreed that J-schools should place emphasis on teaching critical thinking, but at the same time, should not neglect teaching technical skills.

News professionals were asked, "If you wish to possess the technical skills you don't have now, do you prefer to learn them at work or wish you had learned in school?" Editors were given the same question with a slightly different wording. Chi-Square test shows that the difference between editors and news professionals is significant. This finding well supplements the findings from the preceding questions. It suggests that editors not only looked at future journalists' critical thinking ability, but also hoped that future journalists would already possess the skills needed in a converged newsroom when they are hired.

On the other hand, most professionals preferred that they spend most of their school time on gaining critical thinking ability and learn skills largely at work. The professionals' general preference, to some extent, also reflected their need for technological update at their current positions, so that they can better qualify for multimedia productions.

Many editors and reporters said that school is the best place for journalism students to explore every facet of the media and acquire basic technical skills, though some advanced skills can only be learned on the job. Learning skills while in school, they said, can build confidence and an expansive and broad understanding of the entire field and help with damage control and communication in newsrooms.

"If editing and the technical skills were more prevalent in college courses," wrote a multi-tasking editor, "I think I could stave off a lot of headaches when the students become professionals." An internship was the news professionals' and editors' most recommended venue for enhancing and learning more technical skills and gaining other practical experience. Reporter said: "While I value my college education, my internship and first job provided me with the most valuable skills today." Another reporter said: "While education is great, students who work in media while in school fare much better in the real world."

Some editors had complaints about graduates with a 3.5 GPA but no practical experience and no published news work. An anchor/reporter said that it is important even "for a freshman or sophomore in college to visit a newsroom and shadow someone.

So many students wait until they are juniors and seniors to do this and then they realise they made a mistake in selecting their major. You will learn more by watching and doing". One reporter said, "To remain competitive, education must continue throughout a career".

The implication of the discrepancy from this finding suggests that Jschools should place emphasis on teaching critical thinking, expose students to new technology, and design a comprehensive internship Progamme for students to gain real-world knowledge and further develop their crossmedia technical skills.

Both editors and news professionals were given this unstructured question with slightly different wordings. We read through all the answers, and categorized them into the following nine facets in random order: Multimedia production: producing and editing news stories on video, for the Web, and for print; re-purposing the same story for different media.

New technology: knowledge of software for producing video, Web sites, graphics, newspapers, and magazines; knowledge of how to operate a computer and use the Internet. Good writing: knowing how to write to make people remember and/or take action, write about the beats with an expert's view. Good editing is also expected. Critical thinking: having good news Judgement, understanding what is legal and ethical, knowing how to report with insight, knowing how to crunch statistics.

Computer-assisted reporting: expert's knowledge of conducting online information search, database knowledge. On-camera exposure: how to report like a TV news anchor before a camera for a newspaper reporter. Visual production: A newspaper writer must know how to take photos, or a TV reporter must know how to shoot video.

SECOND LANGUAGE KNOWING HOW TO FLUENTLY SPEAK AND READ A FOREIGN LANGUAGE

Time management: well organizing time to work for multiple media platforms; the ability and willingness to work as a team to produce multimedia news stories. Then we ranked these facets according to the percentage scores each facet got separately from the editors and the news professionals:

This ranking shows more agreement than disagreement between editors and news professionals. No matter how technology changes and whether media are converged, editors and news professionals believed that learning how to write good stories is still the top priority and writing is the very basic skill all news professionals should learn. One editor pushed the importance of good writing to the extreme: "I've worked in markets 170 to 20, and having training in multiple media will not help you get a job, but being a good writer will". Most editors and news professionals, however, did believe that learning multimedia production, new technology, and computer-assisted reporting are also among the top priorities.

"I would strongly urge students to prepare themselves to the best of their ability to be able to report/edit the news in a variety of platforms and to learn how to truly engage readers/listeners/viewers in what they are writing about," said Editor.

Editors and news professionals both believed that it is not very important for a newspaper reporter to learn how to talk like an anchor in front of a video camera. This skill was even regarded as being less important than knowing how to speak a second language. Some editors and news professionals also mentioned learning how to manage time for producing multimedia news stories.

Editor hoped that journalists in a converged environment would learn to avoid "extra" work by working "smarter" and with greater awareness of the requirements of the different publishing media.

This finding, again, shows that editors valued critical thinking ability more than news professionals did. Editors wanted news professionals to be good thinkers first, and the latter wanted most to learn how to express their thinking in different media.

Since some authors such as Haiman expressed the concern about the possible decline of work quality if news professionals have to "re-purpose" stories for multiple media platforms, we tried to find out to what extent this concern was shared by editors and news professionals. Opinions split. Thirty-eight percent of the editors and professionals agreed or strongly agreed that the quality would deteriorate, 40per cent disagreed or strongly disagreed, and the other 22per cent were not sure.

Editors and professionals showed no significant difference on this attitude T-test. Such a concern was not prevalent in the news industry.

In response to such concerns, the news director from a converged media company wrote: "When reporters do cross platforms we give them the time to finish the project for all three platforms. Quality does not suffer. If we were to try to force reporters to cross platforms while operating under daily deadlines then quality could suffer depending on the nature of the story and the extra time consumed".

Another editor summed up this issue: "Some employees can capably handle multiple media and tell stories effectively. Others cannot. Certainly strong technical skills and training can help, but it's not just dependent on that; it depends more on the attitude and aptitude of the journalist".

Quality multimedia work also involves a solid understanding of different cultures in different media. Editors both for and against media convergence noted the difficulty of merging different media with different cultures, and editors in those merged media called for flexibility in aptitude and willingness to cooperate across platforms. For instance, Editor wrote: Clarity of what convergence means to the news organization is vital and often lacking. This causes unneeded anxiety.

Managers have to realise that each medium has its own culture, language, skill set and timetable and is naturally skeptical of anything unfamiliar. It is also true that these same journalists' stock in trade is learning a new culture, language, skill set and timetable-on a daily basis.

Therein lies the hope for an efficient news operation running on all cylinders and an effective -maybe even happy-staff. If most editors and news professionals are not concerned about the quality of the work prepared for multiple media platforms and if news professionals are given enough time to complete their cross-media work, there is little reason to worry that future journalists, if well trained both theoretically and technologically for multiple media platforms, will produce work of poorer quality.

Training students to practice news in multiple media platforms will help bridge newsroom cultures from different media and eventually erase such differences. We have noticed that no significant statistical differences existed between the editors and news professionals from the converged media companies and their counterparts from the not-yet-converged media companies when they answered the questions reported above.

How are J-schools Coping with Media Convergence?

From 1998 to 2002, about 60per cent of the J-schools in the United States redesigned their curricula or developed new courses to prepare students for practicing news in multiple media platforms. A typical journalism professor was a man (71per cent) between 46-55 years old (42per cent) with a doctoral degree (63per cent) who worked in news media for one to ten years (48per cent), may still be practicing news (45per cent) in one way or another, and conducted academic research (66per cent).

More professors claimed that they were theoretically equipped (81per cent) than technologically prepared (53per cent) to teach students how to report news in multiple media platforms. More than half of the professors (57per cent) had not taught any journalism courses in the last five years where skill sets were beyond their own expertise; 25per cent of the professors taught one such course and 11per cent taught two.Nevertheless, the majority of the professors (84per cent) added content about media convergence either to their existing courses or to new courses or participated in cross-media team-teaching in the last five years.Worries, concerns, and, sometimes, misconceptions about media convergence appeared in professors' textual answers. For instance, a professor from Montana said: "convergence is not happening".A professor who no longer practiced news said, "In my Judgement, the writing portion of preparing news for print and for the Web is exactly the same". Another professor maintained that it was not necessary to teach cross-media news practicing because "few 'want ads' for newspaper reporter and editor positions specifically listed multimedia platform skills as required or preferred experience for new hires".

Many professors worried that media mergers would restrict the number of voices in a community. They regarded media mergers as a grand experiment in the profession and waited for the FCC's ruling on the cross-ownership of different media in the same market.

Wait-and-see-that was the strategy some universities took for teaching media convergence. One professor said that he needed to see the substantive contribution media convergence could make before he would be more serious about this phenomenon.

He said that J-schools should be cautious about embracing convergence. Some other universities didn't have the time and resources to teach convergence courses or make major curriculum changes.

Most professors, however, did believe that media convergence was a reality; and "anybody serious about practicing media needs at minimal an acquaintance with various media and at best multiple competencies," as Professor said.

Many professors (and editors and news professionals as well) had a clear opinion as to which comes first, teaching critical thinking or teaching technical skills. While acknowledging the need for incorporating media convergence content in curricula, especially the technological components, professors cautioned against sacrificing conceptual and theoretical courses such as law, ethics, history, cultural studies, critical perspectives, etc.

Professor analogized critical thinking as meat and potatoes and technical skills as dessert and side dishes and argued that "the meat and potatoes need to come before one begins to worry about the dessert and side dishes (or side shows)." This viewpoint was popular. Professor wrote:

It's the message, not the medium, that is of paramount importance. If students cannot understand and appreciate the underlying concepts, principles and ethics of journalism, then they cannot produce the type of content that will be of value to a free society. A thorough grounding in journalism must come before any training in tools. The tools are means to an end, not the end in and of themselves.

Incidentally, a reporter had similar thoughts: The medium isn't the message, the message is the message. In short, the fundamental analytic and synthetic skills of the news writer are paramount to the message. The medium does not alter the reporter's craft of interpreting news events in the context of the society in a way that will make sense for the receiver of the information.

Additional skills may be desirable, but for the most part they can be learned on the job. Obviously, the more skills one can offer, the better the employment opportunity. Those ancillary skills should not come at the expense of thorough proficiency as a news writer.We fully understand why these respondents emphasize the teaching of critical thinking and the fundamentals of good reporting over the teaching of technical skills, and we strongly agree with their opinions.

But, we also see the danger of over-stretching the point by treating the two sets of knowledge as two opposing poles. Those arguments are based on the presumptions that message and medium can be easily separated, content and form can be detached, and readers for different media are from the same population.

But, is that right? It is true that content is the king. It is true that "the medium does not alter the reporter's craft of interpreting news events." News practice, however, is not only about news-gathering and writing. It also includes production, editing, and delivery. Without a solid grasp of grammar and style, how can a writer effectively express his/her good analytical thinking?

Without knowing the available features and limitations of online news delivery, how can messages be constructed to their fullest potential? Without understanding the technical difference between video news and print news, how can messages be constructed appropriately? In the digital era when almost all steps of news transmission involves technology, if professors don't teach students technical skills, will the computer majors, who know little about news practices, be expected to produce newspapers, TV news, and online news?

Writers, for instance, do not necessarily have to be conversant in constructing news reporting with Flash for online presentation or know how to operate a video camera to shoot video stories. But knowing the principles and rules of news video-taping and what Flash or other software can offer will surely help writers more effectively convey their messages and better cooperate with visual reporters. Creativity distinguishes artists and artisans.

Critical thinking ability distinguishes master journalists and technical writers. But artists must first know what artisans know and a master journalist must possess all that a technical writer knows for a living. Skills are intrinsic instead of extrinsic to ideas.

Teaching critical thinking and teaching technical skills are not mutually exclusive. Teaching journalism students how to express their critical thinking with conversant technical skills in different media seems to be a big challenge for J-school professors in the years to come. From the professors' textual answers, we have observed different philosophical approaches to teaching convergence.

Unlike some professors who took the wait-and-see approach, a professor from the University of Texas at Austin claimed that "convergence is already happening, and journalism schools should be leading the parade and not following it". A popular viewpoint was that "skills across platforms must be taught, but more importantly storytelling, ethics, and critical thinking skills should be even more important in the journalism school curriculum". One professor from Texas Christian University said that it maintained the existing sequences but required broadcast students to take print courses and vice versa.

Team-teaching was an often-used approach in some J-schools such as Indiana University for courses involving multiple sets of skills while professors learned from each other. Another professor, from the University of Colorado at Boulder, said convergence meant that "students work together to produce multimedia content for the Web-not that each individual should attempt to become proficient in all media".

To overcome the hurdle of the ratio limited by the ACEJMC accreditation standards between journalism courses and liberal arts courses, a professor from Bowling Green State University suggested that journalism undergraduate students stay for five years and devote the fifth year entirely to practice.

Some professors said that journalism students only need to know a little about the practices in media other than their own while some other professors firmly maintained that students should "be the master of many arts and the explorer of all".All respondents were asked, "Do you think that merging media companies such as television station, newspaper, radio station, and online news from a local area will benefit any of the parties listed on the left?

Check all entries that apply." The entries included "The general public," "News professionals," "Media companies," "Nobody," and "Not sure." We designed this question about the legitimacy of media merger as a barometer for testing the respondents' political view on media convergence.

We presumed that a respondent's answer to this question could be related to his/her way of answering other questions regarding teaching media convergence or requirement for new hires. Most respondents (66per cent) from all three groups pointed to media companies as the beneficiary of media mergers. In comparison, only 37per cent of the respondents said that media mergers also benefit the general public, and even fewer (27per cent) said that media mergers benefit the news professionals.

By reading the percentage numbers horizontally, we can find that consistently fewer respondents believed that media mergers benefit the general public or news professionals; also consistently more respondents believed that media mergers benefit media companies.

It is also noticeable that 47per cent of editors believed that media mergers benefit the general public while the other 53per cent didn't. Editors' opinions on this point were roughly equally split. This finding indicates that media merger is a grand experiment in the media industry. Its benefits to the general public, which can better legitimize media mergers, are to be explored in the years to come. By reading the percentage numbers both vertically and horizontally, we also find that editors were the most positive about the benefits media mergers could bring to all three parties while professors were least sure of such benefits. It is logical to reason that management personnel, such as editors and news directors and the companies they represent, are the primary forces behind today's media merger movement.

The question is that, since most professors, editors, and even news professionals believed that media mergers do not benefit news professionals and hardly benefit the general public, why do most news professionals still want to be trained to be cross-media practitioners and why are so many Jschool professors enthusiastic about training such graduates?

Considering the editors' most positive attitude Towards media convergence, we wonder if news professionals are under the pressure to do so, and J-school professors are under the pressure to follow the industrial trend. Our surmise is partially corroborated by some textual answers.

A news anchor from a merged media company agreed that new hires should have received cross-media training in writing and visuals and should possess multiple sets of skills. She showed her understanding for media mergers:

The merging of media companies is almost a daily occurrence. The pool of entities providing news services is shrinking. I think there is a danger that the public will lose in this race for media giants to accumulate wealth. At the same time, with the amount of competition in the industry from cable networks, the Internet, DVD's etc., I see the financial need for companies to merge to survive.

A newspaper reporter also from a merged media company expressed a similar feeling: "I am not all for the media convergence At the same time I find it quite beneficial to be savvy in all branches of the industry. It helps the journalist become more knowledgeable about her or his job". News professionals were not alone in having such feelings. Here are two excerpts from two professors who have expressed similar feelings: It's a harsh reality that I checked the box saying that news companies are the ones that are sure to benefit from media convergence. It may not be great for the public or even for news professionals who are going to be asked to bring more and more skills to the table and to have more and more responsibility on the job. Even so, convergence in one way or another is gonna happen and we need to prepare our students.

Finally, my answer on merging media companies reflects my disdain for the corporatization and concentration of control in the media. I think we ought to train mass communicators for a converged world, but as professors we ought to fight like hell against media mergers.

Very few respondents (19per cent) believed that media mergers benefit all three parties, the general public, news professionals, and media companies, but about one third of the respondents (35per cent) believed that media companies are the only beneficiaries to such a practice.

These 35per cent respondents, who were almost equally proportionally found in editors, news professionals, and professors groups, could be regarded as the most critical Towards media mergers. We compared these 35per cent respondents with the rest of the sample and found no significant difference in their answers concerning the necessity of teaching journalism students cross-media writing and visuals and teaching multiple sets of skills.

Always, more respondents believed that professors should teach all those things. In short, the respondents' political view was not directly tied to their views of teaching students cross-media practices.

As an experimental industrial trend, media convergence in the sense of media mergers is still in its formative stage. Whether it will sustain its momentum to reach popularity in the nation and how its advantages balance against disadvantages are yet to be seen.

While there seems to be a good deal of support for cross-media education, on some questions, professors are more gung-ho than editors and news professionals about the trend. The legitimacy of media mergers needs repeated tests before such mergers can be truly accepted as a healthy development and a full-force education of media convergence can be seen in many in J-schools.

Media convergence, however, is not tied to media mergers. Media convergence, initiated and made possible by digital technology, is more than media mergers propelled largely by financial considerations. More pervasive is the media convergence in the senses of content convergence, technological convergence, and especially role convergence, which have occurred not only in merged media companies but also more in non-merged ones.

No matter whether media mergers will continue, the other three forms of media convergence, which are not subject to the FCC regulations, are likely to continue to develop. Most editors and news professionals in this survey are not from merged media companies.Many editors, news professionals, and professors do not yet see media mergers as beneficial to the general public and news professionals. But, their backgrounds and political views do not prevent them from sharing with other respondents with different backgrounds and political views many opinions regarding where future college journalism should go.

Such common understanding is shaping a force to push forward the education of media convergence in campuses nationwide.To better direct newsroom businesses in a converged media environment, many editors need cross-media training. Many opportunities are out there for news companies and universities to work together to explore the issue of media convergence and provide mid-career professionals and editors cross-media technological training.It seems sensible that opportunities for learning multimedia skills should be made available both on campus and through off-site continuing education Programmes that are geared for midcareer news professionals as technological developments continue to evolve. Multi-dimensional news reporting in multiple media platforms will be tomorrow's way news is presented.

Therefore, dealing with media convergence in college journalism education is an urgent necessity. The wait-and-see strategy will place a Jschool in a disadvantaged position over the long run.

These findings tell us that J-schools do need to provide cross-media knowledge and experience to their students, so that the latter can better qualify for cross-media jobs in the future. Media convergence poses both challenge and opportunity to J-schools for them to reconsider their current curriculum design, sequence setting, faculty composition, teaching methods, and internship approaches.

Many professors, editors, and news professionals have expressed concern that media mergers will eliminate voices in a community, thus potentially eroding democracy. However, media mergers did not start only these days. As a TV reporter wrote in the textual answer, when she first went to Philadelphia years ago, there were five daily papers.

Now, there are two; and they are both published by the same company. Philadelphia is not alone in such media reduction. The question is whether the general public feels that it is less well-informed than it was thirty or forty years ago and that democracy has been eroded by such media reduction prior to media convergence.

This is a topic for another study. Nevertheless, students should be exposed to such a legitimate concern and learn to take a critical look at the phenomenon of media mergers.

J-schools should continue to teach critical thinking courses and meld critical thinking components into the teaching of all courses. Critical thinking is the cornerstone of journalism education. However, technology courses or course components should also be given the status they deserve.

In other words, there should be a balanced curriculum to include both kinds of courses, and many cross-media related courses should contain both components. An ideal curriculum should balance the load of technical skill-based courses and critical thinking courses, weighting Towards the latter. Critical thinking and technical skills can go hand in hand rather than being competitors for class time. A balanced curriculum can help students better gather, produce, edit, and deliver quality news; more creatively and professionally materialize their ideas; and make them better fit into the market, especially in an economic downturn.

University of Florida professor Melinda McAdams, one of the Washington Post's first online editors, told colleagues that if colleges don't teach journalists the technical skills they will need, no one else is likely to take on the responsibility." The reality they'll face in the world is they'll have to teach themselves".

The classroom should be the first stop for students to at least get exposed to and get familiar with the technology for cross-media practices, though they can become more proficient with such technology through internship and their future jobs. With all that said, technology courses should not dominate journalism students' education, and technology should not be taught for the sake of technology. Technology must serve the purposes of doing good journalism.

Apart from teaching students multimedia productions, new technology, and computer-assisted reporting, J-schools still need to place good writing-the very basics of being a journalist-as the top priority for all journalism students regardless of sequences or specializations. Many respondents point out that the teaching of technology should not be at the expense of the teaching of critical thinking. Many J-schools have no more elective hours for students to learn cross-media technology within the existing parameter of curriculum. For such schools, curriculum redesign is a necessity.

Though some J-schools such as Indiana University School of Journalism have eliminated sequences to provide a comprehensive education to all journalism students, we expect that sequences will continue to exist for some time in some other J-schools. However, it has become increasingly important to encourage students from all sequences to learn technology and reporting skills from other platforms.

Sequences in many J-schools are regarded as dinosaurs because it no longer makes sense to teach broadcast and newspaper, for instance, as two unrelated bodies of knowledge in the era of media convergence and students can opt for a specialization without sequences but with professors' advice.Most respondents expect that future journalists will be competent in producing news in multiple media platforms while being particularly strong in one area. It appears that students will be prudent to opt to specialize in either print or television and take several electives in a secondary platform, either radio or online journalism. Versatility and specialization should be equally important.

The majority of the editors do expect that future writers will be able to and willing to write for multiple media platforms, and photographers and designers will create multimedia visuals, though such expectations will not be converted into requirements in job ads for a while because "too many newsroom dinosaurs have to die off first," as Editor put it. But chances are they will, as Nelson (2002) predicted. Most editors even expect that new hires will possess multiple sets of skills to become "superhack masters of multimedia," to use Gates's term.

The needs are out there, but whether the training of such superhack masters will become the norm, as Gates questioned, largely depends on whether J-schools are willing and able to develop those "avant-garde" courses. Apart from the technological aspect, students also need to learn to cooperate and collaborate across newsrooms so as to bridge different newsroom-cultures. Students need to be both theoretically and technically prepared for media convergence. The findings from this study show that more than half of the J-schools in the United States have redesigned their curricula or developed new courses to cope with media convergence, but professors need to be better prepared technologically.Team-teaching is one approach to solve the problem, but will the teaching of media convergence be more effective if a professor at least knows as much as a student in a convergence class will learn? Does the Gestalt psychological principle "the whole is more than the sum of its parts" also apply in such a context? Professors normally learned little or no technical skills while studying in a J-school doctoral Progamme.

Their technical knowledge inherited from their previous media experience is easily dated. More than half of the professors (54per cent) no longer practiced news after they began to teach, as we found out in this study. In some cases, professors know less technical knowledge than their students do. Therefore, in the middle of heavy teaching and research, updating and learning more technical knowledge for teaching convergence is a big challenge for many professors.Learning from each other during team-teaching is, of course, a good way of learning, but professors also need to find time to do self-teaching to gain more in-depth knowledge. J-schools should provide financial support for professors to attend new technology workshops.

Being exposed to or involved in community news reporting in a multiple-media-platform environment, if possible, is an even better way of learning new technology for professors. Attitude and aptitude, together with time management ability, will be the key to producing quality work in newsrooms.

Since editors and news professionals are not prevalently concerned about the quality of work currently re-purposed for multiple media platforms, there is no reason for them or professors to be concerned that students being trained on multiple media platforms will be jacks of all trades but masters of none. Students need to learn how to re-purpose their work in a timely manner and control the quality of their work in a professional manner.One editor said it best: "To sum things up, journalists need to be prepared to hit the workplace running. With limited resources and cutbacks across the country, the new hire will be the person who is the most skilled, coupled with energy and willing to be flexible as needed." Media convergence is a comprehensive topic.

Many sub-topics related to this study are yet to be explored. For instance, how can the general public benefit from media convergence? Does the general public in markets where media are converged think that they are less well-informed and that democracy has suffered in their areas? How can news professionals benefit from media convergence? What are the typical differences between the career lives of the news professionals in converged media and the career lives the same news professionals led before the media were converged? We call on mass communication scholars to continue to study media convergence to shed more light on this phenomenon that will affect every one of us.

3

Journalism in the New Millennium

ORAL HISTORY AND THE NEW CENTURY

Oral history has always been formed by interaction and change. Oral memoirs pivot upon a unique interaction between historian and historymaker. Changing or redefining the subject of history—integrating the actions, experiences, and ideas of "ordinary" women and men—is crucial to the attraction of oral history. And the promise of oral history goes further, seeking to transform the relationship between historian and audience, looking for ways to make study of history more accessible, more engaging, and ultimately more participatory. For inherent to oral history are the democratic notions that everyone can be a historian; that memory is in itself a meaningful form of historical interpretation; and that, through oral history projects, students and others can make a meaningful contribution to our understanding of the past.

As the twentieth century ends, new technology is emerging that may significantly enhance our ability to realise these aspects of oral history's promise. Our growing ability to digitize—and thereby control and transmit—information will affect many aspects of oral history in the century to come.

Already, surveying the World Wide Web, we can see indicators of significant change that will greatly improve the accessibility, usability, and transparency of oral history collections; transform the use of oral history in teaching and learning processes; and spur our return to orality, to the fundamental core of oral history as process that involves speaking and listening. New technology is no panacea for oral historians (or anyone else). Many challenges will remain and new ones will emerge, some directly related to technology itself. But digital media is providing us with new tools that will affect the ways we do—and think about—our work.

LET A THOUSAND FLOWERS BLOOM

The first signs of the changes taking place in oral history are already visible on the World Wide Web. An examination of web sites related to oral history reveals some interesting ways we are utilizing new digital technology. There is no consensus on the best way for oral historians to use the Web. As a field, we are still figuring this out. But important trends are already visible. Most oral history-related web sites are created by established archives and provide lists of the memoirs archived by the institution. There are literally thousands of such sites, ranging from Hogan Jazz Archive of Tulane University to the U.S. Naval Institute Oral History Project. One elaborate site, the Chicago Architects Oral History Project site, constructed by the Art Institute of Chicago, offers for each respondent a photograph, a biographical summary, lists of interview highlights and related interviews, and a one-paragraph transcript excerpt. A master index can be searched and transcripts can be ordered online. While limited in scope, such sites make it much easier for users, working from home or school, to quickly assess the quality and relevance of the collection.

Other web sites go further to provide larger transcript excerpts. Probably the richest transcript site is the American Memory Collection, created by the Library of Congress, which presents tens of thousands of items, from George Washington's papers to historic baseball cards. Among its most used collections are the transcripts and notes from more than 2,900 oral narratives created by the Federal Writers' Project of the 1930s, addressing work and family, memories of slavery and immigration, and stories about local history.

Though constrained in various ways, these narratives provide abundant opportunities to examine the nation's collective memories; on-line presentation opens the collection to teachers, students, and the public, as well as to scholars. The size of the collection is exciting and daunting. Fortunately, the collection's search engine allows Boulean searches across all the transcripts. For example, if you are researching sharecropping, a search can quickly find (and take you to) every mention of sharecropping in every transcript. The computer's ability to quickly analyse digitized text can significantly speed the research process, allowing users to deal more effectively with the collection's massive size.

Few archives can match the Library of Congress, but some have started the process of digitizing and web-publishing. The University of Florida Oral History Programme web site offers excerpts from transcripts focusing on the Seminole Indians and the Florida activities of the Civilian Conservation Corps. Out of 200 interviews conducted on the Seminoles, the site provides seven page transcript excerpts for each of five interviews. The Oral History Office of the Sacramento Air Logistics Centre provides complete transcripts of half a dozen interviews. As archives add electronic avenues to traditional routes, access to oral memoirs will expand, encouraging the growth of the field.

Other sites use the Web differently. The Women's Centre at Virginia Technological University has created a small but fascinating site on the Black Women at Virginia Tech History Project, tracing the 1960s experiences of the university's first African American female students. For each interview, the Centre has published yearbook photographs, family snapshots, period newspaper articles, and papers and letters written by the women at the time. A timeline places the narratives in a chronological framework. Similarly, the Hoover Dam Visitor Centre site contextualizes its transcript excerpts from interviews with workers who built the dam by providing photographs of the workers and the dam, background on the construction process, and a virtual tour of the dam today. Given the particular nature of oral memoirs, the ability to link transcripts to contextual information can be vital in helping users situate and analyse the interviews.

Both the American Memory Collection and the Black Women at Virginia Tech site help us see how technology can do more than provide increased access to oral memoirs. Using the search engine provided by American Memory—or even the "Find" function provided by Netscape or Internet Explorer—not only helps researchers to find what they are looking for; it also allows researchers to examine patterns of word usage and language formation within and across interviews.

Enabling scholars to more easily consider who uses certain words and in what situations and in what ways, the supple search tools provided by digital technology can clarify the extent to which oral memoirs are not merely data (or evidence) but also databases. And while technology can be used in this way to get inside an oral memoir—what could be called a "micro" usage—it can also be used to draw "macro" connections to broader issues and other relevant sources. The promise of the electronic environment, in this case, is that it can facilitate both the "micro" and the "macro," without threatening the integrity of the oral history archive itself.

YOU MUST BE MADE TO WEAR EARPHONES

As we move from web-published finding aids to transcripts, search engines, and contextual information, the amount of labour and the degree of technical difficulty required goes up; and, not surprisingly, the number of Web sites goes down. The next category—offering interviews in audio form over the Web—is significantly more demanding and more rare.

One Web site for audio presentation of oral memoirs is History Matters, constructed by my organization, the American Social History Project of City University of New York. History Matters offers approximately sixty audio excerpts (and related transcripts), most of them five to ten minutes in length. Unlike most sites, which are created by archives and present only their own collections, History Matters assembles material contributed by scholars nationwide and organizes it for classroom use.

In addition to oral histories, the site includes other primary documents, classroom lesson plans, links to related sites, and on-line discussions of topics in history teaching. The material is organized to fit with the chronological framework of the U.S. History survey, and is searchable by theme and document type.

(History Matters is closely tied to ASHP's Who Built America? CD-ROM, which presented oral histories, archival songs and speeches, photographs, and other primary documents. CD-ROMs offer a more contained but reliable way to present digitized audio material, and some oral history archives are exploring ways to use this medium as well as the Web. A new audio CD, Stories from the Collection, created by the Columbia Oral History Research Office, provides excerpts from sixteen interviews.)

Other Web sites offering digitized audio include the Archives of the Billy Graham Centre of Wheaton College, which documents the lives of evangelical Protestant missionaries, providing fifty full interview transcripts and ten audio excerpts.

The Web site of Voice and Visions: Holocaust Survivors Oral Histories provides audio excerpts of interviews with a dozen concentration camp survivors. The Journal of MultiMedia History Web site demonstrates another approach, in which audio excerpts of oral memoirs are integrated into a scholarly article. In the first issue, an article by Thomas Kriger traces the story of a 1939 strike by dairy workers of New York State and features a dozen audio excerpts, which function both as supporting footnotes and as audio illustrations.

Listening to audio excerpts on the Web or CD-ROM has its problems. On the Web, audio is often slow to download. And various sites use different software, requiring users to invest additional time downloading the software itself. Downloading the audio excerpts can be frustrating; if the software is not working right, you wind up at a screen that says "Sound File Invalid." Audio publishing on the Web is new, and there is work to be done to smooth the process. CD-ROMs tend to be easier to use, but problems are not uncommon.

That said, when the software works right, the results can be transformative. One oral memoir on History Matters is the narrative of William Brown, who recalls what it was like growing up black in the South at the turn of the century. Interviewed by Charles Hardy, he tells the story of a lynching of a local man that took place when he was five years old, and recalls how the smell of burning flesh spread for miles. His printed words are powerful.

But hearing his voice, listening to him struggle for the right words, hearing him move in his chair and slap the table in anger as he recalls his feelings of that day, adds layers of meaning to the story. The same is true for listening to the lilt and the relief of Shad Weiss' voice (on Voices and Visions) as she recalls her first sight of the American soldiers, the "beautiful, beautiful young men in uniform, on tanks," who liberated her from Auschwitz. And true as well for heating the mix of strength and pain in the voice of Mary Thomas as she recalls her efforts to fill the rifles of the striking miners fighting for their lives at Ludlow, Colorado in 1914.

The oral quality of oral memoirs is, in many ways, essential to their meaning. In conversations and in interviews, we convey meaning with pitch and tone of voice, giving cues both subtle and obvious to our listeners. Pacing and pauses, volume and inflection, pronunciation of words and sounds that are not even words—coughs, sighs, exhalations, and moans—all give nuance and depth to the choice of words themselves. Some speakers are almost singers, playing their voices as instruments. Transcription, no matter how skillful, inevitably flattens the spoken quality of oral memoirs. Reading a transcript and listening to the interview are vastly different experiences. While not the same as witnessing the original interview, listening to a recording connects us to the speaker both affectively and cognitively, facilitating empathy and deepening our understanding.

Oral historians have, of course, long discussed the relationship of audio and text, and the difficulty of providing broad access to audio recordings. For the most part, the audio record has been confined to archives, or to brief excerpts available through radio and film documentaries. Now, through the Web and CD-ROM, it is increasingly feasible to offer the audio record to millions of people, to anyone with even modest access to computer technology. Ironically, in this case technology, instead of distancing us, can help us get closer to the real human interaction at the heart of oral history.

The Web and CD-ROM not only make longer audio recordings more widely available. These media also make it easier to connect audio with text, including transcripts, scholarly commentary, and related primary documents. Comparing the written and audio versions of an oral memoir is a rich exercise in understanding the process of transcription, the kinds of choices made by transcribers and editors, and the complex relationship between written and spoken language. Juxtaposing the print and audio formats encourages deeper understanding of the memoir than utilizing either format by itself. Examining such juxtapositions has been largely limited to special sessions at scholarly events. The Journal of MultiMedia History suggests the possibility of making that experience integral to scholarly presentation. And sites such as History Matters open the experience to students and the public, offering the possibility of making it a common step in developing a clearer understanding of the nature of oral memoirs.

Everyone A Historian

Over the past three decades, oral history has lent itself to thousands of classroom projects, where students conduct interviews and develop their understandings of the historians' craft. Digital technology opens new possibilities in this area. In the past two years the software for creating Web sites has grown easier to use, and this trend will continue. It is increasingly feasible for students to construct their own oral history Web sites and share their projects with the world. One of the most impressive student-constructed oral history sites is "1968: The Whole World Was Watching," produced by the students of South Kingston High School, with help from the Brown University Scholarly Technology Group. In the spring of 1998, guided by librarian Linda Wood and English teacher Sharon Schmid, students asked thirty local residents for their memories of the 1960s in general and 1968 in particular.

Their well-organized Web site presents these interviews in their entirety, both in transcript and audio format. The site also offers a detailed index of each interview, hotlinked to the relevant sections of the transcript. The user can easily compare the audio and textual versions of the interview and trace the process of transcription, editing, and selection. Finally, students wrote "stories" based on the interviews, summaries which assemble selected interview excerpts into cohesive and well-framed narratives.

The "1968" site also offers other valuable hypertext features. At the end of each transcript is a list of vocabulary words, such as "sit-in," or "teach-in" or "Woodstock." Clicking on the word takes the user to a glossary where the reference is explained. A timeline provides a chronological framework; some items are hotlinked to other sites.

For example, clicking on the timeline item of Lyndon Johnson's January 17, 1968 State of the Union speech takes the reader to the text of that speech, on the Web site of the LBJ Presidential Library. Together, the timeline and the glossary provide a contextual framework for understanding the memoirs.

Presenting the interviews in different formats, with contextual information, makes them more accessible and useful; it also makes the process more transparent to outside readers. And the hypertext quality of the Web makes navigation between different elements quicker and easier.

Web publishing also makes the project accessible to the whole field—and to other students. When South Kingston students discussed this project at this year's OHA convention, they highlighted the excitement of publishing their work on the Web, and the ways that having a global audience made their work feel particularly meaningful.The number of student-created oral history archives available on the Web is slowly growing. The South Kingston site is exceptional, but other sites are interesting as well.

The Miami Valley Cultural Heritage Project, created by Miami University of Ohio professor Marjorie McClellan, offers student-generated interviews on women's history, the steel industry, and local history topics. The Behind the Veil site, created by the Centre for Documentary Studies at Duke University, offers interview transcripts generated in student projects on African American history.

Interviews at all student sites are uneven, as one would expect. But they are impressive in many ways, and point Towardss future possibilities for training students and sharing their research with a broader audience. If such projects flourish, they will significantly increase students' ability to contribute to the on-going construction of a new, more multivocal narrative of American history.

Many Rivers to Cross

These Web-based projects suggest ways that our use of digital technology may change our field. Utilizing the Web to publish transcripts could feed growing interest in oral memoirs and attract new users. Drawing on the multimedia capacities of the new technology to provide audio access to digitized interviews can help bring oral history back to its roots in spoken language. The constructive aspect of the Web should facilitate the visibility and value of student oral history projects, allowing oral history to better realise its democratic promise. At the same time, however, oral historians will face many challenges in the coming century, including some generated by new technology.

One limitation of oral history has been its labour-intensive quality. Generating and recording quality interviews is, in some ways, the easiest step in an oral history project. Transcribing, checking, and indexing are incredibly time-consuming and/or expensive. Many oral history projects have foundered on this rock. And the process of publishing interviews on the Web or on CD-ROM can multiply the amount of time and energy involved.

Moreover, the new technology itself can be expensive. Impressive school-based projects such as the "1968" site usually require the involvement of an outside university or cultural institution, providing funds and expertise. Voice-recognition and audio-indexing software now becoming available may soon facilitate or greatly reduce the need for transcription, and further the trend towards audio presentation. But the issues of time and expense are likely to remain, if not grow in size.

Another major challenge is the question of appropriate access. Archivists are struggling with what transcripts they should publish on the Web. Permissions for most existing collections do not address the issue of Web publishing. And archivists are justifiably concerned about losing control of their collections; once an interview is published online, the archive loses any ability to control its use. The spread of digital technology is forcing archives to rethink their role and function, and to confront difficult questions of security, protection, and accessibility.

The closely related issue of reliability confronts those who use the Web to study oral memoirs. The increasing ease of Web publishing is a double-edged sword. It encourages a free flow of information, always valuable to a democratic society. But it also highlights questions about accuracy.

Scholars have traditionally relied on archivists and publishers to serve as gatekeepers; now the gates they control are less vital.

While most oral history sites are still posted by archives, the possibility for flawed or even counterfeit sites is undeniable. Those who use oral memoirs from the Web must carefully evaluate who created the site and their point of view. Developing critical thinking skills is important for any use of the Web. Happily, oral historians are no stranger to the issues of subjectivity, critical thinking, and the evaluation of sources. In this sense, the challenges long confronted by oral historians may be particularly relevant for the emerging issues of the coming decades. This highlights another problem for the field: the on-going need for sophisticated training. Since the 1980s, American oral historians have become increasingly aware of the theoretical questions and approaches modeled by European scholars.

Raising questions about narrative, identity, and historical memory, Ronald Grele, Michael Frisch and others have deepened our thinking about the nature of oral memoirs. But many practitioners have had limited exposure to this sophisticated discussion.

The "how to do oral history" guides now published on the Web, while valuable, are in themselves not sufficient. There is a great need for training in oral history theory and methodology; and if technology spurs the growth of the field, the need will only increase.

This last point reminds us of an obvious but fundamental troth that may be reassuring or troubling, depending on your point of view. No matter how the technology evolves, the human element will remain crucial to the future of our field. Digital technology may provide us with tools that can help us build our field, transform our representational craft, and move Towards our vision of a democratic practice. Ultimately, however, the impact of the technology—and the vitality and direction of our field in the twenty-first century—will depend on us.

ORGANIZATIONAL THEORY TO MAKE SENSE OF CHANGE

The study of "organizations" is a relatively new discipline. Drucker wrote that "no one in the United States - or anyplace else - talked of Organizations' until after World War?" Drucker said that the modern idea of an organization - as a purposely designed and specialized entity that is defined by its task and is distinct from society's other institutions - emerged in the second half of the 20th century with what he calls the "management revolution." Initial theoretical assumptions of this revolution were largely shaped by turn-of-the-century scholars:

Taylor's views on "scientific management" and Weber's ideas on the rational and specialized bureaucracy. This organizational model is characterized by a hierarchical division of labour where managers are the "thinkers" and laborers are the "doers". Employees develop highly specialized skills that increase performance and productivity, while management's job is to ensure the conditions exist for the organizational "machine" to run smoothly.

Recognizing that organizations must evolve and adapt to survive in changing environments, Lewin suggested a "natural" (as opposed to mechanical) metaphor to explain organizational dynamics; change, he wrote, can be best understood and managed through a process of "unfreeze, change, refreeze."

These early attempts to understand organizations and their dynamics prepared the intellectual soil for the growth of organizational development, which attracted the interest of U.S. scholars and corporate managers in the last quarter of the 20th century as the changing global marketplace threatened U.S. dominance.Although Taylor's and Weber's (and to a lesser extent Lewin's) ideas are considered outdated, they have proven resilient and modest adaptations of them are still very much alive in both theory and practice. Bergquist wrote that most organizational theorists have conceived organizations as pendulum-like mechanisms, which value "simplicity in motion" and homeostasis. When organizations experience turbulent times, they tend to seek equilibrium by returning to their previous form and function. However, the structured and predictable environment in which U.S. companies once thrived no longer exists, and Bergquist contends a more accurate metaphor in the postmodern world is that of the organization as a liquid, "poised on the edge of order and chaos".

The liquid system, he wrote, contains at the same time both elements of stability and change, especially along the edges, or shifting boundaries. In an organizational sense, it is the shifting boundaries that offer potential for understanding the change process. It is these places on the "edge" where innovation occurs and where organizational traits such as mission, communication, and leadership become integral to success.In perhaps the seminal book on organizational change and development, Kanter wrote American companies that value "innovation" are better placed to use their employees' creative capacities and stay ahead in changing environments. Interviews with 65 corporate executives led Kanter to conclude the innovative companies are integrated (my italics); they grant power to individuals to encourage fresh thinking and create opportunities for new ideas to cross organizational boundaries.She juxtaposed integrated companies with "segmented" companies, which are characterized by an "ovorspecification" of resources and consider themselves successful when every segment works well independently, without much need for communication. Segmented companies, Kanter wrote, seek stasis, because they are constantly looking to the past to define the future; accordingly, habits and routines that maintain the course are valued.

Kanter identified five major building blocks in change initiatives that increase the company's capacity to meet new challenges:

- Departures from tradition: activities or ideas that require the organization to think and behave in new ways.
- Crisis or galvanizing event: a critical event that cannot be solved by traditional means. This allows a non-traditional idea to be pushed forward.
- Strategic decisions: the opportunity for management to create a vision by articulating a deliberate and conscious direction.

- Individual "prime movers": people who push the innovative strategy through the organization by communicating strategic decisions and manipulating the symbols of the organizational culture Towards the direction of change.
- Action vehicles: mechanisms that allow new action. These include training Programmes, successful results for people using new practices, new organizational rewards that support new practices, and ongoing messages of the benefits experienced by individuals using the now practices.

Kanter wrote that managers need three new sets of skills to operate effectively in integrated, innovative environments: "power skills" used to persuade others to invest in new initiatives; ability to manage problems associated with teams and greater employee participation; and understanding of how organizational change is designed and constructed. She concluded that "the art and architecture of change" requires managers to abandon their reliance on traditional analytical tools, which measure what already exists or has occurred.

"Change efforts have to mobilize people around what is not yet known, not yet experienced... they require a leap of faith that cannot be eliminated by presentation of all the forecasts, figures, and advance guarantees that can be accumulated". Accordingly, the paradox of managing changes, she wrote, is "there needs to be a plan, and the plan has to acknowledge that it will be departed from".

Most attempts at organizational development involve efforts to transform an organization's culture. Schneider, Brief, and Guzzo wrote that the values and beliefs that are the foundation of an organization's culture can be changed by focusing on the tangible things - such as practices, policies, and procedures - that define daily life in the organization. It is these tangible phenomena that comprise an organization's climate, and for real cultural change to occur, management must change the climate in which the employees exist. The authors contend that many efforts at cultural change are focused on "macro" issues such as values and beliefs, while overlooking the more tangible issues that create the organizational climate in which employees experience everyday life. They wrote: "Sustainable organizational change is most assured when both the climate - what the organization's members experience - and the culture - what the members believe the organization values - change".

Successful companies have increasingly educated workforces, and they are creating cultures that are more innovative and flexible. The new, desired culture is one in which power and accountability are shared between managers and employees in a manner that allows companies to respond quickly to challenges and opportunities. The goal of these efforts is to unleash and channel the power of employees' knowledge in an organizational "culture of contribution." Fisher acknowledges that this is a major cultural shift for most U.S. companies because - unlike the Japanese, whose collective society adapted easily to a team-building, egalitarian corporate model - "America's professional workers value their individualism and often express it in counterproductive ways".

Corporate America also clings to some values that work against creating a culture of contribution; most prominent among these, Fisher wrote, is the corporate view on job attachment. Workers are expected to accept such surprises as downsizing, job reclassification, or relocation with quiet stoicism, which contradicts companies' claims they are striving to empower employees as co-partners with management.

Fisher contends that U.S. managers need to be aware that there is no single ideal corporate culture; rather, corporate culture is better understood as a combination of macro and micro cultures. Many senior managers claim to embrace a culture of contribution, but Fisher contends that few have ideas about how to put a programme or process in place to let the transformation occur. On the other hand, the changing nature of professional work, driven by new technology, has organizations acting as though they are horizontally constructed even though most corporate organizational charts still reflect a vertical hierarchy.

If management is to be successful creating the culture of contribution, it must cede some of its "span of control" and forge a "span of relationships," with workers and managers acting more as "learners than knowers, listeners than tellers, partners than adversaries". Fisher cautions that management should not be too optimistic that a reorganization into teams will solve the ills of the company; rather, a culture of contribution is more likely to develop in a climate where workers are trusted and have the freedom to think and act like owners.

At the core of many organizational development efforts over the past two decades has been the restructuring of organizations from vertical hierarchies into more horizontal, "flattened" designs where most of the work is done by self-directed teams.

In theory, teams "empower" employees by giving team members more decision-making authority and eliminating vertical chains of command. However, empowerment efforts not only require management to share power, they also demand that individual team members think differently about the nature of work.

Labianca, Gray, and Brass found that empowerment efforts require a change in "schemas" - cognitive frameworks that give meaning to experience - for both management and lower level employees. The authors analysed a 2-year organizational development project involving team building and increased participation of lower level employees in decision making. Before the project, the "schema-in-use" for organizational decision making was that management should maintain control of events and decision making, and this schema was understood by both management and employees. The expected new schema for management included: making the organization more team oriented and collaborative, empowering lower level employees, aligning organizational structure effectively, and keeping current workers. For the ruiik-aiid-filu, the expected new schema was characterized by working on team building, creating more avenues of communication, and encouraging employees to air their "beefs."

The authors found: a great amount of employee skepticism at the outset about the likelihood of real change; despite a series of organization-wide meetings, interviews revealed both managers and Non-managers were unclear about the project's goals; resistance was heightened when managerial behaviour failed to conform with its stated expectations; and management incorrectly assumed that employees would postpone Judgement of the reorganization plan until after it was implemented. The authors concluded that employees' resistance to the empowerment plan was motivated less by intentional self-interest than by constraints of well-established, ingrained schema.

Randolph (2000) wrote that few managers or employees fully understand how empowerment affects traditional patterns of corporate hierarchy and behaviour. Management confuses empowerment as "giving people the power to make decisions," and this perception misses the essential notion of empowerment, that a great amount of power already exists in employees' knowledge, experience, and motivation. Rank-and-file perceive empowerment to mean they will be given the freedom to make all major decisions about their jobs. Randolph wrote that empowerment efforts do require a cultural shift; however, the shift is from one person making decisions to team-based shared decision making. he asserts that empowerment makes employees more accountable than the older, hierarchical culture, and it is best understood as a strange combination of opportunity and risk. An organization moves Towards team-based empowered culture through three stages:

- Starting and orienting the process of change,
- Making changes and dealing with discouragement,
- Adopting and refining empowerment to fit the organization.

Each stage utilizes three "interlocking tools" - sharing information, creating autonomy through boundaries, and replacing the hierarchy with self-directed teams.

Hirschhorn, a management scholar whose work focuses on team-based organizations, wrote that the entire philosophy of management is changing as corporations flatten hierarchies and adopt new team environments. Successful managers develop roles for team members and "managc thc boundary," communicating the company's needs to the team and the team's needs to the company. Managers lead by creating a structure in which the team can be successful and by positioning themselves to defend the team's efforts. Managers must realise they are both cause of and solution to many team problems. To be successful, managers must show their vulnerability (a traditional management faux pas) and willingness to learn from team members. Exhibiting these traits shows that managers are open to new ways to solve problems and encourages team members to respond to challenges that can enhance team performance.

Although development efforts are characterized by dispersing power throughout an organization, management's ability to provide leadership remains a key to organizational success. Kets de Vries (1993), a psychologist who focuses on the "psychodynamics of organizations," wrote that organizational culture depends on the psychological contract that exists between its leaders and followers.

Effective leaders need to: articulate a vision of the future; create symbolic impressions to communicate the vision; build networks; empower followers; make choices (often painful ones); and keep perspectives of the followers based in reality. he wrote that the leader/follower relationship a process of social comparison that involves power, authority, hero worship, flattery, ambition, and attention seeking - provides tremendous opportunities for distorted management reasoning.

The key is for managers to "preserve their hold on reality." Trust is essential for a healthy organization, and trust is dependent upon communication, support, respect, fairness, competence, and consistency on the part of the leaders. he concluded, "In order for the leader to understand the meaning of these words, it is important that he or she realise what it means to be a follower, how it feels to be in that position".

The importance of communication in organizations, especially during times of change, has spawned its own discipline of study. Lewis wrote that a growing body of empirical research indicates that the communication process and organizational change efforts are "inextricably linked processes".

Communication plays an important role in several aspects of the change process, including: creating and articulating a vision; soliciting input and channeling feedback to and from all levels of the organizational hierarchy; and propelling and altering the paths of change. The organizational communication literature reveals that communication has been shown to reduce uncertainty associated with change efforts, increase accuracy in perceptions about the reasons and goals of change, and increase willingness to participate in planned change.

Studying the methods and channels organizations use to communicate change, Lewis found change agents consider themselves to be the primary sources of change-related information, and they solicit input much less frequently than they disseminate information. She suggests that management's lack of use of channels of communication, especially upward channels, limits feedback from lower level employees who do the work of the organization. This approach can affect the success of change efforts, as "changes in status, reward structures, job descriptions, roles, work methods, work relationships, and procedures bring significant organizational issues to the surface" that increase rank-and-file employees' need to communicate with their supervisors.

There is a small body of literature; on organizational attempts to initiate market-oriented cultural change. Narver and Slater described a market-oriented culture as one that most effectively and efficiently creates superior customer value. Harris defined a market-oriented culture as "the dominant, dynamic segment of an organization whoso orientation, attitudes and actions are geared towards the market".

Harris contends that most reseachers err when they assume an organization has a single, unitary culture. This approach ignores the dynamic interaction of many aspects of an organization's culture and denies the possibility of the existence of multiple cultures. Generally, developing a market-oriented culture can be understood as a means to improve organizational efficiency and effectiveness.

However, Piercy maintains the success of developing such a culture is largely dependent on internal power relationships and organizational politics, which - at least in the short term - do not necessarily lead to high levels of organization-wide motivation, commitment, or satisfaction. When understood in this context, developing a market-oriented culture can be seen as one of many ways that an organization can impose cultural control over the attitudes, actions, and behaviors of its members.

Overall, Harris and Ogbonna wrote that the literature on the effects of developing market-oriented cultures is inconsistent, with some studies suggesting that the new culture improves employee satisfaction and commitment and others indicating this is not the case. However, researchers tend to agree that the success of any attempt at creating a market-oriented culture is contingent on employees who have to implement it.

In nearly all cases, this is the front-line employees who are the primary link between an organization and its customers. The authors also contend that developing a market-oriented culture should be concerned with the long-term generation of values, attitudes, and behaviors, but the underlying assumption of the market culture is continuing responsiveness to customer needs. The dilemma for organizations is how they can craft short-term responses to "increasingly fickle" customer needs in a manner that does not conflict with long-term organizational objectives. Harris and Ogbonna concluded that this condition is "a contradiction yet to be resolved or fully understood".

Change, because it requires giving up what is known and routine for something new that may not be understood, is often met with resistance. De Jager wrote that many managers perceive employees who resist change as a problem. he contends this a short-sighted view that fundamentally misunderstands the causes of resistance and the potential benefits resistance can exert on an organization. De Jager wrote that businesses today acknowledge the need to change, but there is so much change that employees become confused and see themselves pushed in conflicting directions.

Management is wise to understand that resistance to change is a tool that can be used to guide an organization. "Another way of looking at resistance is as a gateway or filter. Resistance to change helps us select from all possible changes the one that is most appropriate to the current situation". Because change involves replacing old organizational routines and values with new ones, managers must be able to provide answers for employees to some fundamental questions:

- Why is the old status quo no longer sufficient?
- What will it cost to make the transition from the old to new ways of doing things? De Jager identified several likely costs: disruption of routines, training, temporary low morale, new hires, people leaving, and the emotional cost of destroying what was.
- Is the cost of change justified by the incremental benefits of the change proposed?
- Does the proposed change support and reinforce existing core values?

As the millennium approached, the newspaper industry faced imposing, concurrent challenges on several fronts: stagnant circulation and a slowly dwindling base of readers; a fragmenting mass modin market; new electronic media that are changing the way people access and use information; threats to traditional sources of advertising; and unpredictable but rising costs of production. In the wake of a mid-1990s recession that saw significant cutbacks, layoffs, and downsizings, newsrooms were restructured and reorganized. Hierarchical newsroom designs were flattened, and the beat system of coverage centered on social institutions was replaced by a team system that defined coverage areas by topics believed of greater interest to readers and consumers. What becomes apparent from the industry trade journals is that "change" became the guiding light of the industry in the late 1990s.

Feeling out of step with the social patterns and interests of the public, the industry questioned its news values and management has focused on changing the culture of the newsroom to include greater marketing awareness and knowledge.

Editors are increasingly taking on marketing duties, working in cross-departmental teams with advertising, circulation, and marketing directors to create strategies to attract readers, often in specific demographic groups that advertisers are willing to pay to reach. Rank-and-file journalists are expected to accept restructuring, redefined news values, and a greater sensitivity to marketing as part of a larger cultural change process that is redefining their jobs and norms as journalists.Organizational theory suggests that integrated organizations are more innovative and flexible and respond more quickly to opportunities and challenges. The basis of power and decision making in integrated organizations shifts from being solely in the hands of management to a shared arrangement that empowers employees to use their knowledge and skills in team-based systems. Teams, and their individual members, respond to more decision-making power and autonomy by taking more responsibility for the quality of their work and becoming more productive.

Organizational change and development is understood as a process with several stages, including planning, executing, and monitoring the progress and results. Because organizations have different values and goals, the study of OD has usually focused on one organization at a time, identifying the impact of site-specific variables on organizational development. This approach, while making theory building more difficult, has, however, led to researchers identifying several variables that impact the success of OD efforts.

These variables include an organization having a clear mission, employees who understand the mission and organization's core values, effective organizational communication, employee participation in Grafting and implementing change initiatives, strong leadership, trust, flexibility, and mechanisms that monitor the progress of change initiatives and reward desired behaviour. The effect of successful OD efforts should be empowered employees who, in self-directed work teams, are more motivated, productive, and responsible for their work. In theory, at least, successful OD efforts should in the long term improve employee morale.

However, change is also understood as a difficult and risky process. It requires employees (both management and rank-and-file) to embrace new values, to alter routines, and to think differently about their organizational roles and the nature of their work. It requires greater accountability from empowered rank-and-file and a new, less autocratic style from management. Accordingly, resistance to change should be expected, and in some cases is rational. For management, successful OD includes understanding the reasons for resistance and having the flexibility to find ways of working through resistance.

In short, the challenge of conceiving and leading change falls on management, while rank-and-file are expected to enact and embrace change initiatives that affect many of their conventions and values. Management perceives it is initiating change in the best interests of the organization and industry, while rank-and-file ponder the reasons for change and are sensitive to how it is implemented. Organizational theory and change models provide conceptual guidelines that should help predict effective organizational development (OD) initiatives.

Given the vast amount of change in the newspaper industry and the relative dearth of research studying these OD initiatives, this study of top newsroom managers and rank-and-file journalists at newspapers leading industry change explores the following research questions and tests three hypotheses.

*RQ*1: What are the attitudes and opinions of management and rank-and-file journalists Towards organizational change?

*RQ*2: How do management and rank-and-file perceive the change process in relation to organizational development theory?

*RQ*3: How do management and rank-and-file perceive organizational change in relation to the normative values of journalism and marketing?

*RQ*4: Have change efforts affected rank-and-file perceptions of news values and organizational structure?

*RQ*5: Have change efforts affected rank-and-file morale?

*RQ*6: Does organization size (measured by circulation) affect how rank-and-file perceive change?

*H*1: Management will perceive it has done significantly better at organizational development than rank-and-file.

*H*2: Morale among rank-and-file will be low.

*H*3: Rank-and-file perceptions of organizational development will predict morale.

CHALLENGES TO RESEARCH: QUESTIONING WHAT WE KNOW

There are important challenges to readership research that must be tackled at the end of the millennium. Each requires that we question existing assumptions about newspapers and newspaper readers. The most radical challenge is whether readership research should continue to bother with the printed newspaper at all. Another challenge is to our assumptions of indisputable truths about newspapers and their readers - are we prepared to forget the truisms about what we think readers want, and address plausible alternatives instead? We are further challenged to consider the strategies that newspapers have used to compete in the changing marketplace, and whether those strategies have been effective. Newspapers could best compete in the new markets from their points of strength, but how can research help us find, capitalize on and market the functions that newspapers do best?

QUESTIONING EXISTING ASSUMPTIONS

First, many critics - and cynics - would have us assume the printed newspaper will disappear anyway, whether accompanied by research or not. If more than a quarter of the population in Western societies has access to a personal computer, isn't it time to abandon our worries about the printed newspaper and begin to focus our research and resources on a glitzy electronic newspaper, save the high distribution costs, and let the old newspaper slowly die a graceful death?It's an easy assumption to make when hundreds of U.S. and internationally-based newspapers are on-line and more are added regularly.

Yet one of the great strengths of the printed newspaper is that its format and its principal layout have been successfully tested now for almost 400 years. It has faced and survived the challenge of many new media - journals and magazines, telegraph and telephone, cinema, radio and television. It's probable that newspapers displayed on paper or on something similar to paper (such as a large, foldable transparency connected to the newsroom on-line) 10 will persist for several decades to come.

Regardless of the delivery mechanism - paper or on-line - we should not forget what makes the newspaper so indispensable for many people. It offers a combination of guidance and surprise, a selective non-selectivity. No other medium performs this function with quite the style and grace of the newspaper, nor as completely or efficiently.

On the one hand, a newspaper provides a preselected array of information that gives readers a sense of prioritized community concerns.

It serves as a "central, shared information source and guide to help us find order and regularity in a helter-skelter world." Within this "representative resume of the relevant facts concerning the last 24 hours," however, readers still can discover new and surprising stories and events.Their curiosity is served much better by a newspaper than by a menu or search engine on a computer screen, asking them what they want to learn about.

A data-bank approach is obviously not what most readers expect from newspapers. How many people, for instance, are really interested in printed news updated throughout the day, or in quick searches for highly specific topics? "People don't actually read newspapers," Marshall McLuhan once said. "They get into them every morning like a hot bath." They look at them instead.

They scan the headlines, read a few lines here, a paragraph there. "Reading a news story is like coming upon an accident," Kevin Barnhurst suggests. "We don't want to see it but can't stop ourselves from looking."Good newspapers offer both their variety of information and their preselective guidance in a professional (*i.e.* in a trustworthy and competent) way. When it comes down to it, "the franchise is journalism, not newspapers." If this is true, however - if the major purpose of newspapers is to provide a multitude of carefully selected and written stories at a glance - then the paper product physically delivered to our mailbox or to our doorsteps every morning may indeed not be the newspaper of the future. And yet, it's unlikely to be a small computer screen, either.

Eventually, the typical combination of surprise and guidance that a newspaper has to offer requires, as an alternative to what it looks like today, either a large newspaper printed on demand at home, or the wide, flat, foldable and easily transportable TV screens of the next millennium. In sum, then, there is still a lot to do to make printed newspapers better and more attractive to the reader. The second major challenge to newspaper research is in adjusting our reliance on truisms about newspaper readers. We all know them - the more local coverage, the better; the more pictures and the more colored graphs, the better; newspaper readers like little bits of information better than long stories; writing styles should be simple, funny, entertaining.

This is exactly what most facelifts in recent years have tried to accomplish. But are these objectives plausible in an era of increasing alternatives for local and national information; for brief, comprehensive summaries of current affairs; and for entertainment?

The indisputable propositions that have guided many decisions fall apart when we consider that newspaper readers and newspaper editors simply don't see eye to eye when it comes to the important attributes of the newspaper. In a recent U.S. nationwide reader and editor survey, George Gladney found that aggressive, original reporting was an attribute far less important to newspaper subscribers than to newspaper editors.

The same pattern applied to strong local coverage limited to the newspaper's immediate distribution area - an entirely plausible result.

While the rationale behind ever-expanding local sections is that events that are geographically close are also interesting for readers, this truism has only partly been true - all events that are close are not interesting to all readers just because they are close.

Don't readers have to be concerned about an event to be interested in it? Geographic proximity is only one possible way to increase interest, and probably not even a good one. Do we really expect readers to find fascinating the annual convention of the local rabbit breeders, just because it takes place close by?

So far, most layout and typographical changes have been based on the taste of newspaper designers. Their language is revealing in that respect.

They declare that something looks impossible or boring. But why? Do readers really have the same opinions, and even if so, does it sell the newspaper? Gladney's reader and editor survey reveals that, once again, readers found an attractive presentation of news through use of visual tools such as typography, photography, graphics, colour, layout, design far less important than the editors did.

Yet a recent customer satisfaction study with almost 5,500 respondents in Germany showed that liking the layouts of 50 newspapers correlates strongly with the evaluation of their contents as topical and informative.

In other words: The better people evaluated the newspaper, the more attractive they found its appearance - independently of what it actually looked like. Do we have to accept that formalities do not matter as long as the contents are interesting?

STRATEGIES FOR COMPETING IN NEW MARKETS

While we've been busily focusing on changes of newspaper substance and form, our research has lacked a central concept - one might even call it a theory

- which in outline could look like this: In principle, media threatened by new forms of communication have always had two choices, they either copy the more successful competitor, or they try to distinguish themselves from it the best they can.

The copying strategy accepts both television and print magazines as the most successful competitors of newspapers. Newspapers all over the world seem to imitate both. They use magazine layout; they mimic television by presenting lots of pictures and graphs and brief sound bite-type stories - the USA Today approach to saving the printed newspaper.

But let's think twice about this popular strategy. It's entirely possible that those who like television may simply watch television instead of reading a more or less well-crafted copy of it. The stereotypical response to this suspicion, of course, is that people - particularly adolescents - are used to a video approach to the world.

Newspapers, then, would be simply forced to comply with this truth by publishing newspapers as close to videos as possible. We must be careful to remember, however, that these same young people are already readers - readers of books and magazines, more than ever in history. So, one might as well ask: Why do we not tap their great reading skills instead?

This leads us to the other strategy for the survival of the printed press - doing what the newspaper can do best. In our view, this strategy so far has been somewhat neglected. What is it that newspapers can do best?

The following attributes are winners:

- The newspaper is a multi-purpose medium; it offers not only information but also entertainment and guidance - even advice - and all of it is in the hands of its readers at the same time. Newspaper readers don't have to wait for access as they would with television and radio - even at a time when 160 and more specialized TV channels may be available for some people.
- The newspaper provides an immense variety within its information, a diversity of voices and standpoints every day.
- The newspaper has space for explanation and interpretation, for everyday orientation and context.
- The newspaper offers easy access to all information, it is a simply but efficiently structured data bank that doesn't need any technical devices and computer skills. And, there's no waiting for the next screen to appear.
- The newspaper provides the aesthetic pleasure of layout and typography, and even the haptic nature of unfolding a newspaper and paging through it.
- The newspaper is mobile; it can be read almost everywhere.
- The newspaper provides a low threshold for readers to participate in

public discussion. Letters or calls to the editor do not require particular professional skills or the self-consciousness that speaking up on television or radio may take.

Certainly, every one of these advantages of a newspaper can be challenged by other media - above all by magazines, by the way. But it is the mix of functions it serves every day that makes the newspaper special. Over and above their advantages, newspapers can still draw on an almost perfect image. Surveys show that they are regarded as trustworthy, credible and competent. But this image seems to create more awe and reverence among the public than the sympathy, the sense of familiarity, that is necessary for actually reading it.

HOW TO CAPITALIZE ON NEWSPAPERS' STRENGTHS

So, should research not be directed to how these particular characteristics of newspapers may be fortified? Compared to marketing a target group magazine or a narrowly formatted radio or TV station, marketing the typical mix of purposes is probably the major challenge for newspaper readership research.

An easy way out could be to give up the mass appeal of newspapers. Should we try to make them a target group medium, a daily magazine, a medium with class appeal for instance, for loyal and affluent readers only, ready to pay higher prices for quality both in contents and appearance? In Editor and Publisher, George Garneau, for instance, suggests that newspapers cut mercilessly what he calls ego circulation - that is, copies that may contribute to better circulation figures but are sold to people that advertisers are not interested in.

Newspapers should be careful, however, not to engage in the deplorable practice of cutting back on circulation areas that, with or without research, are deemed of little value to advertisers - inner cities and rural areas with fringe distribution are already being abandoned by many U.S. newspapers under the rubric of cost efficiency.

Providing cheaper coverage that doesn't harm circulation numbers is problematic because newspapers serve more than a strictly commercial function. Many studies show that newspaper reading increases political knowledge and furthers political participation. It is much more efficient in this respect than watching television or listening to the radio. It both reaches more people and it helps them learn better.

So, we have a dilemma - the one between our responsibility for an informed audience and the need to sell newspapers. And taking a poll to see what the readers want and then giving it to them provides no easy solution. In a recent study in the German city of Dortmund, readers called newspaper articles high quality if they were complete, easy to read, well-structured and brief.

Newspaper journalists, however, ranked much higher the topic of the story, the quality of research and the objectivity of an article. With that evidence in, do we now abandon the well-researched, objective stories because readers don't ask for them explicitly? This is where the well-meaning friends of the newspaper who fear that research will diminish the quality of journalism have a point.

The American newspaper researcher Philip Meyer warns us:

- A newspaper audience is a mosaic of many small but intense interests, and if you cut back on those interests when space is short, you stand to lose more net readership than a cutback of more general material would.
- So, taking a poll to discover that numbers are low on certain features of the newspaper can backfire if those are the certain features to which particular readers are intensely attached. Lose those features and lose those readers.

LET'S ASK THE RIGHT QUESTIONS

If we still believe in newspapers as a universal medium for everybody, on what then should readership research focus? Successful newspapers with universal appeal face multiple critical dilemmas, and this makes applying research results challenging. Consider the following:

- Probably the most basic dilemma of newspapers is in finding and maintaining the counterpoise between reliability and surprise - that delicate balance between the elements that help structure the newspaper for its readers without destroying the possibility to make unexpected discoveries and to come upon interesting stories by chance alone. This dilemma leads to very practical questions for research, such as:

How long should articles be, if they are not to keep busy readers from being surprised but, on the other hand, provide enough background and context?

Do the growing number of inserts and the unbundling of the newspaper make it a bunch of magazines instead of the universal resume of the last 24 hours? How far can we go to make a newspaper more portable, probably smaller in size, without losing the surprises that two large unfolded pages provide? Whe re are the limits of a more hedonistic, less serious approach, to newspaper reading? It should be a plea sure, not a chore, to read the newspaper. Perhaps the lack of time named as a reason by so many non-readers may be due to the fact that reading a newspaper is simply not enough fun for them.

There are legitimate doubts, of course, that funny, infotainment newspapers are a good idea for the majority of readers. Certainly seriousness and competence belong to the image of the newspaper, and care must be exercised in protecting that reputation.

- How can we attract young people? Do pop music, computer games and young love as topics really do the trick? These are topics, after all, that they can find out about elsewhere and often with more competence. Some other ideas, however, are waiting to be tested:

Does newspaper reading become more attractive for adolescents if we stress its function as a rite of initiation into adulthood? Or is it exactly its grown-up image that keeps young people from turning to it? Ac cording to a 1991 U.S. experiment, young people found newspapers enjoyable if their front pages contained longer stories and more pullout quotes.

The impression of attractiveness was enhanced by more and smaller photographs and larger graphics on the front page. The use of colour and design principles like vertical or horizontal designs did not matter. The results - puzzling as they are - provide at least some indication of what could be worth looking at more thoroughly.

In the United States, it looks as if a major reason for young people to turn to newspapers is the presence of advertising geared Towards them? Attractive weekend sections are another one? Eile en Lehnert suggests there might not be the monolithic youth market for newspapers but several segments of the adolescent audience that demand differently prioritized offers from newspapers.

- Newspaper reading has suffered not only among young people but also among less educated ones and those with little interest in conventional politics. So, a fourth challenge for research is a question of balance: How can we make newspapers more readable for less sophisticated readers without simplifying their contents too much for everybody else?
- Still another research question is derived from the idea of strengthening what newspapers can do best: Would public or civic journalism help the newspaper? This concept - growing in popularity in the United States - regards newspapers as a citizens' forum, a neutral place where the issues of a community can be discussed, where views can be exchanged. Civic journalism also emphasizes the digest function of newspapers - to tell readers precisely where they can find more material outside the newspaper about an issue and how good that material is.
- One last question of balance: How much does diversification of newspaper services distract from its major functions? Additional electronic offerings are beginning to spread. But is it, for instance, a good idea to provide elaborate audiotex systems where users can get the latest news, sports, stock prices, horoscopes, etc., via telephone? In other words, how much exclusive information and service can a newspaper offer to attract an audience online before it harms the printed newspaper in turn?

NOT NECESSARILY AN ARM AND A LEG

A major prejudice readership research has to deal with is its cost. Is it really expensive? Of course, the more useful it is, the less important this question becomes.

But in any case, empirical studies are costly once they involve long-term research designs, large representative surveys, or difficult data-collecting techniques: panels, copy tests, field experiments with different versions of a newspaper. But consider some cheaper and nevertheless useful alternatives:

- Important research questions can be addressed legitimately by closely listening to carefully selected readers and non-readers: In-depth interviews and focus groups are a somewhat inexpensive device. Even copy tests can obviously be conducted as tracking studies administered by the readers themselves.
- Content analyses of the newspaper and its competitors can reveal differences and commonalties in topics, pictures, language, the tone of the articles etc. - again, nothing that has to be overly expensive. This type of evidence may suffice to explain, for instance, what makes a competitor more attractive than one's own newspaper.
- A well-maintained file of subscriber data provides both useful and inexpensive information: Who are the long-term subscribers? Which types of readers are the most susceptible to canceling their subscriptions?
- Socio-demographic data of the distribution area can be bought. They are often very elaborate - lifestyle characteristics of potential readers may be segmented by postal code areas, streets and even blocks. So, these data produce a relatively intricate picture of the housing situation, income, education, household size, voting behaviour etc. They allow both micro-zoning of newspaper editions and finely tuned marketing measures both for actual and potential readers.
- Some questions can be satisfactorily answered by desk research, by using census data, for instance, or other official statistics. Even better: a data bank of evidence gathered by other newspapers - still a dream, of course, as long as newspapers do not feel the need to close the ranks. Instead, many newspapers have maintained a virtual blackout of information they have gathered from their readers. If at all accessible, research on the other newspaper ends up years later in scholarly publications - publications that many practitioners may not read regularly.

JOINT RESEARCH EFFORTS: A PROTOTYPE

Increasingly, severe threats to the newspaper make joint research efforts inevitable. As a nice side effect, cooperation also saves money. An example of fruitful cooperation for the sake of the printed newspaper is an analysis of 350 West German newspapers. On a large scale, it deals with a very practical question that, so far, every single newspaper has tried to answer for itself and only for itself: which of all the measures taken in readership marketing have really been successful?

In a first step, the German research team systematically compared both contents and appearance of the same 350 newspapers in 1989 and in 1994. We now know about all major changes in substance and formalities, such as the structure of the paper; the amount of background and commentary, of local information, of service, of target group offers; the accessibility of its contents, its readability, the tone of its headlines (do they sound friendly, emotional, aggressive?).

But also changes in format, layout principles, colour, graphs, photos, size of articles, etc. were investigated. This part of the study already shows that West German newspapers have become lighter, fluffier, in their layout and typography; their number of pages has increased - mostly in favour of the local section. All in all, they look more serious, less tabloid. Layout and other structuring principles are observed more rigidly.

In a second step, all the other marketing measures directed at the audience were studied, such as attempts to advertise the newspaper and to work on its image, discounts and rewards for subscribing to the paper, sponsoring activities, and readership forums, among others. In a third step, all these ideas to make the newspaper more attractive were evaluated.

For this purpose, circulation and the MA data sets of 1989 and 1994 were used. With more than 50,000 respondents in West Germany, the latter provided information about the success of a specific newspaper in its distribution area.

We know now which ones among the measures that newspapers had been trying out between 1989 and 1994 were the most successful to keep or even enlarge certain groups in the audience: structured, not too crammed layouts, for instance, more variety in the daily offering (not too many inserts), a strict separation of reporting and entertainment, just to name a few. The same study has been conducted in Israel and is now underway in the United States and in Sweden.

The German study was possible only because the participating newspapers gave up some of their egocentrism. Funded by the BDZV, the German Newspaper Publishers Association, and the Stiftervereinigung der Presse, the German Press Foundation, and with the support of the Regionalpresse, the marketing organization of the German regional newspapers, we were given access to the necessary information for such an endeavor.

In France and Britain, for instance, newspapers have also joined - in SPQR and The Newspaper Society - to do research of a scale that a single enterprise could not afford alone. More cooperation between all newspapers is certainly a model for future readership research.

A FINAL CHALLENGE: PREPARING JOURNALISTS TO MAKE USE OF RESEARCH

We've listed the dilemmas - one might even say, the contradictions - in what newspapers are for their audience. These dilemmas make readership research and the application of its results particularly challenging. But let's not forget that it often is a difficult task for publishers and editors to use readership evidence appropriately - for the best of both the public and the paper itself.

Journalism scholar and frequent newspaper consultant David Weaver from Indiana University envisions a trustee editor as the ideal person who applies and uses the results of readership research. Such a trustee editor - he says - "does not sacrifice his or her editorial Judgement to the readers, but he does not ignore readers' opinion either." For this purpose, journalists have to be trained in making use of readership research instead of being warned of it.

ELEVEN BASIC GS IDEAS AND THEIR RELEVANCE TO JOURNALISM AND MEDIA ETHICS

The word is not the thing: General semanticists say, "The map is not the territory." The symbol is not the object or event that is symbolized. For example, when we describe a "flower" we should be aware that the "real" flower is an ever-changing process that entails air, light, water, and soil. When using words, we should not fool ourselves into thinking we are fully describing an actual flower.

The word is not the thing. This principle is even more important when we are discussing abstract terms like freedom, justice, patriotism, democracy, and responsibility. The concluding paragraph reads "President Bush believes that 'democracy,' in the way we use that term, can move the Iraqi people to have happier and more productive lives. Maybe it can.

But maybe people who have been conditioned to accept orders from authorities such as clerics have a different conception of democracy. Maybe they believe, like America's founding fathers and the citizens of ancient Athens, that it is within proper democratic bounds to restrict the rights of women and other groups. Only time will tell which definition of democracy will prevail."

Stay low on the abstraction ladder: In communicating with others, don't use abstract terms when you can use more meaningful—more specific—ones. For example, when expressions like pornography, good Christians, arrogant government officials, fundamentalists, or concerned voters are used in a story, it is helpful for the journalist to explain them. If possible, the journalist should give specific examples of what the subjects do or what they believe, in order to clarify a story's meaning.

Make clear distinctions: reports, inferences, and judgments: Reports are based on observable data and verifiable. Bill Smith, age twenty-five, was sentenced last week to fifteen years in prison. Inferences are assumptions made from known data. Bill Smith will soon be in prison. Judgments are conclusions made from inferences. A Judgement: Bill Smith is an evil and dangerous individual. Journalists frequently confuse or mix reports, inferences, and judgments, which is unfortunate, as flawed inferences or flawed judgments can have a negative impact on "objective reporting." Recognition of non-allness: One can never completely describe anything. Certain characteristics are always left out. For example, a report may say, "He is a New York attorney." But he is a great deal more (a husband, a Baptist, an alcoholic, an ex-military man, etc.). Journalists, when using language, must leave out much significant information. Ethical reporters (ethical in the sense of dedicated to "truthful, accurate, and objective reporting") must avoid intentionally biasing their story by what is omitted, and they should be aware of the omissions.

Delay your reaction: A hunter lived with an infant in a cabin, guarded by his dog. One day the hunter returned from the fields and saw the cradle overturned and the baby nowhere in sight. The room was a mess. The dog had blood all over his muzzle. The hunter, enraged, shot the dog. He then found the baby, unharmed under the bed, and a dead wolf in the corner.

Uncritical assumptions can result in negative consequences. Ethical journalists understand this and so, following the general semantics recommendation to delay one's reaction to more accurately assess what is going on, they do not precipitously rush when gathering facts for a story. Unlike many of us, such reporters do not take for granted the human ability to delay one's reaction.

They know the capacity to delay reacting, and bring our higher brain functions into play, is a key characteristic that distinguishes our species from the rest of the animal kingdom.Reality is dynamic: The Greek philosopher Heraclitus famously said that one can not step in the same river twice. What he meant by this is that life is perpetually in flux, people and situations are constantly shifting. While language may impose, as Nietzsche suggested, a "stabilizing fiction" on events that transpire in our restless universe, the fact is change is ever present.

Because reality is dynamic, ethical reporters will not use an old quotation, as if it were currently valid, to give someone's views on a subject nor will they automatically assume that the views individuals hold today are the same they espoused thirty years ago.The eminent general semanticist Irving J. Lee asserted that we tend to discriminate against people to the degree that we fail to distinguish among them. Indexing, a GS tool that involves using mathematical subscripts to break down larger categories into their component parts, is an effective technique for addressing Lee's concern.

The use of indexing can remind journalists that members of the same group are not the same and that it is dangerous to make assumptions about them because of their nationality, race, religion, party, or other characteristics.

Multivalued orientation: Aristotle's law of the excluded middle (A thing is either "A" or "not A") encourages us to think that every question can be answered in terms of "either-or." The structure of the English language also pushes us in that direction. With its many polarizing terms (good/bad, tall/short, liberal/conservative, etc.), English supports reasoning through extremes rather than with gradations.

General semantics notes that either-or thinking keeps us from seeing the great diversity in the world. For example, rather than being tall or short, or liberal or conservative, most people fall "height wise" and politically somewhere along a continuum.Ethical reporters are mindful that accurate descriptions of people and events involve more than just assigning them to one of two dichotomous categories.

Beware the "is" of projection: "She's a knockout." "That painting is not art." "King Kong was a great movie." When individuals make statements like these they tell us precious little about what they are describing. Instead, they say something about themselves. They are projecting their ideas of what they consider to be "beautiful," "art," and "outstanding cinema." They are confusing opinions with facts.

To demonstrate awareness that our thoughts or comments are products of our internal condition, rather than reports of external "reality," general semantics advocates the use of qualifying expressions like "it seems to me," "as I see it," "apparently," "from my point of view," etc. These phrases signal to others that we are transmitting personal observations about reality, not divine truths.

The "meaning" of words: What's the difference between a "freedom fighter" and a "terrorist"? Were the victims at the Abu Ghraib prison in Iraq subjected to "abuse" or "torture"? Are organizations that comment on news reporting "media watchdog groups," or are they "pressure groups"? Don't look to the dictionary to answer these questions. Their answers depend on how people perceive things.

General semantics observes that strictly speaking, words don't "mean;" people do. The physicist P. W. Bridgman put it this way, "Never ask 'What does word X mean?' but ask instead, 'What do I mean when I say word X?' or 'What do you mean when you say word X?'" Words do not have "one true meaning." For the 500 most used words in the English language, the Oxford Dictionary lists 14,070 meanings. Ethical journalists understand that conveying meaning is a complex and tricky matter, and that possibilities for confusion are a constant threat.

Natural penchant for partiality: General semantics recognizes that there is a tendency for individuals to select (or abstract) from reality those portions that are consistent with personal values. In reporting a story a newsperson may choose what is appealing, what coincides with preferences, what gives pleasure. Ethical journalists guard against such egotistical inclinations and are able to force themselves to include information in stories that is uncongenial to them and with which they disagree.

JOURNALISM PROFESSIONALIZATION AND ORIENTATION

As suggested by the review above, journalism professionalization reflects the political, social, and economic system of which a given press system is a part. Indeed, the elements of professionalization, in general, are related to the factors of press systems just summarized. These elements are specialized education, a public service rather than commercial orientation, autonomy, and a high level of related ethical standards in practice.

It has been argued that journalists acquire these attributes through three levels of socialization: the societal, the professional, and the organizational. Societal socialization refers to the overall impact of the social system on individuals and their values, and it accounts for differences among countries even given comparable politics and economies. The professional level refers to processes such as education, training, the development of particular orientations, and the articulation of values and standards through journalism associations. As will be further explained soon, there is an increasing global harmonization in this respect, though differences remain.

The third level of socialization, the organizational, is the process by which individual news media inculcate their particular values and preferences in their journalists. This level of socialization distinguishes, say, one newspaper from another within the same press system in their professional orientation. Beam has suggested that professionalism is best studied at this level. Such an approach does, indeed, have empirical advantages, but it is limited in its representation of professionalization. Analyses that reflect all three levels of socialization better reflect the reality.

Various categories have been developed for classifying journalists' orientations. In a psycho-social taxonomy that reconciled the contradictory claims that journalists are autonomous rebels and that they are motivated by altruistic service to society, Schwartz demonstrated that they fall in either category, what he labeled "inner-directed" or "other-directed."

Janowitz identified two orientations as the gatekeeper and the advocate, the gatekeeper being committed to scientific detachment and objectivity and the advocate being oriented Towards interpretation and criticism. A similar taxonomy developed by Johnstone, Slawski, and Bowman classifies journalists as neutral and participant.

In a more recent study of American journalists, Weaver and Wilhoit rejected the neutral-participant typology as a misnomer and developed a four-type classification as adversarialist, interpreter, disseminator, and populist mobilizer. They found that the dominant orientation was the interpretive, which entails a blend of investigative reporting and analysis.

This is followed closely by the disseminator orientation, which emphasizes rapid transmission of information to the widest number of people. The adversarialist orientation, with its emphasis on skepticism Towards government and business, was found to be a minority orientation. Only a small percentage of journalists were classified as populist mobilizers, those who stressed giving voice to the public and setting public agenda. The various orientations were found to co-exist in various degrees, creating what Lahav has described as "the inherent contradiction between the press as a political organ and the press as an objective medium."

Press systems and the nature of professionalization may be said to be characterized by the dominant orientation at a given time. Historically, press systems have started out in the partisan-advocacy orientation and, to various degrees, moved Towards more detached reporting. Janowitz concluded in his analysis that the gatekeeper approach to journalism enhances professionalization and that professionalization, in turn, makes the advocacy orientation more viable.

In the United States, the drive Towards professionalization has been traced to the Civil War, when partisanship became so extreme and crude that embarrassed practitioners began to seek reform. The impetus re-emerged after World War I following the resurgence of sensationalistic propaganda. Some early trade publications, undertook the articulation of values and standards and were embraced by journalists. Ultimately, the need to mass-market news accelerated the drive Towards objective and non-partisan news.

In the 1920s, Walter Lippmann articulated what became "a central principle in the professionalization of journalism": careful gathering and accurate, balanced, and objective reporting of facts.

Lippmann proposed a scientific orientation to news, which requires "the habits of ascribing no more credibility to a statement than it warrants, a nice sense of the probabilities, and a keen understanding of the quantitative importance of particular facts." Though it cannot be said that Lippmann's high standards have been attained anywhere, journalism professionalization has advanced along the lines of his recommendation. Various professional organizations have long emerged in part for this purpose.

Their canons typically reflect the need to maintain credibility with the public, a goal that is broadly defined to encompass the press's independence, social responsibility, and adherence to the standards of facticity, accuracy, objectivity, fairness, and balance.

With varying degrees of emphasis, these standards are subscribed to by journalists in various regions of the world. Studies have shown that even in systems where the press is not independent, some journalists aspire to these values or at least subscribe to them in principle.

For instance, while acknowledging that its founding charter imposed "certain political responsibilities," the Pan African News Agency Non-etheless stipulates as follows in its stylebook:

A news agency exists to provide news to newspapers, radio and television stations and it lives on credibility. Those who subscribe to its service have the confidence that its news and features will always be factual, objective and balanced and that it can always be relied upon to provide good quality service promptly. Indeed, as Head and Ibelema have noted, professionalization in various press systems has to be judged in terms of journalists' exemplification of these ideals to the extent possible within their systemic constraints.

Studies have shown that professionalization provides some protection from outside interference and attacks. Dimmick's study shows that various media industries moved Towards or intensified efforts at professionalization during periods of intense scrutiny or threats from the outside. Some scholars have gone as far as to characterize the practice of objectivity as a mask for journalists' agenda or as a "strategic ritual" and professionalization as an "agent of legitimation."

The rise of journalism professionalization has, however, raised concerns that the watchdog role of the press might be blunted. Merrill contends, for instance, that the American press was becoming so socially responsible that it was "in danger of becoming one vast, gray, bland, monotonous, conformist spokesman for some collectivity of society." Some studies have indicated, however, that professionalization has no such effect. This study provides some insight on this debate.

ORIGINS OF PARTISAN-ADVOCATORIAL ORIENTATION

As already noted, the Nigerian press's partisanship has origins in its history, and that history bears on its fate and performance during the June 12 crisis. The history may be broken up into four periods: the nationalist, regionalist, state-oriented, and independent press eras.

This classification reflects major ownership and editorial orientations dating from the early years of the press to the present day. The Nigerian press became politically aligned quite early in its history. Though the first newspapers, dating back to 1859, were published for educational and entertainment purposes, political advocacy soon became a major thrust.

The first noted case of political journalism in Nigeria was in 1863, when R. Campbell, a West Indian of African descent who has been described as a "brilliant and courageous" writer, "practiced journalism to fight the then existing slave trade." In 1891, John Payne, a Liberian trader in Nigeria, began publishing the Lagos Weekly Record, in which he attacked the policies of the colonial government.

The thrust of the Nigerian press became decidedly political from the 1920s, with the formation of political parties and their establishment of newspapers as organs of agitation. Though most of the papers had obvious regional interests, they aligned in their crusade for independence or some form of self-determination or political rights for Nigerians and other Africans. The pre-independence press was thus largely nationalist in ideology and orientation. A major exception was the Daily Times, which was established as a commercial enterprise rather than a political instrument and was funded largely by foreign investors. The rest of the Nigerian press began making the transition from nationalism to regionalism as political independence became increasingly a reality and internal political rivalry emerged as a preoccupation.

However, the birth of the regionalist press was not complete until the late 1950s and the years just after independence. This period witnessed the flourishing of newspapers sponsored by the regional and federal governments.

After the Eastern Nigerian government established the Eastern Outlook (later renamed the Nigerian Outlook), other regions and the federal government followed suit. The federal government established the Morning Post in 1961, the Western Regional government established the Daily Sketch in 1964, and the Northern government established the New Nigerian in 1966 (to replace the Nigerian Citizen). The Midwestern Region, which was excised from the West in 1963, established its own newspaper, The Observer, in 1968. The rise of the regionalist press presaged the demise of the nationalist newspapers, most of which were defunct by 1975.

The regionalist newspapers maintained Nigeria's advocatorial press tradition through the early years of independence and democracy. The vibrancy of the press reflected a political structure in which four powerful ethnic-oriented regional governments competed among themselves for resources, while vying for control of or influence at the federal government. As noted earlier, such inherent political pluralism is usually accompanied by a contentious press.

Just before Nigeria's civil war between 1967 and 1970, the country was broken up into 12 states to replace the four regions as political divisions. The state-oriented press emerged during and after the war, as each state sought to establish its own news media. Among the state-owned newspapers established at this time were the Chronicle (South-Eastern State), Daily Sketch (Western), Nigerian Herald (Kwara), Nigerian Standard (Benue Plateau), Renaissance (East Central), and Nigerian Tide (Rivers).

It was during this period, in 1976, that the federal military government bought 100 per cent interest in the New Nigerian, the North's dominant newspaper, and 60 per cent interest in the Daily Times Company, which till then was Nigeria's largest and most successful publishing house. Significantly, the acquisitions were made the same year that the federal government-owned daily Morning Post and Sunday Post ceased publication after years of falling circulation and revenue losses.

The acquisitions, coupled with the limited geographic appeal of the state-owned newspapers, created a vacuum for national non-governmental newspapers and so gave rise to the birth of the independent press - the fourth (and current) press era - beginning in the early 1980s. This era is marked by the rise and dominance of newspapers and magazines established by wealthy entrepreneurs and groups of journalists. The first major publications in this era were the National Concord and The Guardian. The papers soon became major rivals of the government-owned newspapers, including especially the Daily Times and the New Nigerian, both of which had begun to decline in circulation as well as influence. The Concord, The Guardian and their respective founders - Moshood Abiola and Alex Ibru, respectively - also were to feature prominently in the June 12 crisis.

Though independent, the National Concord became identified with the National Party of Nigeria, the country's ruling party during the four years of what Nigerians call the Second Republic. Dissenting senior staff members subsequently left the Concord group and founded Newswatch in 1984/85, and the magazine gained instant popularity.

This development established a trend that would soon characterize the independent press era, namely the founding of publications by journalists intent on pursuing editorial orientations which though often still partisan were less circumscribed by political affiliation.

Among other publications established this way were the dailies Vanguard and This Day and the weekly magazines Tell and TheNews. The decline of the federal and state government-owned newspapers intensified at this point, and most were reduced to publishing less frequently and in skeletal forms.

Thus, the independent press era is characterized by the dominance of national publications that were not owned by governments or political parties, though their political sympathies or even agendas were transparent in most cases. This era is also marked by the influx into journalism of "a well-educated and politically committed crop of reporters." Olurunyomi writes that "Not only were these young men and women prowling their beats with the confidence of brilliant college graduates, they had also undergone an activist baptism of fire from the anti-apartheid and student movements." This explanation is similar to Flacks's analysis of the ideological ferment within American professions resulting from the influx of graduates radicalized by the campus activism of the 1960s.

The founding of Tell magazine in 1991 and TheNews magazine in 1993 and their subsequent role in the June 12 crisis are particularly illustrative of the ownership trend that characterize the independent press era and the impact of that trend on press performance. The departure of some senior staff members of the Concord group to found Newswatch in 1984 was replicated in 1991 when editors at Newswatch who felt the magazine was becoming too staid and conservative left to found the more radical Tell.

Tell's philosophy was to be more advocatorial in the tradition of the nationalist press. Nosa Igiebor, Tell's executive editor and one of the founding publishers, cited the activist journalism of Nnamdi Azikiwe, Obafemi Awolowo, and other nationalists of the colonial era as his inspiration. That philosophy characterized Tell's performance during the June 12 crisis and kept it in the forefront of defiant opposition throughout the crisis. Like Tell, TheNews was established by a group of senior journalists who left the Guardian group after it was briefly shut down by the military government in 1992. The journalists left the Guardian group rather than agree to an apology for a story as demanded by the government as a condition for ending the shutdown. Like Tell, TheNews was established with an activist journalistic philosophy. The founders believed that "the military had hijacked the [Nigerian] polity," resulting in "a loss of federalism." They saw the magazine then as an "instrument of social engineering" "to catalyze debate and [its] direction," to fight against corruption, and to resist any attempt to muzzle their effort. As will be shown later, the consonant philosophy of the two magazines, along with their relative youth and non-establishment status, informed their reportage and enabled their resilience in the face of concerted effort by the government to muzzle them.

Indeed, it is useful at this point to summarize the factors whose confluence determined the course of the events described below. In politics, there was a legitimation crisis involving military leaders who usurped power at a time the populace was weary of military rule and the economic hardship it helped engender. Along with the ensuing civilian-military divide, there was inter-ethnic tension resulting, in part, from the military's domination by an ethnic/regional segment of the population. Despite the economic difficulties, the press - especially the independent press - also grew at this time, spurred in part by the general resentment of the military government and in part by the growing availability of new technologies that facilitated newspaper and magazine production.

The government also began to license commercial broadcasting at this time. This rapid growth of the news media put a strain on the availability of trained and experienced personnel (despite the influx of graduates noted earlier) and the weak economy strained their viability.

The June 12 crisis therefore featured an illegitimate and insecure government that sought to perpetuate itself through co-opting and coercion, an expanding press that was developing true independence for the first time and was still searching for its professional compass in the midst of an inhospitable economic climate, and a weary populace that included significant numbers of radicalized people. As will become evident below, the tenor of the repression and the press performance reflected all of these factors.

In their systems analysis of the mass media and politics, Gurevitch and Blumler propose an approach that emphasizes the "complementarity of roles." They posit that any given political system would tend to produce a corresponding role for journalists and a matching audience expectation. Conversely, any given journalism orientation would tend to produce a certain audience orientation which would put pressure on people in politics to perform in the appropriate direction. As with most structural/functional analyses, Gurevitch and Blumler's tends Towards harmony. However, one could envision a situation in which the circumstances and roles in a system become conflictual rather than complementary. That was the situation in the June 12 crisis.

THE CRISIS

The June 12 crisis may be said to have its intermediate origin in the military overthrow of the just re-elected civilian government of Shehu Shagari on the eve of January 1, 1984. General Muhammadu Buhari, who headed the ensuing military government, was himself overthrown in August 1985 and succeeded by General Ibrahim B. Babangida. After numerous transition Programmes that stopped short of actualization, the Babangida regime finally conducted presidential elections in June 1993.

Unofficial results of the election showed that Moshood Abiola, a wealthy businessman from Western Nigeria, won the election decisively, but the Babangida government withheld the results and subsequently annulled the election on June 23. In response to the ensuing outcry, Babangida stepped down and picked a civilian, Ernest Shonekan, to head a transition government that would conduct another election. Though Shonekan is also from the West, the gesture did not mollify the opposition.

Given that his appointment was brokered and signed on to by top members of the two parties that contested the election, including Abiola's party, the press might have embraced the agreement if it was still tethered to political parties as it used to be. But the era of the independent press ensured that it maintained its own course.

Subsequent strikes and other forms of resistance made the interim government virtually ineffective. In a few months, General Sani Abacha, the defence minister who was left over from the Babangida administration, forced Shonekan to resign and hand over power to him. What, in effect, was another coup essentially marked an end of the transition to an elected government. Opposition to military rule intensified, as did concerted advocacy for reinstatement of the June 12 election. When Abiola sought to declare himself president in 1994, on the anniversary of the election, he was arrested and imprisoned until his mysterious death in 1998.

The annulment rubbed hard on three sensitivities: the political, the ethnic, and the economic. Politically, there was a strong yearning for electoral democracy, resulting from a near-consensus that the military had overstayed and had, in any case, failed to fulfill its rationalization for seizing power. Nigeria's worsening economy, perhaps more than anything else, intensified disillusionment with military government. And then there was the ethnic factor, the increasingly vociferous complaint of Southerners that Northerners had presided over the federal government since independence. Nullification by a

Northern-dominated military of a national election that was won by a Southerner for the first time in Nigeria's history was seen as confirmation of a Northern conspiracy to dominate.

Therefore, reaction against the nullification was immediate and determined, propelled especially by the ethnic and political factors. There were street demonstrations, especially in the West, Abiola's home base, along with national labour union strikes, which were pronounced across the South. Strikes by workers in the crude oil production industry, Nigeria's economic mainstay, all but crippled the economy.

The Nigerian press weighed in heavily on the June 12 crisis mostly along partisan lines. As Patterson and Donsbach have shown, even journalists in non-partisan press systems are influenced by personal feelings in their news Judgement. With the issues so weighty and emotions so high, the traditionally partisan Nigerian press became wholly advocatorial. The concentration of the news media in the West determined the thrust of the advocacy. An essayist for the Vanguard newspaper noted this reality in a scathing column written after Nigeria's return to democracy in 1999:

By sheer numbers, most of Nigeria's print and electronic media are headquartered in Nigeria's South-West zone. From there, ensconced smugly in a cocoon of sorts, they exert an awesome influence. And even though some of them are not owned by the Yorubas who populate this zone, the media in the South-West zone Non-etheless capture the atmospherics of this zone.

Thus, the thrust of press advocacy was a campaign against nullification of the June 12 election, which took on the dual hue of ethnic agitation and pro-democracy activism. Whereas the broadcast press, most of which was government owned, downplayed the crisis and generally covered the issues so as not arouse the government's ire, the major newspapers and magazines took on a crusading role, publishing anti-government/military investigative pieces and searing editorials.

GOVERNMENT REPRESSION

The military government reacted harshly. However, despite the massive security apparatus at its disposal and its grim determination to perpetuate itself, its repression was made ultimately ineffectual, at least in part, by its simultaneous and confused quest for authority and legitimacy. The government combined harsh measures with attempts to gain approval from the Nigerian public and world opinion, as studies of dictatorships would predict. The contradictions inherent in such an orientation resulted in harsh but haphazard actions against the press.

In 1994 alone, the Committee to Protect Journalists (CPJ) listed about 40 incidents of assault on the press in Nigeria, not including intimidating phone calls and interrogations by members of the State Security Service. Among the incidents were 22 instances of detention or jail, 9 instances of occupation and/ or closure of news media, and several cases of physical assaults and confiscation of publications, including up to 300,000 copies of various issues of Tell magazine.

The Babangida and Abacha regimes legalized the repressive actions through numerous decrees, some of which were promulgated and applied retroactively. This is an instance of searching for authority to legitimize a coercive exercise of power, a practice the military government continued throughout the crisis.

Though Babangida abrogated his predecessor's Decree No. 4 of 1984, he promulgated the Treasonable Offences Decree in May 1993, about a month before the election that he annulled. The Treasonable Offenses Decree went beyond Decree 4 to impose the death penalty against anyone whose speech or writing is determined to be disruptive of "the general fabric of the country or any part of it."

Following denunciations from within and outside Nigeria, the decree was suspended a few weeks after its announcement. The next month, the government announced the promulgation of another law, the Offensive Publications Decree No. 35, under which law enforcement could confiscate publications deemed disruptive of the transition programme. Under this decree, several journalists were jailed and thousands of copies of publications seized.

When Babangida nullified the June 12 election, attacks against his government became even more vociferous. On August 16, the regime announced two additional significant decrees to rein in the press. Newspapers Decree No. 43 of 1993 required annual registration of newspapers with costs to each paper totaling about $10,000, a considerable amount in the context of a developing country. Newspapers Decree No. 48 of 1993, which was retroactive to July 22, proscribed the Concord group, Punch Newspapers, Sketch Press, and the Bendel Newspaper Corporation, all in the West and Mid-West. These publishing houses had been raided and occupied since July 22, 1993.

When Abacha ousted Shonekan in December 1993, he released the jailed journalists and re-opened the closed media houses in a gesture to pro-democracy activists. But he also issued the ominous warning that he would close the media houses again if offended. It did not take long before the threat was effected. On June 11, 1994, security officials again shut down the offices of the Concord and Punch groups, and on August 15 did the same to the Guardian group. The publications' Offence was probably their insistence on de-annulment of the June 12 election and, in the case of the Guardian, a report of conflict within the administration.

To nullify federal courts' damage awards against the government and orders that the publications be allowed to reopen, the Abacha regime, on September 5, announced decrees No. 6, 7, and 8 of 1994, which retroactively proscribed each media house for six months from the dates of their closure. Here again, the government sought, on the one hand, to appear to be law abiding in not ignoring the court's order and, on the other hand, to keep its harsh measures in place. In December, the proscription of all the three publishing houses was extended for six months. Then in June 1995, the government announced a second six-month extension, after the three media houses refused the government's conditions for their deproscription.

The conditions included a pledge to not publish embarrassing information about the government and to not press legal actions over the proscriptions. That a military government included such a requirement is clearly indicative of its strong concern for its image and its quest for approval. And that the press turned it down is also indicative of the extent of its defiance and resilience. Thus, for about 18 months during the height of the crisis, the government effectively silenced three of Nigeria's four largest media houses, which among them published 15 newspapers and magazines and accounted for half of the newspaper market.

The comparable though somewhat different fate of Tell and TheNews, two of the most defiant publications during the June 12 crisis, further illustrates the determined, though uneven, nature of the government's repressive measures. TheNews was proscribed by the Babangida government in July 1993, barely five months after the magazine's debut. However, rather than negotiate with the government on the terms of its deproscription, as was the norm when the press was largely an instrument of political parties, the editors founded another magazine, Tempo, which published underground and, in the words of the editor, "was extremely pungent and uncompromising." Such adaptability would have been improbable without new technologies or had TheNews been a part of the political or even corporate establishment. The government hunted unsuccessfully for the publication's site and for the editor, Dapo Olorunyomi.

After Abacha took over power in 1993, he deproscribed TheNews, which, along with Tempo, resumed searing reportage and commentaries on the government. When the Abacha regime sought to muzzle both publications, they again went underground, in what the editor described as "guerilla journalism."

The Abacha regime could have formally proscribed TheNews and Tempo, even without locating their premises, but it did not. Rather, after trying unsuccessfully to arrest the editor, security officers in exasperation arrested and briefly detained his wife, a freelance journalist.

Unlike TheNews, Tell was never proscribed though it carried equally searing commentaries and damning reportage. However, Tell's staff was readily the most harassed during the crisis.

Several were jailed and assaulted by security officers. To minimize the risk, they too began to practice guerilla journalism. For periods of time the senior journalists avoided their newsrooms, homes, the airports, and other places where they could easily be identified. So frequent was the visit of plain-clothed security officers that even food vendors near Tell's premises began to recognize the security agents and to alert Tell's staff. Any editors present would escape through back doors. But frustrated agents soon began to assault whomever they found. "They took anybody they see, for as long as you worked with Tell. It didn't matter whether you were big or small, it didn't matter whether you were an accountant or a reporter."

Once, the newsroom librarian was so severely beaten he spent several days in the hospital. Members of the State Security Service soon took to keeping a regular surveillance on the magazine's premises and the editors' homes, sometimes openly, sometimes disguised as visitors. The editors sometimes got caught and imprisoned, and copies of the magazine were routinely confiscated by security personnel.

The harassment took its toll on Tell's operating expenses. For a period in 1996, the magazine shed its glossy-colour cover to cut expenses and minimize losses in event of confiscation. Still, along with TheNews and a number of other publications, it maintained a defiant editorial stance against the government until the end of the crisis.

For the most part, the government was reactive and did not seem to have any coherent policy, other than the desire to rein in the press. Therefore, though the government did not seem to deem any measures too harsh, the application was haphazard and inconsistent.

Often journalists were jailed and publications shut down for the same material that others carried without sanction. It seems, however, that on the whole, the government seemed less concerned with excoriating press attacks, which were routine, than with reports that raised doubts about its legitimacy or viability, cast aspersions on its intent, or revealed inner scheming or maneuverings - whether or not the reports were true. This is consistent with the concerns and actions of dictatorships in other parts of the world, including Brazil and Indonesia.

In addition to the contradictions of power inherent in the Abacha regime, several other factors seem to account for its inconsistency and the harsh measures themselves. To begin with, the Abacha administration did not seem to have a coherent philosophy of governance.

Abacha seemed insecure and distrustful of his immediate formal subordinates. Accordingly, he surrounded himself with personal aides to whom he delegated responsibilities that would ordinarily go to portfolioed members of the cabinet. Such authority was haphazardly delegated as deemed necessary to manage particular situations. Decision-making was, in effect, ad hoc. Inevitably, there was a degree of disorder in the military and disarray in the administration.

Second, there was Nigeria's traditional politics of pluralism and the inherent robustness in public discourse, which made totalitarian censorship difficult to implement. This structural impediment to repression, coupled with the courage of journalists and fueled by anger and resentment, facilitated defiance and proved difficult to manage. Third, the introduction of mobile modern communication technologies such as laptop computers, online technology, and fax machines also facilitated "guerilla journalism," which seems to have confounded the military regime. Thus, technology facilitated resistance in much the same way that it helped thwart the military coup against Mikail Gorbachev in 1991.

But, again, the most important factor in the Abacha administration's dealing with the press is the contradictions inherent in the government's determination to retain power by all means and its need to legitimate itself through public approval, both internal and external.

The contradictions were comparable to that faced by Anwar Sadat of Egypt when, possibly to please American policy makers, he sought to liberalize Egyptian politics while also stifling criticism. Similar contradictions have also been identified in the media policies of Zimbabwe's Robert Mugabe, who crafted a media system which though independent in principle is controlled through an intricate ownership and governing structure.

Given that such contradictions reflect on all but one of the above factors and explains both the government's gestures Towards and repressive measures against the press, they will be more extensively discussed. Despite Abacha's image as unresponsive to public opinion and political pressures, he seemed concerned about internal and external acceptance, even as he employed harsh measures to retain power. Accordingly, he undertook repressive measures as he thought necessary to ensure his viability even as he extended gestures intended to facilitate acceptance.

As already noted, when Abacha assumed power in 1993, he revoked several repressive decrees and released journalists who were detained by Babangida's government, of which he was a powerful member as the minister of defence. Among the journalists he released was Nosa Igiebor, the editorin-chief of Tell.

He also deproscribed TheNews. When the gestures did not mollify the opposition press, Abacha re-imposed harsh decrees and began massive arrests, including again of Igiebor in December 1995. Also, in 1994 Abacha appointed Alex Ibru, the owner of the Guardian, one of his fiercest critics, as the interior minister.

The gesture was consistent with authoritarian governments' tendency to find legitimation through inclusiveness. When the Guardian remained adversarial in its coverage and commentary, Abacha's government, of which Ibru was still a member, shut it down. Ibru resigned soon after. Then in February 1996, about two years after the Guardian was proscribed, Ibru barely survived an assassination attempt.

The contradictions may also explain why publications were no longer proscribed after the Concord, Guardian, and Punch groups were deproscribed in 1995. The Abacha government seemed thereafter to have abandoned that approach to repression, possibly because proscriptions, unlike the arrest of individuals, affected the larger public and was patently draconian. Accordingly, arrests and detentions continued, and there was an increased incidence of attacks on news houses, including bombings, assassinations, and attempted assassinations, which could not be directly linked to the government.

The contradictions may be most manifest in the resort of the government or its agents to counterfeit journalism as another counter measure to the opposition press. During the height of the crisis, counterfeit editions of Tell, TheNews, and other publications were occasionally distributed in major cities in Nigeria, carrying news stories that lauded the military government. By 1996, a number of pro-Abacha publications had also come into existence, headed by people with no known journalistic background. The publications were believed to be funded by Abacha's operatives. They, however, never gained the stature of the opposition press. Thus, the contradictions in the government's goals engendered drastic, sometimes desperate, measures but also helped ensure their ultimate failure.

4

Technology and Journalism Research

INTRODUCTION

Numerous scholars have recognized the role of communication technologies in shaping newswork, as well as the information that reporters may or may not acquire by using them. The most prominent channel types, mentioned in the literature as tools of sourcing, are new technologies such as the Internet and e-mail.

The other two are non-mediated channels, such as news-scene attendance and face-to-face interviews and more traditional technologies such as landline telephony.The importance of communication channels in journalism lies in their possible impact on news information, enhancing or limiting its scope, quality, diversity, depth, and accuracy, as well as their role in shaping the epistemological qualities of news information.

For example, the face-to-face interview is considered a channel that enables Non-verbal information to be obtained, and thc tclcphonc intcrview is one that allows reporters to negotiate source versions and implement interview techniques. E-mail, in turn, is described as a dubious channel that strengthens a source's control over messages and invites untraceable involvement of PR practitioners.

The connection between episteme (knowledge) and techne (art) is an ancient concept, dating back to Greek philosophy and addressed by modern thinkers such as Innis and McLuhan.

In this study, however, the concept of epistemological technologies is employed neither as an embodiment of scientific or practical knowledge nor as a tool for shaping the knowledge of media consumers, but rather as the means that media producers use to obtain information.

Not all scholars agree that new technologies necessarily change news practices: "Reformists," probably the largest school of thought, claim that technologies created a significant shift in the work of reporters; "Traditionalists," apparently the smallest group, identified long-range trends in news production methods that may limit the effects of the new technologies significantly; while "Selectivists" assert that journalistic work has changed dramatically for television reporters, whose speed of reaction and ability to gather information have been accelerated by new technologies.

Three shortcomings of the existing body of empirical research may thwart theory-building that would address both journalism and epistemological channels:

- Fragmentation. Most studies focused on a small subset of technologies and sometimes even on one technology only. This fragmented scope limits their generalizability, inviting overestimation or underestimation of the technologies studied. Multi-technology studies were not only scarce but also limited to the public relations field.18 At least one study exhibited a multi-technological and multi-source perspective, but was restricted to print press reporters, who are not necessarily the most advanced among technology users. Moreover, the study was conducted before the new generation of mobile and broadband technologies became popular and possibly revolutionized newswork.
- Non-journalistic Theories. Most studies applied Non-journalistic theories - such as diffusion of innovations or uses and gratifications - that are virtually blind to the specific context of the journalistic field.
- The Novelty Bias. Naturally, new technologies attract extra research attention, especially when perceived as a remedy for the weaknesses of journalism. Nevertheless, exclusive focus on new technologies as "one of the biggest hopes (and hypes)" of journalism, with some studies appearing "upbeat and at times even Utopian in their conclusions," renders all but brand new conduits symbolically extinct.

The current study tries to overcome these shortcomings, supplying a comprehensive picture of old and new channels, both mediated and non-mediated, determining their actual contribution to published news and integrating the results within a broader journalism theory.

Following McManus, the present study distinguishes between two principal stages of the newsmaking process:

- News discovery, during which the reporter becomes acquainted with the existence of a potential new story, and
- News gathering, in which the reporter obtains the building blocks of the news item, as news discovery data is often incomplete and insufficiently substantiated.

Both phases were studied only regarding items that were subsequently published or aired, however. In keeping with its exploratory nature, the study addresses research questions and expectations rather than formal hypotheses.

RQl: What are the relative contributions of the respective communication channels to news published in the three media studied? With some caution, based on several of the studies mentioned previously, one might expect to find that while most news information is technology-mediated, telephony is still widely used and textual channels serve primarily as news discovery conduits.

RQ2: How often do reporters use the Web as a news source? Do online reporters do so more than their counterparts in other media?

According to several prominent studies, journalists use the Web extensively. Furthermore, online reporters are expected to rely on the Web more often than their counterparts in other media, as they also use it as a vehicle for display and consequently acquire considerable Web savvy.

Traditional methods might prove problematic in examining the journalistic role of technology, as surveys and interviews capture per- ceived functions of the various channels that may differ substantially from their actual use; moreover, observation alone cannot detect the full spectrum of channels operated by different reporters in different settings to obtain information from different sources.

Consequently, the present study uses face-to-face reconstruction interviews, a method that has proven its ability to identify the respective contributions of different entities to the production of news.

The procedure consisted of three steps (prior to the interviews):

- Random Selection of Beats: Ten parallel print press, online, and radio news beats were chosen randomly from nine leading Israeli national news organizations.
- Identification of All Published Items within Beats: The sampling period extended over four weeks (beginning November 15, 2006), reflecting the attempt to achieve a fair balance between variety of stories and use of material still fresh in reporters' memories. News Web sites were visited four times a day.
- Random Sampling of News Items: Ten items per reporter were selected randomly (average monthly output per reporter: fifty-three items) to address the necessities of source confidentiality. The sample is thus large enough to allay any concern that stories could be matched to their descriptions but not so large as to tax reporters' focus and patience.

Further measures to maintain source confidentiality included asking reporters to describe how they obtained each of their sampled items without revealing any identifying details about them, as well as the seating arrangements: the reporter (with a pile of sampled stories) and the interviewer (with a pile of coding sheets) sat on opposite sides of a table with a screen between them. Reconstruction interviews were conducted during the month following the sampling period, each approximately ninety minutes in duration.

Although nearly all interviewees cooperated, the goal of deciphering 300 items per medium was not entirely achieved because of structural constraints applying to the organizations studied, such as insufficient number of business items for one of the radio stations and the need to avoid double-length interviews of Haaretz reporters who work for both print and online media.To preclude the distorting effect that the missing items may exert on comparability, each medium was weighted to 300 items, maintaining the internal proportions of the sampled newsbeats.

For the most part, data were displayed and analysed as percentages, thus presenting an overall picture of the channel mix with each channel displayed in the context of other channels and other media. Because of its exploratory nature, the study uses effect size measures (D-statistic) rather than significance tests. Effect values of 0.20 through 0.49 are customarily considered small, 0.50 through 0.79 medium, and 0.80 and above large.

Obviously, no method is without its shortcomings. The current method's drawback is that data deal very specifically with recollected sources for information subsequently used in published (or broadcast) stories. To compensate for this shortcoming and study the uses of technology beyond the specific item, a supplementary personal interview was introduced. As these interviews were conducted after the rather long reconstruction interviews, however, only 49-61 reporters out of a total of 80 agreed to respond to them (depending on the specific question). The data display unambiguous differences between common and rare uses of the Web and as such will be used only in the Discussion as a general indicator of Web use for purposes other than news sourcing. The findings supply an initial overview of the ways in which reporters in three different media operate a comprehensive set of epistemological channels to obtain their news.

RELATIVE CONTRIBUTION

The data show that channel use across media is highly homogeneous except for a few aberrations, concentrated in the discovery phase, that may be explained chiefly on organizational grounds.

The greater use of landline telephones among online reporters is not really substantial, as their total use of telephony is very similar to that of their counterparts and the greater use of pager messages among radio reporters is counterbalanced by their limited use of e-mail.

Furthermore, greater use of pagers may reflect the correspondence between the short and instant nature of both pager messages and radio items, as well as the mobility and urgency of radio newswork, at least in the Israeli case.

Similarities across media intensify if the data are clustered according to the three major channel types embodying the epistemological qualities of the interactions they enable:

- Non-mediated channels, involving the reporters' physical presence at news scenes and face to-face interviews, constitute the smallest group: ranging (across media) from 7per cent to 10per cent of the contacts in the discovery phase and 15per cent to 18per cent in the gathering phase. The remainder consists of technology mediated coverage.
- Oral channels, led by telephony-mediated contacts (landline + cellular), contribute the main course to the news menu: ranging from 46per cent to 50per cent in the discovery phase and 54per cent to 65per cent in the gathering phase. This cluster's share is actually even greater, as it also includes the non-mediated channels.
- Textual channels comprise a rather formidable cluster, particularly in the news discovery phase, in which it accounts for 39per cent-43per cent of the contacts, decreasing to only 18per cent-29per cent in the gathering phase.

INTERNET USE

RQ2 focused on the actual contribution of the World Wide Web, the most celebrated technology in journalism literature, across different media. The Web's contribution to published content as a news source was no more than 3per centin both phases. Even online reporters do not use their publishing platform as a sourcing tool to any greater extent than their old-media colleagues do.

The Internet's contribution rises substantially if we include e-mail: ranging from 8per cent to 21per cent in the discovery phase and 4per cent to 15per cent in the gathering phase. This increment is puzzling, however, as reporters play a proactive role when using the Web and generally adopt a passive or reactive one in e-mail use.

DISCUSSION

Four aspects of reporter behaviour are particularly challenging. The discussion begins with the more general aspects, namely the surprisingly modest use of non-mediated coverage and the lack of any substantial differences among the three media. The remaining two aspects are oriented towards specific technologies: the Web's marginal role as a news source and the enduring dominance of telephony.

The image of extensive non-mediated coverage is fostered not only by scholars (who contend that such coverage prevails in conjunction with telephone interviews), but also by the traditional ethos that extols "shoeleather reporting" as the supreme news gathering method, as well as by journalists themselves, who do not go out of their way to expose the truth behind a deteriorating work pattern that still establishes their occupational legitimacy and authority.

Many have even developed a set of practices to conceal their remote coverage. Although some American reporters declared that face-to-face interviews are their second choice as a newsmaking channel, the current findings indicate that, in practice, non-mediated coverage is far rarer than might be expected, or, as the legendary Jimmy Breslin observed, "in many newsrooms, the shoe-leather reporters are regarded as throwbacks or has-beens."

The overall similarity of channel use across media challenges the widespread belief that at least online reporters embody "new regimes of content creation" with a distinct media logic. Apparently, tendencies Towards journalistic "isomorphism" overshadow medium differences, at least insofar as methods used to source information are concerned, reflecting similarities in organization around newsbeats and news sources, perceived newsworthiness, and the inclination towards homogeneous news products.

Two of these relatively homogenous patterns challenge common wisdom regarding specific technologies: the use of telephones and the Web for news sourcing.

THE WEB AS A NEWS SOURCE

The limited use of the Web observed in this study appears to challenge findings suggesting that the Web had become a "dominant" and "indispensable" newsgathering tool that had changed the face - if not the soul - of journalism. Interestingly, the Web's contribution as a source for published news is not only marginal but also stagnant, having displayed no growth over time - at least with regard to the Israeli print press, studied in 2001 using the same method and research tools as the present study.

However, in contrast to its limited use for sourcing, the Web is widely used for more general newswork functions. Personal interviews with reporters show that they use the Web for two hours and fifty minutes a day for journalistic purposes, plus one hour and twelve minutes for personal matters - about four times more than the average Israeli citizen and about an hour less per day than American computer reporters, who are probably among the most intensive Web users.

During those long hours, reporters were using the Web for the functions. The rich assortment of Web functions used by reporters may be categorized into three basic types:

- Productive: These include core journalistic functions directly involved in sourcing publishable news materials, such as discovering and gathering news information, followed by two types of auxiliary functions that exert less direct impact on news products and more on news processes and news environments.
- Referential: Including self-updates, monitoring other publications, fact checking, locating potential news sources, and finding background material.

- Communicative Functions: Communicating with different stakeholders-superiors, news sources, counterparts, and competitors, mostly via e-mail.

Functions performed routinely (*i.e.*, on a daily basis by at least half the reporters) are mostly referential. The only exception is the highly frequent use of e-mail for receipt of press releases. This still does not guarantee an impact on publications, however, as many if not most press releases are discarded during the selection process.

The highly infrequent use of e-mail for interviews may surprise scholars who described e-mail as "the killer [Internet] application" for journalists. On the other hand, it will relieve those who condemn e-mail interviews as a "method of last resort for conducting anything approaching a candid interview" because it avoids real interaction and invites hoaxes and "canned" PR responses.

Journalists' paradoxical use of the Web - seldom for sourcing and often for more general newswork assignments - suggests that although journalists enjoy "cutting edge gizmos," they are choosier about using them for core journalistic assignments such as sourcing.

Hence, until another study refutes the current findings by taking the exhausting route of investigating - source by source - a sample of published items outside Israel, using the current method and research tools, one cannot rule out that limited use of the Web for sourcing, together with extensive use for more general newswork assignments, extends beyond the case at hand and may even be a relatively universal phenomenon.

It is definitely not an Israeli peculiarity, as shown by initial findings of another study employing the same method and research tool to study Chilean national press reporters in the summer of 2007. Those reporters used the Web for only 5per cent of discovery contacts and 7per cent of gathering contacts. There is some indication that figures for the United States, Portugal, and Greece do not differ dramatically.

At least part of the difference between the current study and those claiming vast use of the Web may thus be rooted in method (reconstructions of specific published items versus general estimations of technology use in surveys and interviews) and research focus (specific uses for sourcing of published items versus more auxiliary uses for reporting).

This line of reasoning is supported by current findings reflecting heavy daily use of the Web, mostly for functions other than sourcing. Some American scholars agree that the Web has not become a major news source despite its numerous advantages. According to one observation, American newsroom adoption of computer-assisted reporting yielded mixed results.

Another opinion maintains that the journalistic advantages of the Internet "are counterbalanced by a number of inherent weaknesses," some of which have already been mentioned in the relevant literature: poor quality of information; limited reliability, believability, and accuracy; as well as time constraints, lack of training and navigation and design faults.

The following drawbacks should be considered as well:

- The Proactive Role: While most other textual channels, including e-mail, assign reporters a passive or reactive role, the Web calls for their proactive performance in such tasks as database analysis or investigation - demands that go against the grain of mainstream news reporting, which is reactive in nature.
- Impersonal Data: While other channels enable and improve communication with human agents, the Web usually bypasses them in favour of largely impersonal data. Hence those who perceived the Web as a promising news source were not wrong about the technology, only about its users. Journalists, it turns out, are not in the general information business but rather supply information originating among human agents.
- The Extra Burden of Corroboration: Constant suspicions concerning the trustworthiness of Web materials could have been resolved by crosschecking with additional sources. As their time frame shrinks, however, reporters may wonder why they ought to use a news source that requires additional sources a priori instead of simply contacting these sources themselves.
- Unqualified Material: Apparently, the Web's marginal contribution to published news (and that of other mass media) contradicts the nature of news producers as heavy news consumers above all, who start each day by reading one another's publications. Media consumption does not necessarily contribute directly to specific news items that are subsequently published, however, but rather informs reporters about current events in general and the output of competitors and counterparts. Furthermore, the Web offers "too much information or [.] too little information" and is loaded with previously published items that are useless to reporters who refrain from plagiarism unless they find their own angle or follow-up, employing an independent sourcing process.

Some of these weaknesses are the strengths of a much older technology, whose contribution to the public news menu tends to be overlooked.

THE ENDURING DOMINANCE OF THE TELEPHONE

The enduring dominance of telephony challenges the assertion that newsmaking was conquered by new technologies, especially when combined with insistence that the golden age of the telephone in journalism ended during the 1950s. Some scholars have mentioned the ongoing prominence of telephony together with face-to-face interviews but did not specify the respective contributions of each.

The continuing dominance of the telephone in the new technology-saturated news environment, after a hundred years of service and despite more sophisticated alternatives, can no longer be explained in simple terms such as the immediacy and efficiency of the given technology.

At first glance, it may appear that numerous factors motivate reporter and source alike to avoid oral communication. Why should reporters trap themselves between oral input and textual output, adding the burden of translating vocal utterances into written stories?

Why would they work with loosely structured, ephemeral raw material that leaves no paper trail and is replete with redundancies, inconsistencies, and multiple, interwoven threads of thought?

And why would news sources, in turn, use channels that impede realization of a speaker's full potential and downgrade control over verbalization, precision of expression, lexical richness, and grammatical sophistication, thereby forgoing the advantage of imperceptible emendation and rendering themselves vulnerable to audible self-correction that sounds like "denial and patchwork"?

Several considerations may explain the persistence of the present situation:

- *Naturalness:* Oral channels are a "primary form of communication for humans." They are "addressed by a real, living person [.] at a specific time in a real setting" and are more "natural to thought and speech" than writing, more spontaneous and more dynamic and vivid, as vocal expression is itself a live event in space and time, anchored in the "life-worlds" of real people.
- *Informativeness:* Oral communication always includes "much more than mere words." Even telephone conversations retain many attributes of face-to-face interactions, including "use of language [.] the way words are pronounced, elements of intonation or prosody, syntax and semantics [.] variations of loudness and pitch beyond that involved in intonation, tempo, resonance, pauses and Non-fluencies, as well as Non-language sounds such as laughing and sighing."
- *Unavailability of Suitable Texts:* Journalists generally search for news within a narrow time slot once a new event or story begins to unfold and before others cover them - at least in the same news market. During this short period, texts may be unavailable, unsuitable, already published, or authored by PR professionals.
- *Participatory Role:* Oral channels are actually the only conduit through which reporters may play a participatory role in shaping the raw materials of news.

This role corresponds with four aspects of newswork:

- As a "negotiated phenomenon" (*i.e.*, an output of bargaining between reporters and sources), news tends to flow through channels such as the telephone, that enable negotiations between the parties.

- As news constitutes a co-production by reporters and their sources, the former perceive their authorship as including mandatory participation in the formation of raw news material and not only post hoc reduction of source-initiated texts.
- Oral channels increase reporters' control over their raw material, whereas written versions accord their writers the advantage, giving them more leeway to hide, slant or frame information as they see fit.

Oral channels enable interview techniques that may not only improve source accountability but also reinforce the status and legitimacy of reporters as trustees of the public who pose questions on its behalf.

- *Competitive Advantage:* While many written materials are distributed to or may be approached by numerous journalists, oral channels give reporters a chance at exclusivity. Most of the time, such exclusivity does not apply to the items as a whole, that are shared by their counterparts and competitors, but rather to certain details thereof.
- *Smaller (Perceived) Risk:* When leaks are involved, both sources and reporters are especially careful to avoid textual channels, as they may leave clear traces in case of investigation. Although they cannot promise full protection, oral channels are perceived as safer than others except in cases of serial leaks, such as the Pentagon Papers, in which randomly chosen pay phones were the instrument of choice.

Epistemological channels, a collection of communication technologies and non-mediated conduits of news coverage, are probably the keystone of technology and journalism theorization, thanks to their crucial role in shaping the scope and quality of information that subsequently becomes the public news diet.

The current study suggests an initial theoretical outline for the role of these channels in news sourcing, based on a careful analysis of their contribution to a random sample of about 850 stories from three different media.

Just as a hierarchy of credibility prevails in the realm of sourcing, according precedence to certain informants over others, a technological hierarchy governs the world of communication channels that echo the logic of sourcing, determining which conduits are to be given priority.

The subordination of these channels to a higher order of sourcing considerations is observed both in the combined tendency of the reporters studied to rely on human agents (in 87per cent of their contacts in the discovery phase and 92per cent in the gathering phase) and to communicate with them orally (57per cent and 75per cent, respectively).

Heavy reliance on technology-mediated coverage suggests that reporters accord much lower priority to the demands of space than to those of time. Hence the basic role of communication technologies is to release reporters from spatial constraints, thereby enabling them to meet temporal demands.

According to the findings, reporters sourcing their published news prefer various remote data excavation technologies to first-hand witnessing, and prefer reliance on human agents to technological sources such as the Web and oral communication to textual. Hence the principal role of epistemological technologies is to enable remote coverage while keeping close to human informants.

The methods journalists employ to obtain published news indicate that news is a social product, fabricated chiefly through interpersonal reporter-source contact. As such, news is more a matter of trust between humans than of independent witnessing, fact finding, or fact checking.This process is none too compliant with "foundationalist epistemology" that expects validation of facts by empirical findings or rational substantiation, but rather conforms with social epistemology that makes do with facts established by communal agreement within "specific epistemic communities."

Furthermore, news is a textual product of oral processes. This "oral culture" allows reporters to omit, edit, select excerpts, and "tidy up" quotes in a manner that often bears the seeds of tension between parties. To a certain extent, this may explain the vast quantities of journalistic errors, misunderstandings, misquotes, and source statements taken out of context.

As one Wall Street Journal reporter put it, "It's your notes against their word." This study focuses on the most substantial role of communication channels as conduits for generating the public news diet. Despite the meticulous methods employed, however, it is not free of weaknesses and blind spots, as it addresses involvement of different channels only in items that were subsequently published or aired, relying on the recollection of reporters themselves.Hence, the current study sets a broad agenda for further studies, especially those considering other types of reporters who probably employ different patterns of channel use, particularly TV reporters, investigative reporters, citizen journalists, multimedia and multi-skilled reporters, and so on.

Subsequent studies should focus on other news cultures especially that of the United States, testing the hypothesis of limited use of the Web as a news source and extensive use for other newswork functions. Newsroom observations may contribute another missing link by mapping the inevitable gaps between reported and actual uses of communication channels. These may also focus on the oral culture that associates reporters and sources, the patterns in which oral raw materials are transformed into final news texts and the extent to which this transformation is susceptible to errors, misunderstandings, and disputes between the parties.

SCIENCE-TECHNOLOGY INDUCED DEVELOPMENT AND ENVIRONMENT

In modem times, much is said and written about the human environment, both physical and social. The print and electronic media put out almost a daily dose of news and features about the environment. Many people wave these away as being a fashion or a fad. For others, the word "environment" is almost like a mantra. You, as a science reporter, must be cautious not to fall into such traps. That means, you must have a deeper understanding of the environment. The deeper your understanding of the environment, the higher would be your scientific temper. How often do you think about the environment? How often do you wonder about your physical surroundings? We live in an environment which is as complex as life itself. Delicate, too! Look from any angle of human development, and the fast changing environment condition will become evident to you.

One basic principle of mass communication is that you should not clutter up your news reports with too many facts. Also, you must not talk or write in complex terms. That way, people with different levels of understanding will not be able to grasp your meaning. Now, let us see the impact of development on the environment. Let environment awareness begin at home. Suppose you are living in a small house in one of the suburbs of a city. Suddenly, you realize that the density of population has increased in the area. Real estate values are shooting up. As a result, tall buildings are coming up all around. Now, observe your home environment. Very little sunlight enters your house. The cross flow of breeze, which you used to enjoy, is no more there. There is the stench of garbage in the air. Your breathing becomes heavier, as if you are suffocating. More illness in the family. The water supply comes only for an hour in the morning and an hour in the evening. You find the noise in the neighbourhood oppressive. As self comes before charity, you tune up your music system. Suddenly, the electricity goes. You open your bedroom window to get some fresh air. All you get is a rush of stench. The tree from which you used to hear the chirping of birds is no more there. The moldy backside of a tall building comes bang in your line of vision. You run out of the house. The roads and lanes are littered with cars, people and garbage. Now think about all the technology inputs in your home and neighbourhood. You cannot deny that the neighbourhood has developed by "leaps and bounds". Then, why this environmental degradation? Think.

The house, that was small and comfortable in the beginning, faces a decay in the home environment due to the pressure changes in the neighbourhood. And the boom in construction and the highest density of population have caused the decline in the environmental quality of the suburb itself. Then, you can set the cause and effect principle in the urban growth and decline, as well as in the rural underdevelopment and in the fall in the quality of life. The chain goes on: rural underdevelopment population pressure migration of people to urban areas-growth of slums in towns and cities-urban environmental decline due to development and under-development-urban pressured on rural areas-further fall in rural life quality-and so on. Similarly, you will see the rampant tree-felling for fuel and timber, and for agriculture, which leads to deforestation, topsoil erosion, floods, reduced rainfall, desertification etc. If you build big dams for irrigation and energy, fertile land which is the much-needed input for development, is submerged, people are displaced, and the course and effect chain goes surging forth. Similarly, you can see the industrialization and pollution chain. And, the lack of industrialization and poverty syndrome will present another startling picture. All that calls for balanced development and caution about leaping in any one direction. The science-technology correspondents, in concert with economic and political reporters, can play a significant role in development journalism. As a young reporter you may not cover big conventions and conferences, though your turn will come. Even for the beginner, there will always be lots of stories to cover. One story will lead to another. The questions always will be: Do you have a keen scientific temper? Are you alert?

LANGUAGE IN SCIENCE-TECHNOLOGY REPORTING FOR POPULAR APPEAL

Journalistic writing must be a precise form of communication. Science is reporting calls for even greater precision. Science deals with the laws of nature. Ideas and images in science communication should flow in logical progression. The written language must be like a precision instrument if it is to register the meanings in the minds of those in a hurry. The skill of good writing improves with usage. Writing and rewriting are machines which sharpen your language. But you as a reporter will have deadlines to keep. There may not be time for re-writing. Therefore, your writing should be patterned after recognizing news writing structures in a daily newspaper. Easily understandable news writing is more than simplicity in the use of words, defining difficult and uncommon ideas and including background material. All these are required and ought to be used appropriately. But, all important news explanation and background packaging may fall flat before the reader. Why this, after all your enthusiastic news collections and packaging efforts? What more does the reader expect from you? You must ask yourself these searching questions when you are preparing a report. The answer? Good science technology reporting needs language that communicates clearly. Here comes the matter of grammar and usage.

Don't be intimidated by the dictates of stiff necked grammarians, which were driven home to you by your language teachers. Give them due respect but go with the contemporary times, and where you are functioning. You have to follow the grammatical practices that make your writing orderly for others to follow. Grammatical practices bestow continuity and universality to a language. These are the very elements of language used in mass communication. The discipline and standards must be followed in any language. Otherwise, a language becomes anarchic and bursts into minor dialects. On the other hand, if the straight jacket approach for grammarians is blindly followed over a period of time, a language gets ossified. That is the death of a language. If the English language has come to be virtually accepted as the global language of the science-technology era, it is because of three reasons:

- It has had a global spread.
- Since Newton's time, major developments in science and technology have taken place in the English-speaking world. Certainly there have been developments in areas speaking other languages. Non-etheless, there is a chance that the people may be acquainted with the English language and they may have published their discoveries and inventions in English.
- The English language is a changing language. It keeps in tune with the changing times. While keeping the basic standards of grammar, it is amenable to improvisations.

The English language is today considered as the window to the science-technology information about the world. Even the non-English science-technology intensive areas of Europe, the Russian Commonwealth of Independent States and Japan, are introducing English language studies in a big way. Therefore, no matter in which language you propose to write as a science-technology reporter, a keen knowledge of the English language is also a must for you.

Words, Sentences and Readability : Words denote images. Nouns evoke images of objects, subjects, actions, etc. Verbs work the Nouns. All other forms of words are accessories to the chains of words, which we call sentences. There are tested patterns of constructing newspaper stories. The opening sentence must say the most important point of the news. The first sentence, on its own, or the first two or three sentences should give the gist of the story. The paragraphs must be small. Fifty-to-sixty word paragraphs are considered to be ideal in news writing. Remember, the story must move on from sentence to sentence, and paragraph to paragraph. Otherwise, the reader will feel the jerk. Readers have a tendency to abandon a news item at the point where it begins to jerk or waver, unless, of course, they have, a specific and special interest in it.

Report Structure : The science-technology news report structure is not different from that of any other news report. A good beginning (intro), followed by the more important news points at the top of the story, and the lesser ones mentioned as you go down. That is the accepted pattern. This has been explained to you in the general news reporting unit and other specialized area reporting units. All the five W's and H—who, what, where, when and why and how—need not be cluttered in the intro. But these elements of beginning a news story must appear at the top. Nothing is ever printed without being edited. Every report you produce goes through the creativity of editors, particularly news editors and sub-editors. If your copy is badly written, no one on the editorial desk has the time or inclination to rewrite it. Science-technology news reports are almost never rewritten, because nobody wants to be accused of having tampered with its precision. Normally, there is no sense of loss if one of the paper's reporters messes up a report because reports from the news agencies are waiting—they get through the teleprinter before you, as a local reporter of the paper, manage to produce your copy.

Unless your copy has the merit of being a well-written piece, the news desk has the option of using the news agency report. You may be called to the news editor's desk the next day, to explain. You do not want this to happen to you ever; never for the second time. That is why you are told to practice the art of news writing before you launch yourself as a professional reporter.

Human Interest : People are interested in reading something which concerns them directly-young or old, man or woman, you or yours. If your science-technology story says something which people are interested in, just make it fit. If it is about a fuel-saving device, just start: "An automobile user can now save 20 per cent of his fuel cost by opting for the 'so and so' engine system, claimed the makers of etc." Similarly make the readers feel that you are their monitor and reporter. Do not fall for the advertisement techniques of selling. Instead, seek to be the best source of information for your reader, the consumer.

Avoiding Exaggeration and Sensationalism : Everyone knows that exaggeration and sensationalism catch the attention of the reader. But Science technology facts simply cannot hold exaggerations. If a discovery, invention, or improvisation bas an element of sensation, you should not be inhibited in including same of the senses in your story. But do not make an inventive look like something the world has been waiting for, when it is just an improvement on something that already existed. Just think about the following. During the last three decades, they have several claims of drugs with curative and preventive properties to deal with cancer.

News reports on the claims have been blown sky high. An expectant public has been waiting for the miracle to happen. The world of cancer continues to remain without the miracle drug. This is where the ethics of a science-technology reporter come into play.

Do not take your reader for a ride on baseless and sensationalized points. Sensationalism and exaggeration can only do harm to the publication and to the credibility of a reporter. A reporter whose credibility is repeatedly doubted, can never grow professionally. Just like the scientist, a science reporter also should be a seeker of truth. Like a technologist, technology reporter too should be one who believes in precision and in updating knowledge.

The Importance of Rewriting : A sentence, a paragraph or a piece of writing can never be perfect. That is because of the very nature of language. There are two sides to linguistic communication-the communicator and the receiver. Only when a reporter makes sense to the largest section of readers does he or she qualify to be a professional writer.

The first draft of any writer may need a lot of tightening up, chipping and polishing. So rewrite whenever your first effort is unsatisfactory for the reader's sake.

Even so, a reporter hard-pressed to meet deadlines may be left with hardly any time to rewrite his or her copy. So, when you sit down to write, be disciplined and alert in the structuring and construction of your reports. Place the important points at the precise junctures of your story. Invariably one needs to revise the copy and make it crisp. If you are left with some time before the deadline of handing in your copy and you feel the need for it, rewrite the story or part of it. You may have to miss a coffee break and the chance to chit-chat with your colleagues. But you will be gratified in many ways if you find time to rewrite your copy.

COMPARING GOOD, BAD AND INDIFFERENT SCIENCE-TECHNOLOGY REPORTS

Every reader, and any reader, is impressed by an excellent news report. Such a report carries all the elements of good news writing. While being a reporter, you must continue to be a keen reader too. Read stories by reporters who are recognized as better writers by the profession and the public. Think about what makes them outstanding. When you see an excellent piece of reporting in a newspaper, and also a lousy one in another, just compare them. The very exercise of doing so will discipline your reporting sensibilities.

ONLINE JOURNALISM

Online journalism is reporting and other journalism produced or distributed via the Internet. An early leader was *The News and Observer* in Raleigh, North Carolina, USA. Many news organizations based in other media also distribute news online. How much they take advantage of the medium varies. Some news organizations, such as the Gongwer News Service, use the Web only or primarily. The Internet challenges traditional news organizations in several ways. They may be losing classified ads to Web sites, which are often targeted by interest instead of geography.

The advertising on news Web sites is sometimes insufficient to support the investment. Even before the Internet, technology and perhaps other factors were dividing people's attention, leading to more but narrower media outlets. Online journalism also leads to the spread of independent online media such as open Democracy and the UK, Wikinews as well as allowing smaller news organizations to publish to a broad audience, such as media-strike.

NEWS COVERAGE AND NEW MEDIA

By covering news, politics, weather, sports, entertainment, and vital events, the daily media shape the dominant cultural, social and political picture of society. Beyond the media networks, independent news sources have evolved to report on events which escape attention or underlie the major stories. In recent years, the blogosphere has taken reporting a step further, mining down to the experiences and perceptions of individual citizens.

An exponentially growing phenomenon, the blogosphere can be abuzz with news that is overlooked by the press and TV networks. Apropos of this was Robert F. Kennedy Jr.'s 11,000-word *Rolling Stone* article apropos of the 2004 United States presidential election, published June 1, 2006. By June 8, there had been no mainstream coverage of the documented allegations by President John F. Kennedy's nephew. On June 9, this sub-story was covered by a *Seattle Post-Intelligencer* article. Media coverage during the 2008 Mumbai attacks highlighted the use of new media and Internet social networking tools, including Twitter and Flickr, in spreading information about the attacks, observing that Internet coverage was often ahead of more traditional media sources. In response, traditional media outlets including such coverage in their coverage. However, several outlets were criticised as they did not check for the reliability and verfiability of the information.

News is shifting from being a product — today's newspaper, Web site or newscast — to becoming a service — how can you help me, even empower me? There is no single or *finished* news product anymore. As news consumption becomes continual, more new effort is put into producing incremental updates, as brief as 40-character e-mails sent from reporters directly to consumers without editing. (The afternoon newspaper is also being reborn online.) Service also broadens the definition of what journalists must supply. Story telling and agenda setting — still important — are now insufficient. Journalism also must help citizens find what they are looking for, react to it, sort it, shape news coverage, and — probably most important and least developed — give them tools to make sense of and use the information for themselves. News people are uncertain how the core values of accuracy and verification will hold up. Some of the experiments, even the experimenters think, are questionable. And people are being stretched thinner, posing hard questions about how to manage time and where to concentrate. But the hope is that service, more than storytelling, could prove a key to unlocking new economics.

A news organization and a news Web site are no longer final destinations. Now they must move Towards also being stops along the way, gateways to other places, and a means to drill deeper, all ideas that connect to service rather than product. "The walled garden is over," the editor of one of the most popular news sites in the country told us. A site restricted to its own content takes on the character of a *cul de sac* street with yellow "No Outlet" sign, reducing its value to the user. "Search has become the predominant ... paradigm," an influential market research report circulating throughout the industry reads.

That means every page of a Web site — even one containing a single story — is its own front page. And each piece of content competes on its own with all other information on that topic linked to by blogs, "digged" by user news sites, sent in e-mails, or appearing in searches. As much as half of every Web page, designers advise, should be devoted to helping people find what they want on the rest of the site or the Web. That change is already occurring. A year ago, our study of news Web sites found that only three of 24 major Web sites from traditional news organizations offered links to outside content. Eleven of those sites now offer them. Some of this may simply be automated, which may be a service of limited value.

The prospects for user-created content, once thought possibly central to the next era of journalism, for now appear more limited, even among "citizen" sites and blogs. News people report the most promising parts of citizen input currently are new ideas, sources, comments and to some extent pictures and video. But citizens posting news content has proven less valuable, with too little that is new or verifiable. (It may thrive at smaller outlets with fewer resources.) And the skepticism is not restricted to the traditional mainstream media or "MSM." The array of citizen-produced news and blog sites is reaching a meaningful level. But a study of citizen media contained in this report finds most of these sites do not let outsiders do more than comment on the site's own material, the same as most traditional news sites. Few allow the posting of news, information, community events or even letters to the editors. And blog sites are even more restricted. In short, rather than rejecting the "gatekeeper" role of traditional journalism, for now citizen journalists and bloggers appear to be recreating it in other places.

Increasingly, the newsroom is perceived as the more innovative and experimental part of the news industry. This appears truer in newspapers and Web sites than elsewhere. But still it represents a significant shift in the conversation. A decade ago, the newsroom was often regarded as the root of journalism's disconnection from the public and its sagging reputation. "I think we may need to just blow up the culture of the newsroom," one of the country's more respected editors told a private gathering of industry leaders in 1997. Now the business side has begun to be identified as the problem area, the place where people are having the most difficulty changing. "My middle management in advertising and distribution is where I see the deer-in-the-headlights look," one publisher recently told us.

"Advertising doesn't know how to start to cope," said a major industry trade association leader. A survey of journalists from different media (being released with this year's report) reinforces this sense. Majorities think such things as journalists writing blogs, the ranking of stories on their Web sites, citizens posting comments or ranking stories, even citizen news sites, are making journalism better — a perspective hard to imagine even a few years ago. These new technologies are seen as less a threat to values or a demand on time than a way to reconnect with audiences. News people also are less anxious about credibility, the focus of concern a few years ago. Their worries now are about money.

The agenda of the American news media continues to narrow, not broaden. A firm grip on this is difficult but the trends seem inescapable. A comprehensive audit of coverage shows that in 2007, two overriding stories — the war in Iraq and the 2008 presidential campaign — filled more than a quarter of the newshole and seemed to consume much of the media's energy and resources. And what wasn't covered was in many ways as notable as what was. Other than Iraq — and to a lesser degree Pakistan and Iran — there was minimal coverage of events overseas, some of which directly involved U.S. interests, blood and treasure. At the same time, consider the list of the domestic issues that each filled less than a single per cent of the newshole: education, race, religion, transportation, the legal system, housing, drug trafficking, gun control, welfare, Social Security, aging, labour, abortion and more.

A related trait is a tendency to move on from stories quickly. On breaking news events — the Virginia Tech massacre or the Minneapolis bridge collapse were among the biggest — the media flooded the zone but then quickly dropped underlying story lines about school safety and infrastructure. And newer media seem to have an even narrower peripheral vision than older media. Cable news, talk radio (and also blogs) tend to seize on top stories (often polarizing ones) and amplify them. The Internet offers the promise of aggregating ever more sources, but its value still depends on what those originating sources are providing. Even as the media world has fragmented into more outlets and options, reporting resources have shrunk.

Madison Avenue, rather than pushing change, appears to be having trouble keeping up with it. Like legacy media, advertising agencies have their own history, mores and cultures that keep them from adapting to new technology and new consumer behaviour. The people who run these agencies know the old-media methods and have old-media contacts. New media offer the promise of more detailed knowledge of consumer behaviour, but the metrics are still evolving and empirical data have not yet delivered a clear path. Advertising executives, in other words, do not have answers any more than the news professionals. In the short run, this may be helping traditional media hold onto share of advertising revenue. For now, the future seems to point to more confusion and fragmentation before new models emerge. But the losses could begin to accelerate when answers come. The question of whether, and how, advertising and news will remain partners is unresolved.

These trends add to those we have discussed in earlier years of this report. In the inaugural State of the News Media report in 2004, we outlined the broad contours of the revolution in news. Journalism is not disappearing, we concluded, but it is changing. Consumers trust and rely on journalists less, and expect more of them, because they have alternative sources of information. In subsequent years we have tracked the splintering of journalism into new norms, including the rise of a new commercially driven Journalism of Affirmation, the shift at many traditional news outlets Towards becoming niche products, the emergence of what we call the new Answer Culture in news, and growing doubts about the ultimate potential of advertising online. We have also outlined ways in which newsrooms of the future probably need to change.

The study, which we believe is unique in depth and scope, breaks the news industry into eight sectors (newspapers, magazines, network, cable and local television, the Internet, radio and ethnic media) and builds off many of the findings from a year ago. The world is currently facing serious challenges in advancing democratic governance and human development. Progress is threatened by the deep recession in the global economy, the looming challenge of climate change, and the persistence of deep-rooted conflict and terrorism. Within this environment, what ideal roles should the mass media play as watchdogs, agenda-setters, and gatekeepers to strengthen democratic governance and human development? Under what conditions do media systems succeed or fail to meet these objectives? And, strategically, what reforms would close the gap between the promise and performance of media systems?

Working within the notion of the democratic public sphere, the report emphasizes the institutional or collective roles of the news media as *watchdogs* over the powerful, as *agenda-setters* calling attention to social needs in natural and manmade disasters and humanitarian crisis, and as *gatekeepers* incorporating a diverse and balanced range of political perspectives and social actors. Each, we argue, is vital to making democratic governance work in an effective, transparent, inclusive, and accountable manner. The capacity of media systems (and thus individual reporters embedded within these institutions) to fulfill these roles is constrained by the broader context of the journalistic profession, the market, and ultimately the state.

Media systems are compared in places as diverse as Kenya and Mexico, Iraq and Ethiopia, Burma and North Korea, Egypt and Qatar. The evidence suggests that, in reality, the performance of media systems often fall far short of lofty aspirations, with important consequences for the workings of the public sphere. The report identifies the most effective strategic interventions designed to overcome these constraints. These include policies directed at strengthening the journalistic profession, notably institutional capacity building, such as press councils, press freedom advocacy NGOs, and organizations concerned with journalistic training and accreditation. Other important reforms seek to overcome market failures, including developing a regulatory legal framework for media systems to ensure pluralism of ownership and diversity of contents. Lastly, policies also address the role of the state, including deregulation shifting state-run to public service broadcasting, overseen by independent broadcasting regulatory bodies, and the protection of constitutional principles of freedom of the press, speech, and expression.

This study brought together a wide range of international experts under the auspices of the Communication for Governance and Accountability programme (CommGAP) at the World Bank and the Joan Shorenstein Centre on the Press, Politics and Public Policy at Harvard University. It provides a fresh perspective on all these issues, covering in a wider range of countries and regions than ever before. The report is designed for policymakers and media professionals working within the international development community, national governments, and grassroots organizations, and for journalists, democratic activists, and scholars engaged in understanding mass communications, democratic governance, and development.

News organizations need to do more to think through the implications of this new era of shrinking ambitions. The move Towards building audience around "franchise" areas of coverage or other traits is a logical response to fragmentation and can, managed creatively, have journalistic value. To a degree, journalism's problems are oversupply, too many news organizations doing the same thing. But something gained means something lost, especially as newsrooms get smaller. There is already evidence that basic monitoring of local government has suffered. Regional concerns, as opposed to local, are likely to get less coverage.

Matters with widespread impact but little audience appeal, always a challenge, seem more at risk of being unmonitored. What do concepts like localism and branding really mean? Should only national newspapers maintain foreign bureaus? Does localism mean provincialism? Should news organizations, so as not to abandon more high-level coverage, enlist citizen sentinels to monitor community news? To what extent do journalists still have a role in creating a broad agenda of common knowledge? Those issues, debated in theory before, are becoming real. And the wrong answers could hasten, not stave off, the decline of news organizations.

The evidence is mounting that the news industry must become more aggressive about developing a new economic model. The signs are clearer that advertising works differently online than in older media. Finding out about goods and services on the Web is an activity unto itself, like using the yellow pages, and less a byproduct of getting news, such as seeing a car ad during a newscast. The consequence is that advertisers may not need journalism as they once did, particularly online. Already the predictions of advertising growth on the Web are being scaled back. That has major implications, (which some initiatives such as "Newspaper Next" are beginning to grapple with). Among them, news organizations can broaden what they consider journalistic function to include activities such as online search and citizen media, and perhaps even liken their journalism to anchor stores at a mall, a major reason for coming but not the only one. Perhaps most important, the math suggests they almost certainly must find a way to get consumers to pay for digital content.

The increasingly logical scenario is not to charge the consumer directly. Instead, news providers would charge Internet providers and aggregators licensing fees for content. News organizations may have to create consortiums to make this happen. And those fees would likely add to the bills consumers pay for Internet access. But the notion that the Internet is free is already false. Those who report the news just aren't sharing in the fees.

The key question is whether the investment community sees the news business as a declining industry or an emerging one in transition. If one believes that news will continue to be the primary public square where people gather — with the central newsrooms in a community delivering that audience across different platforms — then it seems reasonable that the economics in time will sort themselves out. In that scenario, people with things to sell still need to reach consumers, and the news will be a primary means of finding them.

If one believes, however, that the economics of news are now broken, with further declines ahead, then it seems inevitable that the investment in newsrooms will continue to shrink and the quality of journalism in America will decline. One thing seems clear, however: If news companies do not assert their own vision here, including making a case and taking risks, their future will be defined by those less invested in and passionate about news.

There are growing questions about whether the dominant ownership model of the last generation, the public corporation, is suited to the transition newsrooms must now make. Private markets now appear to value media properties more highly than Wall Street does. More executives are openly expressing doubt, too, whether public ownership's required focus on stock price and quarterly returns will allow media companies the time and freedom and risk taking they feel they need to make the transition to the new age. The radio giant Clear Channel made that point when it went private. So have a host of private suitors emerging in the newspaper field.

What is unknown is whether these potential new private owners are motivated by public interest, a vision of growth online, having a high-profile hobby (like a sports team), or as an investment to be flipped for profit after aggressive cost-cutting. Public ownership tends to make companies play by the same rules. Private ownership has few leveling influences.

And the new crop of potential private owners is unlike the press barons of the past, people trying to create their legacy in news. Most of them are people who made their fortunes in other enterprises. The Argument Culture is giving way to something new, the Answer Culture. Critics used to bemoan what author Michael Crichton once called the "Crossfire Syndrome," the tendency of journalists to stage mock debates about issues on TV and in print. Such debates, critics lamented, tended to polarize, oversimplify and flatten issues to the point that Americans in the middle of the spectrum felt left out. That era of argument —R.W. Apple Jr. the gifted New York Times Reporter who died in 2006, called it "pie throwing" — appears to be evolving. The programme "Crossfire" has been canceled. A growing pattern has news outlets, Programmes and journalists offering up solutions, crusades, certainty and the impression of putting all the blur of information in clear order for people.

The tone may be just as extreme as before, but now the other side is not given equal play. In a sense, the debate in many venues is settled — at least for the host. This is something that was once more confined to talk radio, but it is spreading as it draws an audience elsewhere and in more nuanced ways. The most popular show in cable has shifted from the questions of Larry King to the answers of Bill O'Reilly. On CNN his rival Anderson Cooper becomes personally involved in stories. Lou Dobbs, also on CNN, rails against job exportation. Dateline goes after child predators.

Even less controversial figures have causes: ABC weatherman Sam Campion champions green consumerism. The Answer Culture in journalism, which is part of the new branding, represents an appeal more idiosyncratic and less ideological than pure partisan journalism. Blogging is on the brink of a new phase that will probably include scandal, profitability for some, and a splintering into elites and non-elites over standards and ethics.

The use of blogs by political campaigns in the mid-term elections of 2006 is already intensifying in the approach to the presidential election of 2008.

Corporate public-relations efforts are beginning to use blogs as well, often covertly. What gives blogging its authenticity and momentum — its open access — also makes it vulnerable to being used and manipulated.

At the same time, some of the most popular bloggers are already becoming businesses or being assimilated by establishment media.

All this is likely to cause blogging to lose some of its patina as citizen media. To protect themselves, some of the best-known bloggers are already forming associations, with ethics codes, standards of conduct and more.

The paradox of professionalizing the medium to preserve its integrity as an independent citizen platform is the start of a complicated new era in the evolution of the blogosphere.While journalists are becoming more serious about the Web, no clear models of how to do journalism online really exist yet, and some qualities are still only marginally explored.

Our content study this year was a close examination of some three dozen Web sites from a range of media. Our goal was to assess the state of journalism online at the beginning of 2007. What we found was that the root media no longer strictly define a site's character. The Web sites of the Washington Post and the New York Times, for instance, are more dissimilar than the papers are in print.

The Post, by our count, was beginning to have more in common with some sites from other media. The field is still highly experimental, with an array of options, but it can be hard to discern what one site offers, in contrast to another. And some of the Web's potential abilities seem less developed than others. Sites have done more, for instance, to exploit immediacy, but they have done less to exploit the potential for depth.

THE ROLE OF INFORMATION TECHNOLOGIES

According to Lesly, a number of factors have contributed to the creation of the current human climate. These include new information technologies which extend the geographical and social spheres of individual experience and influence, and which also create a growing sense of entitlement, particularly to information, and immediate gratification and need fulfillment.

He noted that communication technologies can be both "a force for bringing the world closer together and a force for segmenting people into more and more separate groups." A result of this, Lesly explained, is what he termed the "glorification of democracy," the expectation that "every individual can interfere with any process — demand, block, sue, or harass." He explained:

Many follow no leadership and respect no rules. They feel they can interfere with the working of any organization - that they can thwart government, business, education, the armed forces and law enforcement. Refusal to follow any rule is a rejection of all leadership, and without leadership there can only be disorder.

The forces I've mentioned create activist pressures to force their type of change. And even when activists attain any of their objectives, they are not likely to fade away but will then seek new and more demanding causes. The pressures for change are now a force in themselves, not to be satiated by the achievement of change.

"SINGLE-ISSUE" PUBLICS

These activist pressures, according to 1980 Schranz Lecturer Douglas G. Hearle, occur as public attitudes become factionalized around highly volatile, self-defining single issues. Hearle explained:

The growing national single issue orientation on both sides of the political aisle coupled with the continued disillusionment with political institutions has meant more independence of mind for the Voter - or fickleness of attitude, depending on your point of view. And when you add to that the growing effect of intractable economic problems inflation, unemployment as well as energy - effects which are as much psychological as they are material - we are likely to continue to have a public which is highly volatile in its attitudes as voters and as consumers.

CONFRONTATION AS A TACTIC

As single-issue publics increase and, in particular, as these publics form around sensitive, divisive and volatile topics, Dilenschneider predicted that "confrontation" would increase as a tactic of choice. "Confrontation," he explained, "is definitely back in and not just on the boarders of Croatia or in the alleys of Ulster." More than likely, he said, these confrontations will be played out in the media and in the courtroom. The emergence of "tabloid values" in the media fuels the need for "stories" in which raw emotion becomes more important than simple facts. He explained:

The information revolution is also fueling the trend. The ready availability of vast stores of details about personal lives is helping to etch the character lines of potential victims.And in the courtroom, the opportunity to make public confrontations may be the ultimate goal of single-issue activist groups. Hearle explained:

The courtroom is increasingly where the action is and will continue to be. In that legal arena, special interest groups, like the environmentalists, do not have to "win" by getting a judgement in their favour, by convincing a judge or jury of the correctness of their point of view or by getting a damage award for their cause.

INFORMATION "CLUTTER"

Another bi-product of the information revolution, Dilenschneider explained, is "information clutter." As publics form around all-consuming single issues, their span of attention for, and ability to recall, other information, including corporate messages, becomes seriously eroded. He explained:

I think that we are just now beginning to recognize a clutter problem in recalling messages. There is just too much competition for storage space. If George Bush has trouble leaning on his war laurels within weeks of victory, imagine how hard it is for the average firm to say: Remember the good things we did back in 1989 and 1990.

ACCOUNTABILITY

Perhaps an ironic characteristic of the new "human climate," Dilenschneider argued, is the double standard in how people feel about the "value" of accountability.

Americans, he suggested are ambivalent about accountability. While personal accountability is out, corporations, public institutions, and businesses should expect even closer scrutiny in the future than in the past, he said.

The implications for this, according to these Schranz lecturers, is that in the era of the new human climate, organizations will be judged less by their products and services and more by their policies and behaviour related to those values that are "hot" or "politically correct." One "value" is community involvement. Corporations, Ann H. Barkelew argued, will be judged by their involvement in local communities: Strengthening communities has been and is a part of our business strategy - as much a part as operations, distribution or human resources.

THE "NEW" ORGANIZATION

A second "force" frequently identified by the Schranz lecturers dealt with the changing nature of organizations themselves. According to these practitioners, organizations are slowly responding to what has been described as a new "social compact" between employers and their employees. Dilenschneider explained:There are plenty of disenfranchised white-collar workers out of jobs these days and I expect that you will see more militant efforts Towards job entitlement and job protection legislation — closer to what we see in Europe today — arise in the United States.

Companies, he concluded, should expect to face a growing number of accusations that they are not managing work and their employees properly or fairly. Others suggested that the role of the CEO would go through dramatic changes in response to the public's perception that corporate management has become arrogant.The "new" CEO. "The CEO of the era beginning in the year 2000 will face a legacy unlike anything in our century," explained 1989 lecturer John Budd Jr.

By then, Europe will have faced up to its 1992 challenges; Hong Kong, its reunification with China in 1997; free enterprise will be implanted in the booming nations of East Asia; we'll see deregulation of the economies of eastern Europe and in the bastions of socialism, the Soviet Union and, I'm convinced, in China, under the pressure of its one billion restless population.

Perhaps the biggest challenge to be faced, he suggested, would be a crisis of public confidence in corporate management's competence. Dilenschneider called it the "CEO disease" - the overwhelming perception that corporate leaders have become arrogant and have lost touch with employees and customers.

According to Budd, a continuing drop in employee loyalty Towards their employers, combined with the crisis of a lack of public trust, is an indication that corporate managements may have to be restructured. He predicted that the nature of the CEO's position will be the first to change. Corporations will create an "Office of the CEO," he said, in which two individuals will serve: one as the CEO for external affairs and the other as a CEO for internal affairs. Reporting to these two individuals, and working to guide their decision making, would be a "cabinet" of executive vice presidents that might include an executive vice president of ideology, an executive vice president of legal affairs, and an executive vice president of human affairs. He explained that what has been traditional public relations would, in this model, fall under the director of "ideology":

I think it's time to recognize that public relations as a term has been debased by misuse, overuse, and abuse. More importantly, in a decade's time the enhancement of - and the protection of - the credibility of a company - and its CEOs - will have outdistanced the rote, formula thinking of public relations' accepted wisdom. It will require, as a prerequisite, people skilled in the advancement of ideas, in building broad non-political coalitions and support. It will need people comfortable in dealing with abstracts and converting them to realities. In short, it requires people with minds of originality, endowed with the intellectual resources needed to deal with subjective views, attitudes and behavioral patterns. In short, an ideologist.

Senior management, he concluded, has never been more "in need of truly creative, objective counsel, externally and internally, as now. And, never before has it been in such limited supply."

This may in fact, according to Carole Howard, facilitate the "metamorphosis" of the public relations practitioner to senior management "counselor." This change, she explained, may be so natural that the profession may not even be aware of it until it has occurred. Kerryn King, the 1985 Schranz lecturer, quoted the CEO of a major oil company, who explained:

The modern corporation is no longer perceived solely in economic terms, but as an institution which contributes to society as a whole. These changes in public expectations and in the perception of business are transforming public relations from an ancillary role in the corporation to an essential one.

Globalization. In addition, the opening of new markets in Eastern Europe and Asia have sent many firms looking for overseas opportunities, creating what Carole Howard described as "stateless corporations" with "borderless offices." This, she said, would bring challenges and opportunities:

That's certainly true in my job. With the technological advantages of FAXes, voice mail and satellite hookups at my fingertips, backed by a superb staff at our global headquarters in New York and Reader's Digest Association colleagues in more than 50 offices worldwide, I am as comfortable brainstorming magazine promotions in Sydney as I am giving a speech in Stockholm.

The "human climate," particularly consumerism and environmental movements, may be stronger abroad than in the United States now, and public relations practitioners must be aware of this, she noted.

The Changing "Face" of Public Relations: A third, significant force affecting public relations is the very composition of the field itself and the way in which public relations firms will be owned and operated in the future. Several of the Schranz lecturers intimated that recent studies which have examined the "velvet ghetto" and "glass ceilings" may have been harbingers of what may be the most serious challenge to face the profession in coming decades.

The role of women. As many as 70 per cent of the college students currently preparing for careers in public relations are women, according to Budd. These women, he explained, must be willing to take on leadership roles needed to elevate the profession's status:If public relations is to achieve the higher destinies its leadership regularly projects for it, women are going to be the catalyst because they will increasingly represent numerically the majority of practitioners. The professional gauntlet is theirs to pick up. Women have to push determinedly upwards by the same measures of personal discipline some men adopt. Men, who currently hold the majority of seniorlevel positions must, for the good of the profession in the long run, must be willing to create opportunities for this to occur. Budd explained:

Male executives - and they hold sway in the agency management echelons - for their part have got to be less chauvinistic and give the same encouragement, the same level of mentorship and opportunity they readily provide male interns.

A return to smaller agencies? In the mergerhungry 1980s, small public relations agencies became prey for publicly owned "mega-agencies," whose own gluttony turned themselves into uncreative, non-risk taking, bottom-line-driven shops in which hundreds of clients were served, but none with the close attention that is supposed to be at the heart of what public relations is about.

Budd argued that mega-agencies cannot give personal services to hundreds of different clients at one time. This, he suggests, is a violation of the very tenets of the profession. Because of this, public relations will have to rethink its need to create these mega-agencies. He suggested that future trends will be Towards small, specialized agencies looking after the needs of a handful of select clients:

In my opinion, the mega-agencies will not be a material factor then. They will have dematerialized one way or another, most likely cannibalized by new owners to extract maximum profit from the pieces.... These very special needs will become the province of small boutiques - or niches - of senior professionals who bring mature perspectives, independent judgement, front-line experience and a degree of irreverence to conventional wisdom to the assignment.

Generalists and Specialists? "The old notions," Fraser P. Seitel argued, "that people in public relations must be generalists, rather than specialists, simply won't cut it in the years ahead." While it will be important to master the "general" skills of communication, Seitel recommended that future practitioners understand they must become "generalized specialists" who are particularly conversant in and knowledgeable either of a specific aspect of public relations work investor relations or government relations or speech writing, etc. - or of a particular industry - computers or health care or sports or the arts or, as in my own case, banking and finance, or whatever.... Increasingly in the future, specific public relations jobs will be awarded to the practitioner who demonstrates specialized expertise in the particular area at issue.Douglas Hearle suggested that many of the needed "specializations" will include history, science, law, engineering, education, political science, international affairs, and television production. The Schranz lecturers shared the belief that public relations practitioners must be better trained to understand the dynamics of the business world and, in particular, the international marketplace. At present, public relations has "too many mechanics and too few counselors truly capable of helping management understand the complexities of today's dynamic business environment," David Ferguson explained. As a result, public relations education, he argued, must move away from its exclusive emphasis on "communication mechanics":

Public relations will never reach the status of a profession, as long as people can get into the field and prosper without having completed a fairly rigorous course of study in the field. And, until educations in public relations become sufficiently broad to include study in such subjects as economics, philosophy and law....Any attempt to expand the vision and reach of public relations education must include significant involvement in international affairs and the international business climate.

One approach to this, according to Ann H. Barkelew, would be to train future practitioners in "implications thinking." Like issues management or issues tracking, "implications thinking" requires that practitioners be able to critically evaluate the impact of external forces — business ethics, diversity, time-poor customers, health care reform, the economy - on their organizations:

We bring our thoughts to the strategy table, because that is the role of public relations at the table: to identify issues, to respond to concerns, and to position the organization effectively to meet these challenges.

In a sense, this requires practitioners to become what 1981 Schranz Lecturer Dorothy Gregg described as organizational "futurists," forecasting social trends and preparing the organization for their bottom-line impact. "Implications thinking" may be a critical skill in an era of globalization and international business. Douglas G. Hearle explained:

A generalist must have the detailed knowledge and expertise of the specialist when dealing with problems... which have far-reaching legal, social, political and economic implications. Only the specialist can know in full detail what interest groups will be aroused by a particular stand on an issue or by a particular decision. Only a specialist can know how a specific social issue is affecting a country in Europe and might, therefore, affect the United States or a country in the Pacific area. It is this combination of "generalist managers" and "specialist counselors" that "will characterize a successful public relations profession over the next decades," Hearle concluded. While these three principal "forces" have been identified through the observations and reflections of practitioners who represent the senior leaders of the field, it is likely that the "forces" will continue to change and evolve over time - as communication and information technologies improve, and as social and political revolutions continue to dot the globe.

Because of this, Philip Lesly suggested that public relations professionals and students should be committed to a "lifetime" education, constantly reading "the best thought in this field, on the social patterns, on the psychology of people."

David Ferguson, in his lecture, "A Practitioner Looks At Public Relations Education," argued that the only way the discipline will be able to successfully prepare current and future practitioners to respond to these changing global forces is through a partnership between professionals and educators. "It is essential," he explained, "that mutual respect be developed between those who teach and those who practice public relations."

It was recommended by several of the lecturers that public relations professionals be given the opportunity for greater involvement in the education process — through visiting lectureships, presentations, and inclusion in active advisory councils. And it was also suggested that public relations educators increase their involvement with working professionals.

Finally, a consistent theme among the lecturers was the need to move the focus of public relations education away from simply teaching "process" or mechanical skills Towards greater efforts at developing critical thinking abilities through the study and application of theory, human psychology, economics, and business philosophies.

Curriculum developers in the field of gifted education raise many critical questions such as:

- What should gifted and talented students learn?,
- For what purpose?

In this chapter, these two questions will be discussed as they relate to and affect the world of gifted and talented students in the first decade of the 21st century. Most of the issues that gifted students will face in the new world landscape, such as ethnic conflict, arms escalation, overpopulation, environmental problems, poverty, and genetic engineering, cannot be solved without integrating knowledge from the natural sciences, the social sciences, and humanities.

This balance is currently not found in the teaching and learning of gifted students, since teaching what is of value, which is called "Philosophy," has less importance than teaching what is, which is called "Science."

I propose that, in order to teach our gifted students elegant problem solving in the arts and sciences (*i.e.*, the parsimonious and e vocative description of patterns to make sense out of a confusion of detail), curriculum developers need to renew their interest in philosophical inquiry in gifted classrooms.

WHY CONSIDER PHILOSOPHICAL INQUIRY

The value of teaching and learning through philosophical inquiry is not only an intellectual adventure, but also enables learners of all ages to discover and understand elements of the human condition. It is not a new approach, nor is it necessarily unique. Vygotsky valued works of art, philosophical arguments, and anthropological data when building a theory of learning with thought and language early in the 20th century. Bruner believed a curriculum for excelling students ought to be constructed around the great issues, principles, and values that the society deemed worthy of continued concern.

Gardner has said that a culture identifies truths, beauties, and virtues it finds valuable and then gathers resources to ensure their understanding in young learners. These virtues are always being redefined and refined. Educators can not only expect students to learn about virtues such as truthfulness, goodness, and beauty, but can also help students pursue truth, beauty, and goodness in their own lives. It is essential for our gifted and talented youth to become immersed in curricula that inculcate the understanding and application of these virtues.

Especially in the new millennium, our brightest students need to discover their deepest ties to the rest of humanity and thereby help ensure that nature and culture survive for future generations.

Recently, a colleague of mine, a historian and educator, offered a historian's perspective of the value of teaching gifted students through philosophical inquiry. He said that the way we think—thought at the most reflective levels—determines what will be important in a culture. If the brightest learners have a foundation in philosophical thinking, then the nature of a nation's technology for example, will reflect that thinking. If the brightest learners know only the mechanics or the science of technology, then it is that knowledge alone that will drive its direction. Teaching through philosophy balances the personal worldview with the technical knowledge of a student as he or she becomes a stakeholder in a society.

Philosophy Within the Humanities

One may take the point of view that the legitimate study of mankind is man. The humanities comprise the study of all formal and informal acts of humankind that have resulted in creative products that portray and enhance the human condition in some form. In this light, developers of gifted curricula may view the humanities as providing a link for many disciplines interesting to gifted learners. Important theoretical models considered for conceptualizing humanities curricula for gifted students include those of Ward and Phenix. Each of these important models incorporates philosophy as a core element in the curriculum experience. Ward's model of teaching philosophy as an integrated learning experience has sought to provide a meaningful structure to gifted curriculum, emphasizing systems of thought and great ideas as organizers. The work of Phenix is a cornerstone of the approach taken by gifted educators as a curriculum-modification procedure designed to provide more in-depth learning experiences for gifted students.

Philosophy as Curriculum

The search for meaning within the domain of philosophy and its subdisciplines is sometimes referred to as ethics, metaphysics, and epistemology. Inviting gifted students to reflect on such philosophical questions as the meaning of knowledge (epistemology), for example, can help them become receptive to all levels and types of experience. It can help prepare them to maximize their knowledge in as many subjects as possible, especially in areas of special interest to them.

Teaching ethics to gifted students expands the teaching of authentic practices in various fields. For example, making explicit to individuals their personal ethical system can help them respond to specific ethical dilemmas. This is an increasingly vital skill to possess when a talented student enters the worlds of microbiology, genetics, fiscal management, journalism, business, or education. Currently, however, teaching gifted students in the philosophical domain of metaphysics seems to be limited, and this may hinder a student from attempting to find meaning personally, as well as in the surrounding world.The main task of the coming era is...a radical renewal of our sense of responsibility. Our conscience must catch up to our reason; otherwise we are lost.

One perplexing problem in the teaching of philosophy to gifted students is that existing curricular models, such as those discussed above, have been too abstract conceptually for easy translation and use by teachers. That can be fixed. As students from one country can easily learn the language of another by extended visits, so teachers of gifted students can allow their students regular extended visits in the realms of truth, beauty, and happiness, all the while doing the business of reading, writing, and arithmetic.

Csikszenrmihalyi has explored the possibility that the next steps in human evolution and human survival will depend on the ability to find flow in activities that nurture human community and protect the environment. In order to do this, schools could promote the activities that bring about flow, including those that could inculcate in students a kind of love for the Cosmos, a cosmic conscientiousness. You don't want to only teach book learning or skills, but also a kind of feeling that the universe is a wonderful place to inhabit and that somehow you love every part of it. Gifted and talented students, their teachers, and their teachers' teachers should be thinking about, talking about, and doing something about these philosophical ideas as they learn in school. Students need to know that teachers are seekers, too. As educators of the gifted, we must question what to teach our students and to what end. The answers become important as we look beyond the year 2000 and realise the problems facing the next generations of students. Developing curricula for the gifted that incorporate teaching through philosophy is my answer to the first question. Establishing the teaching of philosophy as a cornerstone of the integration of knowledge from the natural sciences, social sciences, and humanities so that gifted students may be able to solve the problems of the new millennium is my answer to the second question.

Once a commitment is made to the teaching of philosophy to gifted students, theoretical models can be developed that are easily understood and used by teachers who then become active partners with students, joining together to build meaningful paths to the future.

SCIENCE AND TECHNOLOGY REPORTING

BRUSHING UP KNOWLEDGE OF SCIENCE

Teaching science is beyond the scope of this unit. But all those who have learnt science at school can become science reporters if they brush up their knowledge of the subject and go on adding to it.

Recapitulate School and College Science Studies : Recapitulation here means going over again, or revising the main points—laws, theories, principles, etc. All science reporters must have a basic knowledge of the elementary principles of science. A knowledge of scientific vocabulary is necessary. That does not mean only science graduates can report happenings in science. In a way, such education helps, but science education at school is broad-based and can be built upon.

All students are given the basics of science and mathematics at school. Is it possible to go over what we learnt in our early years at school? Yes, memory has it all stored for re-call. If you have the school books put away, bring them out, dust them and re-read them. If you do not have the books, borrow the science textbooks from the next-door child who is studying them. Read those books with an open and enthusiastic mind. A whole world of scientific thought will come rushing back to you. If you are a science graduate, so much the better. A Ph.D. in a science does not necessarily make one a good science reporter. With your keyed-up scientific temper, observe the happenings in science and technology. We live in the age of science. The age of science is the age of reason. It is by reasoning that human beings have unlocked the secrets of nature. Again, it is by reasoning that human beings have applied the laws of nature in developing technology. Do you try and reason it out when you see something strange? Do you investigate it? If you do, you are a person with a scientific temper. If someone says "rainfall has diminished because of sinful activities of humans", will you accept it blindly? If you do, you are not reasoning. But if you reason it out, you will find the scientific truth unfolding for you. Here, the meaning of the word "sinful" is involved. Sinful activities could include deforestation, water and air pollution, heating up of the atmosphere by industrial activities. Yes, these activities can lead to climate change, including less rainfall in some places. This is how scientific temper works. Now, apply it to all the happenings around you.

Tips on Science Communication Awareness : When the ancient Greek philosopher Archimedes discovered the principle of buoyancy while relaxing in a bathtub, what did he do? He shouted "Eureka!" and ran into the street, without even dressing up. Why? It was because of the overwhelming desire to share his new knowledge. Communication is sharing of information. You, as a science reporter, must have the curiosity to know the latest happenings in the field you are covering. The moment you have learnt enough about a particular happening, go to your desk to write it as a report for publication. Your work involves three stages:

- Search and research,
- Understanding it completely, and
- Writing it in a simple style to make your readers know what you have learnt.

The best way to develop science communication awareness is by reading good popular science books and journals. Also, watch popular science programmes on Indian and foreign television channels. Ask yourself why you liked a particular report. You will realize that the particular report appealed to you not necessarily because it brought out some startling facts, but because of its clarity of style so that the lay person can understand it.

Checking the Facts through Reference : There is no scope for factual errors, half-truths, bluff, exaggeration and hoax in science. So also in science reporting. Scientific truths and technological facts are verifiable. In the modern world, reference books and computerized knowledge banks are there to verify your findings. When you hear about a discovery by an individual or an institution and if it has an element of half-truth or exaggeration in it, you will smell a rat if you have a scientific bent of mind, or a scientific temper. Yet, in a tired moment of your hurried life, this may not happen.

Therefore it is always safe to check the facts with the source of the news or from other sources. Documented reference books and journals are available in all the major libraries and scientific institutions.

Go through the alphabetically-arranged index and reach the information you are looking for. The very exercise will reveal new facts to you and widen your mental horizon. Thus, while you are working on one story, your mind is working itself to show the way to another story. A reporter who verifies facts as a matter of habit will earn the reputation of being credible.

Verification through Interviewing Those Who Know : Who can verify scientific facts and principles better than scientists themselves? Who call give a more credible opinion about technological developments and projects than technologists themselves? Therefore, always keep a list of scientists and technologists of merit, living in the city or town where you are functioning as a reporter. Make sure your list contains both residential and office addresses and telephone numbers. Nothing readymade will be available to you. Look up the telephone directory, Who's Who, etc. Then, go ahead and, cultivate an acquaintance with these scientists and technologists. When you visit a scientific institution, go up to the PR or Information Officer and get the list of the scientists. Ask one scientist to put you on to another. This way, you would have a fund of experts to look up to, when you need to check facts or obtain an opinion. Make sure that you approach the scientists whose area of study and research is appropriate to the theme of your story. Take up an appointment. Be punctual. Have the questions ready with you. Note down your questions and the interviewee's answers carefully. Ask supplementary questions when needed. Such interviews can be woven into your main story or written as boxed items. Make sure you get a photograph of the scientist/expert interviewed.

Personal Glossary of Common Science-Technology Terms and Phrases: A science reporter, like all reporters is hard-pressed for time. You have deadlines to keep. Every writer needs a good dictionary on his writing desk. As a science reporter, you will often be faced with technical terms. Scientists and technologists, and indeed all specialists, are fond of, or used to, speaking in their own technical language, or scientific jargon. While taking down notes, you may not be able to translate these into common language. You have to do so while writing. Therefore, prepare and keep your own glossary of commonly used technical terms. Arrange the words and phrases in alphabetical order. You can prepare such a reference material by working in the reference section of a science-technology library, or a good general library. Keep updating as you progress in your reporting career. The exact commonly used words and meanings of certain science and technology terms may elude your memory in moments of stress. If you have a glossary of technical terms handy, your report will make smooth reading. Newspaper offices do have reference libraries. But do not depend entirely on them. They have too many customers. And avoid making a spectacle of yourself running between the news reporters' room and the reference library several times while doing a story. If you do, you may miss the deadline, or your colleagues may laugh at you.

SOURCING OF SCIENCE AND TECHNOLOGY NEWS

Do not wait for news to drop into your lap. Go and look for it. If you wait for a news story, by the time it reaches you, it would have reached a whole lot of other people. So, be alert. Be on the look out. You have a beat. Do your regular checking. Develop friendly relations with the information officers of the institutions. In the town or city where you work as a science reporter there are bound to be scientific institutions which you may use as your source. Do not think institutions which bear "science" or "technology" in their names are the only sources of science-technology news. The government departments dealing with public health, water supply, electricity, telecommunications, construction, transportation, etc., have all applied science in multiple ways.

Banks and government offices may go in for computerization. Industries may go in for new technologies. The real estate business may opt for taller and taller buildings. All such activities are sources of technology news. And, there will be the ever-present problem of environmental degradation and, of course, efforts to solve it. All these will give you a constant supply of news stories which your readers will appreciate. Let us consider a hypothetical story. You read in the local paper the headline, "Rampur to have a 18-storey building—tallest in the district". This is a general report coming from a construction company, or from the town planners.

A whole lot of people in Rampur will feel happy that their town has started growing skywards. People in Sitapur, a neighboring, town of Rampur, will wonder why their town can not have a 20-story building. As a science-technology reporter, you will have to approach the story from other angles. You can go to the town-planning department and ask whether such a tall building is appropriate in Rampur. Will it not set the trend for other property developers? Will Rampur not end up as an urban concrete jungle? What about water supply, electricity, etc.? An endless stream of questions will come to you. Then, you can seek out the architect of the building and talk to him. You can meet the building contractor and ask him about his experience in building tall structures. What about fire safety? What about the foundation? What about structural stress analysis? If you write your findings in simple language, the story will lead to a debate. The people of Rampur will begin to see beyond status symbol traps. You may be instrumental in creating a scientific temper among the general public. Press conferences, press handouts and policy announcements by ministers are alone not sources of news for a science reporter. Events and phenomena in any area of the subject throw up news stories. For instance, epidemics, soil salinity, good and bad water management, population densities, non conventional energy sources, and observation of fauna and flora of the region are all sources of news. A science reporter will not only recognize the existence of problems, but also their causes and effects. By talking to the right people, you may come out with the right answers. Think while you observe. Observe while you think. Your source may not be far to seek.

INSTITUTIONS OF RESEARCH A DEVELOPMENT (RANDD) IN INDIA

As a reporter covering science and technology in India, you must have a comprehensive knowledge of the institutions of research and development in the country. India has the world's third largest reservoir of technical and scientific manpower. India has also built up one of the world's largest networks of RandD facilities. In the present liberalized industrial and economic climate, these laboratories and research stations will get new goals and work towards achieving them. They will be a major source of science-technology news. The Department of Science and Technology (DST) of the Government of India looks after the policy planning and administrative details of the largest chain of national laboratories. These come under the Council of Scientific and Industrial Research (CSIR). There are about 40 major research laboratories under the CSIR, besides a network of multi-disciplinary extension centres. Among the premier national laboratories under the CSIR, are the National Physical Laboratory, New Delhi; National Chemical Laboratory, Pune; Central Drug Research Institute, Lucknow; Central Glass Research Institute, Dhanbad; Indian Institute of Oceanography, Goa; Electrochemical Laboratory, Karaikudi; etc. The list, and the range of disciplines handled can be mind-boggling. The CSIR headquarters at Rafi Marg, New Delhi-110001, will be only too glad to furnish a science reporter with all the information one may inquire about, in a professional capacity. Atomic Energy and Space are two of the areas where India can boast of frontier research and development. The atomic power stations and rocket development and satellite launching events, capture the headlines.

The Bhabha Atomic Research Centre and the Tata Institute of Fundamental Research, both in Bombay, and research facilities linked with these and scattered over the country, have been doing multi-disciplinary, high technology RandD which have success stories to be written about. The Indian Space Research Organization (ISRO) has done outstanding RandD work at its various facilities, which speak volumes for the Calibre of its scientists. Both the work and the scientists are news. Technical departments under other central ministries to have their research programmes under specialized agencies. Departments of Agriculture does a wide range of crop research through the laboratories and research stations of the Indian Council of Agricultural Research (ICAR).

The Union Ministry of Health and Family Welfare has under it, the Indian Council of Medical Research, which runs a major chain of research laboratories. Then, there is the Research Development Service Organization under the Railway Board. Every department —communication, irrigation, power, surface transport, mining coal, petroleum, environment, etc. has an R and D wing to run its laboratories. All of us know that every university has research programmes going on in their postgraduate departments. These may be in pure science, such as Physics, Chemistry, Geology and Biology or in applied science such as Medicine, Agriculture, Engineering etc. The Indian Institutes of Technology (IITs) do considerable frontier research. The Indian Institute of Science at Bangalore, is rated among the world's top basic science research organizations. All that when pooled, becomes an ocean of science and technology news. The attempt in this unit is only to give a fleeting vision of the mega picture of the potential for science and technology reporting and writing. The vastness of the opportunities awaiting you. If you have your scientific temper heightened, science reporting can be one of the most exciting fields of mass communication. After all, we live in the age of science.

PERSONS WHO MATTER IN SCIENCE AND TECHNOLOGY

Why must you have a cursory knowledge of outstanding scientists and technologists? Because leading names make leading the headlines. Here, we are talking shout living men and women of science, particularly Indian. You may write about their latest achievements. In such reports you must make a reference to their earlier achievements. A leading scientist may visit the town where you are working. Your editor may ask you to interview the person. Or, you may be covering a lecture, which (s) he delivers at a local function-a memorial lecture, a foundation laying ceremony, or whatever else. If you are familiar with the highlights of that person's life, your interview or news report will be that much more interesting and evoke the reader's interest. Biographical knowledge of three categories of scientists and technologists must be in your memory or in your reference recall system:

- Outstanding men of science of the past who made path-breaking, or epoch-making inventions. Their work is globally recognized. Reference to them can be found in an Encyclopaedia of science, or even in general knowledge books. In day to day reporting, such names may not and cannot figure. But the science reporter's knowledge should extend beyond the usual current affairs.
- India's outstanding scientists and technologists of the past-say, since the Renaissance. Here will figure names like C.V. Raman, Jagadish Chandra Bose, M.S. Krishnan, K.S. Krishnan, Homi Bhabha, Meghnad Saha, S.S. Bhatnagar, Vikram Sarabhai, etc. They have tremendous significance because their contributions led to India's present-day achievements in science and technology. Their connections and interactions with India's first prime minister, Pandit Jawaharlal Nehru, enabled the latter to lay the foundations of independent India's science-technology progress. If India is in a position to import, adapt and cope with the very latest technologies, it is because of the institution building efforts of the Nehru-Bhabha-Bhatnagar team.
- India has scores of living world-class scientists and technologists. They are to be found in every discipline and sphere of science and technology. It is beyond the scope of this unit to list them. Look up the Who's Who, Year Books and General Knowledge Books, etc.

5

Evolution of Journalism

INTRODUCTION

Our purpose here is not to present a history of journalism using intervals of 30 years or any other vantage point. That is a massive undertaking for another book. Rather, our purpose is to make the point that the nature of journalism constantly evolves in response to the social, technological and creative environment in which people work.

Furthermore, the defining characteristics of this evolution need to be made explicit and the subject of intense scrutiny and debate, especially in this time when a rapidly changing technological environment arguably offers more options than at any time in the past.

Not all of these options—or even the current emphases of news, however long they last—are beneficial ones for society or for journalism. It is especially important to note "wrong turns" along the way or the failure to shed some bad habits.

And there is the need to more explicitly guide this evolutionary pattern of the new journalism, not a new style of newspaper journalism or broadcast journalism, but rather a journalism resulting from the convergence of many media on the contemporary stage.

JOURNALISTS ARE COMMUNICATORS

One identifying mark of journalists is that they are participants in the process of human communication. Since at least two parties always play a part in the process of human communication—one who transmits stimuli and another in whom a response to that stimuli is evoked, often referred to as senders and receivers or, even more simply, as writers and readers or speakers and listeners—it is important to note which of these parties the journalists most characteristically are. Journalists do an enormous amount of reading and listening. That work as receivers of communication is, in fact, along with observation, among the chief means by which they gather the knowledge that they formulate into messages. But those who *only* do this are not recognized as journalists. Greeley, Douglass, Tarbell, Murrow, and all the others we identify as journalists are most noted for originating the messages that are part of the communication process.

Journalists are those who are responsible for the *content* of what is sent out, transmitted, and conveyed to others. Greeley began his career as a typesetter and printer, but that was not the work of a journalist, for he was not then responsible for selecting or creating the messages that he set into type and then duplicated.

Pressmen, studio technicians, laboratory workers, delivery people, and many others may greatly assist the process of journalism, but their work is not the work of journalism. Journalists have control over what is said; the others may be responsible for the reproduction or circulation of what the journalists produce.

The signs that journalists use to convey their messages are most often verbal and probably more often written than oral. Graphic signs such as pictures, graphs, and drawings also play a part in both the print and oral media. Most of the messages that we will consider will be those that are expressed by written words, but unless stated otherwise, the comments will refer also to the other means of communication.

OTHERS ARE COMMUNICATORS, ALSO

Journalists, however, are not the only ones who create messages. Poets, novelists, playwrights, and others are also responsible for the content of pieces of communication. How do they differ from journalists?

Journalists send out messages that purport to be literally and at least preponderantly true or factual. Such words as "true" and "factual," of course, almost cry out for definition and explication will be given their due. For now, it will suffice to restate this characteristic in negative terms.

Journalistic messages, let us say, do not purport to be false, erroneous, made up, invented, imagined, or fictional. They may, of course, actually be false or invented, but the journalists do not introduce them that way. Journalists are responsible for messages about things that they claim have really happened, are really happening, or are really intended, planned, or likely to happen.

The media in which pieces of journalism appear, it is true, are rarely occupied only by journalistic communications. Commercial television gives most of its time to pieces of fiction. Some may be *based* on fact, a circumstance that, can cause serious confusion, but usually the viewers are provided with sufficient clues to enable them to distinguish the journalistic fact from the fiction. Radio devotes much of its time to music, a Non-verbal form of communication.

The periodical media that rely heavily on the written word are the forms most strongly devoted to journalism, but they also are likely to contain at least some material that is not to be read as though it were literally true.Historically, newspapers are the media most frequently associated with journalism, but newspaper work and the work of journalism are not identical.

Not all newspapermen or -women are journalists. In general, therefore, journalism is a function that should not be identified with any of the media, although it does rely on some of them.

NOR ARE JOURNALISTS THE ONLY NON-FICTION COMMUNICATORS

Journalists, however, are not alone as originators of what they purport to be Non-fiction communications. Philosophers, economists, sociologists, physicists, and many others also devise messages that they intend their readers to accept as literally true. Among them, the group that seems most akin to journalists are the historians.

Journalism, in fact, is sometimes referred to as contemporary or current history. But a careful examination of the differences between historians (as well as philosophers, economists, and similar communicators) and journalists will reveal a crucial characteristic of journalism.

Does the difference consist of this: historians write about the past whereas journalists write about the present? Not at all. Although historians commonly say such things as "the task of the historian" is "to order and interpret the events of the past", the time factor is not critical. What is the present? It is but a moving edge between the past and the future. Most journalistic messages, just like historical writings, deal with what has happened, not with what is happening or will happen. The historian's past is often more remote than that in which the journalist is interested, but that is only a matter of degree, not of essence.

What, then, is the essence of history? That is a difficult question and historians themselves disagree on the answer. Erich Kahler insists that "history is to be understood as the happening itself, not the description or investigation of this happening." Edward H. Carr does not think so. History, he says, "is a continuous process of interaction between the historian and his facts, an unending dialogue between the present and the past." R. G. Collingwood says, "Every historian would agree, I think, that history is a kind of research or inquiry... generically it belongs to what we call the sciences: that is, the forms of thought whereby we ask questions and try to answer them."

Collingwood has surely overstated the degree of agreement, yet his does seem to be the preponderant view.

Arnold Toynbee, for instance, has a similar opinion: "I do not think that history... is a succession of facts, nor history-writing the narration of these facts. Historians, like all human observers, have to make reality comprehensible, and this involves them in continuous judgments about what is true and what is significant."

THE MEANINGS OF MASS COMMUNICATIONS

The term "mass communications" means different things to different writers and speakers. Another excellent scholar, Charles R. Wright, a contemporary of Schramm, presented a somewhat clearer explanation—clear enough, at least, to show what modifications must be made if we are to see the relationship between journalism and mass communications.

Wright makes quite clear that he is writing about "modern mass communications", but he does not identify or describe any mass communications before the modern period. At least he does not do so explicitly. One can look at what he has to say about modern mass communications, subtract the modern and qualify a few other items, and then set forth the characteristics of basic mass communications.

But why go to all this trouble? Why not simply accept Wright's formulation as he expressed it? Well, even if one extends the modern period back to the middle of the last century, limiting mass communications to that time forces a dilemma: either journalism did not exist before approximately 1850 or journalism, if it did exist before that time, must not be a type of mass communications.

The first choice would ignore the hundreds of books on the history of journalism that set earlier dates for those working in this field, including one of our prototype journalists, Horace Greeley, who was already an experienced journalist when he founded his *New York Tribune* in 1841. The second removes an effective means by which we can distinguish journalism from other practical communications, such as law.

Another, perhaps stronger, reason for removing the "modern" qualification is that the notion of "modern mass communications" is no longer apt. Wright distinguishes modern mass communications from earlier individual communications in this way:

Mass communications is organized communication. Unlike the lone artist or writer, the "communicator" in mass media works through a complex organization embodying an extensive division of labour and an accompanying degree of expense.

To be sure, in the 1950s when Wright was preparing his book, mass communications seemed to be moving in the direction of complexity, expensiveness, and a division of labour that resulted in more workers per communication enterprise but fewer and fewer independently controlled media institutions. What Morris L. Ernst had ironically called the "sweep of progress" had continued, seemingly unabated, a decade later. The tide apparently was moving Towards bigger but fewer media institutions. Both print and broadcast outlets were getting larger, but their number, and the competition between the members, was decreasing. This movement, especially among daily newspapers, had flowed along steadily since the second decade of this century.

A new type of mass communications, therefore, seemed to be acquiring characteristics that were the inevitable flooding from the past. Thus it could have seemed quite reasonable to Wright to ignore the fact that the communications operations of a century or two earlier were *not* complex and expensive, for the flow of history seemed to show that those days were gone forever.

But technology outwitted the course of history. The machines that had been growing larger, requiring more people to operate and vastly more money to acquire, suddenly began to move in the opposite direction. Computers that had occupied enormous air-cooled rooms shrank until they fit on the lap of a businessman jetting from Chicago to Los Angeles. Minicams plus public access channels brought the possibility of television journalism within the financial range of even the lower middle class.

Desktop publishing moved the production of periodicals into small offices, even into homes. Computer bulletin boards opened a vast range of new ways of distributing messages. In other words, technology opened doors back into the mass media environment that had existed at the beginning of the nineteenth century: once again, a single person with only a modest investment could convey messages to large numbers of persons in a very short period of time.

If those processes that possess the characteristics of mass communications, except that they involve simple and inexpensive production, are not included in the category of mass communications, then we would have to create another category to accommodate them. But what are we to call the broadsheets introduced by the missionaries in Nigeria a century before that country's independence? They were examples of mass communications, but they were not produced through complex or expensive facilities.

The handwritten newsletters circulated among the refusniks in the USSR; the wall posters that appeared in China during the Cultural Revolution; the mimeographed sheets of church agencies, universities, and justice and peace groups in South and Central America; the *Drudge Report* that appears on the web pages of the Internet: these and many other relatively contemporary communication activities have all the characteristics of early nineteenth-century mass communications. It seems unnecessary to invent another name for the category that merely lacks the complex organization, the division of labour, and the great expense mentioned by Wright.

Many others of Wright's points about mass communi-cations, however, help clarify this confusing term. He says, for instance, that the audience of mass communications is relatively large and that so many people are exposed to the message in a short period of time and are of such numbers "that the communicator could not interact with its members on a face-to-face basis". He also says that the audience is anonymous so that its members "generally remain personally unknown to the communicator".

Moreover, mass communications are public; because the messages "are addressed to no one in particular, their content is open for public surveillance." Also, "They are rapid because the messages are meant to reach large audiences within a relatively short time, or even simultaneously." And, "They are transient because they are usually intended to be consumed immediately".

Even so brief an account tells us enough to help us distinguish journalistic communications from lawyer-courtroom communications. When lawyers address juries, they are addressing several people, but not so many that the lawyers are unable to be aware of them as individuals.

Jurors cannot normally respond verbally to the words of the lawyers, but they have available many Non-verbal means of communicating. If one jury member's facial expression indicates skepticism at what the lawyer is saying, the latter can modify his or her communication to take that into consideration.

If another juror shows surprise, the lawyer may realise that an opportunity for pressing a point now exists. If still another juror is falling asleep, that may tell the lawyer it is time to request a recess.

Thus interpersonal communication can exist even when a number of people are involved. How large can that number be? There is no magic figure. Normally, the limit is the number of people to whom the communicator can react as individuals when they provide verbal or Non-verbal responses to what the communicator is saying. Consider, for example, the politician who is addressing a thousand people at a political rally. They may cheer or they may boo at what the politician has to say.

The speaker may modify what he had intended to say as a result, but the reaction is to the audience as a collectivity, not to them as individuals. The speaker is engaging in mass communications. But let's say that one person leaps up and begins to engage the speaker in a debate. If the speaker responds, what had been only mass communications then becomes a mixture of mass and interpersonal communications.

When a young couple sends out a thousand wedding invitations to friends and relatives, the process is interpersonal communications in spite of the large number of persons to whom the message is sent. Each person to whom that message is sent can--and is probably expected to--respond individually. Some will attend. Some will send regrets. A few might ask whether they may bring a friend. But when the commander of a thousand troops orders them to attack at dawn, no individual responses are expected and none is likely to take place.

Then the process is solely mass communications. Thus, although in mass communications one or a relatively few people send a message to relatively many people, the exact size of that receiving group is not important.

More important is what Wright refers to as the anonymity of the audience. The audience may be known as a certain category of persons, as when the army commander knows he is addressing infantrymen rather than pilots or when the publisher of a religious newspaper knows the readers are Lutherans rather than Methodists. But these people are not individually spoken to or even precisely thought of as individuals.

Likewise, when a magazine publisher goes to a list broker to buy a thousand names and addresses of people who the publisher hopes will become subscribers, the subscription offers will go out to individually named persons, but they are persons unknown to the publisher. They are as anonymous as "occupant."

The last example reveals a slight modification of Wright's statement that mass communications messages "are addressed to no one in particular" and that the messages are "open for public surveillance." What Wright says is very often true, especially when broadcast mass communications are involved.

But it is less true when the mass communications medium is a periodical sent to a list of subscribers. Large circulation magazines are usually open for public scrutiny at newsstands and libraries, of course, but there are many hundreds of highly practical and specialized publications--for example, trade journals such as Implement and Tractor, China Glass and Tableware, and Western Outfitter-that are not. They are rarely available for inspection by anyone other than subscribers.

Wright's point concerning the transience of mass communications also needs qualification. Mass produced novels, poems, and other works of fiction may endure for centuries, and so also may theoretical nonfiction works such as books of philosophy or natural science.

Such works as Charles Dickens A Tale of Two Cities and Albert Einstein The Meaning of Relativity possess all the qualities Wright attributes to mass communications except transience.

Interestingly, however, the mass communications that are transient are likely to be the journalistic ones, for once they have served their practical purpose, once the decisions have been made from the knowledge that journalism supplies, then the messages cease to be useful, cease to be journalism, and become, like treaties, diaries, and other artifacts, the raw materials of history.

BASIC MASS COMMUNICATIONS

Thus there is a type of mass communications that not only exists in the modern period but also has existed for many earlier centuries.

In this basic mass communications, one person or a relatively few people (relatively few in comparison to the number of people who receive the message) convey one or more messages to a relatively large number of persons.

Often the receivers perceive the messages simultaneously; if not simultaneously, at least they perceive them more quickly than they would if the message had to be originated for each individual. Even if the messages are individually addressed, the receivers are not thought of as individuals; they are thought of as groups or types or masses of people; for all practical purposes, the receivers are anonymous. Each of those who receive the message does not prepare and deliver an equivalent response to those who send the message. They may, however, respond as a group (as when Pontius Pilate asked the people what he should do with Jesus and they all replied, "Let Him be crucified!"). Sometimes the group reply will be through action rather than through words (as when soldiers, in response to the commander's order "Charge!" go dashing into the field of battle). Thus, although mass communications seem to be one-way, they are not totally so; the sender may well get a response, but not an equivalent response, from each one who receives the message.

A few situations require special attention. Although not all the receivers will give an equivalent response, some of them might do so. For example, a newspaper reader might respond to an editorial with an equivalent letter to the editor. If this letter is delivered to the editorial writer, that person may or may not provide a personal reply.

If the editorial writer does so, then there has been a transition from a mass communication to an interpersonal communication between the letter writer and the editorial writer. Or the editor may decide to publish the letter in the newspaper; if so, a new phase of mass communications takes place, one in which the letter writer is the sender and the other readers of the paper are the receivers.

Quite clearly, not everyone who is involved in a mass communication process is a mass communicator. That name is reserved for those who have control over the content of messages and intend to deliver their messages to masses of people. The readers of newspapers, although participants in the mass communications process, are not normally mass communicators.

Nor are the printers, delivery people, newsstand salespersons, and others who lack the authority to originate or modify the content of the messages. Writers, speakers, editors, photographers, cartoonists, and the like, however, can be mass communicators, if they intend their messages to go out to the masses.

To clarify this latter point, let us consider for a moment the call-in Programmes often heard on radio, often late at night. The subjects discussed are sometimes quite personal: the sex life or economic problems of the callers, for example.

The host of the show is clearly a mass communicator. He or she wants the program's messages to be heard by as many people as possible. The host's popularity and income depend upon a wide, anonymous, unrestricted audience.

The host, in other words, is not communicating only with the person who calls in; the host would like to think that he or she is communicating with "the world." But what about the person who calls in? That person is also involved in a mass communications process and originates a portion of the messages that are sent out. But is that person also, like the host, a mass communicator? Perhaps not. Although the caller participates voluntarily in a mass communications process, he or she does not, in many instances, really desire to do so. To obtain free advice, the caller tolerates one type of communication, mass communication, but would probably prefer another type, interpersonal communication.

If the caller happens to be an exhibitionist or propagandist, however, then the caller does become, like the host, a mass communicator.

But because we cannot always establish the truth of intentions, it will sometimes be difficult or impossible to know whether or not a certain person is a mass communicator. Yet in most instances, the evidence and circumstances are so clear that we have no doubts. To those who participate in the mass communications process regularly and for a living, it is particularly easy to grant the title of mass communicator.

Two additional glosses on Wright's mention of anonymity as a characteristic of mass communications are relevant. First, not only do mass communicators not know the recipients of their communications as individuals, but those recipients usually do not know one another as individuals.

They often think of themselves as existing in isolation. Second, partly because of the anonymity of the audience, mass communicators must guess at the level of background knowledge, literacy, and sophistication of the message recipients. The messages are often directed at a level somewhat below the median, to the distress of those who exist at the extremes.

LAWYERS AND JOURNALISTS RECONSIDERED

With all this in mind, we can perhaps better understand how journalists differ from lawyers, even when both groups employ the communication of literally true, practical knowledge.

The former are mass communicators; the latter are not. Courtroom lawyers may direct their messages to a number of people—the judge, jurors, witnesses, the other lawyers—but they are people with whom it is possible for the lawyers to interact as individuals. Although there are prominent exceptions, most lawyers in the courtroom are not interested in addressing the nebulous, anonymous public at large.

The lawyers defending civil-rights activists in the 1960s and 1970s may have been extending their remarks to an audience far outside the courtroom. They may have wanted their words to be political statements to the entire nation about racial injustice.If so, to that extent they were assuming the role of mass communicators. But, usually, trial lawyers direct their messages to the limited group of persons at hand in the courtroom. Their aim, like that of journalists, is a practical one, but their audience is the relatively few people who are able to determine the outcome of legal proceedings. In most instances, lawyers control their messages so that they impact on that select group. In addition, this is an immediate group, one whom lawyers, simply by a turn of the head, can address face-to-face. Any overt reactions by members of this group can be readily known and dealt with by the lawyers. Thus, not only in their private relations with clients in their offices but also in the public arena of the courtroom, lawyers are normally interpersonal communicators. Journalists, on the other hand, are mass communicators.

THE DIFFERENCE BETWEEN HISTORY AND JOURNALISM

Even if one accepts the dominant view about the nature of history, what, if anything, does it say that will help us distinguish history from journalism? First, we must be careful not to be misled by one obvious but not unimportant difference. Journalism is a type of communication. History is not that. If one accepts Kahler, it is what has been going on.

If one accepts Collingwood and most other historians, it is knowledge, organized knowledge, of what has been going on. Thus the parallel with journalism is not history itself but rather the *communication* of history. But this is not the crucial point. Both journalism and history deal with knowledge. Journalism is the communication of a type of knowledge that has been acquired.

History is the acquisition of a type of knowledge that will be communicated. Both are concerned with the communication of knowledge. But the important factor is neither when the knowledge is acquired nor *when* it is communicated. Rather, what requires our attention is the *type* of knowledge that is acquired and communicated.

Traditionally, two broad categories of knowledge have been recognized. One is knowledge that is acquired for the sake of knowledge. It is knowledge for its own sake. It is knowledge for the sheer pleasure of knowing. This is called theoretical knowledge. The other is acquired to procure by some kind of activity the good of people. It is knowledge that is put to use. This is called practical knowledge. In *How to Read a Book*, Mortimer Adler and Charles Van Doren explain the difference this way:

Some books and some teachers are interested only in the knowledge itself that they have to communicate. This does not mean that they deny its utility, or that they insist that knowledge is good *only* for its own sake. They simply limit themselves to one kind of communication or teaching, and leave the other kind to other men. These others have an interest beyond knowledge for its own sake. They are concerned with the problems of human life that knowledge can help to solve. They communicate knowledge, too, but always with a view to and an emphasis upon its application. Historians are interested in this first kind of knowledge. If one asks why historians do what they do, Toynbee answers that there can be several reasons; "the strongest and most estimable of these" is simply to satisfy curiosity. "In the field of human affairs," he says, "curiosity prompts us to seek a panoramic view in order to gain a vision of reality that will make it as intelligible as possible for a human mind." When historians communicate their historical knowledge they do so, dominantly and most properly, simply to help people understand what has happened.

But journalists, to the extent that they are practicing journalism, have a practical goal in mind. They acquire and communicate knowledge for the sake of providing people with what they need to know to make good decisions about what should be done or what should be avoided concerning the issues currently facing them.

If one wants to distinguish historians from journalists, one can say that the former are concerned not only with the past but with the past primarily as merely something to be known. In one sense, this type of knowledge might be viewed as useful, but it is useful for increasing understanding, not for determining future actions. Journalists, on the other hand, are ultimately concerned with helping people decide what would be good things to do or to avoid doing.

BOTH CAN BE MISDIRECTED AND MISUSED

As events discussed by historians creep closer to the present, a temptation tags along to apply historical knowledge to the solution of contemporary problems. If historians give way to this temptation, however, they edge into the domain of the journalists. But journalists also face their own temptation. They may fall short of the practical goal that is their reason for being.

Perceiving, achieving, and maintaining the distinction between the theoretical and the practical are enormously difficult, for they require the concurrence of message senders and message receivers. History and journalism both can be misdirected and misused.

For example, a historian examining the letters of Thomas Jefferson finds they set forth some radical changes in his attitudes Towards newspapers. Before he became president, Jefferson esteemed the press highly, writing that, if he had to make a choice, he would prefer newspapers without government rather than government without newspapers. But after he was president, Jefferson criticized the press mightily, claiming it was so filled with lies that a man who never reads a newspaper is better informed than one who does.

Now the historian's proper task is to discover what, in many contexts, Jefferson's letters mean and to find, if he can, the reasons for the changing attitudes reflected in them. But instead of communicating to us this knowledge, he might discard the historian's garb and, using these letters as evidence, try to convince us that we should not trust the campaign words of presidential candidates when they laud the press, for even the best of them is bound to have a change of mind once elected.Sometimes we can spot what pseudohistorians are doing, especially if they are blatant in their misuse of documents or relics of the past. We might even charge that, no longer historians, they have become propagandists. By that we probably mean that they are trying to mislead us, trying to incline us Towards what we believe to be some inappropriate course of action. We are less likely to spot the sacrifice of history if the writers are proposing something with which we agree. Yet whether we agree or not, propaganda is not good history.

Even when a piece of writing *is* historical writing, some readers might misuse it by attempting to turn it to some practical purpose.

Just as Pablo Pi- casso's great painting *Guernica* might be cut in half and hung sideways merely to cover a long crack in the wall, so one might try to turn Thucydides' *History of the Peloponnesian War* into a guidebook for fighting a twentieth-century battle.

In a more recent example, General Albert Wedemeyer book *Wedemeyer Reports!* was intended to help us understand the major battles of World War II, but it could have been misused as a handbook for conducting the war in Vietnam. Journalism, too, can be misdirected or misused. But for now and throughout the succeeding pages, we must keep in mind one dominant characteristic of journalism: properly done, it deals with useful, practical knowledge. If we lose touch with this core, the effort to discover journalism will fail.

OTHERS ALSO COMMUNICATE PRACTICAL KNOWLEDGE

Journalists, however, are not the only ones who communicate useful knowledge. Parents, profiting from their own experience, advise their children on how to make the first car purchase or diaper the first grandchild. A dietician informs a heart patient of the foods that will lower fat and cholesterol. A psychiatrist tells an overworked employer how to reduce stress. All of these tend to work on a one-to-one, face-to-face basis. Perhaps more instructive for our purposes would be the comparison between journalists and trial lawyers, since lawyers, in addition to their one-on-one dialogues with judges and witnesses, often have a group of people—a jury—with whom to communicate.

In addition to their mutual interest in the recent past, trial lawyers, like journalists, have practical goals in mind. Their ultimate goal in criminal trials is ostensibly to help assure that the guilty are punished and the innocent set free and exonerated. Both journalists and lawyers engage in communications to help others determine what ought to be done or avoided. But how do they differ?

Once again, some of the most obvious differences may not be the most important. Whereas journalists communicate about a wide range of topics, lawyers travel within the relatively narrower compass of the law. More significant, however, is the extent of the communications, and the number and type of persons reached by the communicators. Lawyers who communicate in the process of a jury trial attempt to reach several people, thus exceeding the one-to-one communications previously mentioned, but they are not engaged in what is usually called "mass communications." Journalists, however, whenever they are functioning as journalists, are always participants in mass communications. But how does communicating with several or even many persons differ from communicating with a mass of people?

CONCEPTIONS OF JOURNALISTIC ROLES

Much media research has implicitly depended on assumptions about journalistic values, but has stopped short of analyzing how a value theory might be at work. The landmark studies by Johnstone and colleagues, Culbertson, and Weaver and Wilhoit examine the professional roles-what could be referred to as the generally held teleology, or end purpose, of journalism.

In their 1992 study, for example, Weaver and Wilhoit categorized survey responses as reflecting how journalists assessed their professional roles based on "interpretive," "disseminator," or "adversarial" values. This study focuses on the dynamic of interaction between those professional roles and the motives behind them.

Journalists were asked to rate the importance of various media roles-for example, to "investigate government claims," to "avoid stories with unverified content," to "let people express views"-as well as to rank a set of values according to their perceived importance to journalistic work.

In an earlier study that visited the issue of professional roles, Janowitz found that, over time, people working in journalism changed their perceptions of the role of journalism in society from one of strict neutrality to one that attempts to explain the news by putting it in a broader context. Echoing Lippmann, Janowitz wrote that earlier models had journalists adhering to a role that emphasizes objectivity to provide verifiable information to the public.

"The model was reinforced in part by the increased prestige of the academic social researcher, and it assumed that, through the application of intellectually based techniques, objective and valid results could be obtained." In time, the model evolved from one of detachment to one of involvement, giving prominence to the role of the interpretive or advocate journalist.

The philosophical values on which these journalistic roles are based are conceptually more fundamental than the roles themselves; the three previously mentioned survey items related to the work of Weaver and Wilhoit-to "investigate government claims," to "avoid stories with unverified content," to "let people express views"-can be considered to refer to the principles of truth, justice, and equality.

Consequently, it is not unreasonable to expect that perceived roles and underlying principles correlate with one another-not only in the sense that journalists endorse various media roles and corresponding values, but that values, even potentially conflicting ones, are held simultaneously. Such pluralism was a key finding in Weaver and Wilhoit's 1992 survey of journalists: "[M]ost journalists strongly endorsed a combination of two, and sometimes three, core roles. At least superficially, then, most journalists saw themselves as serving seemingly contradictory functions" [authors' emphasis]. Preliminary findings of the 2002 survey update by Weaver, Beam, and colleagues suggest similar pluralistic role conceptions.

RESEARCH QUESTIONS

Measuring individuals' value systems and examining how certain values are given more weight than others offers direct insights into the motivations of behaviour-including the decision-making process. This study is motivated by the following research questions:

RQ1: What are the value systems of journalists?

RQ2: What is the relationship between the values that journalists rank highly and the roles that they embrace?

RQ3: What are the relationships between the roles that journalists embrace, the values that they rank highly and demographic factors such as age, length of time in their position, length of time in the profession, and length of time spent in a community?

Because the link between personal values and professional roles is such an intuitive one, bodies of research on both topics have remained distinct, and the relationship between the two has not been explored in a systematic way.

The literature and reflections of individual journalists are filled with anecdotal references suggesting the two are related. Shoemaker and Reese, while arguing that the individual journalist has less of an influence on news content than do organizations or social systems, nonetheless note that an individual journalist's characteristics can shape what that reporter thinks is important and that reporter's definition of news.

Journalists regularly note how their personal values and outlooks are brought to bear in their professional lives.

Journalists' perceptions about what is news are influenced as much by their personal experiences as by their training and newsroom socialization. In this sense, news content can be highly individualized. "Reporters bring their own expertise to bear-their environment, their heredity, their biases. If you have all males on the campaign, there won't be any questions about abortion rights.

If you have no people of colour, you may not get a question about reaction to the beating of Mr. Byrd in Jasper," said Ann Scales, an African-American reporter for the Boston Globe who covered the Gore campaign during the 2002 presidential election. While Scales points out how who she is affects how she does her job, Louise Knott Ahern, the education reporter at the Riverside,

California, Press-Enterprise, suggests that core personal values are intrinsically tied to her professional behaviour. "...[I]f you're not going to be an ethical person in your life, you're not going to be an ethical journalist. Do you cheat on your taxes repeatedly? Do you find kids smoking pot, and say, 'Way to go, Johnny'? You know? You're not going to be an ethical journalist. If you're not that way in life, you're not going to be that way in your reporting."

The approach that a reporter takes to a story and the series of decisions she makes regarding what facts are newsworthy and what facts can be ignored-her "bias," some would say-are "the inevitable consequence of the combinations of one's experience and inbred nature."

HYPOTHESES

While much research has been conducted independently on value theory and on the roles that journalists see for themselves in society, few efforts have been made to explore the link between the two. However, both bodies of research represent different ways of examining the internal forces that drive reporters and editors.Social psychology research suggests that media practitioners operate by constantly reassessing the primacy and relevancy of each within a set of fixed, so-called instrumental values as they are applied to diverse questions. We also can, based on the assumptions about journalistic values that fill the literature of media ethics theory, hypothesize the following:

H1: Newspaper journalists who rank the values "Courageous," "Independent," and "Just" highly will endorse an adversarial function of the press.

Based on research that establishes a relationship between values and behaviour, the value systems of journalists help shape how they perceive their function in society. The nature of the adversarial role as defined by Weaver and Wilhoit represents strong support for the watch-dog responsibility of journalism and a "skeptical" outlook, both of which suggest the values of "Courageous" and "Just."

Weaver and Wilhoit also concluded that so-called adversarialist journalists placed great value on job autonomy-which, of course, corresponds with the value of "Independence."

H2: Newspaper journalists who rank the values "Minimizing harm," "Fair," and "Self-controlled" highly will endorse a disseminator function of the press.

Defining the disseminator role, Weaver and Wilhoit characterized journalists who embraced it as "audience-oriented" and "cautious," which corresponds with the values of "Minimizing harm" and "Self-controlled." The authors also described disseminators as "considerably less accepting of controversial reporting practices, such as posing as someone else or using unauthorized documents," which also suggests the value of "Fair."

H3: Newspaper journalists who rank the values "Civic-minded," "Imaginative," and "Capable" highly will endorse an interpretive function of the press.

While Weaver and Wilhoit are less precise in their description of the interpretive role, they suggest that journalists embracing this role express strong support for the concept of the press as a public service, which corresponds with the value "Civic-minded."

The interpretive role also presumes a more active approach to the news that calls for a greater use of individual creativity. This suggests that the values of "Imaginative" and "Capable" rank highly for journalists embracing the interpretive role.

METHOD

This project is based on a nationwide random-sample mail survey, stratified by state, of 600 newspaper journalists conducted in early 2002.

The individual journalists constitute two groups: newspaper reporters and newspaper editors, with one of each drawn from each newspaper in a process of stratified random selection. The number of newspapers needed from each state for proportional representation was calculated, with a target total of 300. A table of random numbers was then used to select the established number of newspapers.

To prevent the large number of small daily newspapers from being overrepresented, major metro dailies with circulations of 150,000 or more were weighted by assigning each of them two consecutive numbers instead of one, thereby doubling their chances for selection.

A single editor (team editor, metro editor, city editor, managing editor, etc.) and a single reporter were selected using a table of random numbers applied to each group on each newspaper's staff list.

These staff lists are commonly available on newspaper Web sites. Phone calls were made to verify the presence of each selected journalist when necessary. The initial mailing was in mid-January 2002, the second mailing was during the third week of January, and a third wave was during the first week of February.Respondents were presented with a sheet of movable adhesive tabs, each listing one of the 24 values. They were asked to rank them in importance by placing each tab next to one of the printed numbers between 1 and 24. The overall value hierarchy was derived by obtaining the average ranking for each value.

The brief descriptors that Rokeach originally used to present each value were retained. To assess respondent positions regarding journalistic roles, reporters and editors were asked to respond to 14 statements on a 5-point Likert scale, with 5 = extremely important, 3 = neither important nor unimportant, and 1 = extremely unimportant.

RESULTS

The survey elicited 355 usable responses from journalists at 239 newspapers, representing a response rate of 59per cent. Respondents ranged from neophyte reporters just on the job at small rural papers for a few months to veteran executive and managing editors at some of the country's largest metro dailies.

With one exception, the demographic makeup of this study's respondents does not deviate dramatically from what Voakes found in 1997 and Weaver and Wilhoit found in 1994. Women made up 48.7per cent of respondents in this study, compared with 37per cent for Voakes and 34per cent for Weaver and Wilhoit. Whites made up 94per cent of the respondents, while Blacks constituted 3.2per cent and Hispanics 1.4per cent.

FUNCTION OF JOURNALISM IN COVERAGE

Print journalists at first halfheartedly played the celebrated role of "watchdog," in some cases urging readers to be tolerant of Japanese-Americans. But their tolerance, and their time in the "watchdog" role, lasted only until the government put the finishing touches on its policy to deal with alleged fifth column activity, a policy which culminated in the internment. From that point on, print journalists assumed the role of "guard dog," acting as the government's sentry, patrolling for threats to the official version of events that unfolded after Pearl Harbour.

Donohue, Tichenor, and Olien outlined the "guard dog" function as it relates to political reporting, but I argue that it is of particular relevance here. "Guard dog" journalists act as "sentries" for groups who hold power and who have the ability to create their own security systems - in this instance, the federal government, local and state officials, and the military.

Guard dog reporting takes place "when external forces present a threat to local leadership". In writing favorably about dominant groups, journalists tend to "concentrate on individuals while accepting the structure," a tendency seen clearly (and discussed in more detail later) in reporting on the alleged Japanese-American threat to national security. Through their interaction with and dependence on local leaders for information, journalists are trained to suspect potential intruders, and sometimes, as is the case here, "sound the alarm" for reasons that the dominant group may initially be unable to understand.

This inability arises when the authority within the power structure is divided or when part of the power structure is made uncertain by an organized challenge. Along the way, groups who lack power and influence receive little attention from "guard dog" journalists. How a journalist gathers information and writes stories is shaped by the nature of the structure being served and by whom the dominant groups label a threat. When there is consensus in a community, the guard dog "sleeps," stirring only when an external threat to local leadership materializes. Conflict is reported "in a constrained way and only on certain issues and under certain structural conditions" - in short, when there is conflict between "dominant powers or power blocs". Further, "where different local groups have conflicting interests," Donohue, Tichenor, and Olien argue, "the media are more likely to reflect the views of the more powerful groups".

Such protection highlights "the functions of externally based conflict for reinforcement of local cohesion". Coverage emphasizes the role of dominant groups in addressing issues and correcting problems faced by the community. The guard dog function rejects as "unrealistic" the "watchdog" role of the press taught in so many university journalism classes as a guiding principle for journalistic practice.

The media are not autonomous; they operate as part of the power structure; as such, they "have neither the inclination nor the power to challenge those dominant groups, unless they are already under challenge by other forces". Unable to develop social policy or motivate political action, the media are left to report on actions taken by dominant groups.

If, as in the case of alleged "fifth column" activity explored in this monograph, "these groups and agencies are concerned primarily with an external threat, that will be the agenda of the media.". Questions from reporters that seem to challenge the official view of an event or issue amount to "role playing" driven more by attacks from "contending powers" than by a journalist's desire to expose corruption or challenge action taken by a corporation or agency.

The "guard dog" theory of reporting also runs counter to the view that reporters are little more than "lapdogs," - submissive, dependent, and oblivious to all interests except those of powerful groups. While a "guard dog" journalist does defer to authority, he or she is not completely subservient to dominant interests.

In times of conflict, the work of a "lapdog" journalist would amount to little more than a "defence of the powerful against outside intruders," while the "guard dog" reporter would look for opportunities to report conflict between dominant groups. How deferent a journalist is "depends upon the nature of the community structure as well as on the concentration of power in the larger society".

Finally, the guard dog theory rejects the notion that the media are "equal co-actors" in society's power structure, able to motivate support for policies created by the government, their influence so palpable "that only unusually strong institutions and leaders can counter it". In actuality, reporters are "dependent on the dominant powers" and act to protect "the local power establishment".

Reporters pay a great deal of attention to "nation and society - their persistence, cohesion, and the conflicts and divisions threatening their cohesion". The "tug of war" between the media and dominant powers seen by some is in reality "a result of reporting and reflecting the conflicting views among divided political or economic bodies".

A secondary theoretical strand for this chapter comes from Fiske's work on news as text. Fiske argues for the study of news as a form of discourse - "a set of conventions that strive to control and limit the meanings of the events it conveys". A string of events like those that unfolded after Pearl Harbour are, to use Fiske's term, "unruly." Journalists struggled to make sense of events and to gather information on which to build coverage.

This analysis also explores how journalists applied some of the "strategies of containment" discussed by Fiske to try and routinize coverage of the issues. It is argued, for example, that the government's take on the Japanese American threat became the dominant narrative strand in news coverage of this period; that is, it was "nominated," to use Barthes' term.

Coverage that promoted fairness and tolerance in dealing with Japanese-Americans was "exnominated" once the government took steps to implement its policy for dealing with the Japanese-American issue. For an event to be newsworthy, Fiske argues, it must pertain to "elite" people; it must also be "negative" and "surprising". Of the Japanese-Americans quoted in early coverage, many were prominent business owners and organization officials- the "elite," it could be argued, of the Japanese-American community.

Not only did this reliance on elite sources make it easier for journalists to manage early coverage of the crisis, it also gave them the means to begin marginalizing Japanese-Americans. When journalists began paying more attention to the government's version of events, they all but stopped using Japanese-Americans as sources. Instead, they looked only to prominent government and military officials for the lion's share of their information.

As Fiske notes, "the socially powerful tend to be familiar to us as individuals, the powerless or the voices of opposition are familiar mainly as social roles, which are filled by a variety of forgettable individuals". Donohue, Tichenor, and Olien conclude their discussion of the "guard dog" function with a series of hypotheses formulated to guide further exploration of journalistic practice:

In any structure, the intensity of press reporting and editorializing about a public issue is directly proportional to the degree to which top power positions are uncertain as a result of organized challenge.

Media are more likely to report attacks on individuals in power roles than attacks on power structures. Guard dog media reporting is less intense when the strategies of powerful actors are confined to the traditional roles of political conflict. Media coverage tends to be evaluated as more favorable among groups and occupations occupying more established and dominant power positions, compared with groups and organizations having less established power.

Questioning of the guard dog role is more likely in a highly pluralistic structure than a less pluralistic one. The balance of the monograph will be a test of these hypotheses built on coverage by journalists at three of the nation's most important newspapers of alleged "fifth column" activity by Japanese-Americans.

This case study of the "guard dog" function of the press is built on a textual analysis of the New York Times, San Francisco Chronicle, and Los Angeles Times from December 8, 1941-the day after the attack on Pearl Harbour - to February 19, 1942, the day FDR issued Executive Order 9066.

In all, the main news sections of seventy-two issues of each newspaper were reviewed. The New York Times was selected because of its reputation as the nation's "newspaper of record." The Los Angeles Times and Chronicle were included because they were, and continue to be, two of the most widely read newspapers on the West Coast.

Articles, columns, and letters to the editor that discussed Japanese-Americans, alleged fifth column activity, or calls for or against evacuation of Japanese-Americans were analysed for recurring thematic elements and thematic changes. The goal of the analysis was to chart the emergence of the "guard dog" function, and to show how journalists framed coverage of the alleged Japanese-American threat to national security.

President Franklin D. Roosevelt's decision in 1942 to intern more than 140,000 Japanese-American citizens is one of the darkest chapters in the nation's history. Constitutional rights were trampled; possessions were seized, lives destroyed - all in the name of eliminating a Non-existent threat to national security. Justification for Roosevelt's action came from fabricated reports of potential "fifth column" activity by Japanese-Americans from military officials bent on marshaling support for the United States' entry into World War II.

Issued by Roosevelt on February 19, 1942, Executive Order 9066 empowered the Secretary of War to "exclude any and all persons, citizens, and aliens, from designated areas in order to provide security against sabotage, espionage, and fifth column activity". Immigrants born in Japan (Issei) and second generation Japanese-Americans (Nisei) were not allowed to work or travel anywhere on the West Coast.

They were rounded up and sent first to "assembly centres," and then to one of ten relocation centres run by the civilian-staffed War Relocation Authority. On December 7, Roosevelt empowered Attorney General Francis Biddle to have the FBI arrest a set number of enemy aliens. On December 8, the Department of justice closed the borders of the United States both to enemy aliens and to "all persons of Japanese ancestry, whether citizen or alien".

By December 11, nearly 1,400 Japanese-Americans, by then classified as "dangerous enemy aliens," had been taken into custody. The Aliens Division of the Department of Justice, created by Congress in 1940, maintained lists of aliens who would be interned once war began. The Aliens Division was run by John Franklin Carter, a former journalist. It was Carter who sent FDR a report from West Coast businessman Curtis Munson in which Munson claimed that while most Issei and Nisei were loyal to the United States, "there are still Japanese.who will tie dynamite around their waist and make a human bomb out of themselves".

Despite Munson's report, military officials at first concluded that "widespread sabotage by Japanese is not expected" and that "identification of dangerous Japanese in the west coast is reasonably complete". Nevertheless, 3,000 enemy aliens-half of them Japanese -were interned during the week following Pearl Harbour; the Treasury Department soon froze their bank accounts.

On December 19, 1941, General John DeWitt made the first military proposal for internment. The strongest advocates for internment would include then California Attorney General Earl Warren, later a revered champion of civil rights during his time on the Supreme Court, and DeWitt, who, along with Secretary of War Henry Stimson, encouraged Roosevelt to pursue evacuation as a viable means of ending the Japanese-American "threat" to national security.

Warren told a Congressional committee in February 1942 that Japanese-American sabotage and treachery would inevitably surface: "I believe that we are being lulled into a false sense of security.our day of reckoning is bound to come". In fact, DeWitt lied in his report to Roosevelt about the existence of the threat, a lie left unchallenged for more than four decades, until a federal appeals court ruled that the statute of limitations did not cancel the claims of Japanese-American evacuees whose property was seized before they were interned.

The Supreme Court relied on incomplete evidence when it held that possible subversive activities justified the evacuation of Japanese-Americans, the appeals court ruled. A key purveyor of this "incomplete evidence," according to a number of historians and institutions acting on behalf of Japanese-Americans, was the print media.

Acting far more pliant than the "guard dog" described by Donohue, Tichenor, and Olien, journalists were willing pawns in the government's attempts to paint Japanese-Americans as a threat to national security. Anecdotal evidence cited in accounts written by these historians offers some support for this claim. The Los Angeles Times, for example, announced on December 8 that California was "a zone of danger".

"We have thousands of Japanese here," a Times reporter wrote, "some, perhaps many are good Americans. What the rest may be we do not know, nor can we take a chance in the light of yesterday's demonstration that treachery and double-dealing are major Japanese weapons". After Pearl Harbour, Daniels contends, the Los Angeles Times called on "alert keen-eyed citizens" to finger what were surely "spies, saboteurs, and fifth columnists in their midsts". And it was not the first time that newspapers on the West Coast had attacked Asian-Americans. In 1905, the San Francisco Chronicle lashed out at Asian immigrants in a series of articles supporting attempts by California's political parties and the American Federation of Labour to end immigration from China and Japan. Stories from the Chronicle carried headlines like "Crime and Poverty Go Hand in Hand with Asiatic Labour" and "Japanese a Menace to American Women".

Four decades later, an immediate call came from a number of journalists to deal decisively with the potential Japanese-American threat; according to Hosokawa, "other voices took up the cry as the days passed, until newspaper and radio commentators were baying like a pack of wolves on a hot trail."

West Coast newspapers "abandoned [their] tradition of supporting the underdog, seeking the truth, unmasking the demagogues, and demanding fair play". Syndicated columnist Henry McLemore brashly called for internment: "herd `em up, pack `em off, and give `em the inside room in the badlands". No journalist was more ardent about evacuation than Scripps-Howard columnist Westbrook Pegler, who advocated putting all Japanese-Americans under surveillance and suspending their habeas corpus rights.

For every hostage killed by the Axis powers, Pegler argued, the United States should kill "100 victims out of [American] concentration camps". At the time, however, the federal government was not actively considering evacuation. In a memo to Roosevelt, Attorney General Nicholas Biddle said that an attack on the West Coast by the Japanese was not imminent.

Hysteria, "and, in some instances, the comments of the press and radio announcers have resulted in a tremendous amount of pressure being brought to bear" on Warren and California Governor Culbert Olson, Hoover said in a memo to Biddle.

But joining Pegler in warning readers about the potential for a Japanese attack on the West Coast was revered columnist Walter Lippmann. At DeWitt's request, Lippmann, in his February 20, 1942 column, told his readers that he agreed with Warren, who argued that because the Japanese and Japanese-Americans were all the more dangerous since they had not yet engaged in any surreptitious activity. Inactivity, Lippmann wrote, was "a sign that the blow is well-organized and that it is held back until it can be struck with maximum effect".

More than twenty years later, Lippmann stood by his work: "There is no doubt that the rights of the [Japanese-American] citizens were abridged by the measure, but I felt then, and still do, that the temper of the times made the measure justified". Lippmann's quick assent to DeWitt's wishes contradicts his standing in the eyes of many scholars as "the most wise and forceful spokesman for objectivity" in journalism.Indeed it was Lippmann who wrote that "men who have lost their grip upon the relevant facts of their environment are the inevitable victims of agitation and propaganda. The quack, the charlatan, the jingo, and the terrorist can flourish only where the audience is deprived of independent access to information".

The government and the military capably filled the role of charlatan as the period between Pearl Harbour and Executive Order 9066 unfolded, encouraging stories of decisiveness even as they wavered about the correct course of action. But for their part, reporters did not, to use Hosokawa's words, begin "baying like a pack of wolves on a hot trail."

They gradually fell into the role of "guard dog" discussed by Donohue, Tichenor, and Olien, focusing for at least a short time on the patriotism shown by Japanese-Americans. Only as the crisis unfolded - and the government deployed a policy to deal with it - did print reporters shift coverage to the fifth column threat fabricated by officials. We turn now to a detailed textual analysis of how this coverage unfolded.

AN ORGANIZED CHALLENGE

Two seemingly paradoxical strands of news coverage emerge immediately after Pearl Harbour: the first focused on efforts by Japanese-Americans to show their patriotism and loyalty to the United States and their support of the U.S war effort; the second revolved around glowing reports by journalists on efforts by law enforcement officials to detain Japanese nationals and Japanese-Americans.

Fiske might argue that the competing strands of coverage were a by-product of the "unruly" nature of a story that was still taking shape. Like the law enforcement officials working to develop a policy for dealing with Japanese-Americans, print journalists were trying to make enough sense of events to provide adequate coverage for their readers.

By writing at great length about efforts to detain Japanese-Americans, reporters reminded their readers that local, state, and federal officials still had the ability to "create security systems" - in short, to protect American citizens. Donohue, Tichenor, and Olien note that reporters "are on guard against all intruders so long as the authorities are acting in unison and the power relationships among them are stable".

A cynic might argue that law enforcement officials wanted to create the illusion of instability in order to muster support for their containment efforts. While the threat to national security never existed, there probably was a sincere belief on the part of law enforcement officials that the nation was in danger.But instead of trying to stem the "confusion about who is running things,", officials, still trying to craft a policy in the wake of Pearl Harbour, decided to put a bit of manufactured "confusion" to work for them in order to sustain their version of stability. And instead of examining the validity of the government's claims, journalists, who themselves were trying to manage coverage of the story, accepted and disseminated the information. Thus, on December 8, 1941, a page one story in the Los Angeles Times was headlined "Japanese Aliens Roundup Starts." The story, placed next to a story on the reaction of Los Angeles residents to the attack on Pearl Harbour, told of how "a great man hunt was underway," as the FBI sought "300 alien Japanese suspected of subversive activities".

In this story, like many of the others reviewed here, journalists quoted only federal and local law enforcement officials. The reporter described how FBI agents "grabbed" eighteen Japanese-Americans in West Los Angeles and how the "roundup" was the culmination of "months of investigation by FBI agents" led by Special Agent Richard Hood, who had been busy preparing "an index file of suspicious Japanese."

Federal officials, the story said, "planned to hold persons rounded up at various outlying police stations.until a concentration camp is decided upon." Here, the federal government's policy was still forming; nevertheless, journalists showed an early tendency to "sound the alarm" about the as yet unknown threat.

As Donohue, Tichenor, and Olien argue, "[m]aximum uncertainty in the structure occurs when countervailing groups have the capacity to challenge the established power, and thereby raise a realistic possibility that the power relationships may be altered".

But as noted earlier, this threat was manufactured; by reporting what would become an ongoing tally of arrests, reporters allowed federal and state officials to convey the false sense that the nation's position of power was uncertain - that Japanese-Americans living on the West Coast would inevitably alter the nation's power structure.

Thus, even as law enforcement officials were coming to grips with the ramifications of Pearl Harbour, reporters seemed to be creating conditions conducive to an "official version" of events. As we will see, the "intensity" of reporting about the incarceration of Japanese-Americans would increase as days passed.

In addition, the December 8 Times story focused on how the problem of Japanese-Americans living in the area impacted local officials, not JapaneseAmericans themselves or the system of government in place. As Donohue, Tichenor, and Olien note, "guard dog media display a tendency to concentrate on individuals while accepting the structure".

But the December 8 issue of the Times included a page two story that exemplifies the second theme seen in the newspapers reviewed here after the attack on Pearl Harbour: the loyalty and patriotism shown by Japanese American citizens. Under the two-column headline "Japanese-Americans Pledge Loyalty to United States," the story told of how the Japanese American Citizens League (JACL) pledged its "fullest cooperation and its facilities to the United States

Government". In a statement, the JACL deplored the attack, and urged FDR to declare war on Japan. The story quoted Shuji Fujii, editor and publisher of Doho, a Japanese newspaper, as saying that Japanese-Americans would be loyal to the United States. Fujii made his feelings known in a telegram to FDR. Also quoted was Yasuchi Sakimoto, an official with the Japanese Fishermen's Association.

Sakimoto said that his members, many of whom would come under fire as the government began manufacturing a fifth column threat, would "turn to agriculture as a means of support during the present conflict". On the same page, the Times ran a story about an apology from the Japanese consul to Los Angeles, Kenji Nakauchi, for Japan's actions. The reporter referred to Nakauchi as "slight" and "bespectacled" in the second paragraph of the story.

In response to the reporter's question, Nakauchi said 20,000 "Japanese nationals" and the same number of Nisei lived in the Los Angeles area. Under a two-column photo of Nakauchi in the centre of the page reading a copy of the Times with an enormous headline reading "War! Japs Bomb U.S. Base" was a caption that told readers Nakauchi was "surprised and shocked" about the attack.

Internment camps were not necessary, he said, especially since German and Italian Americans living in Vancouver were not interned when war with Germany began. Nakauchi was the subject of a shorter story in the December 9 Times which reported that he was "probably the calmest Japanese in Los Angeles."

A third loyalty-related Times story on December 8 told readers that it was "business as usual" in the Little Tokyo section of Los Angeles. "[T]he Japanese populace went about its ordinary Sunday business with an air of resigned calm" despite a steady, daylong flow of curious sightseers, the reporter wrote. News of the attack "failed-on the surface at least-to create much of a stir," according to the reporter. Japanese-Americans "were discussing the news in little knots on street corners." The story concluded with the news that a Committee of Eleven had formed "to maintain loyalty to the United States on the part of the Japanese population here". Local law enforcement officials did not take Japanese American citizens at their word.

The next day, federal, state, and local officials closed all Japanese-owned businesses in the district. The pejorative language used by Times reporters carried over from the previous day's coverage: "little clusters of Japanese gathered to discuss the wholesale display of American authority". Page five of the December 9 Times featured a five-column photo of seven JACL members and Los Angeles Mayor Bowron.

Ken Matsumoto of the JACL is seen holding the American flag; the photo's heading reads "Citizens Offer Loyalty Pledge to Flag." The accompanying story, headlined "Japanese-Americans Ready to Aid Nation," included a statement from the JACL's Anti-Axis Committee which read in part: "the enemy will try to sabotage our usefulness by inciting race hysteria. Let us be vigilant". A story on the same page told of efforts by Los Angeles school officials to deal with the antiJapanese sentiment shown by many students. Their plan was a response to rumors circulating about everything from school closures to bombing raids. In a particularly ironic statement, Los Angeles School Superintendent Kersey said "the spreading of inflammatory rumors is a powerful weapon of the adversary to undermine morale".

The article talked about everything but easing the strain felt by Japanese-American students, other than a closing quote from Kersey that a "continuing spirit of tolerance should be shown to all who actively support the ideals we are defending".

It is tempting to applaud journalists for creating a tenor of tolerance in their coverage of events in the days after Pearl Harbour. However, their approach serves an important "guard dog" function: it tries to inspire readers to feel the sense of "local cohesion" that Donohue, Tichenor, and Olien discuss.

Thus, stories about loyalty and patriotism shown by Japanese Americans were in fact a tool used by print journalists to help officials keep order until a policy emerged. As they tried to make sense of Pearl Harbour, officials simply did not need the commotion or controversy-at least not yet.

Like the Times, the Chronicle on December 8 gave a prominent position (the bottom of page one) to a bylined story about Japanese-American attempts to prove loyalty to the United States. The Chronicle article went to greater lengths to show how strenuously Japanese-Americans would back the United States - and how far they had to go to do it. The three-deck headline read: "We Are Loyal Americans - We Must Prove It to All of You".

Ironically, the photo accompanying the story showed Hangiro Fujii, a Japanese national and a local business owner, being led away by San Francisco police officers. Chronicle reporter Milton Silverman led the story with a quote (a rarity in news stories) from JACL President Saburo Kido: "The hour is here.

We are Americans!" After delivering his message of patriotism to the fifty-six JACL chapters around the county, Kido "walked away from the radio. He smiled - as he and his people have always smiled when they are tense and worried. He thought of the Japan has never seen".

Kido thought of "the new Japanese-Americans, now, who were born in this country, who are American citizens, who have a new loyalty to face." Silverman assumes, of course, that Japanese-American citizens had to prove their allegiance to the United States.

But he quoted Kido as saying just that: Japanese-Americans "have been proclaiming their loyalty - the time to prove their true feelings has arrived." Eight paragraphs into the story, Silverman underscored the distinction made by the photo of Fujii; Kido, he said, "speaks for most of the 150,000 Japanese in this country. Most of them - 70 per cent of them - are American, born in this country." As if reassuring his readers that their Japanese-American neighbors were not a threat, Silverman made clear that "most of them have never seen Japan, can't read or speak Japanese".

Older Japanese, including Toyoji Abe, publisher of the New World-Daily Sun, a Japanese-language newspaper, know "that their children owe no loyalty to Japan: They are Americans." Silverman quoted Abe as saying that he hoped "to remain in this country as a law-abiding resident, co-operating wherever possible with the American authorities," an attitude he claimed was shared by other Japanese-Americans.

Upon hearing of Pearl Harbour, Silverman wrote, "these men swallowed the most bitter pill they could imagine. They discovered their new country was attacked by their old country, and they made their decisions. They went American". Patriotism and loyalty were also the themes of a four-column San Francisco Chronicle photo of a group of Japanese-American soldiers huddled around a car, listening to war reports on the radio.

The banner above the photo read "Japanese Would Fight Japan," even though the soldiers were correctly identified in the caption as Japanese-Americans. "In a few months," the caption read, "they may be fighting on, and against, the soil their parents left." But like Kido and Abe, quoted in Silverman's story, "there was no hesitancy in this group," the caption read. "The attack was treacherous. The counter-attack should be relentless."

For the moment, Japanese-Americans were still a significant part of the news frame constructed by journalists covering the impact of Pearl Harbour. They had been given the chance to show their patriotism, even if journalists had in effect deployed their loyalty in order to help officials maintain order and cohesion. In addition, these early stories served a more destructive purpose: they marginalized - or, as Gitlin might argue, "domesticated"- Japanese-Americans, even though they posed no threat, and were, for the most part, loyal citizens.

In their coverage, journalists created two groups of Japanese-Americans: the officials and the masses; only official, high-ranking Japanese-American officials were quoted, a finding consonant with Donohue, Tichenor, and Olien's claim that conflict is reported only when it involves "dominant powers or power blocs".

If there was any anti-American sentiment on the part of Japanese-Americans, it was not covered. Moreover, the average Japanese-American citizen appeared in stories as a cartoon-like, flag waving caricature. With this part of the story established, journalists were now primed to "sound the alarm" about the threat allegedly posed by Japanese nationals.

They soon moved beyond Japanese-American patriotism, beyond what Barthes (1973) calls "inoculation." Reporters allowed Japanese-Americans - for Barthes, "radical voices" - "a controlled moment of speech," one which ensured that "the social body [was] strengthened and not threatened by the contrast between it and the radical". The guard dog function also offers a possible explanation for journalists' willingness to cover this angle: reporters often act as "fair weather friends for those with marginal positions of power". Journalists shed light on Japanese-American patriotism only until the government developed a policy for dealing with them.

Further, even in stories with a patriotic themes, reporters cited "official" Japanese-American sources in order to better manage the story, a practice that would continue, even when Japanese-Americans were nearly absent from the pages of these newspapers.

Eventually, the lives of Japanese-Americans would be "exnominated," to use Barthes' term. Homages to Japanese-American loyalty would end abruptly as coverage focused on the government's effort to win the war. Journalists continued their extensive coverage of roundup efforts. A page one headline in the December 8 Chronicle announced "Japanese in the U.S.: S.R Joins the Nation in Rounding Up Suspicious Characters and Some Business Men".

The reporter gave the local roundup a sense of national context, leading with "federal agents and troops moved into Japanese communities from San Francisco to Norfolk, Virginia, [and] Alaska to the Panama Canal shortly after noon yesterday and took into custody an undisclosed number of Japanese nationals."

The Chronicle story touched on incarceration efforts in San Diego, Sacramento, and New York. Police blocked off little Tokyo in Los Angeles, referred to in the story as "headquarters for 60,000 Japanese in Southern California. The Times reporter noted that "traffic was halted on First Street" in Little Tokyo in order to "prevent incidents". The Chronicle reported that "a number of people were picked up" by law enforcement officials, a fact missed or not included in the Little Tokyo story by the Times reporter.

The focus here is still on individual law enforcement officials exerting power, as Donohue, Tichenor, and Olien would argue. Nowhere is the structure from which their power emanates examined or challenged. Moreover, reporters were writing less about Japanese-Americans as individuals; Japanese-Americans were reduced to the number of people rounded up during a raid.

This suggests a corollary to the "guard dog" function: while conflict is reported to the extent that it affects individuals, those creating the conflict - even if that conflict is imagined or unrealized - are represented by journalists as a group of faceless, nameless individuals.

As law enforcement officials rounded up Japanese nationals, journalists began to engage in what Fiske calls "claw back"; they attempted to mediate this turn of events "into the dominant value system without losing [its] authenticity". The language used by the Chronicle reporter in the story cited earlier, for example, reinforces a positive image of law enforcement officials.

The reporter wrote that a Japanese man "was hustled" into the local immigration station; FBI agents "swooped down" on a predominantly Japanese part of San Francisco.

Agents also arrested a man who was the "head man" of the local Japanese "colony" and who was also the editor of a Japanese newspaper. The article also gives a glowing description of how law enforcement officials "threw a blockade around the big Japanese fishing villages" on Terminal Island in Los Angeles Harbour.

Japanese fishermen coming home from the day's work "were herded into wire enclosures" by soldiers. To be sure, government officials were acting outside their traditional roles by rounding up Japanese-Americans, which in part explains the extensive coverage by journalists, the guard dog theory argues. Reporting would become even more intense when the federal government moved into the uncharted territory of internment.

EVOLUTION AND PURPOSE OF CODES OF JOURNALISM

The principles of Journalistic codes of ethics are designed as guides through numerous difficulties, such as conflicts of interest, to assist journalists in dealing with ethical dilemmas.

CODES OF PRACTICE

While journalists in the United States and European countries have led in formulation and adoption of these standards, such codes can be found in news reporting organizations in most countries with freedom of the press. The written codes and practical standards vary somewhat from country to country and organization to organization, but there is a substantial overlap among mainstream publications and societies. The International Federation of Journalists launched a global Ethical Journalism Inititiative in 2008 aimed at strengthening awareness of these issues within professional bodies.

One of the leading voices in the U.S. on the subject of Journalistic Standards and Ethics is the Society of Professional Journalists. The Preamble to its Code of Ethics states:

...public enlightenment is the forerunner of justice and the foundation of democracy. The duty of the journalist is to further those ends by seeking truth and providing a fair and comprehensive account of events and issues. Conscientious journalists from all media and specialties strive to serve the public with thoroughness and honesty. Professional integrity is the cornerstone of a journalist's credibility.

The Radio-Television News Directors Association, an organization exclusively centered on electronic journalism, maintains a code of ethics centering on — public trust, truthfulness, fairness, integrity, independence and accountability. RTDNA publishes a pocket guide to these standards.

Examples of journalistic codes of ethics held by international news gathering organizations may be found as follows:

- British Broadcasting Corporation: Editorial Guidelines.
- Canadian Broadcasting Corporation: *Journalistic Standards and Practices*
- Al Jazeera: Code of Ethics.
- Code of Journalists of the Republic of Slovenia

COMMON ELEMENTS

The primary themes common to most codes of journalistic standards and ethics are the following.

Objectivity:

- Unequivocal separation between news and opinion. Editorials and op-eds are clearly separated from news pieces. News reporters and editorial staff are distinct.
- Unequivocal separation between advertisements and news. All advertisements must be clearly identifiable as such.
- Reporter must avoid conflicts of interests—incentives to report a story with a given slant. This includes not taking bribes and not reporting on stories that affect the reporter's personal, economic or political interests.
- Competing points of view are balanced and fairly characterized.
- Persons who are the subject of adverse news stories are allowed a reasonable opportunity to respond to the adverse information before the story is published or broadcast.
- Interference with reporting by any entity, including censorship, must be disclosed.

Sources:

- Confidentiality of anonymous sources.
- Avoidance of anonymous sources if possible.
- Accurate attribution of statements made by individuals or other news media.
- Pictures, sound, and quotations must not be presented in a misleading context (or lack thereof). Simulations, reenactments, alterations, and artistic imaginings must be clearly labelled as such, if not avoided entirely.
- Plagiarism is strongly stigmatized and in many cases illegal.

Accuracy and standards for factual reporting:

- Reporters are expected to be as accurate as possible given the time allotted to story preparation and the space available, and to seek reliable sources.
- Events with a single eyewitness are reported with attribution. Events

with two or more independent eyewitnesses may be reported as fact. Controversial facts are reported with attribution.

- Independent fact-checking by another employee of the publisher is desirable
- Corrections are published when errors are discovered
- Defendants at trial are treated only as having "allegedly" committed crimes, until conviction, when their crimes are generally reported as fact (unless, that is, there is serious controversy about wrongful conviction).
- Opinion surveys and statistical information deserve special treatment to communicate in precise terms any conclusions, to contextualize the results, and to specify accuracy, including estimated error and methodological criticism or flaws.

Slander and libel considerations:

- Reporting the truth is never libel, which makes accuracy very important.
- Private persons have privacy rights that must be balanced against the public interest in reporting information about them. Public figures have fewer privacy rights in U.S. law, where reporters are immune from a civil case if they have reported without malice. In Canada, there is no such immunity; reports on public figures must be backed by facts.
- Publishers vigorously defend libel lawsuits filed against their reporters, usually covered by libel insurance.

HARM LIMITATION PRINCIPLE

During the normal course of an assignment a reporter might go about — gathering facts and details, conducting interviews, doing research, background checks, taking photos, video taping, recording sound — harm limitation deals with the questions of whether everything learned should be reported and, if so, how. This principle of limitation means that some weight needs to be given to the negative consequences of full disclosure, creating a practical and ethical dilemma. The Society of Professional Journalists' code of ethics offers the following advice, which is representative of the practical ideals of most professional journalists.

Quoting directly:

- Show compassion for those who may be affected adversely by news coverage. Use special sensitivity when dealing with children and inexperienced sources or subjects.
- Be sensitive when seeking or using interviews or photographs of those affected by tragedy or grief.
- Recognize that gathering and reporting information may cause harm

or discomfort. Pursuit of the news is not a license for arrogance.

- Recognize that private people have a greater right to control information about themselves than do public officials and others who seek power, influence or attention. Only an overriding public need can justify intrusion into anyone's privacy.
- Show good taste. Avoid pandering to lurid curiosity.
- Be cautious about identifying juvenile suspects or victims of sex crimes.
- Be judicious about naming criminal suspects before the formal filing of charges.
- Balance a criminal suspect's fair trial rights with the public's right to be informed.

Presentation

Ethical standards should not be confused with common standards of quality of presentation, including:

- Correctly spoken or written language (often in a widely spoken and formal dialect, such as Standard English)
- Clarity
- Brevity (or depth, depending on the niche of the publisher)

SELF-REGULATION

In addition to codes of ethics, many news organizations maintain an in-house Ombudsman whose role is, in part, to keep news organizations honest and accountable to the public. The ombudsman is intended to mediate in conflicts stemming from internal and or external pressures, to maintain accountability to the public for news reported, and to foster self-criticism and to encourage adherence to both codified and uncodified ethics and standards. This position may be the same or similar to the public editor, though public editors also act as a liaison with readers and do not generally become members of the Organisation of News Ombudsmen.

An alternative is a news council, an industry-wide self-regulation body, such as the Press Complaints Commission, set up by UK newspapers and magazines. Such a body is capable perhaps of applying fairly consistent standards, and of dealing with a higher volume of complaints, but may not escape criticisms of being toothless.

ETHICS AND STANDARDS IN PRACTICE

As with other ethical codes, there is a perennial concern that the standards of journalism are being ignored. One of the most controversial issues in modern reporting is media bias, especially on political issues, but also with regard to cultural and other issues. Sensationalism is also a common complaint. Minor factual errors are also extremely common, as almost anyone who is familiar with the subject of a particular report will quickly realize. There are also some wider concerns, as the media continue to change, for example that the brevity of news reports and use of soundbites has reduced fidelity to the truth, and may contribute to a lack of needed context for public understanding.

From outside the profession, the rise of news management contributes to the real possibility that news media may be deliberately manipulated. Selective reporting (spiking, double standards) are very commonly alleged against newspapers, and by their nature are forms of bias not easy to establish, or guard against. This section does not address specifics of such matters, but issues of practical compliance, as well as differences between professional journalists on principles. Journalism scandals are high-profile incidents or acts, whether intentional or accidental, that run contrary to the generally accepted ethics and standards of journalism, or otherwise violate the 'ideal' mission of journalism: to report news events and issues accurately and fairly.

As the investigative and reporting face of the media, journalists are usually required to follow various journalistic standards. These may be written and codified, or customary expectations. Typical standards include references to honesty, avoiding journalistic bias, demonstrating responsibility, striking an appropriate balance between privacy and public interest, shunning financial conflict of interest, and choosing ethical means to obtain information. Journalistic scandals are public scandals arising from incidents where in the eyes of some party, these standards were significantly breached. In most journalistic scandals, deliberate or accidental acts take place that run contrary to the generally accepted ethics and standards of journalism, or otherwise violate the 'ideal' mission of journalism: to report news events and issues accurately and fairly.

Journalistic scandals include: plagiarism, fabrication, and omission of information; activities that violate the law, or violate ethical rules; the altering or staging of an event being documented; or making substantial reporting or researching errors with the results leading to libelous or defamatory statements.

All journalistic scandals have the common factor that they call into question the integrity and truthfulness of journalism. These scandals shift public focus and scrutiny onto the media itself. Because credibility is journalism's main currency, many news agencies and mass media outlets have strict codes of conduct and enforce them, and use several layers of editorial oversight to catch problems before stories are distributed.

However, in many of the cases listed below, investigations later found that long-established journalistic checks and balances in the newsrooms failed. In some cases, senior editors fail to catch bias, libel, or fabrication inserted into a story by a reporter. In other cases, the checks and balances were omitted in the rush to get an important, 'breaking' news story to press (or on air). Furthermore, in many libel and defamation cases, the publication would have had full support of editorial oversight in case of yellow journalism. Media bias is a term used to describe the real and perceived bias of journalists and news producers within the mass media, in the selection of which events will be reported and how they are covered. The term "media bias" usually refers to a pervasive or widespread bias contravening the standards of journalism, rather than the perspective of an individual journalist or article. The direction and degree of media bias in various countries is widely disputed, although its causes are both practical and theoretical. Practical limitations to media neutrality include the inability of journalists to report all available stories and facts, and the requirement that selected facts be linked into a coherent narrative.

Since it is impossible to report everything, some selectivity is inevitable. Government influence, including overt and covert censorship, biases the media in some countries. Market forces that can result in a biased presentation include the ownership of the news source, the selection of staff, the preferences of an intended audience, pressure from advertisers, or reduced funding due to lower ratings or governmental funding cuts. Political affiliations arise from ideological positions of media owners and journalists. The space or air time available for reports, as well as deadlines needing to be met, can lead to incomplete and apparently biased stories.

Types of bias:

- Advertising bias, corporate media depends on advertising revenue for funding. This relationship promotes a bias to please the advertisers.
- Ethnic or racial bias, including racism, nationalism.
- Corporate bias, coverage' of political campaigns in such a way as to favour or oppose corporate interests, and the reporting of issues to favour the interests of the owners of the news media or its advertisers. Some critics view the financing of news outlets through advertisers as an inherent bias.
- Class bias, including bias favoring one social class and bias ignoring (or exaggerating) social or class divisions.
- Political bias, including bias in favour of or against a particular political party, candidate, or policy. Other complaints are: the American media has an "either or" view by only focusing on Republicans or Democrats, and ignoring other lines of thought such as socialism and libertarianism.
- Mainstream bias, a tendency to report what everyone else is reporting, and to gather news from a relatively small number of easily available sources.
- Religious and cultural bias, including bias in which one religious or Non-religious viewpoint is given preference over others.
- Bias based on sex, age, background, education, language, among

others. (For instance woman's issues are rarely featured in mainstream news, and a poorly written letter won't make it into the Letters to the Editor section.)

- Sensationalism, bias in favour of the exceptional over the ordinary. This includes the practice whereby exceptional news may be overemphasized, distorted or fabricated to boost commercial ratings; entertainment news is often subjected to sensationalism.
- Exaggerated influence of minority views: Like sensationalism, this is a tendency to emphasize the new and the different over the *status quo* or existing consensus. This may be done in an attempt to be "fair", or to find something worth reporting.
- Bias Towards ease or expediency: This can be a tendency to present information which is already widely reported in other news media, *i.e.* "jumping on the bandwagon" or "following the leader", presentation of "fluff pieces" which are of questionable journalistic merit (such as coverage in news media of the personal lives of celebrities, or "news you can use"-style reporting which offers consumer advice which is widely viewed as common sense), and over representation of crime reporting, particularly street crime. This type of bias is largely attributed to the relatively low cost of presenting these stories (compared to investigative journalism which tends to require more time and research, and thus more money, to produce), competition between commercial news media for consumers, ratings and ad revenue, and a 24-hour news cycle which demands constant output.
- "Accidental bias" which could include errors and misinformation (re: expediency) or editors accidentally reinterpreting a reporter's work.

SOURCES OF MEDIA BIAS

Whether or not media bias exists is a seemingly endless debate. Yet valid questions remain about media performance and the role of public communications practitioners in shaping perception. There are some researchers who use a "social construction of reality" framework to analyse media and the ways in which information is filtered. According to scholar Richard Alan Nelson's (2003) study *Tracking Propaganda to the Source: Tools for Analyzing Media Bias*, media effects findings suggest that when bias occurs it stems from a combination of 10 factors:

- The media are neither objective nor completely honest in their portrayal of important issues.
- Framing devices are employed in stories by featuring some angles and downplaying others.
- The news is a product not only of deliberate manipulation, but of the

ideological and economic conditions under which the media operate.

- While appearing independent, the news media are institutions that are controlled or heavily influenced by government and business interests experienced with manufacturing of consent/consensus.
- Reporters' sources frequently dominate the flow of information as a way of furthering their own overt and hidden agendas. In particular, the heavy reliance on political officials and other-government related experts occurs through a preferential sourcing selection process which excludes dissident voices.
- Journalists widely accept the faulty premise that the government's collective intentions are benevolent, despite occasional mistakes.
- The regular use of the word "we" by journalists in referring to their government's actions implies nationalistic complicity with those policies.
- There is an absence of historical context and contemporary comparisons in reportage which would make news more meaningful.
- The failure to provide follow up assessment is further evidence of a pack journalism mentality that at the conclusion of a "feeding frenzy" wants to move on to other stories.
- Citizens must avoid self-censorship by reading divergent sources and maintaining a critical perspective on the media in order to make informed choices and participate effectively in the public policy process.

SCHOLARLY TREATMENT OF MEDIA BIAS

Media bias is studied at schools of journalism, university departments (including Media studies, Cultural studies and Peace studies) and by many independent watchdog groups from various parts of the political spectrum. In the United States, many of these studies focus on issues of a conservative/ liberal balance in the media. Other focuses include international differences in reporting, as well as bias in reporting of particular issues such as economic class or environmental interests. A widely-cited public opinion study documents a correlation between news source and certain misconceptions about the Iraq war. Conducted by the Programme on International Policy Attitudes in October 2003, the poll asked Americans whether they believed statements about the Iraq war that were known to be false.

Respondents were also asked which was their primary news source: Fox News, CBS, NBC, ABC, CNN, "Print sources," or NPR. By cross referencing the responses according to primary news source, the study showed that higher numbers of Fox News watchers held certain misconceptions about the Iraq war. The director of Programme on International Policy (PIPA), Stephen Kull said, "While we cannot assert that these misconceptions created the support for going to war with Iraq, it does appear likely that support for the war would be substantially lower if fewer members of the public had these misperceptions."

The Glasgow Media Group carried out the Bad News Studies, a series of detailed analyses of television broadcasts (and later newspaper coverage) in the United Kingdom. Published between 1976 and 1985, the Bad News Studies used content analysis, interviews and covert participant observation to conclude that news was biased against trade unions, blaming them for breaking wage negotiating guidelines and causing high inflation. Martin Harrison's *TV News: Whose Bias?* (1985) criticized the methodology of the Glasgow Media Group, arguing that the GMG identified bias selectively, via their own preconceptions about what phrases qualify as biased descriptions. For example, the GMG sees the word "idle" to describe striking workers as pejorative, despite the word being used by strikers themselves.

Herman and Chomsky (1988) proposed a propaganda model hypothesizing systematic biases of U.S. media from structural economic causes. They hypothesize media ownership by corporations, funding from advertising, the use of official sources, efforts to discredit independent media ("flak"), and "anti-communist" ideology as the filters that bias news in favour of U.S. corporate interests. Their propaganda model first and foremost disuses self censorship through the corporate system; that reporters and especially editors share and/or acquire values with corporate elites in order to further their careers. Those that don't are usually weeded out or marginalized. Such examples have been dramatized in fact based movie dramas as "Good Night, and Good Luck" and "The Insider" or demonstrated in the documentary "The Corporation". George Orwell originally wrote a preface for his book "Animal Farm", which focuses on British self censorship.

"The sinister fact about literary censorship in England is that it is largely voluntary.... [Things are] kept right out of the British press, not because the Government intervened but because of a general tacit agreement that 'it wouldn't do' to mention that particular fact." As if to prove the point, the preface itself was censored and is not published with most copies of the book.

The propaganda model posits that advertising dollars are essential for funding most media sources and clearly have an effect on the content of the media. For example, according to Fair, 'When Al Gore proposed launching a progressive TV network, a Fox News executive told Advertising Age (10/13/03): "The problem with being associated as liberal is that they wouldn't be going in a direction that advertisers are really interested in.... If you go out and say that you are a liberal network, you are cutting your potential audience, and certainly your potential advertising pool, right off the bat."

Furthermore "an internal memo from ABC Radio Networks to its affiliates reveals scores of powerful sponsors have a standing order that their commercials never be placed on syndicated Air America programming that airs on ABC affiliates.... The list, totaling 90 advertisers, includes some of largest and most well-known corporations advertising in the U.S.: Wal-Mart, GE, Exxon Mobil, Microsoft, Bank of America, Fed-Ex, Visa, Allstate, McDonald's, Sony and Johnson and Johnson. The U.S. Postal Service and the U.S. Navy are also listed as advertisers who don't want their commercials to air on Air America."

The academic study cited most frequently by critics of a "liberal media bias" in American journalism is *The Media Elite,* a 1986 book co-authored by political scientists Robert Lichter, Stanley Rothman, and Linda Lichter. They surveyed journalists at national media outlets such as the New York Times, Washington Post, and the broadcast networks. The survey found that most of these journalists were Democratic voters whose attitudes were well to the left of the general public on a variety of topics, including such hot-button social issues such as abortion, affirmative action, and gay rights. Then they compared journalists' attitudes to their coverage of controversial issues such as the safety of nuclear power, school busing to promote racial integration, and the energy crisis of the 1970s.

The book's most thorough case study involved nuclear energy. The survey of journalists showed that most were highly skeptical about nuclear safety. However, the authors conducted a separate survey of scientists in energy related fields, who were much more sanguine about nuclear safety issues. They then conducted a content analysis of nuclear energy coverage in the media outlets they had surveyed. They found that the opinions of sources who were cited as scientific experts reflected the antinuclear sentiments of journalists, rather than the more pro-nuclear perspectives held by most energy scientists. The authors concluded that journalists' coverage of controversial issues reflected their own attitudes, and the predominance of political liberals in newsrooms therefore pushed news coverage in a liberal direction. They presented this tilt as a mostly unconscious process of like-minded individuals projecting their shared assumptions onto their interpretations of reality.

At the time the study was embraced mainly by conservative columnists and politicians, who adopted the findings as scientific proof of liberal media bias. Many of the positions in the preceding study are supported by a 2002 study by Jim A. Kuypers: Press Bias and Politics: How the Media Frame Controversial Issues. In this study of 116 mainstream US papers (including The New York Times, the Washington Post, Los Angeles Times, and the San Francisco Chronicle), Kuypers found that the mainstream print press in America operate within a narrow range of liberal beliefs. Those who expressed points of view further to the left were generally ignored, whereas those who expressed moderate or conservative points of view were often actively denigrated or labeled as holding a minority point of view.

In short, if a political leader, regardless of party, spoke within the press-supported range of acceptable discourse, he or she would receive positive press coverage. If a politician, again regardless of party, were to speak outside of this range, he or she would receive negative press or be ignored. Kuypers also found that the liberal points of view expressed in editorial and opinion pages were found in hard news coverage of the same issues. Although focusing primarily on the issues of race and homosexuality, Kuypers found that the press injected opinion into its news coverage of other issues such as welfare reform, environmental protection, and gun control; in all cases favoring a liberal point of view.

Studies reporting perceptions of liberal bias in the media are not limited to studies of print media. A joint study by the Joan Shorenstein Centre on Press, Politics and Public Policy at Harvard University and the Project for Excellence in Journalism found that people see liberal media bias in television news media such as CNN.. Although both CNN and Fox were perceived in the study as being left of centre, CNN was perceived as being more liberal than Fox. Moreover, the study's findings concerning CNN's perceived liberal bias are echoed in other studies. There is also a growing economics literature on mass media bias, both on the theoretical and the empirical side. On the theoretical side the focus is on understanding to what extent the political positioning of mass media outlets is mainly driven by demand or supply factors. According to Dan Sutter of the University of Oklahoma, a systematic liberal bias in the U.S. media could depend on the fact that owners and/or journalists typically lean to the left.

Along the same lines, David Baron of Stanford GSB presents a game-theoretic model of mass media behaviour in which, given that the pool of journalists systematically leans towards the left or the right, mass media outlets maximise their profits by providing content that is biased in the same direction. They can do so, because it is cheaper to hire journalists that write stories which are consistent with their political position. A concurrent theory would be that supply and demand would cause media to attain a neutral balance because consumers would of course gravitate towards the media they agreed with. This argument fails in considering the imbalance in self-reported political allegiances by journalists themselves, that distort any market analogy as regards offer: (...) *Indeed, in 1982, 85 per cent of Columbia Graduate School of Journalism students identified themselves as liberal, versus 11 per cent conservative*", quoted in Sutter, 2001.

This same argument would have news outlets in equal numbers increasing profits of a more balanced media far more than the slight increase in costs to hire unbiased journalists, notwithstanding the extreme rarity of self-reported conservative journalists. As mentioned above, Tim Groseclose of UCLA and Jeff Milyo of the University of Missouri at Columbia use think tank quotes, in order to estimate the relative position of mass media outlets in the political spectrum. The idea is to trace out which think tanks are quoted by various mass media outlets within news stories, and to match these think tanks with the political position of members of the U.S. Congress who quote them in a non-negative way. Using this procedure, Groseclose and Milyo obtain the stark result that all sampled news providers -except Fox News' Special Report and the Washington Times- are located to the left of the average Congress member, *i.e.* there are signs of a liberal bias in the US news media.

However, the news media also show a remarkable degree of centrism, just because all outlets but one are located –from an ideological point of view- between the average Democrat and average Republican in Congress. The methods Groseclose and Milyo used to calculate this bias have been criticized by Mark Liberman, a professor of Computer Science at the University of Pennsylvania. Liberman concludes by saying he thinks "that many if not most of the complaints directed against GandM are motivated in part by ideological disagreement — just as much of the praise for their work is motivated by ideological agreement. It would be nice if there were a less politically fraught body of data on which such modeling exercises could be explored."

Sendhil Mullainathan and Andrei Shleifer of Harvard University construct a behavioural model, which is built around the assumption that readers and viewers hold beliefs that they would like to see confirmed by news providers. When news customers share common beliefs, profit-maximizing media outlets find it optimal to select and/or frame stories in order to pander to those beliefs. On the other hand, when beliefs are heterogeneous, news providers differentiate their offer and segment the market, by providing news stories that are slanted towards the two extreme positions in the spectrum of beliefs.

Matthew Gentzkow and Jesse Shapiro of Chicago GSB present another demand-driven theory of mass media bias. If readers and viewers have a priori views on the current state of affairs and are uncertain about the quality of the information about it being provided by media outlets, then the latter have an incentive to slant stories towards their customers' prior beliefs, in order to build and keep a reputation for high-quality journalism. The reason for this is that rational agents would tend to believe that pieces of information that go against their prior beliefs in fact originate from low-quality news providers.

The economics empirical literature on mass media bias mainly focuses on the United States. Steve Ansolabehere, Rebecca Lessem and Jim Snyder of the Massachusetts Institute of Technology analyse the political orientation of endorsements by U.S. newspapers. They find an upward trend in the average propensity to endorse a candidate, and in particular an incumbent one. There are also some changes in the average ideological slant of endorsements: while in the 40s and in the 50s there was a clear advantage to Republican candidates, this advantage continuously eroded in subsequent decades, to the extent that in the 90s the authors find a slight Democratic lead in the average endorsement choice. John Lott and Kevin Hassett of the American Enterprise Institute study the coverage of economic news by looking at a panel of 389 U.S. newspapers from 1991 to 2004, and from 1985 to 2004 for a subsample comprising the top 10 newspapers and the Associated Press. For each release of official data about a set of economic indicators, the authors analyse how newspapers decide to report on them, as reflected by the tone of the related headlines. The idea is to check whether newspapers display some kind of partisan bias, by giving more positive or negative coverage to the same economic figure, as a function of the political affiliation of the incumbent President. Controlling for the economic data being released, the authors find that there are between 9.6 and 14.7 per cent fewer positive stories when the incumbent President is a Republican.

Riccardo Puglisi of the Massachusetts Institute of Technology looks at the editorial choices of the *New York Times* from 1946 to 1997. He finds that the *Times* displays Democratic partisanship, with some watchdog aspects. This is the case, because during presidential campaigns the Times systematically gives more coverage to Democratic topics of civil rights, health care, labour and social welfare, but only when the incumbent president is a Republican. These topics are classified as Democratic ones, because Gallup polls show that on average U.S. citizens think that Democratic candidates would be better at handling problems related to them. According to Puglisi, in the post-1960 period the Times displays a more symmetric type of watchdog behaviour, just because during presidential campaigns it also gives more coverage to the typically Republican issue of Defence when the incumbent President is a Democrat, and less so when the incumbent is a Republican.

Alan Gerber and Dean Karlan of Yale University use an experimental approach to examine not whether the media are biased, but whether the media influence political decisions and attitudes. They conduct a randomized control trial just prior to the November 2005 gubernatorial election in Virginia and randomly assign individuals in Northern Virginia to (a) a treatment group that receives a free subscription to the Washington Post, (b) a treatment group that receives a free subscription to the Washington Times, or (c) a control group. They find that those who are assigned to the Washington Post treatment group are eight percentage points more likely to vote for the Democrat in the elections. The report also found that "exposure to either newspaper was weakly linked to a movement away from the Bush administration and Republicans."

Another unaffiliated group, Media Study Group, established seven categories of poor journalistic practice: for example, the journalist stating personal opinion in a report, asserting incorrect facts, applying unequal space or treatment to two sides of a controversial issue; then analyzed The Age Newspaper (Melbourne Australia) for the frequency of infraction of this code of practice. The resultant instances were then analyzed statistically with respect to the frequency they supported one or other side of the two-sided controversial issue under consideration. The goal of this group was to establish a quantitative methodology for the study of bias.

A self-described progressive media watchdog group, Fairness and Accuracy in Reporting, in consultation with the Survey and Evaluation Research Laboratory at Virginia Commonwealth University, sponsored a rigorous academic study in which journalists were asked a range of questions about how they did their work and about how they viewed the quality of media coverage in the broad area of politics and economic policy. "They were asked for their opinions and views about a range of recent policy issues and debates. Finally, they were asked for demographic and identifying information, including their political orientation". They then compared to the say or similar questions posed with "the public" based on Gallup, and Pew Trust polls. Their study concluded that a majority of journalists, although relatively liberal on social policies, were significantly to the right of the public on economic, labour, health care and foreign policy issues.

This study continues: "we learn much more about the political orientation of news content by looking at sourcing patterns rather than journalists' personal views. As this survey shows, it is government officials and business representatives to whom journalists "nearly always" turn when covering economic policy. Labour representatives and consumer advocates were at the bottom of the list. This is consistent with earlier research on sources. For example, analysts from the centrist Brookings Institution and conservative think tanks such as the Heritage Foundation and the American Enterprise Institute are those most quoted in mainstream news accounts; liberal think tanks are often invisible. When it comes to sources, 'liberal bias' is nowhere to be found."

EXPERIMENTER BIAS

A major problem in studies is experimenter bias. Research into studies of media bias in the United States shows that Liberal experimenters tend to get results that say the media has a conservative bias, while conservatives experimenters tend to get results that say the media has a liberal bias, and those who do not identify themselves as either liberal or conservative get results indicating little bias, or mixed bias. This same problem with experimenter bias extends to the studies of experimenter bias, of course. Whether bias is Towards the left or the right depends on where you stand.

The study "A Measure of Media Bias" (pdf) by political scientist Timothy J. Groseclose of UCLA and economist Jeffrey D. Milyo of the University of Missouri-Columbia, purports to rank news organisations in terms of identifying with liberal or conservative values relative to each other. They used the Americans for Democratic Action (ADA) scores as a quantitative proxy for political leanings of the referential organizations. Thus their definition of "liberal" includes the RAND Corporation, a Non-profit research organization with strong ties to the Defence Department. According to Media Matters for America (a non-profit progressive research and information centre), "the study employed a measure of "bias" so problematic that its findings are next to useless". What is "liberal" in the United States may not be "liberal" by world standards. FAIR suggests that a benchmark for each country be set by scientific polling of a cross-section of the citizens. Another source of bias is the fact that some studies are reported by the media, and other stories are not. The case study "A Measure of Media Bias" discussed above was widely reported in the United States. George Orwell pointed out that in the UK during the last century businesses did not undermine their own interests by reporting leftist (anti business or pro-labour) information. In the United States Ben Bagdikian documents a long history of advertisers pulling out support when media content becomes too controversial.

6

Journalism and the News

INTRODUCTION

As we continue to examine the nature and functions of journalism in greater detail, we see immediately that another term is so closely associated with journalists that it is sometimes used as a synonym.

During the prolonged Society of Professional Journalists-Sigma Delta Chi debate on the meaning of journalism, for example, Edward Lindsay, editor of the Lindsay-Schaub newspapers in Decatur, Illinois, sometimes substituted "fraternity of newsmen" for "society of professional journalists".

Indeed, in the mind of many persons, news reporters and newswriters seem to occupy the centermost chambers in the house of journalism. Therefore, although journalism consists of much more than the acquisition and presentation of news, it is appropriate that we now turn our attention to that important but highly ambiguous term.

THE GENERIC MEANING OF JOURNALISM

We have reached the point where we are ready to set forth the basic definition of journalism. Many refinements will be added in the succeeding pages, but the following seems to sum up the comments we have made so far.

Journalism is a type of mass communications:

- That provides useful and practical (rather than theoretical) knowledge;
- That actually is or at least purports to be literally true, rather than invented or fictional;
- That is provided by persons who have at least some control over the content of the messages that are communicated;
- And that aids the recipients of the knowledge in making decisions on issues presently facing them.

Journalism is the type of activity that has all of the attributes just described. Journalists are the persons who engage in that type of activity.

Journalism does not exist aside from the persons who practice it. It is not like a tree or a frying pan or a light bulb; it cannot grow by itself, nor, once made, can it exist by itself. The *products* of journalism—news stories, editorials, video tapes, photographs—can have an independent existence, but journalism itself cannot.

Journalists, however, do exist independently of their journalism. A sleeping Horace Greeley, Frederick Douglass, Ida Tarbell, or Edward R. Murrow would have been identified as a journalist even though, while sleeping, he or she was not practicing journalism.

All of this seems quite clear. What may not be so clear is the correlative point: just as those readily identified as journalists often continue to be called journalists even when they are not practicing journalism, so also those who are not ordinarily identified as journalists ought to be called journalists as soon as they begin to practice journalism.

Journalism is not a custom-made dress or suit available to only a few select people. It is a cloak which almost anybody can throw on.

Journalism is an activity that can be employed by everyone except those who have not yet acquired or who have lost their communicative faculties. Whenever plumbers or clerks or architects or musicians become participants in the activities identified earlier, *they become journalists*.

This point, sometimes ignored, becomes especially important when questions concerning the legal protection of journalists arise.

Such protection belongs to all of us. It is also important when we consider our national educational system, for it means that all citizens should be prepared to practice the arts of journalism, should they ever desire to do so. Thus one of the dangers of attempting to define journalism, now becomes less worrisome. There is no need to license journalists as a restricted class of people when nearly everyone is or legitimately can be a journalist.

SOME OF THE SPECIES OF JOURNALISM

Some people would grant the title of "journalist" only to those for whom the work is a full-time job. But such a viewpoint not only carries with it some of the dangers already mentioned but would be analogous to denying T. S. Eliot the title of poet because he made his living working at Lloyd's Bank or saying William Carlos Williams should not be called a poet because all his life he was a practicing physician.

Thus it seems much better to recognize that, although for some their regular, full-time job is doing the work of journalism, there are many more who practice journalism only occasionally. *New York Tribune* editor Horace Greeley belongs to the first group; Robert Dale Owen, a Democratic congressman from Indiana, who wrote a letter published in the *Tribune* on October 23, 1862, appealing for a Proclamation of Emancipation, belongs to the second. The first are often called professional journalists in the sense that the principal source of their livelihood is the practice of journalism. For the second, we have no well-accepted designation. Perhaps it is adequate simply to call them amateur or occasional journalists. Although professional journalists are sometimes given privileges not available to occasional journalists, access to a press box at a baseball game, for example, or access to the press gallery in the U. S. Senate chambers, the legal rights of both the amateurs and the professionals are the same, and whenever they are doing the work described earlier they deserve to be called journalists.

Another set of species is quite obvious, for it is based on the medium employed by journalists to convey their messages to the public. Thus there are newspaper, magazine, radio, television, film, book, and other types of journalists, even though no journalist is inextricably tied to a single medium. Many, in fact, move from one to another, as did William L. Shirer, who switched from the *Chicago Tribune* to radio, television, and books.

Others use several media at the same time, as did David Gergen, who was an editor of *U.S. News and World Report* at the same time that he was a news analyst on public television. But most professional journalists are usually identified with the medium to which they devote most of their time and from which they derive the greater part of their income.

PUBLIC AFFAIRS AND PERSONAL AFFAIRS JOURNALISM

One of the most important, yet also one of the most ignored, divisions of journalism is that into public affairs journalism and personal affairs journalism.

It is easy to understand why it receives so little attention: although both journalists and the public have a quiet awareness that the distinction exists, they seldom discuss it explicitly. But it is so essential to an understanding of journalism that explicit discussion is essential, briefly here and more extensively later on.

The brief description of the generic meaning of journalism is that it provides useful, practical knowledge. But useful for what purpose? Useful to help those who are consumers of journalism decide what should be done or what should be avoided concerning the issues currently facing them. Journalism exists to help all of us decide what is good to do and what is good not to do.

The concept of good, of course, has a multitude of meanings. Here we think of it in relation to those for whom something can be considered good. We can say that something is good for me or we can say that something is good for us.

That is, we can make a choice in order to improve, profit, delight, enhance, benefit our individual selves or to do one or all of these things for the improvement and benefit of the community, group, organization, or society of which we individuals are members. For example, let's consider a fictitious Hiram. Hiram never married and is now retired from his job as a clothing salesman. He lives in a small apartment, is in good health, likes spectator sports, has a satisfactory income from Social Security and a few investments, pays taxes, and is, in general, a rather average person. Every day, Hiram has to make thousands of decisions. Some are so personal—shall I sleep another five minutes or should I get out of bed right now?—that no other person can be of much help to him in deciding what is the good thing to do. But hundreds of his decisions can be more or less well made depending on the knowledge that is communicated to him from the outside world.

He likes to watch the local baseball team. Is the team playing today? Is the weather likely to be good for baseball? Are the normal means of transportation in operation? Is the admission price the same as last time he went to a game? What time of the day will the game be played? Will it also be shown on television?

How well has the team been doing? Has any starter been injured and thus is unavailable to play? He can probably find the answers to these and to numerous other questions affecting his personal welfare by consulting his daily newspaper or listening to the news reports on radio or television.

The knowledge he receives will help him decide whether or not it would be good for him to attend the baseball game. Learning that the game will be shown on television, Hiram may decide to watch it at home rather than go out to the ballpark. Many others, receiving the same information, may decide just the opposite. Hiram's decision is a personal decision in the sense that he decides what is good for himself. Other baseball fans can make similar or different personal decisions. It is not necessary that there be just one decision.

Now let's say that while reading the newspaper Hiram learns that next Tuesday the city will hold a referendum to determine whether or not money will be borrowed to build a new high school. In this situation, the decision to be made is not what is good for Hiram but rather what is good for the city, not "for me" but "for us." Whatever the decision is, it will be one decision. It will be assumed that even those who might have preferred a different decision will go along with the one that is made.

If the voters decide to approve of the borrowing, that decision will be against Hiram's personal welfare: his taxes will probably increase, and he has no children who will benefit from the new school.

But if the new school is truly needed, the public welfare might well require that money be borrowed to build it. In fact, Hiram himself, recognizing the dominant character of the public welfare, of the common good, might put aside consideration of his own personal good to vote in favour of the referendum.

What, then, is the difference between personal affairs journalism and public affairs journalism? The first type provides the knowledge people can use to make good decisions about their personal, current welfare. Each person decides what is good for him or her, independent of the decisions being made by others. Much of the journalism dealing with sports, business, and entertainment (just to name a few possibilities) is of that type. The second type of journalism provides the knowledge people need for decisions concerning the current welfare of some community, group, organization, or society of which they are a part. Here a decision will be made (perhaps by all the members, perhaps by one or a few) concerning what will be good for that community or group. It will be a decision concerning the welfare of the whole collectivity, and the members will be expected to go along with it even if they would have preferred some other decision.

Most of the activities of federal, state, and local governments are the business of public affairs journalism, but the latter can also extend to private groups: fraternities or businesses, for instance.

The welfare of these, too, requires decisions concerning the good of the whole, and public affairs journalism contributes to the goodness of those decisions. If one company is considering a merger with another, this decision concerns the welfare of both companies and is a decision in which the managements, stockholders, and employees have a stake.

All need knowledge so that the decision can be well made, and most of the knowledge that is needed comes through the work of public affairs journalism. One might ask: Why should members of a public pay attention to issues-such as a proposal to raise tax rates—which seem beyond the public's powers of determination? Some answers will be found in our later discussions of public opinion and electoral processes.

For now, it may be sufficient to recollect that mass communications always extend messages to more people than have a direct need for them. Can we also say that the communications tasks associated with public relations and with advertising ought to be viewed as additional types or species of journalism? That question has been the source of many heated disagreements.

One of the most vigorous of these disagreements took place in the 1950s when Sigma Delta Chi, the Society of Professional Journalists (SPJ), debated the problem of membership eligibility. Having already excluded advertising people from the organization, the members now decided that, in the future, public relations practitioners would also be excluded because neither group was composed of true journalists.Some public relations practitioners do spend their time analyzing situations and providing interpersonal consultation to their clients. Similarly, some advertising people spend time in market and media research and in similar interpersonal communications.

Thus, to the extent they are not engaged in mass communications, they would not fit the definition of journalists.

But the activities of most people in both fields culminate in their preparing messages for the mass media. To the extent that those messages convey useful knowledge that at least purports to be true, the work they do fits the concept of journalism.Why, then, did SPJ claim they were *not* journalists? For years, the society had differentiated between those acceptable persons who prepared and disseminated information in the "public interest" and those Non-acceptable persons who did so in what the members called the "private interest." They concluded that all advertising people were in the latter category; but in 1952, they admitted, at least for a few years, that this was not true of all public relations practitioners.

Those who wrote for civic organizations, social agencies, benevolent foundations, educational institutions, and governmental departments (with the interesting exception of the military) and who had an "acceptable background of experience in news work for newspapers, magazines or in broadcasting" could be considered to be working in the public interest and thus be eligible for membership.

But in the summer of 1958, a select panel had second thoughts about even these exceptions and submitted a report proposing, among other things, that there be no initiation of public relations men in the future. A heated and extensive debate ensued, much of it carried out in the pages of *Quill*, the society's journal, concluding with a vote at the 1958 national convention that endorsed the report.

One of the more interesting contributions to the debate came from a group of distinguished public relations persons themselves. Although they were grandfathered into the society, they said they recognized differences between their work and that of many other members:

We accept your tighter definition of journalism. Although we prepare and disseminate news stories, we admit we do so, at least in part, in the interest of our clients and employers. Newsmen, on the other hand, generally work without obligation to any special interest. Both activities may well be in the public interest, but there is a fundamental difference which is important to Sigma Delta Chi.

Several years later, David Berkman seemed to express a similar thought. In discussing whether public relations courses have a place within journalism Programmes, he wrote, "If we accept—and how can we not do so?—that the purpose of the journalist is to discover and report truth, while that of those in public relations is to serve the interests of their clients or employers, then the answer is clearly 'no'".Even though public relations practitioners serve the interests of clients or employers, it does not necessarily follow that such a type of service precludes the discovering and reporting of truth.

Journalists, no matter whether they are newswriters, public relations practitioners, or advertising personnel, can have a variety of motives when they do their work. They can be working for their own welfare, for the welfare of a cause in which they are interested, for the welfare of their employers, for the welfare of the public, or for many other possible objectives. To say that only one of these goals is good and all the rest are suspect is to assume an arbitrary and unreasonable moral standard. Any or all of them can be good, and no one of them need necessarily exclude the others. Any moralistic approach to the definition of journalism depends in part on the precarious possibility of detecting the intentions of message senders.

Although some journalists are morally good and some morally deficient, it is not the case that all newspeople are in the first category and all public relations and advertising people in the second.

It did not seem, for instance, that former *Wall Street Journal* reporter R. Foster Winans had been acting as a very ethical journalist when he was convicted in 1985 of using his "Heard on the Street" stock market column to further an insider trading scheme that netted him $31,000.

Unfortunately, deceptions on various levels have not been infrequent among newspeople during the history of journalism.

During the first months of 1998, Stephen Glass of the *New Republic*, Patricia Smith of the *Boston Globe*, and April Oliver of CNN lost their jobs for concocting material that turned out not to be factual. But they certainly are not typical of all reporters, columnists, and television producers.Likewise, some advertising and public relations practitioners lack the integrity we ought to expect of people who work in those fields even though most of them adhere to the goals of their professions. The Public Relations Society of America*Code of Professional Standards* says, "A member shall conduct his or her professional life in accord with the public interest."

Also, advertising personnel aim at stimulating business competition, resulting in improved products and more economical ways to produce and distribute them; thus in the end "the consumer benefits by the availability of new and better products".To increase the likelihood of such good performance is one reason for incorporating advertising and public relations instruction in journalism Programmes.The journalism/advertising identification is further complicated because some advertising, like newspaper, magazine, and broadcast editorials, argues for or against public issues.

The Mobil Oil Company produces this type of editorial advertising frequently. The American Federation of Teachers buys space in the *New York Times* on the first Sunday of each month so that its president can discuss matters of public policy.Similarly, political public relations contribute to the public discussion of public affairs. The public relations writer, of course, advances the position of the person or party who is paying the bill, but print and broadcast editorial writers also advance the positions of the editors, publishers, or station managers who employ them.

Ideological, ethnic, religious, and other special interest newspapers, magazines, and cable systems are as much devoted to advancing private agendas as are public relations and advertising practitioners.And at least since the period of the penny press in the 1830s, a strong feeling has existed that some members of the information media function more to sell copies and enrich their owners than to serve the public. The contemporary members of this trend might be the tabloids conveniently placed along the supermarket checkout lanes.

ADVERTISING AND PUBLIC RELATIONS ARE SPECIES OF JOURNALISM

Thus it seems that as long as advertising and public relations people use the mass media to convey purportedly true knowledge that can help people make good decisions about what to do and what to avoid in regard to issues currently facing them, advertising and public relations people ought to be considered journalists as much as anyone else who does that type of work.

They are, in particular, much like print and broadcast editorial writers, columnists, and commentators. Like them, advertising and public relations practitioners are persuaders. It is true that they advance products or causes in which they or their employers are interested, but so also did Greeley, Douglass, Tarbell, and Murrow—and nearly all of those whom we are proud to identify as journalists.

It is also true that, unlike some other journalists, advertising journalists buy space or time in media that they do not own. This makes them different from those who own or those who are employed by those who own their media. But every type of journalist is different from other types: photojournalists differ from word journalists, broadcast journalists from print journalists, public affairs journalists from personal affairs journalists.

The fact that a person is this type of journalist rather than another *type* of journalist need not deprive that person of identification as *a journalist*. Many public relations practitioners produce their own media: newsletters, company newspapers, brochures, slide presentations, annual reports, and video- tapes.

Many of the others supply, at no cost, informational, analytical, and persuasive material to the general mass media. Some studies indicate that more than half of the Non-wire, Non-syndicated editorial content of newspapers comes from releases or memos generated by public relations sources. Some press agents have misused their abilities, it is true, but the same can be said of those in any field of endeavor. Nothing in the nature of the work they do requires either the lying or fictionizing that would exclude them from journalism.

CHANGING STYLES OF NEWS

Much more has changed than the variety of media that deliver the news. The style of that news also has changed significantly.

A succinct portrait of this evolutionary pattern in contemporary journalism during the final decades of the 20th century is found in Thomas Patterson's *"Out of Order"* an analysis of how the news media covered our presidential elections from 1960 to 1992. Again, an interval of approximately 30 years proves a useful vantage point for sketching these changes. In 1960, an interpretative framework—rather than the more traditional descriptive framework used to report the presidential election—was found in only a small fraction of the news stories on the front page of the *New York Times.*

By 1972, there was parity between the two styles of election reporting; in the 1988 and 1992 elections, interpretative stories dominated the front page of the *New York Times* by a ratio of 4-to-l. Over a period of approximately 30 years, the preferred style for reporting the presidential election had turned upside down.

By 1960 there already was an emphasis on politics as a game in which reporting a candidate's strategy for winning and conjuring with such things as "who won the day" and "who is ahead by how much" were key elements.

That is, the thrust of the reportage was on the campaign as a contest between parties and politicians rather than on the election as a method for the public to make a decision about its future.

In that 1960 election, the split between reporting on the game and reporting on the issues was close to 50-50. This already was very different from elections in earlier periods, but that 50-50 split was just the baseline for major changes appearing in the 1972 and 1976 elections.

By 1972, reporting on the game prevailed by about 2-to-l. By 1976, the ratio of game coverage to issue coverage had reached a new plateau of about 4-to-l.Among the most powerful influences driving the startling shift to a 4-1 ratio of strategic, insider reporting over issues reporting was Theodore H. White.Starting in 1960, White, a veteran reporter, produced a best-selling series of quadrennial books, *"The Making of the President.* " Remarkable in their detailed reporting from inside the presidential campaigns, the books set a new standard for depth and insight into the strategic and human calculations that elected presidents.

White was writing history, but the seemingly authenticating details that his books contained proved irresistible to the political press; never mind that they were reported months after the votes were cast.

The Associated Press, for instance, messaged its political reporters, "When Teddy White's book comes out, there shouldn't be a single story in that book that we haven't reported ourselves.

" And A. M. Rosenthal, managing editor of the *New York Times,* instructed his staff, "We aren't going to wait until a year after the election to read in Teddy White's book what we should have reported ourselves. "

The impact of such commands was to drive political reporting further and further inside the campaigns and away from issue coverage. The narrative illusion was if you can report what's in the candidate's stomach, that is, if you know what he had for breakfast, then you surely must also know what's in his head and heart. What journalists failed to recognize was that White's books were not helpful to the public in terms of picking a leader, for the rich details they contained were published months after the votes were cast. They were conceived and executed as history, not contemporary journalism. Nevertheless, the hunger for glimpses into the inner circles and thoughts of the campaigns moved political reporting ever further from anything that could be useful, or even very interesting, to average voters.

Even White himself came to regret his reportorial invention. "It's appalling what we've done, " White said during the 1972 campaign, the fourth of the five he chronicled. "All of us are observing him (the candidate), taking notes like mad, getting all the little details. Which I think I invented as a method of reporting and which I now sincerely regret. If you write about this, say that I sincerely regret it. Who gives a ... if the guy had milk and Total for breakfast?"

Not surprisingly, as shifts occurred among the aspects of the campaign that were emphasized in news reports, the journalist's voice also became more prominent in setting the tone of election reports. Back in 1960, the candidates themselves and partisan participants in the election set the tone in two-thirds of the stories. Praise for a candidate came from his supporters, attacks and criticism from his opponent and the opponent's supporters. By the 1972 presidential election, journalists were setting the tone of most articles.

Looking more closely at the nature of that tone reveals another pattern that turned upside down across those nine elections from 1960 to 1992; good news versus bad news. Back in 1960, the ratio of good news to bad news was about 3-to-1. This ratio seesawed up and down over the next four elections but in 1980 moved to a new plateau where the ratio of good news to bad news was 2-to-3, another 30-year reversal in the prevailing style of political reporting.This 30-year trend is graphically illustrated by the titles on *Time* magazine's cover stories. In 1960, they were simply "Candidate Kennedy" and "Candidate Nixon.

" In 1992, they included "Nobody's Perfect: The Doubts About Ross Perot" and "Waiting for Perot: He's Leading in the Polls, But Can He Lead the Nation?. " Bush's cover story was "The Fight of His Life" and Clinton's cover stories included "Why Voters Don't Trust Clinton" and "Is Bill Clinton for Real?. "

In sum, the pattern of presidential election coverage that evolved bit by bit from 1960 to 1992 resulted in a fundamentally different election journalism. In 1960, journalists described the campaign, issue coverage was priority, partisans set the tone of the coverage, and good news prevailed over bad news. Thirty years later, journalists interpreted the campaign, game coverage was the priority, the tone of the coverage was set by journalists, and bad news prevailed over good news.

The sequence of these steps in the evolution of a new style of political reporting is where the Xs mark elections with significant increases over past journalistic practice. This stair-step pattern is a succinct portrait of shifting professional perspectives, the evolution of a new set of "cookie cutters" that shape contemporary political journalism.Beyond political journalism and presidential elections, there are numerous other cookie cutters used to shape the daily news, many with long histories of use. Noting the repetition of master narratives—even rather specific stories—over and over through the years, even centuries, Robert Darnton metaphorically summarized his time as a journalist:

We simply drew on the traditional repertory of genres. It was like making cookies from an antique cookie cutter.

Among the most ancient sets of journalistic cookie cutters are political, financial and sexual scandals, cookie cutters extensively employed in the final decade of the 20th century whose historical origins are in the broadside ballads, news books and French canards of the 16th and 17th century.

In reporting the news of the moment, journalists depend for the most part on a set of standard conventions about how a news story should be written. Some of these are very ancient, some very recent.The mix of cookie cutters in common use is constantly evolving, and an interval of 30 years is a useful vantage point for observing what has changed and what has remained constant in reporting the news.

Journalism changed in the closing decades of the 20th century, in particular adding a strong interpretive element to the reporting of public affairs in general, not just political campaigns.Undoubtedly, journalism will change again during the opening decades of this century. Part of the change will result from the tremendous changes in communication technology and its diffusion among the public.

In *"Mediamorphosis: Understanding New Media"* Roger Fidler cited Paul Saffo, a director at the Institute for the Future in Menlo Park, Calif., who "posits that the amount of time required for new ideas to fully seep into a culture has consistently averaged about three decades for at least the past five centuries. He calls this the 30-year rule. "

POLITICAL ENGAGEMENT AND THE AUDIENCE FOR NEWS

Among the many reasons citizen had a hard time committing to being newspaper readers, one seems the most important: They found the stories did not touch on the areas of civic activity they encountered in their daily lives.

Although the newspaper retains its meaning as a symbol of adulthood, the young adults often failed to sustain the family ritual experienced in childhood. A second study on television news found that college students who turned away from newspapers did not appear to substitute another news medium to inform themselves as citizens.

Although they held television news in minimal regard, they still credited the first major news story they remembered from television with making them feel part of the larger national community. In spite of this fairly strong generation effect from watching news, many of the young adult participants considered newscasts primarily a form of entertainment, and only a few mentioned any other source far news, such as radio or the Internet.

Surveys and field work confirm that, although some older Americans may experience a strong need for news, the younger generation does not share that appetite. A growing minority of young Americans get along without what the major news organizations serve up daily, and those who do pay attention, especially to television news, do so without attaching great significance to the news as the Fourth Estate in political life. The view of the news arena as a space where the public sphere operates is declining among the young citizenry.

Because of the clear impact on the civic role for news businesses, with the potential to weaken political participation, the trends among young Americans have aroused debate about the future of democracy. Carried on without reference to other countries, the debate raised questions requiring comparative research abroad. Are the increasingly negative experiences with news among young citizens peculiar to the United States? Or do the changes pertain as well to young adults in other contemporary societies? To search for answers, this monograph presents the results of two qualitative studies abroad that closely replicate the U.S. research, examining newspaper and then television news experiences that college students recount in life history narratives.

Spain was selected as a comparative case for several reasons. The most compelling comes from data on the young audience for news: Among Western democracies, only in Spain is news viewership reaching an almost universal national audience and newspaper circulation growing among young citizens. Spain provides a setting within another advanced country that differs from the United States in most particulars: Spain's development came recently, as did its return to democracy. Besides their differing language and parliamentary monarchy, young Spaniards grew up in close-knit extended families and attended highly structured schools that emphasized rote learning. More important, the Spanish media arena diverges greatly from that typical in the United States. Where local newspapers and commercial broadcasting dominate the U.S. press, national newspapers and public television predominate in Spain. In such a contrasting political and media settings, young citizens will likely report distinct ways of informing themselves as citizens.

The decisions of young adults in another country present opportunities to build grounded theory. By looking at groups that contrast strongly with those previously studied, field work can seek cases that break the rule, clarifying the contours of the new relationship to news emerging among the young. The process may also generate concepts useful to understanding subjective experiences of the news arena. Comparing groups reared under a greatly differing news arena permits a search for common patterns. Any strong similarities found to cross cultural or national boundaries would contribute to the general understanding of subjective experience. The comparison could yield insights into the structure of generations as the news media globalize. Expected differences might indicate alternative policy choices for news organizations and their role in informing citizens.

THEORY AND METHOD

The idea of comparing nations has long been employed to build theories of politics and society. Since Durkheim and Weber, "the father of crossnational research", tried to understand modern society by holding it up against historical and primitive groups, scholars have used examples from different nations as a way to illustrate their ideas, from the social Darwinism of Spencer and the functionalism of Radcliffe-Brown, to the structuralism of Levi-Strauss. Herbert Blumer criticized these comparisons to remote societies as an exercise in nostalgia.Comparative studies of contemporary nations, on the other hand, give observers a vantage point closer to home, reducing the danger of romanticizing a traditional or historical society. Interest in comparative research was surging, principally at the intersection between sociology and political science, when Seymour Martin Lipset wrote his classic studies. The new field, political sociology, took on several topics that cross the borders of the two fields, such as the fate of democracy, the role of the media, and the participation of individual citizens as part of different generations.

Defining and measuring "the political culture of democracy" and "the social structures and processes that sustain it" inspired the pioneer study of comparative political attitudes in the United States, United Kingdom, Germany, Italy, and Mexico. The news media clearly took part in these structures and processes. To illustrate the patterns found in survey questions about media use and political interest, the authors also conducted life history interviews.

During the early 1960s Americans facing the cold war, fearing a domino effect if small nations fell to Communism, wanted to know how to encourage the broadest democracy without causing instability. "How can the apathetic peripheral man become the aspiring participant man without a deep seachange in the psychic weather?" asked Daniel Lerner.

The answer was found in Lipset's three requirements for political democracy; a regular means to change officials, a loyal opposition, and (important for this study) a mechanism for the largest possible share of society to participate. Communication seemed to provide one of the most likely mechanisms. "In the world today - whether you like it or not, whether it is advisable or not, whether it is good policy planning or not - tremendous developments in communication," Lerner went on, "are occurring in every country". These changes at mid-century began to shrink the global community, and several contemporary studies identify communications (including newspaper consumption) as a strong indicator of political development. Subsequent studies have paid most attention to voting, but the news media also provide a key to citizens' involvement in democratic governments. As mass communication grows, clusters of older social, economic, and psychological commitments end, and citizens become more open to new patterns of action.

The commitment to participate in politics can clash with the roles the media play in generating economic profits, and this contradiction may limit their legitimacy and effectiveness in the political system. News media can block as well as encourage change, because "the construction of political reality is essentially a 'mediated' process". Young adulthood, when political reality takes firm shape in personal commitments, is rarely studied.

Socialization research emphasizes childhood and adolescence and pays little attention to the media, although media research shows that television often provides the earliest encounters with politics in the United States. Cross-national research on media and politics usually focuses on media content, not audiences, and mass media researchers have called for more comparative study of public communication.

This chapter on young citizens and the media has two theoretical aims. One is to describe and delineate elements in the structure of subjective experience. In his suggestions for studying the media, Blumer proposed that they do not operate within clearly demarcated and distinct outlets and forms, such as newspapers and television, but instead act within a larger zone that he called an arena. Viewed from the perspective of citizens' symbolic interactions, subjective experiences with the news arena have been little studied.

To extend understanding of the political sociology of news, this monograph employs a descriptive strategy to discover grounded theory. After identifying other groups for comparison, a principal task is to describe subjective experience in detail, thus adding to the store of empirical observations of responses to the media arena. To build theory, groups are chosen as negative cases, selected to delimit the news arena and clarify its role in young citizens' experience.

That Americans increasingly reject news invites the search for cases where a different news arena holds sway. Cross-national research looks for similarities between nations because "if the same factor produces the same effects in two very different situations, its influence tends to be confirmed". National distinctiveness makes finding the same processes less likely in more than one country, and so similarities are not only unexpected but also valuable to add to the general understanding of the media arena. Differences contribute as well, and the most important source of contrast, of course, is national history.

As they confront problems, the citizens of various countries find alternatives and reach different decisions. Their contrasting responses can be used to suggest policy options. Another theoretical aim is to examine generational change. Generations are produced only in modern societies, where rapid changes produce longterm shifts in ideology. Events give each new group of children a different set of experiences that tie them strongly to others their age. What people know about politics is influenced by their position in a generation, and studies of generations suggest that their collective memories emerge not only from massive traumatic events such as wars and large scale demographic shifts but also from mass exposure to events shown in the media. Karl Mannheim noted that an actual generation, whose coming of age coincides with a set of common experiences, does not necessarily interpret those shared events uniformly.The conflicting meanings they assign events divide them into what Mannheim called generational units. Maurice Halbwachs agreed that collective memories play a central role in distinguishing different social groups and classes. Mannheim further suggested that, although their life spans may overlap, different age groups experience the same moments of history differently, each generation living in its own subjective era, as he called it.

This has been borne out in subsequent research. Finally, Mannheim proposed that national differences effectively separate people of the same chronological age; citizens in Germany and China in 1800 could not form part of the same actual generation because they could share no formative experiences.

The growth of news organizations that extend beyond national borders, the consolidation of media ownership globally, and the resulting international spread of political reporting styles raise the question whether citizens of nations separated by geography and language had begun to share sufficient media experience by the end of the 20th century to form a generation in effect.

These theoretical considerations guide the study: the search for commonalities that indicate new social and political meanings for news crossing national boundaries, the observation of differences with an eye to discover alternate policies for American news organizations as they inform citizens, and the testing of boundaries of subjective experience between a political generation and its units in the United States and Spain.

As a practical matter, choosing countries is the first task in any crossnational comparison. For the greatest detail and depth, a binary analysis comparing only one country to another -works best. Because it "leaves out neither the specific nor the general," binary study can contribute "to an understanding of general phenomena". The choice of countries requires a balance.

The two should share enough to make reasonable comparisons but also have enough differences to make for robust results. The United States shares with Europe many cultural, political, and economic traditions, including the modern phenomenon of youth culture. Within Europe, Spain differs from the United States perhaps more than any other nation. The United States and Spain stood as complete opposites in the early 1960s. Among developed American and European nations, Spain had the lowest newspaper circulation (70 per thousand population) and the penultimate rate for televisions (13.1 per thousand population) - only the Portuguese owned fewer sets.

During the Franco era, Spain also had no meaningful gauge of voting. By contrast, the United States had newspaper circulation in the middle of the range (326 per thousand population, compared to the United Kingdom, 506 per thousand population) and the highest number of television sets (306.4 per thousand population).

The percentage of U.S. citizens who actually voted, while not high (64.4 per cent in 1960), ranked with those nations lacking mandatory voting laws. The United States also had the highest level of college enrollment (1,983 per hundred thousand population) and Spain (258 per hundred thousand population) the lowest (Britain had 460 per hundred thousand population, but a larger share of enrollees graduated).

Perhaps because of these differences, most Americans know little of Spain beyond the tourist cliches of bullfights and flamenco, necessitating a brief overview of recent political, media, and generational history.

POLITICS

Unlike the United States, Spain experienced an extended pause from democracy during the Franco regime, which had a profound impact on the country. The "executions, the imprisonments, the torture, the lives destroyed by political exile and forced economic migration point to the exorbitant price paid by Spain for Franco's `triumphs' ". Despite these depredations, Spanish citizens remained committed to the ideal of civic culture. Under Franco, citizens in the different regions of Spain preferred democratic rule by "all of us" rather than by one caudillo, even in the most conservative strongholds. The commitment to democracy was based on the culture of Spain, rather than springing from economic factors or social structure.

In Franco's later years, Spain underwent a "Prussian-type economic development . . . beginning in the mid-1950s and promoted by national ruling classes". Preston characterized the 1960s as a period of robust economic growth resulting in broad social changes. Business and professional people became independent-minded in increasing numbers, and unrest from the worker movements applied growing pressure for change.

The Franco regime did institute some liberalizing policies, such as the Press Law enacted in 1966. Liberalization took firm root in such places as the universities, where Marxist publications became widely available and prominent intellectuals criticized the regime, calling for reform, and where "tolerance at the ideological level was unquestionable". Spain also experienced greater contact with the outside world, through flows of migration from Europe and increases in tourism primarily from the western hemisphere.

The assassination in 1973 of Carrero Blanco, the ultraconservative head of Franco's government, "was a factor of overwhelming importance". He was replaced by Carlos Arias Navarro, who, although not progressive, did support limited reforms. In his most important act, televised on February 12, 1974, he announced that "the national consensus in support of the regime must in the future be expressed in the form of participation". Arias Navarro's speech opened the door for Francoist institutions to reflect more political pluralism, although that aim faced repeated setbacks. The regime then enacted a Statute of Associations, which allowed groups to register, although few did (and opposition political parties remained prohibited).

The hopes for reform in the early 1970s clashed with economic frustration over Franco's "paternalistic regulation of the labour market", as well as his policy of keeping Spain out of the European Economic Community.

The energy crisis put a break on increases in the standard of living for the working class, which lacked political rights and became increasingly militant. By 1975, "it had become clear that socioeconomic and institutional change as well as modifications in political beliefs at both the mass and elite level of Spanish society had eroded away the underpinnings of the authoritarian regime". Franco himself became ill, and the media kept a vigil outside the palace. The extreme measures to postpone his death, the machinations to extend the regime, and the hope of installing a new head of the Cortes (Parliament) who would resist change - these things came to light only later. At the time, Spaniards witnessed only the head of government in tears, announcing Franco's death on TVE1, the state channel.

TRANSITION

Franco left behind a constitution that envisioned Prince Juan Carlos becoming king. This went as planned. The king would have ruled only as the successor to Franco, without full dynastic legitimacy, but then his father Don Juan de Borbon renounced his right to the throne. Arias Navarro continued as head of the government from November 1975 until the king replaced him in July 1976 with Adolfo Suarez, who followed a strategy of seeking pacts with the right and the left.

He got the approval of the military and Cortes for a Law on Political Reform, ratified in 1976. The process secured the right to form political parties, granted political amnesty, dissolved the state labour unions and the single Francoist Movimiento party, and then set free elections for the Constituent Assembly.

The consensus completely rejected Franco's plan: "trade unions were legalized, political parties, including the hated Partido Comunista de Espana [PCE], were permitted". Extremists of the right wing began a violent backlash, which reached a nadir in Madrid, January 23 to 28, 1977, during the semana negra or "black week" that left student activists and lawyers, as well as policemen, murdered. The fate of Spanish democracy seemed uncertain. In May 1977, during preparations leading up to the first general, multiparty elections, the Union Centro Democratico (UCD) formed a centre-right coalition of political forces. The communists (PCE) "played a major role in the transition and . . . gained 20 per cent of the vote in the 1977 election", and the socialists (PSOE) won more than a quarter of the vote (28 per cent and 118 seats). The centre coalition (UCD) received one-third of the votes (165 seats) and began a period leading a minority government that lasted until 1982 (in the 1979 general election, the UCD won 34 per cent and 168 seats, and the PSOE won 30 per cent and 121 seats).

The country put its economy on abetter footing with the Moncloa Pacts in October 1977. The accords imposed austerity, with budgetary control, tax reform, limits on wage increases, and a devalued peseta. As a result, inflation decreased (from 29 per cent) and exports went up, but unemployment also increased. The accords caused discontent when many of the promised reforms failed to materialize.

"Inevitably," Preston wrote, "the most dramatic difficulties encountered by Spain's newborn democracy were the direct legacy of Franco's rule". One of these, the Basque separatist movement (ETA), enjoyed some popular support through the 1970s. The rigid centralist policies of the Franco regime had left such regional movements stronger, especially those in the Basque country and Catalunya. Although the new constitution adopted in 1978 recognized regional autonomy, the separatist movements still presented a violent threat. A military trained to distrust democracy presented another difficulty.

This bore fruit when Lieutenant Colonel Antonio Tejero led a group of senior military officers in an attempted coup d'etat on February 23, 1981. The king went on state television to denounce the failed attempt, and the public responded with mass demonstrations. From 1977 to 1982, the socialists remained the principal opposition party. Then the socialist era arrived: "Felipe Gonzalez became prime minister in 1982, after his party's crushing victory in the elections that year. His second administration saw Spain enjoy dramatic levels of economic growth. His third administration was marked by internal party strife, exacerbated by growing evidence of corruption".

Following an unexpected victory in 1993, the government became increasingly mired in charges of corruption and was defeated in 1996 by the Partido Popular (PP), which formed a minority government with Catalan support. The 1996 elections marked the end of the transition from the Franco era. Since the transition, Spain appears to have entered a period of stability, similar to the quiescence characteristic of the mature U.S. democracy.

At a time when the left-leaning socialist party controlled Spanish government, the United States by contrast had a series of conservative administrations. A decline of trust in the U.S. government and its institutions marked the period. Surveys of opinions and attitudes since the transition to democracy indicate a Spanish citizenry consistently moderate in ideology and supportive of democratic principles.

They also have low levels of political interest and information. From the late 1970s through the late 1980s, a consistent share (about three-quarters) said they knew little or nothing about politics. When asked their general response to politics, a majority expressed boredom or indifference, while one-third expressed interest and enthusiasm and one-fifth expressed annoyance and disgust. These survey results lead researchers to identify an "outstanding feature in the political attitudes of Spanish people, namely, their political passivity".

MEDIA

In a study in the 1960s, the United States and United Kingdom plotted high and near the regression line correlating communications (an index computed from newspaper consumption, newsprint used, telephones installed, and mail volumes) and political development. Spain stood near the middle in communications development and the low-middle in political development, well below the average. This combination suggested a country poised, because of its communications development, to experience a spurt in political development - an accurate prediction, as it turned out.

Under the Franco regime, changes in the laws governing the press took a first step Towards liberalization. The 1966 reform changed the process (but not the fact) of censorship, ending it before publication but imposing "post hoc suspension or closure", so that editors had to guess what might get censored. "Franco, the Falange, the Army and the principles of the regime could not be criticized, but for all the limitations, the law constituted a real change, and the most reactionary elements in the regime were furious at the implications".

The policy change "gave rise to hopes of more substantial political change". Under the new law, periodicals such as the newspapers Informaciones, Ya, and Madrid and the magazine Diario 16 published criticism of the government and called for reform, working within the constraints of the regime. Publications also sprang up in regional languages such as Catalan.

Spanish television was founded as a state monopoly in the 1950s. "Under the Franco regime, television held the key to reading the eyes and ears of the Spanish population" because, unlike newspapers in the country, "television commands massive audiences". After Franco's death, government control continued over what were by then two state channels, TVE1 (also called La Primera) and TVE2 (La Dos). Newspapers gained much more freedom, and the transition saw several newspapers start up. The most important national paper to emerge, EI Pais, established a left-leaning socialist editorial line, in contrast to the right-leaning monarchist position of the newspaper ABC. The strong political agendas of Spanish newspapers did not come as a novelty. Much earlier, for example, "Franco spoke of the monarchist daily ABC as an `enemy'".

During the period of socialist rule, two important shifts occurred in the Spanish news media, bringing them closer to their U.S. counterparts. On one hand, the government revised (by some accounts timidly) the broadcasting laws. "In the 1980s, Spanish television evolved from a public monopoly, with only two state channels, into a competitive multi-channel system".

Two new channels began free broadcasting, Antena 3 and TeleS, and a third emerged based on subscription, Canal Plus. On the other hand, Pedro J. Ramirez founded in the late 1980s a national newspaper, EI Mundo. Ramirez, who worked as a young intern in the Washington Post newsroom the day Nixon resigned, introduced investigative journalism at EI Mundo. The paper took a strongly anti-socialist line against Felipe Gonzalez and his government. Ramirez made himself a household name in Spain by pushing the stories of corruption in government to the forefront of the political agenda.

The national newspapers in Spain circulate throughout the country, alongside (and in competition with) the local and regional press, and both continue growing in circulation. By the 1990s, all the older Spanish newspapers had reformatted themselves as smaller tabloids. The press has adopted an aggressive pattern of redesigns and received a number of awards, particularly El Mundo for reporting and EI Pais for design. U.S.-based journalism associations have named both of these among the best newspapers in the world. The changes in newspapers accompanied an erosion of press partisanship, with an increase in claims to professionalism among reporters and in market orientation among publishers.

Television news also has a history of partisanship in Spain, although less overt than the printed press. A study of the 1993 election, for example, shows that the state-controlled TVE1's favorable coverage of Gonzalez and the socialist government became especially pronounced in the pre-campaign period. In that election the private channels, Antena 3, Tele5, and Canal Plus, first covered the campaign in full. The entry of commercial broadcasters "has created a new audience map, and all the networks and stations are increasingly guided by ratings". As a result, public broadcasting, although still dominant, has seen a continual erosion of its audience and income.

Despite some growth, newspapers still do not receive wide readership in Spain, and total circulation reaches only one in ten of the population. The press has been expanding, however, with the number of newspapers published increasing since the 1980s. At the same time, the trends have been Towards greater concentration of ownership, including the growth of newspaper chains and cross-ownership of television and radio stations and magazines. These trends have parallels in the Unitcd States. Electioneering in the news media of various countries has begun to follow a pattern as elections become

Americanized. That trend makes a clear picture of U.S. news essential for understanding the Spanish media. Historically, the U.S. news media have operated under market competition with only limited government regulation. Public broadcasting arrived late and has played a very small role. The press remains predominantly local, with competition at that level declining as newspapers have closed or consolidated.

Coverage of politics has changed substantially since the 1960s, when newspaper reporters and television correspondents gave a largely descriptive chronicle of the candidates' words and movements during election campaigns. Studies show that U.S. journalists have increasingly described presidential campaigns using the metaphors of conflict or the horse race, positioning themselves as political interpreters for the public. As a result, media organizations may have largely supplanted political parties as the principal power brokers in the selection of U.S. leaders.

Competition for readers and viewers has imposed entertainment values on U.S. news. Since the 1960s, television journalists have greatly shortened politicians' sound bites and increased the relative share of time and emphasis given to their own judgments about campaigns. Newscasts became dramatically more visual in the 1970s, at the time when they reached a pinnacle of audience share and advertising revenues. Seeing themselves in competition with television, newspapers followed suit, updating their designs at a rate that accelerated in the early 1980s.

Both television and newspapers began to face audience declines in the mid-1980s, as cable expanded the alternatives for news (including CNN and C-SPAN). Newspaper executives identified and attempted to slow the erosion of readership among young adults. By the early 1990s, news executives viewed computer networks as a potential competitor. Unlike the ideological competition among Spanish newspapers, the U.S. press sees itself as part of a news market, where television broadcast news competes with cable and radio and where newspapers - most of them local monopolies - compete with broadcasters. Driven by market considerations, the U.S. news media aim for the greatest visual and emotional impact within the constraints of the widest possible audience appeal.

YOUNG ADULTS

A persistent puzzle of Spain since Franco has been the political culture that survey researchers characterize as passive, with low rates of participation, weak party allegiance, and limited social capital, as measured by memberships in civic associations and neighborliness. Despite low participation, the levels of cynicism and efficacy in Spain during the transition were no worse than those in the United Kingdom and the United States, and in general the "political culture in Spain did not differ too greatly from the political cultures of stable democracies". The period of rapid change in Spain did, however, produce clear differences between generations. Those in young adulthood during the late 1970s belong to what has been called the transition generation, born after 1951 and reaching adulthood after Franco. In 1980, 21to 25-year-olds had the highest feelings of political efficacy and lowest cynicism of any group.

On the whole, the young voiced more support for democracy, had more interest and confidence in politics, participated more, and had greater party allegiance, while they indicated less trust in the actions of authorities and in their country as a whole than did older Spaniards. General levels of participation ranked lower, but the young were among the most likely to participate in politics. The idea "of a generalized lack of interest in politics among the youngest age group is not borne out" at that time. They culminated a trend in which each succeeding generation, in response to the dictatorship, identified more strongly with the left in Spain.

Young adults of the post-transition generation are even less the product of their country's period under Franco than were their parents. Born near the time he died, they are reaching adulthood with Spain fully integrated into the European Community. They appear to be moving away from the left. Recent surveys show that they have levels of political interest similar to those found in 1980. The highest level of interest appears among those recently of voting age, and the level and growth of their interest corresponds to the availability and access to information such as news about politics. Their most common modes of political participation include voting, informing themselves, joining associations, and discussing politics. They report being most influenced by the media and by friends, followed by their families and by schools. They overwhelmingly support democracy as a political system, although they tend to judge their own country's system harshly in comparison to others in Europe. The survey data tend to contradict popular wisdom among the transition generation that their heirs in the posttransition era are less interested in and knowledgeable about politics, and more disengaged from and cynical about public life. No previous field work has examined this contradiction.

In the young generation's media experience, the newspaper landscape has had regular growth in circulation and in the number of newspapers published. Unlike their parents, they see EI Pais as a fixture and, of course, the anti-socialist, crusading EI Mundo as a novelty. Despite growth, newspapers form a small part of the media environment, but they offer a range of competing ideologies (contrary to the rule in the United States or in Spain under Franco).

Newspapers during the young adults' lives have been constantly changing - not only growing but redesigning and altering formats requiring regular adaptation and adjustment by the audience. Television, however, remained under state control through most of their formative years. Public broadcasting provided the only news on television through the 1989 campaign, when the post-transition generation entered its teenage years. The addition of private channels occurred in the political calendar during the next two elections, just as the young generation reached voting age. In other ways, the new generation of Spanish citizens presents a particularly interesting case. The country saw a baby boom immediately after Franco's death. Upon reaching an all-time high, the birthrate then dropped in subsequent years to reach the lowest level in the world. As a result, the group reaching young adulthood in the mid-1990s is the largest in Spain's history.

Their demographics create a case study in contrasts. On the up side, they have experienced the expansion of education and stabilization of democracy. The number of Spaniards completing college doubled between 1973 and 1992, and successive elections since the transition to democracy have produced rising levels of voting and other participation among the young.

On the down side, the large size of the generation has caused problems. With general unemployment high (22 per cent at the time of the 1996 election), discontent among young voters became a factor cited in the defeat of the socialist party. The counterpart cohort of young Americans is also part of a bulge generation, the children of America's earlier baby boom, and they have suffered similar economic consequences, with the attendant levels of discouragement.

INDICATORS TODAY

By the 1990s, the political and social gap between the United States and Spain had closed substantially. The share of Spanish workers employed in white collar jobs had grown dramatically (from 30 to 44 per cent, 1960 to 1981). Television had reached close to saturation in 1994 (99.3 per cent of households), and half had more than one set (49.9 per cent) and a VCR (57.6 per cent). However, the average electoral turnout remains much higher in Spain (73.9 per cent of eligible voters, since the death of Franco, 1977-1993) than in the United States.

On average, Spaniards use the media in very different patterns (according to 1996 data from ASEP). They view only three and one-half hours of television a day (210 minutes). The state channels still receive a third of the audience share (TVE1 at 28 per cent, TVE2 at 10 per cent), with private channels dividing up most of the rest (led by Antena 3 at 26 per cent, Tele5 at 19 per cent). Satellite channels from abroad play a much smaller role. Large differences appear especially in the printed press (according to 1996 data from FIEJ). The number of newspapers continues to grow (up 13.6 per cent from 1990 to 1994), as does daily circulation (up 36.6 per cent). Over the same period, the number of dailies in the United States declined (by 4.5 per cent), and weekday circulation was also down (by 5.3 per cent).

METHODS OF STUDY

Although political sociology since its founding has relied on data from statistical samples of various nations to use as indicators of political and social life, qualitative methods have also played a role. Personal essays written by citizens were considered a standard technique. In recent guides to crossnational study, half of the recommended methods require field work, and qualitative tools seem especially useful to examine subjective beliefs. Because survey data "necessarily abstracts institutions events, and processes from their unique social and cultural context", field studies become all the more important.

Autobiographical techniques have a long history in studies of the media and citizens, beginning with the groundbreaking examination of Polish peasants and immigrants to the United States. The full length autobiography has generally been used in the social sciences to study foreign or marginalized others. Bv simplifying and focusing autobiography more narrowly, researchers found a way to apply the technique to the mainstream. Blumer asked young people from many walks of life to write shorter narratives about one aspect of their experience, their memories of and reactions to movies. This technique, the limited life history, has found wide application in recent years among scholars in the social sciences and cultural studies.

The limited life history technique is especially effective for spanning time - the longitudinal section - as political culture is transmitted across generations. Life histories also impose an expanded view of political participation, not only including such elements as party affiliation and political interest included in questionnaires but also leaving open a full range of other activities, whatever participants choose to address in their narrative essays.

To find out about young Spaniards' subjective experiences with news, colleagues helped me collect life history narratives from young adults in Spain. During 1996, sixty-two undergraduates at three Spanish universities contributed their news experiences. The universities are located in three very different regions in Spain: the capital, Madrid, the industrial Navarra region, and the depressed autonomous community of Canarias. Because each of the universities draws from a wide area, the mix of participants included many other regions of Spain. The participants form what is called a "saturation sample", the qualitative standard for gathering sufficient examples. Saturation, the point at which any additional examples would add only particulars without increasing the general understanding about the group, is reached in most studies somewhere between twenty-five and thirty.

The study group is appropriate for two purposes. It first allows a close replication of the studies of U.S. college students. Second and more important, it represents the small but significant sector in Spain of the affluent and educated young. They form not only the core of up-scale audience members that news executives seek to attract and sustain but also the source for the next generation of political leaders, activists, and attentive citizens essential to democratic government. The participants were asked to write a short life history essay, beginning with their earliest memories and continuing to their current activities. They received the same instructions as did the U.S. groups in earlier studies, translated into Spanish, one set for television news and another for newspapers. About a third of the participants agreed to write two essays, one on each medium, to allow a comparison of their ways of writing and thinking about the two. All participants also completed a questionnaire with standard demographic, media use, and political items, the same completed by the U.S. groups but translated into Spanish.

The group is not intended, of course, to be a representative sample at the morphological level. The questionnaire was collected to allow a clear comparison to the previous studies as well as to national measurements of young Spaniards. In the survey responses, the volunteers did resemble the U.S. groups from previous studies: mostly communication majors, predominantly white, and roughly two-thirds women. Unlike the U.S. participants, a slightly larger share of Spanish volunteers haled from cities and large towns (80 per cent), with most of the remainder from smaller towns and rural areas (16 per cent). Their parents also differ, the largest share of whom attended only some high school (72 per cent of mothers, 50 per cent of fathers) and work mostly in labour and in the home.

The Spanish students reported higher levels of media use than did the Americans (the mean for each measure is shown). They read newspapers more often (5.4 days "last week") and watched newscasts more (6.1 days). More of the Spaniards said they read a national newspaper (36 per cent), local paper (40 per cent) or both (20 per cent), and none reported reading a student paper. There were no non-readers. For television news, more Spaniards reported watching local news (52 per cent) and national news (54 per cent and some watch both), but satellite and cable received no mention. There were no non-viewers. Besides their higher attention to news, they paid slightly more attention to audio-visual media. They said they watched a bit more television on average (84 minutes "yesterday") and listened to radio somewhat more (58 minutes). In contrast, they spent substantially more time with the newspaper (31 minutes). They read more books (2.1 "last month") but fewer magazines (3.6). They also watched many more movies (8.4 viewed, plus 1.0 rented).

The participants' media use roughly matched audience statistics for urban Spaniards their age. In national surveys (all figures from 1996 ASEP data), young adults generally used print media and radio more heavily than did older adults. Young adults read newspapers more (50 per cent "yesterday") than did all adults (37 per cent), although the gap appears to be narrowing.

The same share of young and older adults watched television (89 per cent), but slightly more of those under 30 watched news (76 per cent compared to 73 per cent "yesterday" for all adults). The study group, although smaller in number than the U.S. volunteers, was much more geographically diverse than either of the U.S. groups. However, the saturation sample did not yield sub-populations large enough to break out for comparison. The differing minority populations in the two countries did not permit comparison in any case.

I also gathered fifteen essays from Spanish adults older than 29, ten about newspapers and five about newscasts. These get mentioned parenthetically in the following sections. The older group, all white, split evenly by gender. They ranged from 30 to 52 years old, with the mode at 36. Their parents hold roughly the same types of jobs and attained about the same educational level as in the younger group. However, the older adults came predominantly from small towns and rural areas (53.3 per cent). They paid much more attention to newspapers, reading more days (6.3 "last week") and for longer intervals (37 minutes "yesterday"). They watched television news less often (5.3 days "last week") and spent less time with television (66 minutes "yesterday"). In fact, all their uses of media fell substantially lower (except movies rented, 4.5 "last month").

To help compare these life histories, I studied the newspaper essays separately from the television essays. For each group, I first read a small number (about a fifth) to look for the recurring themes found in the previous studies and revised the list as needed (this amounted to adding a few items). A Spanish assistant then used the translated and annotated list to code the essays for the presence or absence of each theme. To check reliability, I recoded some of the essays (20 per cent). The reliability coefficients between coders are quite good on average.

In reporting the results, I have stayed as closely as possible to the form and structure of the two earlier studies. Although lengthy, this strategy produced a wealth of description and allowed the maximum direct comparison to the studies being replicated.

The analysis in the next two sections, then, weaves together three strands: qualitative readings and quotations from each group of essays, the quantitative results of coding, and related questionnaire responses. To these dimensions I have added the following types of comparisons: with the counterpart group from the United States, with Spanish national statistics when available, and with records of important news stories since the mid-1970s, drawn from two chronicles the leading national newspapers published.

Quotations from the essays given in the following two sections identify the writer's gender, hometown size, and frequency of attending to the news medium (occasional 3 or fewer days "last week," regular 4 or 5, and habitual 6 or 7). Age is shown because I followed the Spanish norm of including adults under 30 (the U. S. statistics on young adults usually, but not always, include only 18- to 24-year-olds). Unless indicated, the writer came from a town.

Partisan Newspapers and Ritual

In broad strokes, the Spanish essays on newspapers reaffirmed the centrality of daily rituals for acquiring the reading habit. Although they did not present their newspaper experiences as uniformly by periods as did the Americans, the Spaniards did provide detailed accounts of the newspaper ritual for each stage in the U.S. chronology: in early childhood at home, middle childhood in school, and transition to adulthood, with various influences and political consequences in the present.

Unlike the Americans, the Spaniards became newspaper readers (and in quotations from these essays, the writer read the newspaper habitually, unless otherwise noted). Many aspects that make the Spanish press more attractive and accessible to young adults flow from the partisan ideologies newspapers overtly espouse. The partisan distinctiveness was echoed in the Spanish essays themselves, which on the whole seem much more varied and individualistic than the U.S. essays.

CHILDHOOD

At first the newspaper simply existed in the jumble of early childhood memories. Spaniards and Americans alike said they had a hard time remembering their first glimpse of one. An urban male occasional reader, 21, wrote, "It's like trying to remember seeing abed the first time or the bathroom of your house. They've always been there and there just wasn't a first time." A few did report a memorable first encounter:

When I was five, snooping in the old family bureau, I discovered a pile of yellowed papers, gnawed by mice. I unfolded it and found before my eyes a kind of revelation: one of those newspapers from before, on sheets so large you could roll me up in them. That was the first time I saw a newspaper. -a male regular reader, 25

Many of the essays, like the U.S. group, said they experienced newspapers as a constant presence (70 per cent) throughout their upbringing. Once the newspaper emerged from the tog of early childhood, however, the initial uniformity in Spanish and U. S. experiences dissolved.' The strength of habit and family training came through strongly among the Spaniards. A majority of their essays described newspapers as a part of family routine (56.7 per cent), a share exceeding that found in the U.S. essays. None of the Spanish writers concluded from the repetitive nature of their early experience that newspapers therefore had little importance or played no role in their lives.

The Spaniards described many ways the news routine unified them with parents. Two-thirds of the essays said that their first encounters with newspapers occurred in the presence of parents (66.7 per cent), and many of those who did not cite parents instead mentioned grandparents. The essays talked of morning rituals for purchasing bread and newspapers that made them feel part of the adult world. An urban female, 21, wrote, "When he took me to school, we used to stop at some kiosk and he gave me money so I could buy the paper. Since I was very small, it gave me the illusion of going alone to buy it, and I felt grown up." Spaniards reported more parental encouragement than did the Americans. Quite a few essays said parents urged them to read the paper (40 per cent), and on the questionnaire a majority (66.7 per cent) said parents encouraged them either "strongly" or "somewhat" (compared to very few essay mentions and much lower ratings by the U.S. group). The Spanish parents also encouraged their children to read books (83.3 per cent, only slightly below the U.S. group), suggesting that the difference springs from their beliefs about newspapers, not about reading in general.

Some Spanish parents went beyond urging and read aloud or discussed the newspaper. Unlike the Americans, more Spaniards said their parents read to them from the newspaper (20 per cent). They also described the family having conversations based on the newspaper.

I remember my father in the kitchen reading the paper while my mother served lunch. He also, after reading something interesting, commented about it to my mother, and they both began a conversation, filled with constant exclamations. -an urban female, 20

With all the urging they received as children, the Spaniards expressed impatience with parents (6.7 per cent) only about as often as the U.S. group, but they less often defined the paper as exclusively for adults (33.3 per cent, compared to almost half of the U.S. essays).

The gap between the child and the newspaper as an adult activity seems smaller in Spain. Responses to the format of the paper, for example, created less of an issue among the Spanish participants. Children from both countries encountered broadsheet pages as youngsters, but the Spaniards then watched the changeover to tabloid size. About a third of the essays mentioned the change (30 per cent), and none talked about continuing frustration with the large pages, as the Americans did. Instead, they remembered large broadsheets fondly as objects from childhood. An urban female, 20, recalls, "With that enormous paper I could make the biggest paper hats you've ever seen." Although some young Spaniards mentioned the ink rubbing off, none expressed the sort of irony on the subject found in the U.S. essays. An urban female, 21, said she liked newspapers because "it didn't matter if I tore them up or spilled on them because the next morning a new one appeared in my father's hands."

The Spanish essays did not reveal the climate of conflict apparent in the U.S. stories, although the gender and power order for reading the paper worked about the same in both countries. The Spaniards mentioned fathers being first (30 per cent) a bit more often than Americans did, but the Spaniards also mentioned mothers reading first (10 per cent), or "parents" (6.7 per cent), or others, especially grandparents (13.3 per cent). (This represents a change from the previous generation, according to the older Spaniards, who said twice as often that their fathers used the newspaper first.) Only one essay reported sibling rivalry over newspaper access. A female regular reader, 21, said "there were even fights in my house because both of us wanted to be the first to read it. In the end, what always ruled was the strong arm." Although some of the gender issues Americans discussed surely exist in Spanish home life, most of the essays did not seem troubled by the disparity between gender roles.

The Americans expressed much more conflict with the newspaper as a form and object, with its role in defining the power relationships within the family, and, most important, with the adult world it represents. Americans defined their situation by the yawning rift in their social world, between themselves as small children and the distant, sometimes incomprehensible world of grownups.

7

Role of Journalism in a Democracy

ROLE OF THE GOVERNMENT AGENCIES

The Government's anti-corruption agencies conduct stings to nab the corrupt. Numbered and chemically treated currency notes are given to officials demanding bribes. This money is not the Government's, but the complainant's. It becomes case property during judicial processes against the accused. Providing money on Government account for stings is generally frowned upon as a means of encouraging corruption.

In the US, the FBI conducts nearly 170 operations a year, to investigate complaints of bribery, extortion, narcotics smuggling, sale of cigarettes to minors, child abuse, etc. Ground rules have been laid down over the years by departmental instructions and judicial rulings. One is that sting operations can be mounted only against persons against whom some evidence of criminality exists, and such an exercise is considered necessary for getting conclusive evidence.

Permission for stings must be obtained from appropriate courts or the Attorney-General. This safeguard has been put in place since those who organise stings may themselves commit offences of impersonation or criminal trespass under false pretexts so as to catch criminals red-handed. The complainant's identity is not revealed unless he himself makes the details of his complaint public or discloses his identity to any other office or authority.

After concealing the complainant's identity, the designated agency makes discreet inquiries to ascertain whether any basis exists for proceeding further with the complaint. For this purpose, it has to devise an appropriate machinery.

The Central Vigilance Commission, for instance, is authorised, as the designated agency, to receive written complaints or disclosures on allegations of corruption or misuse of office by any employee of the Central Government or of any corporation established by or under any Central Act, Government companies, societies or local authorities owned or controlled by the government. The disclosure or complaint must contain full particulars, accompanied by supporting documents or other materials. The designated agency may call for further information or particulars from persons making the disclosure. If the complaint is anonymous, it should not take any action in the matter. Under the law and Constitution, ministers enjoy no special privileges with regard to corruption or any other criminal offence and are equal before law like any other citizen, has ensured that the media in India is legally unfettered while reporting even if it damages the reputation of a public figure (subject to the laws of defamation). In fact, India prides itself in having one of the most independent, vibrant, fearless media in the developing world. From time to time media exposes have brought to light corruption at the very highest echelons of government - be it ministers or senior bureaucrats, no one is spared.

Even prime ministers have come under media scrutiny, as in the cases of Rajiv Gandhi and Narasimha Rao. Investigative reporting and major scoops have often shaken the foundations of government and even led to the resignation of ministers and have also inspired the courts to take suo motu cognizance of certain cases highlighted by the media.

Thus the media takes its role as the Fourth Estate, the watchdog and conscience keeper of the nation and shaper of public opinion very seriously and functions with a high level of freedom and independence. However, it would be politically naive to assume that extraneous interests do not influence media reports.

The fact that the private media, whether newspapers or TV channels, are owned by business groups who in turn have political affiliations, does have a bearing on the manner of reporting, the slant given to reports, and the editorial content. This invariably leads to newspapers/TV channels committing acts of omission or commission, suppressing or exposing facts according to political compulsions, and so indirectly and subtly promoting the interests of the parties they support.

Freedom of the press is included in the wider freedom of expression which is guaranteed under Article 19 (1) (a) of the Constitution. Here freedom of expression is taken to mean the freedom to express not only one's own views but also the views of others, to propagate, circulate and defend them by any means, including printing. But since the freedom of expression is not an absolute freedom and is subject to clause (2) of Article 19, laws may be passed imposing reasonable restriction on the freedom of the press in the interests of the security of the state, the sovereignty and integrity of India, friendly relations with foreign states, public order, decency or morality, or for the prevention of contempt of court, defamation or incitement to an offence.

Constitution and Censorship of the Press

Censorship of the press is not specifically prohibited by any provision of the Constitution. Like other restrictions, its constitutionality has to be judged by the test of "reasonableness" (both substantive and procedural) within the meaning of clause (2) of Article 19. With the commencement of the Constitution, the question of the validity of censorship came up before the Supreme Court where it ruled that imposition of pre-censorship on a journal was an obvious restriction upon the freedom of speech guaranteed under clause (1) of Article 19. Shortly after these decisions, clause (2) was amended by the Constitution (First Amendment) Act, 1951, by inserting the words "public order" in clause (2). The word "reasonable" was also inserted in clause (2) by the same amendment.

The result was that if censorship were imposed in the interests of public order, it cannot at once be held to be unconstitutional as a fetter upon the freedom of circulation but its reasonableness has to be determined with reference to the circumstance of its imposition. Thus, even in a time of peace, censorship for a limited period may be valid if it is subjected to reasonable safeguards, both from the substantive and procedural standpoints. But if it is left to the absolute discretion of the executive authority, it must be held unreasonable. The mainstream media does, on occasion, expose the nefarious activities of public servants and politicians.

Mass Media systems of the world vary from each other according to the economy, polity, religion and culture of different societies. In societies, which followed communism and totalitarianism, like the former USSR and China, there were limitations of what the media could say about the government. Almost everything that was said against the State was censored for fear of revolutions. On the other hand, in countries like USA, which have a Bourgeois Democracy, almost everything is allowed.

Shifting our view to the Indian perspective and its system of Parliamentary Democracy, it is true that, the Press is free but subject to certain reasonable restrictions imposed by the Constitution of India, 1950, as amended ("Constitution"). Before the impact of globalisation was felt, the mass media was wholly controlled by the government, which let the media project only what the government wanted the public to see and in a way in which it wanted the public to see it. However, with the onset of globalisation and privatisation, the situation has undergone a humongous change.

Before the invention of communication satellites, communication was mainly in the form of national media, both public and private, in India and abroad. Then came 'transnational media' with the progress of communication technologies like Satellite delivery and ISDN (Integrated Services Digital Network), the outcome: local TV, global films and global information systems.

In such an era of media upsurge, it becomes an absolute necessity to impose certain legal checks and bounds on transmission and communication. Mass Media laws in India have a long history and are deeply rooted in the country's colonial experience under British rule. The earliest regulatory measures can be traced back to 1799 when Lord Wellesley promulgated the Press Regulations, which had the effect of imposing pre-censorship on an infant newspaper publishing industry. The onset of 1835 saw the promulgation of the Press Act, which undid most of, the repressive features of earlier legislations on the subject. Thereafter on 18th June 1857, the government passed the 'Gagging Act', which among various other things, introduced compulsory licensing for the owning or running of printing presses; empowered the government to prohibit the publication or circulation of any newspaper, book or other printed material and banned the publication or dissemination of statements or news stories which had a tendency to cause a furore against the government, thereby weakening its authority.

Then followed the 'Press and Registration of Books Act' in 1867 and which continues to remain in force till date. Governor General Lord Lytton promulgated the 'Vernacular Press Act' of 1878 allowing the government to clamp down on the publication of writings deemed seditious and to impose punitive sanctions on printers and publishers who failed to fall in line. In 1908, Lord Minto promulgated the 'Newspapers (Incitement to Offences) Act, 1908 which authorized local authorities to take action against the editor of any newspaper that published matter deemed to constitute an incitement to rebellion. However, the most significant day in the history of Media Regulations was the 26th of January 1950 – the day on which the Constitution was brought into force. The colonial experience of the Indians made them realise the crucial significance of the 'Freedom of Press'. Such freedom was therefore incorporated in the Constitution; to empower the Press to disseminate knowledge to the masses and the Constituent Assembly thus, decided to safeguard this 'Freedom of Press' as a fundamental right.

Although, the Indian Constitution does not expressly mention the liberty of the press, it is evident that the liberty of the press is included in the freedom of speech and expression under Article 19(1) (a). It is however pertinent to mention that, such freedom is not absolute but is qualified by certain clearly defined limitations under Article 19(2) in the interests of the public. It is necessary to mention here that, this freedom under Article 19(1)(a) is not only cribbed, cabined and confined to newspapers and periodicals but also includes pamphlets, leaflets, handbills, circulars and every sort of publication which affords a vehicle of information and opinion. Thus, although the freedom of the press is guaranteed as a fundamental right, it is necessary for us to deal with the various laws governing the different areas of media so as to appreciate the vast expanse of media laws.

THE PROPOSED IT ACT AMENDMENTS IN INDIA

Power of Police office and other Officers to Enter, Search, etc-Deleted

It seems the proposed IT Act no more satisfy the traditional purpose of law making, *i.e.* a measure to preserve and maintain social order. The public interest is different from the private interest that seems to have favoured the Committee while suggesting the deletion of section 80.

The correct approach is to give proper "training" to the police officers and judicial officers dealing with Cyber Laws so that justice can be done to the accused, victim and the society. The power of the police officers should not be taken away.

It would serve the interest of justice if the police officers "consult" the Cyber law experts before taking an action, till they are well equipped with the Cyber Laws.

Compounding of Certain Offences

1. Notwithstanding any thing contained in the Code of Criminal Procedures, 1973, any Offence punishable under this Act may either before or after the institution of any prosecution be compounded by
   (a) The Controller; or
   (b) The adjudicating officers appointed under section 46, where the maximum amount of fine and/or imprisonment does not exceed such limits as may be specified by the Central Government.
   On payment or credit to the Central Government of such sum as the Controller or the Adjudicating officer, as the case may be, may specify.
2. Nothing in sub-section (1) shall apply to an offence committed by a person within a period of three years from the date on which a similar offence committed by him was compounded under this section.

Explanation: For the purpose of this section any second or subsequent offence committed after the expiry of a period of three years from the date on which the offence was previously compounded, shall be deemed to be a first offence.

3. Where any offence is compounded before the institution of any prosecution, no prosecution shall be instituted in relation to such offence, either by the Controller or by the adjudication officer or by any other person, against the offender in relation to whom the offence is so compounded.
4. Where the composition of any offence is made after the institution of any prosecution, such composition shall be brought by the Controller or the adjudicating officer in writing, to the notice to the Court in which the prosecution is pending and on such notice of the composition of the offence being given, the person in relation to whom the offence is so compounded shall be discharged.

This again is not a good suggestion to be accepted. The reasons are numerous and some of them will be discussed here.

Firstly, the Cr.P.C has been totally excluded in this context. The Cr.P.C contains section 320 that provides for the compounding of offences contained in I.P.C. Now section 320 is divided into two parts. Section 320(1) respects the party autonomy and victimology aspects.

The victim can compound the offences specified in Table-1 without the intervention and permission of the court. Section 320(2), on the other hand, allows the victim of the offence to compound the offence with the permission of the court, for the offences mentioned in Table-2. Section 320(8) provides that a compounding of an offence under section 320 will amount to "acquittal' of the accused. Now if section 320 is "overridden" by section 80A then "all the offences" related to Cyber Crimes and Contraventions under the I.P.C and other laws for the time being in force will be made automatically compoundable too because section 80A is not subject to "Tables" unlike section 320. Thus, practically the bar of "specified compoundable offences" is not there under section 80A.

Secondly, the blanket protection of compounding the offences and contraventions either before or after the institution of any prosecution without any safeguard of "specified compoundable offences" cannot be accepted to be rationale and reasonable in any society. If "all" the offences and contraventions can be compounded then there is no need of putting these offences and contraventions in the IT Act.

Thirdly, a "bar of jurisdiction" has been created by section 80A (3) if the offence or contravention has been compounded before the institution of the prosecution. Now suppose the "privacy" of an individual has been violated and he is planning to file a complaint before the competent authority. If that privacy violation is compounded before that complaint, then he cannot file that complaint at all. The worst part about this process is that there is no need of "consulting" the "aggrieved party".

Fourthly, an 'obligation" has been imposed upon the courts to discharge the accused if the compounding has been done after the institution of the proceedings. Thus, no discretion whatsoever has been given to the courts.

Section 81: General Provisions

1. The provisions of this Act shall have effect notwithstanding anything inconsistent therewith contained in any other law for the time being in force.
2. Nothing that is permitted under the Copyright Act 1957 and the Patents Act 1970 as amended from time to time shall render any person liable for contravention of any of the provisions of this Act.

This is a welcome provision that will go a long way in the overall economic development of the nation. This will also reduce the chances of prosecution for innocent and inadvertent IT Act violations that are permitted as per

Copyright Act and Patents Act. It would be better if the protection is also extended to other IPRs as well particularly the Trade Marks Act, 1999.

Section 85: Offences by companies

Where a person committing a contravention of any of the provisions of this Act or of any rule, direction or order made thereunder is a company, every person who, at the time the contravention was committed, was in charge of, and was responsible to, the company for the conduct of business of the company as well as the company, shall be guilty of the contravention and shall be liable to be proceeded against and punished accordingly:

Provided that nothing contained in this sub-section shall render any such person liable to punishment (if he proves-Deleted) unless it is proved that the contravention took place with (without-Deleted) his knowledge and connivance and that he failed to prevent such contravention ;(or that he exercised all due diligence to prevent such contravention-Deleted).

This is a "peculiar" suggestion. It seems the Committee got confused with the "burden of proof" aspect between a "natural person" and an "artificial person".

The law expects every person to act fairly, reasonably and diligently. That is why deviations from these standards are made punishable by the law. One cannot in the zeal of earning profit or in the sense of indifference take the law casually. There are certain well-recognised cardinal principles of criminal laws, which need to be discussed before proceeding further.

These are:

1. The ignorance of law is no excuse,
2. The "presumption of innocence" continues until the guilt of the accused is proved,
3. The guilt of the accused must be proved "beyond reasonable doubt",
4. No person is guilty of an offence unless it is accompanicd by an act/omission and the guilty intention for the same,
5. The law may presume the guilty intention if the commission of the act is proved. This is known as "strict liability offences", and
6. The law may fix the liability of certain individuals on a "notional basis". This usually happens where a company is involved in the commission of an offence or wrong. The imputation of criminal liability to certain "natural persons" is logical because a company, being an artificial person, cannot operate automatically. Thus, to conduct the affairs of the company certain natural persons are required, who alone can be saddled with the liability of the wrongs committed by the company.

Now it is logical and reasonable to fix the "burden of proof" upon the prosecution where natural persons are involved in the commission of an offence. The same yardstick and parameters cannot, however, be made applicable to an artificial person like company, though ultimately it is manned by natural persons. That is why the burden of proof is upon the company to prove its innocence. For instance, a natural person can be held liable for murder, grievous hurt, etc. If we are applying the "normal rules' of criminal law then perhaps the Companies must also be held liable for "manslaughter", grievous hurt, etc. That will bring absurd results.

That is why a "reasonable classification' has been made between natural and artificial persons and the same should not be mixed at any cost. If this suggestion is accepted, then we have to change all the existing laws that contain a "standard form clause" regarding the liability of the Companies. The liability clause in the IT Act is exactly same as is found in all other statutes.

Even otherwise, in the ultimate analysis the prosecution has to prove the guilt of the accused beyond reasonable doubts once the preliminary burden of proof is discharged by the person managing the company. It seems the Committee has fixed the preliminary burden of proof upon the prosecution unlike other statutes where it is upon the company.

PUBLIC SPHERE AND DEMOCRACY

Most directly, "the public sphere is paradigmatically associated with discussions on democracy and its shortcomings". In this respect, the public sphere is viewed as a resource for growth of democracy, promoting discussions of civil society and public life. The concept of the public sphere appeals to the nature of civil society as it attempts to explain the social foundations of democracy and to introduce a discussion of the specific organization of social and cultural bases within civil society for the development of an effective rational-critical discourse. Habermas (1992) saw the public sphere as a domain of social life in which public opinion could be formed out of rational public debate. Ultimately, informed and logical discussion, could lead to public agreement and decision making, thus representing the best of the democratic tradition.

Blumler and Gurevitch (2001) argue that the new interactive media have a "vulnerable potential" to enhance public communications and enrich democracy. Scholars of political sciences also ask if it is possible to foster democratic development with the help of communication technology. Hagen states that research on the relationship between communication technologies and democracy has turned up ample evidence illustrating that concepts of electronic democracy contribute both to democratic theory and our understanding of the working of a democratic political system in the information age (Newhagen, 2000).

Accordingly, it is the condition of the public sphere that differentiates democratic political systems from non-democratic ones. In the absence of the public sphere, people are deprived from a space through which they can govern themselves by themselves for themselves. "The importance of the public sphere to democratic theory and democratic movements cannot be underestimated. For a functioning and purposeful citizenry to develop, it is argued that they must have a space in which to engage debate and make decisions. This space is thought to exist outside of the governmental sphere and the private sphere. The public sphere is seen to lie between these two other parts of social life in order to develop solutions to social problems. Citizens in the public sphere are meant to leave their personal concerns behind, and transcend their limited subjectivities in pursuit of 'the common good'" (Franko, 2005).

Engagement in the public sphere defines the public, and it is best to envision the public sphere not necessarily as a public space, but as a purposeful interaction towards discussion and democratic decision-making. Habermas tells us that, "a public sphere comes into being in every conversation in which private individuals assemble to form a public body" (Franko, 2005).

To better understand the nature of the public space we need to differentiate it from other types of spaces. A space is private when given individuals are recognized by others as having the right to establish criteria that must be met for anyone else to enter it. Thus, we speak of a private room, a private meeting, and private parts. Such a space is belongs to someone that has the right to establish criteria by which access is allowed or denied. Sacred space is different and similar. Such a space is neither made by human action nor can it be owned. It is the God. The sacred space as identified here reflects the European view which is completely different from that of Islam, as there is no separation between private and public spaces from the Islamic point of view. At the other extreme, a space may be common to human beings. There are no criteria for common space. It is not owned or controlled and is open to everyone. Thus, the sea or forests are (or can be) common space. This is not a space to which one goes to speak with others and therefore, it is not a public realm, and its boundaries are not contestable per se. Public space is a space created by and for humans that is always contestable, and it is open to those who meet the criteria, but it is not owned in the sense of being controlled.

In the tradition of Western thought, the very idea of democracy is inseparable from that of public space. It is perceived as a disposition to open and contradictory debate with the aim of making possible a reasoned understanding between citizens with regard to the matter of the definition of institutions, the formulation of laws, and their enforcement. From this point of view, public means simultaneously: open to all, well known to all, and acknowledged by all. Public space stands in opposition to private space, because it is civic space and it belongs to the citizens. Historically, the public sphere has been associated with revolution. The public gathering of individuals, to make decisions and garner support is critical to most reform movements. Thus, Habermas defines the public sphere as "the scene of a psychological emancipation that corresponded to a political economic one". The public sphere and democracy should not be considered as inseparable from one another, because the democratic political systems are based on the voice of the people and the rule of the majority that is likely formed through a liberal public sphere in which people freely discuss the critical public issues.

In Egypt, the situation is different from that of Western countries, as the separation between public sphere and democracy is the most likely dominant principle in the Egyptian milieu. The government is obliged to allow a partly-free public sphere. However, it restricts the formation of real public opinion and establishes the types of laws and legislations that perpetuate the dominance of the ruling party. Simply speaking, it seems that the government allows people to say whatever they want, while allowing itself to act whatever it wants. In this political atmosphere, it is difficult to find a link between public sphere and democratic transformations. However, a free or partly-free public sphere may eventually lead to formation of public opinion that will govern.

Habermas (1989) first conceived of the public sphere as a physical space that first emerged in coffee houses in England and salons in France in the 17th and 18th centuries with the rise of capitalism and the state. He describes the public sphere as a physical place where propertied, educated men who were members of the bourgeois joined together to engage in rational-critical discourse on public matters and other issues of the day. Even in the early public sphere, newspapers and journals were an enabling technology that helped create a network bringing the forums of the coffee houses and salons together to create the larger public sphere. For Habermas and Alexis de Tocqueville, the public sphere was a place where men gathered to rationally discuss issues of the day. Newspapers played a key role in the public sphere by supplying information, creating interest, and helping set the agenda for participants in the public sphere.

Conversation and action oriented around discussion define what the public sphere should be, according to classic theorists. John Keane describes the public sphere as "a particular type of spatial relationship between two or more people, usually connected by a certain means of communication...in which Non-violent controversies erupt, for a brief or more extended period of time, concerning the power relations operating within their given milieu of interaction and/or with the wider milieus of social and political structures within which the disputants are situated" (Rajagopal, 2004). The linkage between people via means of communication is critical here, whether this communication exists via conversation, in the press or on satellite television. Communication is essential for the public sphere, and in many ways, it is the only constitutive element of that space (Franko, 2005).

At a general level, the concept of the public sphere is defined by many scholars as designating a realm related to democratic political discourse. Here, the notion of "public" as in "public opinion" refers to a collection of politically significant shared common interests impacting ideologically upon the exercise of state of power. Of course not all politics (democratic or otherwise) take place through discussion (public or not). The public sphere, however, is a concept applicable to voluntary and violence-free political behaviour. For this reason, Habermas argues that the public sphere needs institutional guarantees of a constitutional state on the one hand, and on the other, a political culture in the broader society of populace accustomed to freedom. This perception helps explain the importance of a democratic constitution and the rule of law as contextual conditions of media's optimum democratic role.

When Alexis de Tocqueville, a French nobleman and political scientist, visited the United States in 1831, he was so impressed with what he termed the "voluntary associations" of men in the United States; he devoted much study and later description of these associations in his treatise on American life, democracy in America. Although Tocqueville utilizes the term "associations" rather than "public sphere," a thorough reading of both men's writings leaves little doubt that they are talking about the same thing. There are obviously some differences between the European and American public spheres. These differences are both political and cultural, but the similarities are more numerous and profound than are the differences. Tocqueville even surmised that the notion of associations in America was imported from England and that the differences can be attributed to Americans' incorporation of their manners and customs.

There are numerous and profound similarities between the American public sphere of the 19th century as described by Tocqueville and the European public sphere of the 17th and 18th centuries as described by Habermas. Non-etheless, there are also discernible differences between the spheres with the greatest difference resting in the relationships between the spheres and their governments. The American public sphere did not clearly reside in the private realm; it was often tied to government. The stronger relationship between government and the American public sphere is logical when one remembers that the Americans were members of a self-governing democracy who believed they had a duty to take an active role in the official governance of their communities. The public spheres of Europe occurred at times and within countries where political power was still very much vested in monarchs and church leaders.

Another difference between the two public spheres is that within the American associations, people pursuing public interests coexisted with people pursuing private interests (Tocqueville, 1956 in Newhagen, 2004) Habermas believed that the pursuit of private interests displaced the pursuit of public interests in the European public spheres (Habermas, 1989in Newhagen, 2004) In Habermas' conceptualization of the public sphere he privileges face-to-face communication, believing the most valuable role for the media is to provide information for intimate exchanges. He accepts that the printed word played a significant role in the development of the bourgeois public sphere, but he did not fully conceive of the key role for media in the public sphere. In his writings he also expresses a distrust for mediated communication, seeing it as an obstacle to "discursive rationality and communicative authenticity".

Taking the aforementioned discussion into account, it is safe to state that public sphere depends to a large extent on the nature of the political system in which it exists. In Europe, the public sphere-which was achieved despite opposition from the state powers, is at odds with what transpired in the United States. Habermas' suggestion that the European public sphere was regulated by its individual members is contradicted by the U.S.'s case, where the media emerge instead as the first and foremost project of nation-building. Starr considers three extended and overlapping "constitutive moments" when political choices and technological developments shaped the media's growth. "America's first information revolution" was the first constitutive" moment," extending from the colonial period to the onset of the civil war" (Rajagopal, 2006). Its distinctive trait was the deliberate development of inexpensive postage, schools, and newspapers through direct and indirect subsidies. The intent was to enable the people of the nascent and geographically dispersed republic to communicate with each other and thereby strengthen their internal ties. The result was a population that actively participated in public and political life. Thus, while European countries discouraged communication by placing taxes on the postal service, the early Post Office in the U.S. saw its goal as promoting intercourse, and reducing the mental distance between town and country. At one point, America's ratio of post offices to people was four times that of England or France.

Starr also notes the government's early realization of the importance of public education, although it was public schools of the North, not the South, that regularly increased enrollment. Starr explains at length the policies that made books and newspapers far less expensive in the United States than in Europe (among these was a disregard for European copyright laws that made windfall profits possible for U.S. publishers). Contemporary observers noted the effects of the early development of the press in the US. The private realm did not arise from a struggle against state absolutism, as in Europe, but as an effect of state formation. Not surprisingly, the constitution and the government are frequently granted cultural sanction to restrict the scope of these customs (Starr, 2004).

On the other hand, Arab political systems have created a politically repressive atmosphere to control the public sphere. The development of media and state in the Arab world confirm the fact that all Arab states controlled the media, especially radio and television, to prevent the establishment of a free public sphere, to restrict the formation of public opinion and to hinder any democratic transformation in the region. "There are several reasons for the predominance of government–owned broadcasting system in the Arab World. However, the most important factor is the intense government interest in the media as political instruments, media reach beyond borders and literary barriers; the government has a much greater interest in controlling them or at least keeping them out of hostile hands" (Rugh, 2004).

In his research on "Arab media and communication systems in the information age", Hamada concludes that democratizing the media and communication system represents a real threat to any undemocratic regime. The majority of Arab governments have never been interested in creating a democratic communication environment in which the citizens can have a voice regarding public issues. Government operated media agencies provide most of the information, and much of the content it supplies is politically biased, incomplete, and of poor quality. Most Arab governments claim that the issues of development must take priority and that the time is not right for democracy. Therefore, democracy is not a part of most Arab leaders' political agenda.. Although democracy and development represent two distinctly different human endeavours, they are both required, to ensure success, sustainability, adequate levels of information and popular participation. The more objective and the wider the scope of information conveyed, the more likely it will be to sustain democracy and development. Modern communication technology is essential in the speed and efficiency with which data and news are processed and disseminated among different citizens of the society. Another common and related requirement for both democracy and development is an active and public participation (Attiga, 2001).

The bulk of the discussion on media pluralism as a political value continues to be based on the conceptual framework of the public sphere. As a general normative concept against which to assess the media, much of the debate draws upon Habermas's early work (1989) but also, more broadly, the public sphere is understood as a general context of interaction in which deliberation and discussion take place and citizens in general inform and form themselves into the public (Karppinen, 2004). Lippman conceives of public opinion as the aggregate opinion of persons whose individual opinions are pieced together from what they hear, read, see and are able to imagine. He also believes that their exposure to information is manipulated to create a certain opinion that meets the needs of elites. Lippman's idea of public opinion is quite different from Habermas' conception. Habermas believes public opinion is what develops in the public sphere as the result of rational discourse. He views public opinion as the culmination of sharing of information among enlightened individuals operating in the public interest.

The author completely agrees with Hbermas's notion of the priority of public interests as a condition for the public sphere. First, in order for the public sphere to exist, priority has to be given to social issues. If people left public issues behind and concentrate on their private interests, there will never be a space for the common good, common grounds for members of the public to exchange experience, but personal interests that work against the collective mind. In Egypt, the overwhelming majority are poor, illiterate, and unemployed people who spend much of their time trying to save their food. Hence, the majority is handicapped by illiteracy, poverty, ills and unemployment to such a great extent that they lack motivation to engage in the "public sphere". Also complicating the problem is the government's intolerance with the activities of the opposing parties and political movements. Due to this atmosphere, the role of new communication technologies, especially the Internet, in enhancing public sphere is limited.

MASS MEDIA AND PUBLIC SPHERE

As Mansson (1999) points out, many scholars regard the media as the main institution of the contemporary public sphere. However, we have to consider the fact that restricted media will never contribute to public sphere. If the media are state-owned, working under direct supervision of the government officials and suffer from political and economic pressures, the government's voice is the only one that will be heard in the public sphere. For Habermas, the real public is the one that assembles and engages in dialogue. There is no public space without "reciprocal communication". For Regis Debray, the real public is the one that reads and writes, that reasons, as opposed to one that allows itself to be influenced by images. In the author's opinion, the public sphere is the freedom of the public to convene via free media space which is detached from the government, providing marginalized people an arena to speak out about public policies and decisions. As my definition illustrates media ownership, media diversity and freedom of speech are requirements for a true public sphere.

Although we can accept the assumption made by Manuel Castells who asserts that "the media have become the essential space of politics", we have to be careful of whether all types of media have the potential to establish a public sphere or not. For the public sphere to exist, the media have to provide equal opportunities for its users to freely discuss and form their opinions which eventually will form an important mechanism to affect state policies.

Thus, any analysis of the contemporary political climate must take into account the interaction between the media and political candidates, issues and citizens. Political participation, citizenship and the media cannot be separated. As Castells points out, "to an overwhelming extent people receive their information, on the basis of which they form their political opinion...through the media. Thus the media space is the space of information, and the sphere citizens depend on to direct them towards relevant issues" (Franko, 2005). Having said this, it is not acceptable to conclude that entertainment-oriented media or government–owned media will play a significant role in shaping an Egyptian public sphere. Therefore, Habermas' was concerned about modern media and his concerns stem in part from the media's reliance on mass advertising for revenue. Although advertising dates back to ancient times, mass advertising sharply increased following the industrial revolution as manufacturers sought markets for their factory-produced goods. So, much of what appears in media today is not meant to be informative and enlightening for participants in the public sphere. It is merely entertainment and designed to attract audiences that will appeal to advertisers.

Michael Robinson's research demonstrates that voters who rely on television for political campaign information are prone to develop a feeling of political inefficacy, distrust, and cynicism. He coined the term "videomalaise" in order to express that television gives rise to political malaise among the public. Gerbner and his collaborators' research seems to justify the interpretation that television viewing cultivates fear, alienation, and interpersonal mistrust. In Europe, similar concerns became an issue in public debate and an object of study in the late 1970s and early 1980s in the course of deregulating and commercializing the broadcasting sector. European television adopted the American model in the 1980s and conquered the market with Programmes emphasizing entertainment, crime and violence. It is quite likely that changes of this kind have an impact on the political system and the public sphere.

With the advent of the technologies of modernity, time has become separated from space and space from place, giving rise to ever more "disembedded social systems". Social relations have been lifted out of local contexts of interaction and restructured across "indefinite spans of time-space" (Giddens, 1990). As a result, what can be defined as a global public sphere emerged. The world trend of democratization starting from the mid of 1980s until now should be understood from the link between global mass media and global public sphere. Political observers like Ted Turner to Robert Kaplan have suggested that many of the changes that led to the breakup of the Soviet Union stemmed from the rapid and uncontrolled spread of information, news, sports, and entertainment across political borders. The Soviet Union spent two decades fighting in vain to control broadcasting into their country. Significantly, they sought to place limits on countries and satellite networks that would seek to beam programming across international boundaries. The Soviet Union's attempt failed and it subsequently broke up. Indeed, the power of satellite broadcasting is powerful.

Though Habermas relates public sphere to face-to face conversations and was skeptical about the influence of mass media, theorists posited suggestions as to how the public sphere was consequently being transformed into the new 'information society'. The national control of governments over the information delivered to the national population was eroded. The new ICTs allowed information to traverse borders and individuals to interact with other audiences beyond the reach of the state. Thus they accelerated and intensified a global social transformation which threatened to make national political structures redundant. Writers like Manuel Castells have notably argued that ICTs provide new opportunities, or spaces, for information to accumulate and be exchanged, not least about what governments do. He has suggested that governments will find it increasingly difficult to control interactive access to this information and thus to assert the power of the state in, or over, the public sphere. He has further suggested that this would progressively lead to a more horizontally networked society in place of current top-down forms of communication.

The power of the state would be eroded, while the individual citizen's capacity to engage directly with an un-bordered society would be exponentially increased. The capacity of the state to exert its authority over the range of information or modes of political participation available via conventional means is reduced. Consistent with assumptions about communication technologies and public sphere, it was the 2002 UNDP report that apparently established a link between communication technologies and freedom and democracy. However, it still rejects a cause–effect relationship between the two. The report concludes that the world has more democratic countries and more political participation than ever, with 140 countries holding multiparty elections. Of 147 with data, 121–with 68per cent of the world people – have some or all of the elements of formal democracy in 2000. This compares with only 54 countries, with 46per cent of the world's people, in 1980. Since then 81 countries have taken significant steps Towards democratization while 6 have regressed.

The impact of communication technologies in fostering democracy is not universal. Satellite television's potential for democratization depends on the overall socioeconomic political context in which it operates. As Noveck comments: it is not technology per se which either fosters or denigrates between communication media and participatory democratic culture. Technology exists within a framework of values and ideals both inherent to it and imposed by the external legal and institutional structures" (2001). Hence, there is no single relationship between ICTs and democracy, and it is safe to suggest that the Internet and satellite television may have different and sometimes contradicting effects on the democratization process in different socioeconomic and political contexts (Hamelink, 1999). The communication revolution has also led several authors to assume that a fragmentation of the public will be the result of a proliferation of channels in an expanding media environment. Fragmentation refers to the process whereby the same amount of audience attention is dispersed over more and more media sources. The public sphere may dissolve into a large number of subcultures and when this occurs, the common experience for all members of society disappears.

DEMOCRACY AND PUBLIC PARTICIPATION

Dewey's concept of public opinion is rooted in an intellectual tradition that can be traced back to Montesquieu. In this tradition of thought, public opinion is understood as a body of shared beliefs and attitudes that emerged within the public sphere. With the decline of absolutism in the Renaissance, there emerged an independent social sphere, dominated by neither church nor monarch, in which an educated class was able to meet, to exchange ideas, and to formulate improved, shared concepts to benefit society as a whole.

The venues for this discourse were neither churches nor the royal courts, but salons, coffee houses, and the pages of the early newspapers, which offered both a forum for ideas and a stimulus for face-to face discussion. The public itself can thus be seen as in some sense a product of the media. It was the early newspapers that provided a common body of knowledge and ideas among urban residents who were not connected by face-to-face relationships.

The participants in this discourse saw themselves as citizens, not merely giving expression to private interests, but rather participating as representatives of the larger society. Public opinion, as understood in this tradition, was the social consensus that emerged as the result of dialogue. Juergen Habermas traces the decline of the public sphere to the middle of the last century, prompted by, among other factors, the transformation of newspapers from political journals into commercial enterprises, and the development of a broader, more heterogeneous audience.

A great deal has been written about the decline of the public and the decline of community. Both issues are complex, but they are distinct. What is meant by community seems generally to be small groups "bound together by history, faith, and fellowship." The notion of a public, by contrast, is that of private individuals, who do not necessarily share a common history, faith, or fellowship, but who come together to participate in critical rational discourse about common concerns on the basis of common knowledge—a common knowledge provided by shared sources of information.

The concern with revitalizing the public sphere goes back at least to the 1920s, when John Dewey worried, in *The Public and Its Problems*, about the eclipse of the public. Recently, there has been a major upsurge of interest in revitalizing the public sphere, evidenced by such works as *The Good Society* by Robert Bellah, Richard Madsen, William Sullivan, Ann Swidler, and Steven Tipton; Benjamin Barber's *Strong Democracy*; and such civic enterprises as Harry Boyte's *Project Public Life* and Frances Moore Lappe's *Centre for Living Democracy*, as well as the writings of Jay Rosen, James Carey, Noam Chomsky, and Douglas Kellner.

Any defender of participatory democracy must address the objection that, as Benjamin Barber phrases it, "popular government carries within it the seeds of a totalitarian despotism." John Dewey's answer is, in part, that if the people cannot be trusted to take an active role in governing themselves, then it is not plausible to imagine that they can play a meaningful role as watchdogs over their leaders either. The real alternative, in this view, is not elite democracy, but oligarchy.

And, argues Dewey, "the world has suffered more from leaders and authorities than from the masses." Dewey was prepared to acknowledge that the average citizen, considered as an individual, does lack the knowledge necessary to play an effective role in governing. But for Dewey, it was not the individual in isolation who was to play an active role in self-governance; it was the individual as the member of a community and as a participant in the processes of debate and discussion who had the ability to draw on the knowledge of others and participate in the formation of a public will.

Non-etheless, our collective memory is haunted by images of masses out of control: lynchings and pogroms and the mass terrorism of a Kristallnacht. But are these really examples of publics that have become overly active, as social conservatives and political realists would argue, or masses of individuals who have become overly passive, as advocates of participatory democracy maintain? Barber argues that "thin democracy has itself nourished some of the pathologies that it has attributed to direct democracy and . . . strong democracy may offer remedies for the very diseases it has been thought to occasion."

The frenzied masses feared by democratic realists are most frequently seen in totalitarian or oligarchic societies, and their participants typically have little access to effective mechanisms of democratic participation. By contrast, the very culture of democratic participation fosters a climate of rationality, deliberation, and respect for persons. In participatory democracies, by definition, power and decision-making authority is decentralized and diffused throughout the society. The capacity for collective willformation at the smallest levels of organization is enhanced, but the capacity for the formation of a mass will is diminished.

In the past few years, the theoretical debate between democratic realists and advocates of strong or participatory democracy has been overtaken by events. There has been a devolution of power from the federal to the state and local levels, and a scaling back of our national commitment to provide, through the mechanisms of government, basic social guarantees in the areas of education, housing, welfare, and other social services.

The responsibility for addressing these needs is being shifted to communities and individuals. With a change in the political reality of who must govern and solve problems comes a change in the institutional definitions of who and what is newsworthy.

The Lippmann model of the citizen as interested spectator must be abandoned as citizens become the key players in the social drama. Some social critics, such as British sociologist John Thompson, question the viability of participatory democracy in a mass media age. The arguments raised by Thompson against the ideal of public participation have less to do with a distrust of the public than with considerations related to technology and scale. Thompson argues that "the idea of the public sphere is largely inapplicable to the circumstances of the late twentieth century," and he offers two arguments for this claim:

- The development of technical media has dramatically altered the nature of mass communications and the conditions under which it takes place, so much so that the original idea of the public sphere could not simply be reactivated on a new footing. The media of print have increasingly given way to electronically mediated forms of mass communication, and especially television, and these new media have transformed the very conditions of interaction, communication and information diffusion in modern societies.
- The second reason why the idea of the public sphere is of limited relevance today is that the idea is linked fundamentally to a notion of participatory opinion formation. The idea of the public sphere assumes that the personal opinions of individuals will become *public opinion* through, and only through participation in a free and equal debate which is open in principle to all. But this assumption, whatever relevance it may have had to eighteenth-century political life (and this may have been considerably less than Habermas suggests) is far removed from the political realities and possibilities of the twentieth century. . . . We live in a world today in which the sheer scale and complexity of decision-making processes limits the extent to which they can be organized in a participatory way. Hence the original idea of the public sphere, in so far as it is linked to the idea of participatory opinion formation, is of limited relevance today.

Neither of these objections seems fatal. If we understand the public sphere as an ideal, realized only in a very partial way even in the Enlightenment, then the prospect of even a partial realization of this ideal in our own era may seem like a partial victory worth striving for, rather than a dream impossible to achieve.

The emergence of new media makes participation more, rather than less possible. It is not face-to-face participation that matters, but rather participation in dialogue, and new technologies have broadened the possibilities for public participation.

However imperfectly realized, such new forms of media as talk radio and electronic bulletin boards offer new forums for public dialogue.

Their potential to serve the common good can only increase if civility is acknowledged as a core value for public communicators. Public access channels on cable television are as yet little used, but they too represent a space in which public dialogue can take place. Although it is true that some decision-making takes place on a scale that makes public participation difficult or impossible, that would seem to constitute an argument for, rather than against, political decentralization.

Even though some decisionmaking must take place on a regional, national, or even international scale, there is also a great deal of decision-making that takes place on a local scale and can be opened up to much greater participation.

DEMOCRACY AS CONTEXT

The Press opens the right pathway here. Democracy provides the framework for The Press's understanding of the structure and function of the news media. The press is considered "an institution of American democracy.... At the centre of this book is the question: What should a democracy expect of the press". Journalism is considered the means; "the end is democracy".

The fourth section in the book deals with the journalistic enterprise, its practice, and performance, but section one frames the issues in the larger context of representative, constitutional democracy-its vitality and ongoing redefinitions. While the standard press-government relation is examined in section three-the first amendment, regulation, and public policy.

The Press sees democracy philosophically and politically as the overriding concern. James Curran represents the flow of the argument with his chapter title, "What Democracy Requires of the Media". John Keane in coming to grips with global politics focuses on civil society rather than state institutions as he struggles with the question of whether "democracy has a chance of taking root in the emerging global order".

The intellectual strategy represented in The Press is analogous to the reorientation we need in media ethics. When we organize our teaching and research around the general morality rather than in terms of professional ethics per se, we participate in the debates over political philosophy and their implications for public communication. Ed Lambeth has demonstrated life-long leadership here on journalism and democracy since his early years as a Washington correspondent and then founding director of the Washington Reporting Programme for a decade.

His Committed Journalism puts ethics in the context of civic life. He published a research essay on "The News Media and Democracy" in the Media Studies Journal and argued in the Journal of Mass Media Ethics that moral reasoning is an essential competence for democratic journalism. Journalism's significance for democratic life was central to two book chapters also. The Missouri School of Journalism adopted a capstone course in journalism and democracy for its news majors and Lambeth designed it.

Democratic entities are not merely political and economic arrangements but moral structures. As a matter of fact, democracy is inconceivable without ordering relations. A limited set of fundamental moral commitments such as tolerance are necessary for collective survival. Sissela Bok labels them minimalist values, and they provide a basis for political dialogue and negotiation but do not call for agreement as to their source or character.

Without a broad acceptance of such common values, a viable democratic order is impossible. Without a framework broadly owned and understood, the resolution of practical issues is inconceivable.

In political philosophy we call it the common good, and the health of democratic life depends on its vitality. Aristotle's "common interest" is the basis for distinguishing constitutional governments in the people's interest from illegitimate ones on the ruler's behalf. Thomas Aquinas insists on the common good as the ultimate end of law and government. Rousseau understood the common good as the object of the general will and the end of the state, in contrast to "particular wills."

Although philosophers have differed on the precise content of the common good and how to promote it, there is a core meaning that the welfare of all citizens should be served impartially, rather than the welfare of factions or special interests.

Mass Media and the Moral Imagination argues for enlarging the moral sensibility as the arena in which the common good can be developed, and offers theological and philosophical reflections on how this expansion might be possible. Democracy will not be successful unless the common good comes into its own conceptually. Citizenship, civic discourse, community activism, and grass-roots participation are only moralistic pleading unless they are grounded in a defensible notion of the common good. The common good is the axis around which communities and politics become a democratic organism.

It is a normative principle, a fundamental concept of social morality, not just the majority results of voting or an opinion poll. Since our public life in democracy is not merely functional, but knit together by social values, the media are challenged to participate in a community's process of moral elucidation.

If societies are moral orders, the various technologies of public communication ought to stimulate the moral imagination.From this perspective, the news media are obligated to appeal to democratic citizens about human values. News ought to further a community's ongoing values clarification by helping people penetrate through the political and economic surface to the moral dynamics underneath. Rather than merely provide readers and audiences with information, the press's aim is morally literate citizens.

In the tsunami disaster, December 2004, the news included the overwhelming acts of kindness around the world, and our moral imagination was invigorated. Historical documentaries on television relive human morality during the horrifies of the Holocaust and WWII-the benefactors hiding Anne Frank in the Netherlands, and the resistance of Dietrich Bonhoeffer.

Out of the turmoil in the Middle East are the inspiring stories of Jews and Muslims working on water projects in Palestine, and teaching their children each other's religion. The great film Hotel Rwanda highlights the virtue of Paul Rusesabagina sheltering 1200 refugees, rather than raw bloodshed and human evil only. The moral dimension of the social order takes on life and inspiration.Editorials have raised our consciousness of anti-Semitism and heightened our moral awareness of racism and gender discrimination. In the debates over war and worldwide trade in military arms, the moral issues in terms of just-war theory and pacifism have emerged at various times in news and commentary.

Affirmative action, environmental protection, health, global warming, gun control, immigration policy, and welfare reform raise moral conflicts that journalists can help the public negotiate. Over time and across the media, one observes a redemptive glow on occasion in which the news and popular culture have facilitated moral discernment by their affirmation of democracy as a people's movement and their insight into humankind as a distinctive species.

Along these lines we redeem the media as an agent of democratic formation.Building on its unique capacities as a genre, we are empowered Towards moral literacy by reporters appealing to our conscience. Democratic life rests on moral principles. Communication ethics is the foundation of genuine democracy. In meeting this challenge, the media are accountable to the widely shared moral frameworks that orient the society in which they operate and give it meaning.

DEMOCRACY AND FREE PRESS IN JOURNALISM

Press in a democracy is known as the Fourth Estate meaning thereby that it is as important as other three known organs of the State *i.e.* Legislature, Executive and the Judiciary. Its main objective is to create a healthy public opinion that may preserve and strengthen the rule of law. The Press in India is however not able to discharge this function properly. There is therefore the need for full and detailed discussion of the role of Press in India. With this in view, the Central India Law institute organised a seminar on-Freedom of Press at Jabalpur on 26th January 1996. The Seminar was presided over by Hon. Justice S.M.N. Raina, Retired Judge of the High Court of M.P. Justice Gulab Gupta.

Executive Chairman of the Institute initiated the discussion on the subject, which was followed by comments, questions and explanation by the audience. Smt. Shobha Menon, Advocate Jabalpur presented here paper on "Need for Limitation on Freedom of Press" which also provoked good deal of discussion by -the audience. Shri K.P. Mishra, Advocate Jabalpur then presented his paper on "Obscenity and the Press" which was very much appreciated. It also provoked good deal of discussion. The Seminar ended with a vote of thanks by Justice S.Awasthy, Director of the Institute. The following is the summary of the main presentations in the Seminar. Justice Gulab Gupta- Obligations of the Fourth Estate Though the Press in the context of Freedom of speech and Expression may also include Radio.

Television and other similar media, the law and public morality imposes similar obligations on them and hence the word 'Press' is us in a comprehensive sense. As regards newspapers they are either national or local and all are not only controlled by business houses but also motivated by economic gains.

Referring to Hindi newspapers of M.P., it was stated that many of them publish their editions from several cities giving some national news and mostly local news. As a result these newspapers do not publish even the regional news. A newspaper in Bilaspur neither publishes news from other centres nor is read in other centres. This localization has reduced their value in our context of democratic social order. Such newspapers are termed as 'regional' only to charge higher advertisement rates.

There is therefore need to have a fresh look in the matter. Referring to Yellow Journalism, Justice Gupta said that local newspapers in particular show this tendency and the same is increasing day by day. Since sensational, morbid or offensive matter easily attract attention of readers, they are considered the basis of good earning and resorted to knowingly. If such reporting relates to law courts, they become subject to the law of contempt. Decisions of the Supreme Court in Vishwa Dev Sharma v. State of Rajasthan,' and In Re. Vinayak Chandra Sharma were cited in support of the view. Yellow Journalism according to Justice was wide enough to include not only contemptuous publication but also obscene publications and since it was against our cultural heritage and values; that deserved to be avoided.

Mrs. Shobha Menon-Need for Limitations 'Freedom' means absence of control, interference or restriction. Hence, the expression 'freedom of the Press' means the right to print and publish without any intereference from the State or any public authority. But, as will be seen presently, this freedom, like other freedoms, cannot be absolute but is subject to well-known exceptions acknowledged in the public interest, which in India are enumerated in Art. of the Constitution. Since in India, freedom of expression is guaranteed by Art. 19(1) (a) of the Constitution, and it has been held by Supreme Court that freedom of the 'press' is included in that wider guarantee, it is unnecessary to plead for the freedom of the Press in this country.

Nevertheless, the principles which lie at the background of the Press and the limitation thereto-are relevant to every legislation relating to the Press. Since its constitutionality can be challenged in India, it would be not only useful but also essential to keep before one's mind's eye the basis and historic principles on which the demand for freedom of the Press is founded. This has become particularly important in India, when the zeal for establishing a welfare and socialist State is apt to relegate all individual rights to the background, for the time being. Need for Limitations If the Press is such a useful or rather an indispensable instrument for information and exchange of views and opinions in a modern democracy, the question at once arises, why should there by any need for regulating or controlling this freedom by law.

The reason is obvious: If no guarantee of individual right can be absolute, so is the freedom of the Press-it must be reconciled with the collective interests of the society, otherwise known as the 'public interest. The need for balancing these with competing interests has been pithily expressed by the eminent English Judge, Lord Denning. "The freedom of the press is extolled as one of the great bulwarks of liberty. It is entrenched in the constitutions of the world. But it is often misunderstood. It does not mean that the press is free to ruin a reputation or to break a confidence or to pollute the course of justice or to do any thing that it is unlawful. It means that there is to be censorship. Not by lacewing system. Not by executive direction, Nor by court injunction. "It means that the press is to be free from what Blackstone calls 'previous restrain'. In short, the press is not entitled to any absolute immunity from unlawful conduct any more than any other individual.

Rights are dependent upon the existence of the State and the maintenance of order so that the rights may be ensured and enforced. Hence, no right or freedom can be allowed to be exercised in such manner as would jeopardize the very existence of the State or the maintenance of public order, or under public normality, or a fair and impartial administration of justice, which are essential for a civilized existence. Again since a pre-condition of the enforcement of individual rights is guarded, the freedom of expression cannot be so exercised as to undermine the reputation of any member of the public. When the danger to such countervailing public interest assumes a serious dimension, the State would be justified in curtailing or controlling even the freedom of the Press.

Freedom of the Press cannot, therefore, mean an uncontrolled license for or immunity to every possible use of language. Every human institution is liable to be abused and every liberty, is left unbridled, has the tendency to become a licence. It should be pointed out that when there is a conflict between the public interest behind a free press and some other competing interest arises, it is for the Courts to strike the balance between the two interests. In India, the Court's role in balancing the two competing public interests is reserved in the Constitution itself by the expression 'reasonable restriction' in C1.(2)-(6)of Art. 19.

In every civilized society whew individual rights are declared and enforced, whether by ordinary law or 13y the Constitution, the right implies a duty not to abuse that right, for, the right being guaranteed to all citizens alike, it would be hollow to others unless one individual respects the similar rights of others or transgresses the bounds of his own right, and affects the other rights of other individuals. As early as 1789, the French Declaration of the Rights of Man, which declared that "free communication of thoughts and ideas is one of the most precious rights of man", in the same breath stated that this freedom of every citizen was "subject to responsibility for abuse of this liberty in cases contemplated by law".

AVENUES OF ABUSE OF FREEDOM OF THE PRESS

The avenues of abuse of the Press in modern times, should be noticed in. brief: The foremost danger is that since the Press is a most potent instrument of mass communication, newspapers are sought to be used by powerful parties and financial groups or even individuals having vested interests, for purposes of 'propaganda', *i.e.*, to further their private interests to the detriment of the public, as a result of which the Press, instead of creating a free market of ideas, tend to become an instrument for suppression of view, and an agency of monopolistic contrail or eve news and reports.

The basic assumption that freedom of the Press is indispensable to offer to the public all points of view involved in public issues and to give a truthful account of events so that the reader may freely form his considered view on each issue is defeated if every newspaper gives a biased or coloured report of news and advocates only one of the solutions, namely, that advocated by the party or group which conducts that newspaper.

SAFEGUARDS AGAINST ABUSE OF FREEDOM OF THE PRESS

Though the likelihood of freedom of the Press to be abused is now evident in all modern countries, the remedy of this serious problem is not so easy. The reason is that it is a necessary evil since freedom of the Press is the ' Ark of the Covenant of Democracy' it cannot be dispensed with. Though it "has some disagreeable results, the wholesome ones are greater and more numerous." If that be so, the Press' cannot be suppressed nor does the remedy lie in State monopoly or nationalization of newspaper, because that would be the assumption by the State of the guardianship of the public mind a very antithesis of democracy.

The result would be the same of the State acquires complete control by a system of censorship of day-to-day regulation. That is why Pundit Jawaharlal once said-" I would rather have a completely free press with all the dangers involved in the wrong use of that freedom than a suppressed or a regulated press". The remedy against abuse of.freedom of the Press has, in fact, been provided, in India, by Art of the Constitution itself. In c1.(2) it empowered the State to impose ' reasonable restriction' in the countervailing social interests such as security of the State, public order and the like, which are enumerated in that clause. "The exercise of these freedoms, since it carries with it duties and responsibilities, may be subject to such formalities condition, restrictions or penalties as are prescribed by law and are necessary in a democratic society, in the interests of national security, territorial integrity or public safety, for the prevention of disorder or crime, for the protection of health or morals for the protection of the reputation or rights of others, for preventing the disclosure of information received in confidence or for maintaining the authority and impartiality of the judiciary". Thus, apart from the interest of security of the State, freedom of the Press may have to be controlled to protect an individual from any damage to his reputation, privacy property and the like, by irresponsible publications through the Press.

"The Press is the servant, not the master, of the citizenry and its freedom does not carry with it an unrestricted hunting license to prey on the ordinary citizen". In short, "Without a lively sense of responsibility a free press may readily become a powerful inst5ument of injustice".

Classification of the limitation In India, a journalist, a printer, publisher or proprietor of newspaper or an author has to take care that he does not violate any of the restrictions which have been imposed on the freedom of the Press by a number of Statute founded on different aspects of the need for social or public control. Some of these statutes, again, have a constitutional foundation, *e.g.* those which have been passed to enforce the grounds of restriction envisaged by cl. (2) or (6) of Art while others are general laws applicable to the public, including the Press.'

Besides statutory limitations, there are certain limitations which are founded on English common law, and are still uncodified, *e.g.*, those founded on the common law of torts, such as the civil wrongs of defamation breach of confidence, invasion of privacy and the like. Some of the limitations, again founded on reasons of State or public policy, such as 'official secrets', while others are founded on private rights, such as copyright.

EXTRA LEGAL RESTRAINTS

The need for an institution to ensure a high standard of responsibilities on the part of the Press arises from the fact that the freedom of the Press is likely to be abused by what is called 'yellow journalism', *i.e.*,. the publication of matters which debase public taste or indulge in intrusion into public lives even though such publication may not be punishable under the provisions of the existing law.

Almost every modern country has therefore set up a body which could serve as a watchdog over the standards of journalism and at the same time maintain the freedom of the Press against unwarranted government intrusion. In England, the Press Council (1953) is non-statutory body, having no legal powers.

It is composed of representatives of journalists as well as eminent men and academicians who constitute about one-third of the Council, and is headed by a non-political Chairman. In India, the Press Council is a statutory body. It was first established by the Press Council Act, 1965, on the lines recommended by the first Press Commission (1954). In the main, its functions followed the British precedent, to include:

- The preservation of the freedom of the Press.
- To maintain and improve the standards of newspaper in India
- To form a code of conduct to prevent writings which were not legally punishable but where yet 'objectionable'?

The Press Council Act, 1965 was, however repealed during Mrs. Gandhi's regime, by enacting the Press Council (Repeal) Act, 1976. The Press Council was, therefore abolished with effect from January, 1976, on the following grounds offered by the Government while bringing the Ordinance which later become the Act: The Press Council has failed to set out and enforce any code of conduct, as envisaged by the Act of 1965. It also failed to build up any respectable body of case-law because only complaints of comparatively minor importance were dealt with by the Council. After coming into power, the Janata Government enacted a fresh Press Council Act, 1978, to re-establish the Press Council, with a different composition and powers. Censorship which, when imposed by law, operates as a restriction upon the freedom of the Press, ceases to be so when it is self-imposed. In many countries, therefore, newspaper and journals have put their heads together to formulate a code of conduct or guidelines they would observe to prevent abuses of the freedom of these. In U.S.A., for instance, such guidelines have been formulated in many States, by the news media in consultation with the Bar, as to matters which should not be published to the prejudice of an accused in pending or impending trial, *e.g.* confessions, opinions on the guilt or innocence of the accused, statements as might influence the outcome of trial.

In U.K. the Press Council itself is an institution of self-censorship. Its 'adjudication' on complaints received from members of the public against the Press are thus regarded as having moral authority and have thus been developing a code of conduct of journalists. Self-censorship imposed by voluntary restraints must be distinguished from guidelines issued by a Censor, an instance of which was when in India during the 1975-76 Emergency.

Newspaper editors hardly have to be told about the importance of press freedom. Nor do they need to be lectured on the virtues of peace. But surprisingly, few editors seem to be aware of or articulate the strong connection between the two. Quite simply, a free press promotes peace; creating a universally free press would promote universal peace. The bridge between the two is democracy.

Only to academics is democracy a complex term requiring elaborate definition. To most people, correctly I argue, democracy is easily defined by certain rights: that of voting and the secret ballot, of being able to run for any political office, including the highest, and of freedom of speech. And the latter, of course, means not only the freedom to publish criticism of the government, but even to advocate revolution. Except in a time of war, censorship and democracy are not only seen as incompatible—they *are* incompatible. This is clear from a survey of governments around the world. For all countries, without exception, as shown by the latest Freedom House survey of freedom, the most democratic have the freest media; the least democratic have the least free media. Indeed, it is inconceivable that it could be otherwise. Plainly, a free press is essential to democracy, but I would put this even in stronger terms: promoting freedom of the press also promotes democracy—a way to democracy is by working to create a free press. I think that most newsmen would agree with this.

Now, on the other side of the coin, research on war and peace has shown the following results. First, democracies do not make war on each other. There has been no war and virtually no threat of violence between two countries that are democratic. The most war occurs between the least free countries. Note that there are 167 sovereign nations in the world today, 60 of them democracies. Not only has there been or is there no war between them, but there is not even the threat of war; none of these democracies arm against each other. Not one. In its long, bloody history, for example, Western Europe is finally at peace. There is not even the expectation of war among these countries. And, it is no accident that Western Europe is also totally democratic.

Second, democracies tend to have the least internal violence (riots, revolutions, guerrilla warfare, civil war); those countries with the least freedom tend to have the most. Finally, democratic governments just do not kill their own citizens for any but the most reprehensible civil crimes, such as executions for murder; the least free tend to kill their citizens by the millions for political, religious, or racial reasons. In many parts of the world, genocide and totalitarianism are almost synonymous. Consider that in this century alone, aside from foreign or domestic wars, totalitarian governments have killed in cold blood more than 115,000,000 people, over three times the number killed in battle in all wars in this century, including the two world wars.

The major perpetuators are well known; disagreement now only exists about the numbers: Hitler may have slaughtered as many as 14,000,000 people, including near 5,000,000 Jews; Stalin surely outdid him by murdering well over 20,000,000; Mao Tse-tung possibly liquidated even more; Pol Pot in Cambodia exterminated around 2,000,000 Cambodians; the Young Turks killed over 1,000,000 Armenians during World War I. And then there were the assorted butcheries in Ethiopia, Vietnam, Syria, Uganda, Rwanda, Burundi, Indonesia, East Pakistan, and elsewhere. A twentieth century, global blood bath of over 100,000,000; over 140,000,000 people when battle-deaths in foreign and domestic wars are included. But not one of these millions were killed in a war or violence between democracies; few, if any, citizen of a democracy have been killed by their own government for other than civil crimes like murder (the number of criminals executed in the whole history of the United State by federal and local authorities up to 1982 is 13,630).

It should be clear that democracies are a way to Non-violence. In fact, promoting democracy is promoting world peace. For were democracy universalized, the lesson of history and contemporary events is that international war would be eliminated, domestic violence minimized, and genocide and governmental mass murder of its citizens ended. The conclusion is now manifest. Since advancing freedom of the press furthers democracy, spreading freedom of the press promotes world peace. And the reverse logic is also true. Without democracies, there will be war; without freedom of the press, democracies cannot exist. Newsmen everywhere should realize this simple equation, then. *To foster peace, foster freedom of the press.*

The recent happenings in Tamil Nadu where six journalists were sentenced to 15 days simple imprisonment for alleged breach of privilege and contempt by the state Legislative Assembly brings back the not so pleasant memories of the Emergency. There is a saying that those who forget history are wont to repeat it. The action is condemnable as the intent of those who passed the Judgement is, itself, questionable. The threat to freedom of the press in this country or for that matter in all of Asia hangs like the proverbial sword of Damocles. In India, no political party can boast of respecting the freedom of the press. There have been numerous instances of newspaper offices being vandalised and editors and journalists being roughed up by political flunkeys for publishing articles that were critical of their leaders whose credentials were suspect, to say the least. This sorry state of affairs has increased in recent years.

Not long ago, an article published by Alex Perry, a foreign journalist, on Prime Minister Vajpayee's fitness, thereby questioning his ability to lead the nation, considerably angered the ruling party. The press is considered the watchdog of democracy. Sadly, there is scant regard for this truism in a country which is, ironically, the world's largest democracy. Self-discipline, which is so crucial for the survival of any democracy, is fast disappearing from the Indian polity. Tolerance levels are declining and arrogance is all-pervasive. More often than not political power is used to further the cause of the power-hungry rather than to serve the masses. When obedience to the enforceable is itself neglected, obedience to the unenforceable is out of the question. Even after more than five decades of Independence, democracy in India has still not matured and the quality of public life is declining alarmingly.

Today, political leaders are voted to power because of their oratory and manipulative skills and not for their wisdom and virtue. We cannot expect better governance if we continue to elect people with criminal track records and malafide intentions. Fortunately, the Indian citizen can depend on a strong judiciary, which has so often come to the rescue. The press, on its part, should bear in mind that freedom of the press does not mean a license to write anything. This freedom is precious and it has to be used judiciously. When this freedom is misused, public respect for this profession will diminish. The press has to guard against this.

There is a common understanding that democracy and press freedom are strongly connected and mutually reinforcing. Mass media fulfill an essential function in democracy as a link between the citizens and their political representatives. The information and representation function of the media is thought to be best performed if the media are free, that is to say autonomous. In all dissident movements in Eastern-Europe the demand for democracy was accompanied by the demand for a free press. In Russia, Gorbachev stressed the importance of glasnost' (not the equivalent of press freedom but a step in that direction) as a sine qua non for democratic reform.

Yeltsin affirmed that he could not conceive of a democratic society 'without the freedom of expression and the press'. And also Putin stressed the relationship: 'without a truly free media, Russian democracy will not survive'. In this paper we discuss the relationship between press freedom and democracy in post- communist Russia. Post-communist Russia represents a unique historical and socio- political setting, which does not readily allow for generalization. Nevertheless, the observations on Russia can contribute to a deeper understanding of the connection between press freedom and democracy in other contexts as well. Although widely used words, the concepts of democracy and press freedom are not uniformly defined.

Different perceptions of democracy cause different perceptions of the role of the media in democracy. In order to avoid confusion of ideas, we start by having a closer look at both concepts. The concept of democracy Press freedom and democracy are words with a highly positive emotional value. Amartya Sen (1999) has pointed out that while democracy is not yet universally practiced, nor indeed uniformly accepted, in the general climate of world opinion, democratic governance has now achieved the status of being taken to be generally right. Because of its positive emotional value the word is highly vulnerable for abuse and 'cooptation' which leads to a shift, and in the end an emptiness, of meaning.

In the Soviet Union a distinction was made between the real 'socialist democracy' and the fake 'bourgeois democracy'. The meaning of the word democracy became even more obscured by the use of the prefixes pseudo-, new-, or 'not consolidated' in combination with democracy. Post- communist Russia has been labelled all of this, due to the gap between its democratic quality and its democratization rhetoric. Other labels have been used that question the genuineness of Russian democracy even more: Russia as 'delegative democracy', 'totalitarian democracy' or 'authoritarian democracy'.

With the same half-heartedness, Olcott and Ottaway (1999) speak of 'semi-authoritarianism', Zhelev (1999) of 'a multiparty authoritarian system', Sergej Kovalev of an 'authoritarian-police regime that will preserve the formal characteristics of democracy and market economy' and the Russian commentator Mikhail Delyagin of a 'liberal dictatorship' and 'manipulative democracy'. Koshkareva and Narzhikulov (1998: 164) speak of a 'nomenklatura democracy'. Diamond (1996) calls this a characteristic of the 'third wave' of democratization: the gap between the so called electoral (formal, political) and liberal (substantial, social) democracies.

At a minimum, democracy is a political system based on free, competitive and regular elections. This 'electoral' democracy presumes space for political opposition movements and political parties that represent a significant range of voter choice and whose leaders can openly compete for and be elected to positions of power in government. The concept of 'liberal' or 'substantial' democracy extends the key element of free competition with a bunch of political and civil rights (freedom of speech, freedom of association, freedom of religion, etc.) and the notions of the rule of law, inclusive citizenship and civil society. The concept of substantial democracy cannot easily be reduced to a set of procedures and institutions but is described as 'a way of regulating power relations in such a way as to maximize the opportunities for individuals to influence the conditions in which they live, to participate in and influence debates about the key decisions that affect society'.

Democracy in this sense is not a dichotomic but continuous variable. The choice is not between democracy or no democracy but between more or less democracy, which comes down very often to 'old' and 'new' democracies. Linz and Stepan (1996) distinguish 'consolidated' and 'transitional' democracies. Consolidation is attained to when democracy became 'the only game in town', constitutionally as well as behaviourally and attitudinally. At this stage, institutions and laws alone are not sufficient anymore, and the element of political culture joins in. The concept of political culture builds largely on the book of Almond and Verba, The Civic Culture, and experiences some renaissance in the last decennia.

The idea however, that one 'culture' - one constellation of values, norms, belief systems, and attitudes - fits democracy closer than the other, is not new. Plato already pointed out that forms of government (oligarchy, democracy, tyranny, aristocracy) differ according to dispositions of men. More recently, Miller, White and Heywood (1998: 66) have expressed this as 'democracies require democrats'. The concept of political culture provides a link between the macro level of the society and the micro level of the individual. The concept of culture also suggests some continuity over time: 'neither an individual's values nor those of a society as a whole are likely to change overnight. Instead, fundamental value change takes place gradually'.

The value that has singled out as most contributive to a 'civic' or 'democratic' culture is trust, and more specifically impersonal trust, in contrast with personal trust. In the 'democratic' culture, the individual is considered an end in itself and a rational being, capable of making independent judgments and choices (eg. voting) and able to construct his own 'truth' out of widely divergent messages. 'Authoritarian culture', in contrast, places truth in the hands of a few 'wise men' whereas the common man is distrusted and considered a dependent, irrational being, a 'cog in the wheel', not capable of making independent judgments and choices.

Merrill and Lowenstein (1990: 159-160) speak of a 'democratic orientation' (with examples such as John Locke and John Milton) versus an 'elitarian orientation'. The former can be linked to individualism, pluralism and trust; the latter to collectivism, dominance (unitary truth) and distrust. Russia has traditionally been an elitist country. Tsarist Russia was characterized by a wide gap between the ruling elite and the common men. Communist Russia was, despite its claims to be egalitarian, very elitist oriented. Lenin stressed the role of the Communist Party as a vanguard party.

Hence, the mass lacked class consciousness and organization and had need of the guidance of the Party. According to Kropotkin, Lenin's attitude was dictated by a fundamental distrust in mankind (cited in Krug, 1990: 106). The American journalist Robert Kaiser (1976: 22) has stated it very crude when he wrote: 'The Soviet system is built on the assumption that the citizenry cannot be trusted'. The sharp dichotomy between the Party and the people outlived Lenin. Pavao Novosel speaks of a division of the Soviet society in 'first and second class citizens', formalized through the nomenklatura system. Postcommunist Russia is characterized by a more diversified social stratification but the contrast between the 'elite' (oligarchs and rulers) and 'the people' remains.

The distinction is expressed more frequently than before in terms of money and standard of living, but remains present in the mentality of the Russians as well. Also Zhelev (1996: 7) sees this as a constant between the past and the present: 'the sense that 'we, the people' are of no consequence' and the tension between 'us' and 'them'. Truth has traditionally been unitary in Russia and so was the community, as words like sobornost' (a kind of mystic unity.) testify to. In the Marxist interpretation too there was only one right position. Opposition and diversity were considered falsehood and therefore deserved no hearing. William Zimmerman (1995: 631) has called this 'synoptic thinking': 'the view that there is only one correct philosophy'.

This view is diametrically opposed to the pluralistic view of truth and the parliamentarian model that 'by contrast is based on the assumption that the existence of groups or factions that express and defend particular interests in a representative institution is not only natural but its sole justification'.

THE CONCEPT OF PRESS FREEDOM

A free press is a cornerstone of (liberal) democracy. It is essential for holding government accountable, and for citizens to get informed, to communicate their wishes, to participate in the political decisionmaking. In principle, and on the analogy of democracy, press freedom has been accepted worldwide as the norm. The Soviet mass media enjoyed, in contrast with 'bourgeois' mass media and on the analogy of 'real democracy', 'real freedom'. Hence, media were freed from the obligation to be profitable: 'Freedom of the press was equated with freedom from private ownership: being freed from the profit motive, the media were free to do their duties as instruments of the state and the Party'. The communist model embraced the notion of the so called 'positive freedom', namely the freedom to, whereas in the liberal view, common in the West, the concept of 'negative freedom' or freedom from, prevailed: freedom from external goals (eg. building of a communist society, class homogenization) and external control and pressures (eg. government, parties, industry).

A free press, in other words, is an autonomous press: free to determine its own tasks and policies. In line with this view of freedom, 'traditional free press theory lacks a prescriptive character. It does not in its simple and most basic form say anything of what the press ought to do'. Media autonomy, or independence, implies that the media are clearly separated from state and political institutions and free from/of inhibiting forms of economic, political or other dependency. Karol Jakubowicz (2000) distinguishes three levels of media independence:

- External independence of media organizations, that is freedom to establish and operate media outlets without legal, political, or administrative interference or restraint.
- Internal independence of editorial staff, that is editorial autonomy, respected by owners, publishers and managers.
- Personal/professional independence of media practitioners, both management and journalists, which implies their impartiality and detachment from social, political and economic interests in their performance of journalistic duties and a sense of high professionalism and dedication to journalistic ethics.

Whereas laws, codes and institutions can contribute a lot to the first two levels of independence (media institutions and editorial staff) – one could speak of a 'formal press freedom' in accordance with the notion of 'formal democracy' – the third level, that is the individual level, is situated more on the field of (political) culture (*i.e.* attitudes, norms, values). And whereas the first two levels can be possibly realized without the third, absence of the third level on the other hand makes external and internal independence to a large degree meaningless. In other words: as democracy, press freedom is not considered a dichotomic but a continuous variable. The choice is not between press freedom or no press freedom but between more or less press freedom. In every country and every system one can distinguish factors that spur press freedom on the one hand and factors that curtail press freedom on the other hand.

The American organization Freedom House (2002) concentrates on the external factors that endanger press autonomy as the most measurable criteria: laws, regulations and administrative decisions that influence media content, political pressures and controls on media content, economic influences over media content and repressive actions (censorship, physical violence, arrests, killing of journalists). On the basis of these criteria Russia enjoys a 'partial press freedom'. Very often the issue of 'press freedom' is linked to the issue of 'press responsibility' or 'social responsibility'.

Together with Freedom House (2002) we want to stress the demand for 'freedom' above the demand for responsibility. Hence, the issue of 'press responsibility' often is voiced to defend governmental control of the press. It is linked more with the concept of 'positive freedom' than with the concept of freedom as such ('negative freedom'). Another frequently made association is that of press freedom with 'freedom of information' and the 'right to know'. This aspect is crucial indeed and complementary to press freedom as it relates to the perspective of the citizen. We'll come back to it later.

THE PARADOX OF DEMOCRACY AND PRESS FREEDOM: THE POLITICIAN'S SIDE

The process of democratization in Russia paradoxically became a justification to curtail press freedom and to keep the media instrumentalized. The instrumental use of the mass media in postcommunist Russia is a continuation of the communist past. Although the external (societal) goal has changed from the building of the communist society into support for the democratic society, the mobilization of the mass media as a means to a goal remained unchanged. Gorbachev considered the mass media main instruments in promoting his politics of glasnost and gaining support for his reforms. As before, mass media mobilized people for the ideology of socialism but now in a more dynamic way. Yassen Zassoursky, dean of the Faculty of Journalism of the Moscow State University, has labelled the media model in the glasnost era (1985-1991) successively the 'glasnost-model' and the 'instrumental model'.

The first label (glasnost- model) points out an element of change, namely the break with the previous 'administrative-bureaucratic model'. Also in this model, however, Zassoursky points at the instrumental use of the mass media. In the name he later used (instrumental model), this aspect of continuity is brought to the forefront. The first Yeltsin-years received from Zassoursky the label of 'fourth power model'. The expectations, however, were pitched too high, and from 1995-'96 onward this label was changed in for that of 'authoritarian-corporate model'. It seems that the press could not meet the requirements for being called an independent 'Fourth Power'. 'Whatever good or bad happened to the Russian media in the 90s was directly tied to Yeltsin's views and acts in the information sphere', states media law specialist Andrei Richter. Yeltsin presented himself as the self-constituted personal guarantor of democracy and press freedom. While it is obvious that Yeltsin 'allowed' more freedom than any of his predecessors, he never questioned his presumed right to allow such freedom. And in exchange he expected loyal support from the mass media for his policy.

Yeltsin embodied the belief that in order to improve the democratic procedures one has to step 'beyond' these procedures. In the name of democracy he fired upon Parliament in October 1993 and banned opposition newspapers. In the name of democracy he ruled largely by decree thus ignoring a whole series of 'horizontal checks'. In times of elections - 'the lifeblood' of democracy– the mobilization of mass media reaches a peak. In the name of democracy Yeltsin blatantly expected the mass media to support and arrange his re-election as President in 1996.

The mass media were committed to an anti-communist crusade. The whole election campaign was reduced to a duel between President Yeltsin and oppositional candidate Zhuganov, between the future and the past, between democracy and communism, between press freedom and press control. The tone of the campaign was set by the sacking on 15 February 1996 of Oleg Poptsov, head of the state-owned television station RTR. The right to appoint and dismiss media functionaries are one of the most powerful means of direct influence in the media for the executive. The President appoints the chairman of the 'public' television channel ORT and the government channels RTR and Kul'tura.

The government appoints the chairmen of the central radio channels. Another way of direct control are the state organizations directly subordinated to the executive, especially the Media Ministry but also an ad hoc institution such as Boris Yeltsin's 'Federal Information Centre of Russia' or an institution with no direct authority over the media such as the Security Council. The possibilities for indirect control are even greater. There is the reliance of many media outlets on economic sponsorship, either through state subsidies or by businesses, either open or secret. There is the use of courts as weapons deployed against journalists (esp. libel and slander). There is the dependency on the Kremlin – instead of an independent agency – for the issuance and revoking of broadcast and publishing licenses.

There is the dependency on state facilities such as printing houses, transmission facilities, and distribution systems. There is the accreditation of journalists and the unequal access to information. There is the use of violence against journalists. To this we can add the legal insecurity caused by the rapid succession of decrees, government orders and procedures, and the unpredictable changes in policy and practice of, for example, tax collection (eg. massively tolerated tax-evasion, followed by repressive controls on a large scale).

The paradox of democracy and press freedom: the media's side It does not appear fair to exclusively blame the authorities for the described system. The label 'authoritarian-corporate model' implies next to the 'authoritarian' aspect (that is, the media subordinated to the authorities) also the 'corporate' aspect (that is, the cooperation and alliances). The distinction comes down to the question whether the media are 'forced' rather than 'free' partners of the authorities. The question of quilt is inappropriate. We can only observe and conclude. In the early years of the Russian Federation, marked by the conflict between President and Parliament, 'most of the Russian media appeared to adopt a strongly pro- government stance'.

A content analysis of central television Programmes in the run-up to the referendum of 25 April 1993, showed 'the obtrusive partisanship of state television'. The majority of media voluntarily opted for the new, hence democratic partiality. Their leaders approached Yeltsin on their own initiative for protection and promised loyalty (read: partiality) instead. In the presidential elections of 1996, the majority of journalists and media professionals rallied behind Yeltsin again and voluntarily agreed with the mobilization function of the media. As Shevelov, vice president of television channel ORT, stated: 'you can only refer to pressure if there is resistance. There is none.'

The journalists adhered to partisanship not only for material reasons but also out of normative considerations. Igor Malashenko, president of the private television station NTV, who joined the Yeltsin re-election campaign in April 1996 as chief media advisor, explained this logic as following: if the private media provided "unbiased, professional, and objective" campaign coverage, Zyuganov would win the election, and journalists would lose their freedom permanently. Better to become a temporary "instrument of propaganda" in the hands of the Kremlin, Malashenko argued. Partijnost' was justified for the protection of democracy and consequently for press freedom. In the name of democracy the journalists voluntarily gave up their autonomy and their freedom.

Elections in general, and the 1996 elections in particular, can be considered critical but not atypical periods. Hence, it is not possible to treat the electoral period as being distinct from the context in which media normally operate. Quite the reverse, if we may believe Brzezinski: '

A perceptive formula is easier to articulate in a moment of special stress. (..) The situation of crisis permits sharper value judgments'. In general, and apart from election context, research has shown that many Russian journalists do not reject the paternalistic character of power and therefore accept its tutelage in mass communication. The journalist considers himself, in line with the tradition, a missionary of ideas, not a neutral observer or autonomous information disseminator.

The concept adhered to is that of the active or participant journalist as described by the Hungarian writer Janos Horvat: someone who wants to influence politics and audiences according to his political beliefs. The restriction to the presentation of mere facts is even commonly regarded as a devaluation of the profession of journalist. The attitude of the individual journalists suits the media-owners who like to use the argument of press freedom to protect their own freedom and their particular interests. As the majority of media-holdings form part of larger financial-industrial groups and as money is still made through political connections, political, economic and media-interests go closely together.

Political and economic elites try to secure via the media their own positions. Oligarchs and media magnates like Boris Berezovsky and Vladimir Gusinsky are the classic examples. When the media outlets of Vladimir Gusinsky became the target of prosecution, Gusinsky immediately alarmed that press freedom and in extension even democracy was endangered. His alarm was taken over by other journalists in Russia as well as in foreign countries (the USA in the first place).

There were, however, also skeptical voices. Robert Coalson (2000) wrote in a column in The Moscow Times: 'Gusinsky has shown very little genuine concern for press freedom. Like the other oligarchs, he only appears when his own interests are directly at risk'. In the same way Sergej Markov noticed with reference to a rally on freedom of speech, organized in connection with the NTV-case: '.. all speeches by NTV stars were about NTV's freedom. Such egoism could not inspire champions of freedom of expression'. Also in line is the following reflection: 'Where were the voices of protest from this 'independent' press when Yeltsin attacked the legitimate Russian parliament with military force, when the Soviet Union became dissolved by the signatures of a few officials, when the country's resources passed into the hands of a few oligarchs, and when corruption allowed Yeltsin's chosen family and friends to suddenly acquire wealth and transfer this wealth out of the country? That 'independent' press manipulated a government that served its interests.'

'The concept of freedom of speech has become hackneyed after Gusinsky and somewhat awkward to use' concludes the however not neutral General Director of Gazprom-Media, Alfred Kokh (2001: 20) and the public? As Price and Krug (2000: 4) state: 'for free and independent media to 'work', the community in question must value the role that the media play'. The public however seems to accept the 'Russian interpretation' of press freedom. Or, in any case, is adapted to it. The people react to mass media information by asking themselves not 'is this true' but 'komu eto vygodno?' (to who's advantage ?). News is interpreted in function of the news source, whether 'Berezovsky's channel', 'Gusinsky's channel' or 'the government's channel', or whether Potanin's newspaper, LUKoil's newspaper or the Communist Party's newspaper. It is telling that 'independent' media in Russia are identified with 'opposition' media. Media independence is considered illusory, and partisanship the norm. Many Russians endorse the proposition that the mass media have the obligation to support 'the system'. A poll at the end of 2000, for example, shows that 34per cent of the Russians agree that the mass media have to give 'full support' to the President and that opposition is not desirable. 'In today's Russia, media freedom is not the most fashionable and popularly supported notion' declared television presentator and journalist Evgeny Kiselev in an interview with Jeremy Drukker. And Elena Androunas (1993: 35) points to the absence of 'freedom as a state of mind'.

FREEDOM OF OPINION, NOT OF INFORMATION

The result is a pluralist but not an independent (autonomous) press. Pluralist, in the sense of representation in the media system of a broad range of political expression, opinions and interests. In this sense, postcommunist Russia is hardly less pluralistic than older democracies and probably even more, as it is not hindered to the same degree by 'political correctness' or 'la pensée unique'. Peter Humphreys (1996: 312) points in his book on media policy in Western Europe at a systematic decline of pluralism in the 20st century, caused by a de-ideologization of the traditional politics and commercialization, standardization and concentration of the media.

While the Russian media system is characterized by a high degree of concentration as well, this concentration is not at all linked with depolitization: 'money in the CIS is still made through connections in the government, and in this game it helps to own newspapers and stations as instruments of political influence'. Ivan Sigal (1997) has named Russian news coverage 'a part of politics'. 'In such circumstances', says Izvestiya-journalist Sergej Agafonov, 'a free independent press is doomed, but an unfree and dependent press can flourish'. Alexei Pankin speaks of a unique result: 'a genuinely pluralistic unfree media'.

However, a pluralism that derives the right to exist from the presence of different power groups in society is an uncertain pluralism. Hence, when the different power groups join forces because they feel threatened in their positions, as was the case in the 1996 presidential elections, this pluralism dies. The greatest victim of this kind of pluralism is the (factual) information. Every newspaper and every television channel brings its own versiya of the facts. In order to get an accurate picture of what happened, one has to read daily about six newspapers and watch several television stations, claims Andrei Fadin (1997). But who does? 'What we have is not freedom of information, and this 'freedom' is not exhaustive stimulating readers to buy half a dozen newspapers, but rather discouraging them from reading anything other than gossip columns and cheap sensations, and even more importantly, from organising their own actions on the basis of information received' reacts Alexei Pankin (1997).

The skepticism of the public is illustrated by its small confidence in the media: down from 70per cent in 1990 to only 13per cent in 2000. To fulfil their information function, the media need not only to break with the view of journalism as 'politics conducted with other means'. They also are in need, more concretely, for guaranteed access to information and transparency of governance. Press freedom presumes that, though independent, the press is not shielded away from government and industry. Worldwide, a correlation is determined between press freedom and transparency, and consequently between transparency and democracy: 'Information gathering is a vital component of freedom of information.

Without access to information, journalists are engaged primarily in the presentation of opinions. And while openness in the statement of opinions is an important element of democratic society, it is not sufficient for its development and maintenance. The possibility for an informed citizenry depends on the ability of journalists to have access to sources. Without this kind of journalistic effectiveness, a society can have free and independent media, but their utility Towards advancement of democratic institution-building might be severely limited.'

A climate of open access clings to the principle of information as a universal right, adjudged to everyone on an equal basis according to laws and procedures (universalism) whereas a culture of secrecy considers information a privilege, dependent on position or connections (particularism). Laws concerning transparency include those that recognize and guarantee public access to government-controlled information and institutions, with limited exceptions for national security, protection of personal privacy, crime prevention, and other goals. Laws concerning the licensing and accredititation of journalists also relate to his question. Russia has always been characterized by a culture of secrecy rather than transparency.

Always in Russian history, information was considered a privilege not a universal right - a property of the 'elite' who could dispose of it arbitrarily. In the Soviet Union, access to news sources depended on one's hierarchical (Party) position. The privileges of the nomenklatura 'first class' citizens not only included material goods, such as high salaries, access to 'diplomatic' shops, country houses, and the like, but also enhanced access to information: from the right to see foreign movies, or to read books, declared unsuited for general distribution to the receipt of special foreign news bulletins, on a daily basis compiled by TASS and distributed on paper of different colors according to the degree of detail and the intended public.

Though the high-placed functionaries received significantly more information, they too received their information on a 'need-to-know' basis. The result of this information policy was an information deficit: information became one of the most sought after commodities in the Soviet Union. Informal networks and rumours filled the vacuum. Parallel to the official information circuit, and on the analogy of the 'black market', an unofficial information circuit (*e.g.* samizdat) was functioning. The use of personal networks and informal contacts for obtaining scarce information, services or goods is indicated in Russian by the word blat or the term ZIS (znakomstva i svyazi). In the Soviet Union, the use of informal information networks primarily had an economic function, namely the survival in an economy of scarcity.

In the transition to a free market economy, privileged access to information played a key role in the process of privatizations, which became indicated as 'insider privatizations'. Personal (particularistic) relations (*e.g.* corruption, loyalties, privileges) continue to dominate the post-communist Russian economy and politics alike. Postcommunist leaders continue to see secrecy as a method to control the information flow. The panelists that IREX brought together to discuss the media situation in Russia agreed unanimously that 'access to some publicly relevant information is not free: authorities continue to view information as their property, and want to control access.' Defence-related security topics that are not state secrets have the status of classified information.

As a result 'obtaining publicly relevant information has become an increasingly challenging and dangerous job for Russian journalists, especially in cases of investigating authorities' abuses, corruption, fraud during election campaigns, and the war in Chechnya'. Banai sums up the three most efficient processes of information gathering in Russia as 'trust, relationship and integration'. Authorities still offer privileges to some periodicals and journalists. Mikhail Gulyaev names as 'privileged media' under President Yeltsin the news agencies ITAR-TASS and Interfaks, the newspapers Kommersant' and Izvestiya, and the weekly Argumenty i Fakty.

More recent examples support the enduring culture of secrecy. The way in which the Kremlin handled the disaster with the sunken submarine Kursk in the summer of 2000 fuelled speculations that the government was trying to withhold information from the public. Media coverage of the disaster was restricted, only state-controlled television channel RTR was granted full access to the disaster scene. The dissemination of false and misleading information led to confusion and government officials provided obscure answers to justified questions. The adoption by the Security Council of the 'Doctrine of the Information Security of the Russian Federation' on September 9th, 2000 roused fear that the government intended to limit the free flow of information and conceal information from the public.

Among others, the doctrine promotes a feeling of distrust towards the foreign press whereas the unrestricted access to foreign media nowadays is guaranteed by the Russian mass media law of 27 December 1991. The Russian mass media law gives the citizens only an indirect right to information that is they have the right to efficient reception through the mass media of correct information on the activities of state organs, societal organizations and their functionaries. Mass media however have guaranteed access to government and administration information. Unlawful refusals from government or administration functionaries to communicate information requested upon are punishable by law.

In reality however, refusal of information remain a problem. Since 1993, the Glasnost Defence Foundation draws up an inventory of all infringements of the rights of journalists and mass media. The majority of violations are tied up with precisely the refusal and restriction of access to information. What's more, the number of infringements increases throughout the 90s. Very few journalists however, claim their rights before court. Again, we have to conclude that the existence of laws alone is not a sufficient condition for their implementation. Kathryn Hendley (1999) points out that the 'demand for law' lags behind the 'supply of law'.

The demand for law implies respect for the law and trust in law, or, in other words a 'juridical culture'. We started from the common understanding that presses freedom and democracy are closely associated concepts. Both concepts, however, are not unequivocally defined. Democracy implies participation of the citizens in the decision making process, at the least in the election of the government. But gradations are legion. Press freedom implies media autonomy, freedom from external goals and controls. Again, gradations are numerous. Having said that, the correlation seems to exist: in the sense that there was 'no democracy' and 'no press freedom' in the Soviet Union and only 'partial democracy' and 'partial press freedom' in post-communist Russia.

A third concept should be added, crucial to both press freedom and democracy, namely the right to know or the right to information coupled up to transparency of governance and administration. Information has to be considered a key concept in democracy and, at times, an antidote to opinion. The close integration of democracy with press freedom and in extension of politics with mass media has to be considered not only in terms of manipulation and force but also in terms of sharing a common political and information culture. Hence, the same values underly both 'cultures'.

All observations come down to the same conclusion: laws and institutions alone are not sufficient. Attitudes and values do play a role - whether named juridical culture, political culture, information culture, or culture tout court. The concept of culture suggests some communality of values: politicians, media workers and public alike share the same political culture and in extension the same information and communication culture. The concept of culture also suggests some continuity over time: not only over the communist and postcommunist period but also dating back to the time of the czars.Culture is not unchangeable, but too high expectations concerning the role of media as triggers of democracy are doomed to fail. Media and society's development go together in coherent patterns. Howie Severino raises an interesting question in his latest blog post: how can a country that supposedly enjoys so much press freedom, such as the Philippines, be so corrupt? Isn't sunshine the best disinfectant? If we are a nation of tattletales, how come many are still stealing and cheating? Howie cites data that suggest that countries with high press-freedom rankings are less corrupt.

The conventional wisdom is that a free and courageous press exposes, thus helps to eliminate, corruption. One of the exception, Howie points out, seems to be the Philippines. We all have our own theories on why this is so. I'm not about to offer mine, except to point out my disagreement with the premise of this whole democracy-equals-press-freedom thing in the context of the Philippines. Press freedom, as we all know, does not exist in a vacuum. In a truly functioning democracy, press freedom should flourish. It is a gauge of democracy's efficacy. Without genuine democracy, it would be impossible for press freedom to exist.

The key word in that last sentence is "genuine." If we define democracy by its classic meaning — that people are free to choose their leaders and chart their own political course - then it would seem that what the Philippines have is indeed a democracy. But Philippine democracy has gone through a lot of permutations ever since the Americans introduced the concept to us more than a century ago. (It was, to be sure, an alien idea, which is probably why for much of the period since then, we were merely experimenting with democracy, not quite sure what to do with it, not quite fully grasping its potential.)

We have been told, since 1986 at least, that a military coup d'etat that is subsequently backed by a throng of people rushing to Edsa is democracy in action. We were told about this again in 2001. Today, we tend to equate democracy in action with the upheavals of a mob - a well-meaning mob, sure, but a mob just the same. The bastardization of democracy continues to this day. Every election time, we are told that a few select families ruling over us for years and years is democracy in action.

An elite political family is good for us, we are told. Political dynasties in the Philippines are the antithesis of democracy and yet we are relentlessly made to accept them as part of our democratic way of life. Never mind that the evidence that elections in the Philippines are far from democratic has always been plain for all to see: the fraud, the vote buying, the violence, the manipulations, to name a few. The consequence of this bastardization, of course, is the poisoning and emasculation of our democratic institutions. This allows politicians to easily steal elections and make us all believe - through the media — that that is the work of God.

We have a Commission on Elections that has shown its capacity to be the chief agent not in upholding democracy but in subverting it. We have a judicial system that tends to favour the rich and those in power. We have an executive branch that is populated by a few select families who Harbour a sense of entitlement to the positions that they had either stole or bought. Not surprisingly, we have had a media that, through all these years, has served the cause of the elite, the rich and the powerful more than they do the common man. The Philippine press, with a few exceptions, has not changed since the end of World War II, which is to say that it remains either a weapon or a plaything by those rich or influential enough to literally buy a newspaper or a broadcast network or pay off reporters, editors and news managers.

Filipino journalists work on pittance wages, if at all, making them the most abused of professionals. As such, they are easily corrupted not just by the owners of their newspapers or stations but by those who have the money to buy them and influence how they write or present the news. Again, there are exceptions but these exceptions are not significant enough to empower the press to function properly and professionally.

Perhaps with the exception of the mosquito press during the martial-law years, the Philippine press has never quite shown us why it deserves to be called the "fourth estate," supposedly a vanguard for the people that would come to democracy's rescue if the other three estates — the executive branch, the legislative branch and the judiciary — failed. So what we have now is a democracy that is not quite the democracy that many of us may have wished for. And what we have is a media that is an outgrowth of this anomaly of democracy, a corrupted and incompetent press so weak it cannot function as the sunshine to disinfect the rot in our system.

8

Mass Communications and Journalism

META-ANALYSES OF MASS COMMUNICATION RESEARCH

Previous meta-analyses of mass communication research have focused on the following topics. Qualitative versus Quantitative Methods, The emphasis on qualitative and quantitative research in mass communication journals has interested many researchers and scholars in general. Some studies have examined changes in methodology over time. Each has found an increase in the use of quantitative research. Cooper, Potter, and Dupagne investigated the assumption that the amount of qualitative research has increased during the past decades. They studied eight journals during the 1965-1989 period. A systematic interval of three years was used to choose the sample from a population of twenty-five years. They did not find an expected increase in qualitative research. Instead, they found that qualitative research was actually more common in the late 1960s, but in the 1970s and 1980s quantitative research far exceeded it.

They argued that this finding did not mean that qualitative research was losing favour with researchers, but rather that the journals sampled might not have been ones that qualitative mass media researchers sought out, considering that many of the high circulation journals were still heavily quantitative in orientation during this time period.

Weaver, surveying trends in the field, urged more studies that combine qualitative and quantitative methods. Previous research has shown that very few such studies have been published.

In those studies that combined more than one method, the combinations tended to be quantitative. Weaver argued that there was an increase in research combining the two approaches in the 1980s. This trend was expected to continue. But subsequent studies have shown that qualitative research has not increased, at least not in high circulation communication journals. Their primary focus is still quantitative research, even though more researchers continue to attest to the larger role that qualitative research should be playing.

THEORETICAL FRAMEWORKS

Several reviews of mass communication research have focused on whether there was an explicit theoretical framework evident in the articles. Riffe and Freitag found that only a fourth of the articles employing content analysis included an explicit theoretical framework, and fewer than half of them had clearly stated hypotheses or research questions that guided the analysis. Overall, research in mass communication has been found lacking in theoretical development by this and other reviews.

MEDIUM

Print media have been the focus of many research studies. Weaver and Gray found that 56per cent of the articles between 1955 and 1974 in Journalism Quarterly dealt with print media. Electronic media or a combination of electronic and print media constituted 26per cent.

They attributed this dominance to numerous historical articles on newspapers, magazines, and books. Other studies have also demonstrated the dominance of research on print media in mass communication journals. But these results were derived from only one journal-Journalism Quarterly. Since then the journal has widened its scope, and in 1995 it changed its name to Journalism and Mass Communication Quarterly.

One might ask today whether studies of print media still dominate. Television is the medium with the highest exposure among most groups in society. It is only logical that it will receive attention in proportion to its reach in society. There are newly discovered areas in television research that have drawn increased interest. In the past, visual aspects of television have not received a great deal of attention.

Television has mostly been studied in terms of its verbal messages (for theoretical and methodological reasons), but now there is an increased interest in studying visual images and how they interact with the verbal content of television to affect the audience. The Internet does not seem to have dethroned television yet as a focus for research, although there are increasing numbers of communication studies about the Internet.

FUNDING

Mass communication research has traditionally received less frequent funding than any of the other social sciences, according to studies by Weaver and Gray, and Zhi and Swiencicki. Weaver and Gray, studying the period from 1954 to 1978, found only one-fourth of the mass communication studies reported in Journalism Quarterly and Public Opinion Quarterly acknowledged funding, while the average funding rate for journals from the three disciplines of psychology, sociology, and political science was 55per cent. Zhu and Swiencicki studied the 1983-1993 period for these two journals plus Journal of

Communication, Journal of Broadcasting and Electronic Media, Critical Studies in Mass Communication, and Communication Research. They found only 22per cent of the sampled articles reported funding compared to 56per cent in the other disciplines. In their analysis of two major journals from 1954 to 1978, Weaver and Gray found that research funding was evenly balanced among university, government, and private sources. This present study checks on this balance during the 1980s and 1990s.

METHOD

The objective of this present study is to investigate trends in published mass communication research during the decades of the 1980s and 1990s in ten major journals. We were particularly interested in the use of qualitative and quantitative methods, the presence of theoretical frameworks, the medium (or media) being studied, and acknowledgment of funding (its presence or lack of, and sources of).

SAMPLE

As mentioned earlier, many meta-analyses have focused on single journals, but generalizing from one journal to most journals in the field is questionable. Studying more than one journal allows for wider generalization. We have analysed mass communication research published in the twenty years between 1980 and 1999 in ten major mass communication journals in the United States. We have excluded book reviews, essays, and commentaries as well as articles not dealing with mass communication. "Research-in-brief" articles also were not included.

Major mass communication journals were defined as those that have a circulation of more than 1,500, employ a blind review process, and have a typical acceptance rate under 20per cent. Based on these criteria, the selection was made from The Iowa Guide. Four of these journals-Journalism and Mass Communication Quarterly, Journal of Communication, Journal of Broadcasting and Electronic Media, and Critical Studies in Mass Communication-are the official publications on mass communication research of four major professional societies.

We realise that the results of this study are influenced by the sample used. From the outset, for example, excluding "research in brief" meant that a certain line of research published in the selected journals was not included in our sample. We excluded these reports because they rarely included information on many of our key variables. The choice of "major" or "big" journals also restricts the kind of research we analysed, but we thought that studying the more general and larger circulation journals (as opposed to the more narrowly focused and smaller circulation publications) would be the most representative of mass communication research since these journals likely reach more scholars in the field than the newer journals. The fact remains that our findings can only be generalized to these journals and that different results would be likely from a wider selection of journals and publications than we analysed.

For each journal, one issue was selected randomly to represent each year. Thus there are a total of 196 issues analysed in this study. A table of random numbers was used to make the issue selection for each journal. A range was set (from 1 to 4 if the journal was quarterly, or 1 to 6 if it was bi-monthly). A random starting point was chosen, and then the researchers moved down the table taking the first number that fell within the range. Twenty numbers were selected for each journal, each representing a year. A total of 889 research articles related to mass communication published in the ten journals between January 1980 and December 1999 were included in this analysis.

CODING INSTRUMENT

Variables coded for each article included the general method of research (qualitative, quantitative, or a mix of both), the data gathering procedure (survey, content analysis, etc.), the theory behind the study (if any), the source of funding, and the time period from which data were gathered. If the method by which the results were determined involved numerical or counting procedures and statistics were used to report data, the chapter was classified as quantitative. Quantitative research included mostly content analyses, surveys, and experiments.

Qualitative research involves being closely involved with the subjects to increase depth of understanding. It does not convert what is observed into numerical form in order to perform mathematical procedures. It often includes focus groups, direct observation, in-depth interviews, and case studies, as well as legal, policy, and historical research.

If more than one data gathering procedure was used, the method was coded as a mixture of quantitative if all the methods were quantitative, a mixture of qualitative if all the methods were qualitative, or a combination of both qualitative and quantitative when both kinds of methods were used. For example, a survey in addition to in-depth interviews would be coded as a combination of qualitative and quantitative methods.

We also coded the communication medium studied. An article was classified as print if it dealt exclusively with print media (newspapers, magazines, trade journals). It was considered broadcast if it dealt with television and/or radio. When print and broadcast were both studied, the article was coded as a combination. Studies of the Internet were coded separately. Some studies that did not mention any particular medium were coded as "media in general." Finally, an "others" option included other mass media studies too infrequent to have their own categories. These included videotext, cinema, wire services, public relations, and video games, as well as non-media studies (such as studies of mass communication students or faculty).

Theory was among the most difficult variables to code. We specifically looked for any theory mentioned. When no theory was specifically mentioned, we re-examined whether any theory was strongly implied but fell short of being mentioned. When more than one theory was mentioned, the dominant one was coded. When more than one seemed dominant, the first one mentioned was coded.

Funding source options included university, government, and private. More than one funding source could be checked for a single article; the category "combination" was included to be used for this situation. The funding status and funding source were coded based on the acknowledgment made by the author(s) in the text, footnotes, or the endnotes.

Study length was coded as an interval variable. It was later receded for ease of analysis. The categories created were (1) less than three months, (2) from more than three months to one year and (3) more than one year.

DATA COLLECTION

One mass communication doctoral student did the coding. An intercoder reliability test of a sample of 26 articles using Krippendorf's alpha showed 78per cent agreement. The lowest agreement was over data gathering method (65per cent) and the highest agreement was over the theory mentioned (100per cent).

STATISTICS

Considering the exploratory nature of this study, the statistical significance level was set at.05 to minimize Type II errors (overlooking real relationships). The statistic most employed was the difference of proportions test, mainly to examine whether the changes over the decades were significant or not. These tests are usually two-tailed.

FINDINGS

Methods. It has been widely asserted and assumed that qualitative methods have re-emerged in mass communication research. This assumption is evident in U.S. mass communication Programmes where the number of courses in qualitative methodologies appears to be growing. Contrary to expectations, however, qualitative research was not given as much attention as quantitative research in the 1980s in the 8 journals studied by Cooper, Potter, and Dupagne.

They speculated that these journals might have been biased against publishing qualitative research, and that such research might have been published in other journals that were more qualitatively oriented. But their analysis included most of the leading journals with the largest circulations in the field. A reanalysis of the 1980s using our 10 journals (7 of which overlapped with those analysed by Cooper, Potter, and Dupagne), and an analysis of the 1990s, confirms their findings. The use of qualitative methods did not increase significantly during the twenty-year period we analysed. There was a slight increase of 4per cent from the early 1980s to the late1990s. Even in the 1990s, non-qualitative studies clearly dominated in the 10 mass communication journals we analysed. Incorporating 1970s data from Cooper, Potter, and Dupagne, the gap between qualitative and quantitative research seems to have increased from the 1970s to the 1980s and then leveled off in the 1990s. The use of both methods jointly in single studies has been rare, especially in the 1980s and 1990s.

Experiments ranked third, nearly doubling in frequency from the early 1980s to the late 1990s. One reason that these three methods are used the most may be related to funding, considering that studies employing quantitative methods are more likely to have received funding than those not using such methods. Increased use of experiments is consistent with the rise of the cognitive approach that uses experiments as the main method of data gathering and also with an increase in funding of experimental research.

USE OF THEORY

The use of theory was not common, even for articles using quantitative methods. Of the 889 studies only 39per cent referred to a theory (30.5per cent specifically mentioned and 8.7per cent implied). Most of these theories were cited in quantitative studies, especially surveys.

The theories most frequently mentioned were ones relating to uses and effects of media, and also that only three theories (Information Processing, Uses and Gratifications, and Media Construction of Social Reality) were cited in 10per cent or more of the studies.

MEDIUM

The traditional broadcast and print media were most likely to be studied in leading mass communication research journals during the last two decades. Studies on broadcast exceeded studies on print in both decades. The overall difference of 13.5per cent between the two areas is statistically significant.

Although we are now in the age of the Internet and the World Wide Web, this was not yet reflected in mass communication research published in major journals in the 1990s. There was a slight increase from the 1980s to almost 7per cent in the late 1990s, but overall studies about the Internet constituted only 2per cent of all the articles we analysed. Almost all of these studies appeared in the1990s, when the Internet began to be considered a mass medium.

Broadcast research exceeded print research in all the five-year intervals studied. When broadcast research increased, print research decreased, and vice versa. Looking only at the first and last time periods, it is clear that broadcast research decreased about 10per cent while print research remained at the same level. The decrease in broadcast research seemed to be due mainly to an increase in research on the Internet and other media, and non-media studies.

FUNDING

For the two decades combined, only 254 or slightly more than one-fourth (28.6per cent) of the published studies we analysed acknowledged receipt of financial support from an intramural or extramural source.

Weaver and Gray, studying funding between 1954 and 1978, found a similar pattern: only 26per cent of their studies mentioned a funding source. This funding rate is also roughly comparable to the one found by Zhu and Swiencicki who studied mass communication research funding from 1983 to 1993. Overall, 22per cent of their studies were funded. A clear trend can be detected from our data. There has been a gradual decrease over the years in frequency of funding. While 36.2per cent of all studies were funded in 1980-1984, this decreased significantly to 23.8per cent in 1995-1999.

Funding in the early 1980s for published studies was nearly evenly split between university, government, and private sources with no one source dominating, similar to Weaver and Gray's findings for the 1950s, 60s and 70s. They regarded this diversity in funding sources as healthy. But Towards the late 1980s and early 1990s, we found government funding decreased proportionally with a small rebound in the late 1990s. Private funding increased slightly in the late 1980s, but decreased notably in the 1990s, especially in the last half of the decade.University funding increased steadily during the 1980s and 1990s, becoming by far the dominant funding source in the 1990s. The dominance in university funding can be regarded as a positive development because of the freedom of inquiry usually supported by academic institutions, but as Weaver noted, the relatively low level of funding provided by universities as compared with government and private sources also restricts the kind of research that can be done.

We found no correlation between funding and the time period covered by a study. In other words, there was no significant difference in proportion of funded studies by time span of the study (less than three months, from three months to one year, or more than one year). But there was definitely a greater tendency for quantitative studies to receive funding.

DISCUSSION

This study sought to analyse and update trends in mass communication research published in ten leading journals during the past two decades, with special attention to whether the debate over approaches has resulted in changes in methods used, which media are most and least studied, how theory-guided the research is, which theories are most often relied upon, and whether funding levels and sources have changed. One notable finding is the lack of any increase in qualitative research articles in the journals sampled and the continued emphasis on the funding of quantitative studies. The reasons why qualitative research is not more prominent in major journals could be further investigated.

Is this due to the perceived orientation of these journals or to the actual orientation of these journals? In other words, is there a "bias" among the major journal editors in favour of quantitative research or do qualitative researchers not submit to these journals because of a perceived bias, page length restrictions, or other reasons? These questions could be further examined in surveys of journal editors and qualitative researchers.One of the limits of our findings is that using the article as the unit of analysis does not account for the space devoted to such articles.

Qualitative research generally requires more pages to report than does quantitative. Thus we would expect journals that carry fewer articles to publish relatively more qualitative research per issue. In the six journals with lower article frequency (they carried 12per cent of total articles analysed), both methods of research are represented equally, while in the four journals with higher article frequency (they accounted for 88per cent of the sampled articles) qualitative methods are significantly less likely to be used, confirming our expectation.

Because our sample of articles came mainly from the four journals that averaged more than three articles per issue, these articles are most likely to be shorter and thus to employ quantitative methods. These findings confirm the dominance of the quantitative social science research approach in major mass communication journals in the last two decades of the Twentieth Century. However, these generalizations can be applied only to the ten journals studied here.

Our findings may create the impression that relatively little qualitative research is conducted in the mass communication field, but it seems likely that more qualitative research is published in other more specialized (and lower circulation) journals, book chapters, monographs, and books. Our sample of journals did not include many of the journals that qualitative researchers typically read and publish in, although it did include some, such as Critical Studies in Mass Communication and Journalism and Mass Communication Monographs.

Another major finding of this analysis is the dominance of mass communication studies focused on traditional broadcast and print media, especially television, and newspapers. Will these media continue to dominate research as we enter further into the "Internet age"? So far there has been only a slight decrease in traditional media research and a slight increase in mass communication research about the Internet. Some of the reasons may be the difficulty of conducting Internet studies, the slow acceptance of the Internet as a mass medium, the failure of the Internet to replace traditional media, and its fairly limited reach. Yet more research on new media is expected in the coming years, at least more than was evident in our sample of articles. One indication of this is a recent analysis by Kim and Weaver of the index of

Communication Abstracts from 1995 through 1999. This abstracting service includes studies broadly related to communication from more than 200 journals, as well as reports and books. Kim and Weaver found that Internet-related publications increased rapidly from only ten in 1995 to 188 in 1999, an increase from 0.7per cent to 9.5per cent. In addition, some new online journals have emerged, such as Convergence and the Web Journal of Mass Communication Research, and much research about the Internet is published in such journals as Journal of Computer Mediated Communication and New Media and Society.

Theoretical development is probably the main consideration in evaluating the disciplinary status of the field. As our field grows in scope and complexity, the pressure for theoretical integration increases. It seems that scholars in the field should be developing and testing theories to explain the process and effects of mass communication. However, that was not widely evident in our sample.

Overall only 39per cent of the studies referred to any theory, and most of these references were to previously existing theories. DeFleur's analysis of the state of theory building seems to apply to our results. Most of the articles we analysed seemed to be one-shot studies without a theoretical trail. This information is not news to mass communication researchers. A 1991 survey of major scholars in the field of communication revealed that only 37per cent of them thought theoretical development of the field was either good or very good.

Funding is of central importance to any field of research. However, the data we have about funding for mass communication research is limited, as few studies have empirically investigated this issue, which almost all communication scholars must face. While mass communication has been growing in terms of more and new media channels, a larger labour force, and more colleges offering mass communication education, there has been no corresponding increase in the proportion of funded research. This study finds that overall funding for mass communication remains low; there has been a steady decline in proportions of funded research from the early 1980s to the late 1990s, at least that research published in major journals analysed in this study.

In addition, a balance between university, government, and private funding sources was no longer evident in the 1990s, when the university became the main source of funding. This has one advantage: unlike government and private sectors, the university typically does not have an agenda favoring one sort of research more than another. Thus, theoretical as well as applied research can be pursued, but university funding tends to be lower in actual dollars than that from private and government sources. The decline of government support for mass communication studies may be due to government funding agencies not recognizing mass communication as an academic discipline. Mass communication scholars have a long way to go before being fully recognized by funding sources within the government. The decline in private funding is harder to explain. The increase in university funding may imply that within the university, mass communication is becoming more accepted as a legitimate field. More systematic investigation as to the cause of the changes in funding patterns would be useful.

Contrary to Berelson's 1959 declaration that the field of mass communication research was "withering away,"51 the field has actually grown and blossomed in the five decades that have followed. This is apparent from the proliferation of communication schools, doctoral Programmes, associations and divisions in the associations, graduate student enrollment, journals, and books.

In spite of such growth, the findings of this review of mass communication research published in ten leading journals suggest considerable stability in methods, media, and funding patterns during the 1980s and 1990s, as compared with the previous two or three decades. There were some changes in methods and in the theories most and least studied, but the general picture was one of more stability than change, at least in these major journals.

It must be remembered, however, that this observation does not include the dozens of conference papers, books, book chapters, and articles in newer, less widely circulated journals. There seems to be much change already going on in the mass communication field, but not yet in the major journals of the field.

Depending on one's view of the value of continuity and change, this can be interpreted as positive or negative. It does seem likely, however, given the dramatic changes in communication media and scholarship during the past decade, that research in the major journals in mass communication will also change in the coming decade.

This study examined one issue from each of the twenty years of investigation for each of the ten journals selected. Thus while this research of mass communication research trends is one of the most ambitious so far in terms of population studied and variables examined, we are aware that the sample may be skewed in favour of quantitative research. A larger sample that includes different journals and books (and even conference research papers) would likely yield different results. We leave that formidable task to others to explore.

THE IMPORTANCE OF COMMUNICATION SCHOLARS RESEARCHING THE INTERNET

Within the discipline, a handful of articles has addressed the importance of communication scholars studying the Internet. The reasons for study as well as the ways in which the Internet should be studied are varied. For example, in 1996, the Journal of Communication devoted the majority of its winter issue to "The Net." Within this issue, in a dialogue between Newhagen and Rafaeli,

Rafeali pointed out that the development of the Internet, in part, is rooted in academe and, as such, "this alone behooves our involvement" in its study.

Beyond this statement Rafeali suggested that researchers focus on what he called the "five defining qualities of communication" on the Internet which, although somewhat abstract, included "multimedia, hypertextuality, packet switching, synchronicity, and interactivity." Newhagen argued that communication researchers must take a more active role in understanding the Internet by first understanding computer architecture, an area often left to engineers.

A bridge must be constructed between the worlds of communication and engineering so that communication researchers no longer find themselves in the position "where the engineers roll out a new technology, and we hold up numbers from 1 to 10, rating it."

Concerning the benefits of studying virtual reality, Biocca stated, "Communication researchers rarely have had the chance to observe the introduction, diffusion, and sociocultural presence of what may become the next dominant communication medium." However, he cautioned against viewing new communication technologies as a revolutionary by stating that many "new" technologies build upon, and borrow from, existing ones.

As such, researchers are likely to start out using existing theories and methods to study a new technology. He suggested focusing on questions such as the shape the medium is taking, and how the medium shapes and is shaped by the user-areas well suited to communication research. In a 1993 article, writing more broadly about humancomputer interface design, Biocca, as Newhagen was to do later in 1996, called for communication scholars to be more proactive in researching computer-mediated communication (CMC) by taking part in the design and development of new communication technologies.

Although, both of Biocca's articles were written just prior to the Internet's widespread public diffusion, his ideas, as if in anticipation of its introduction, are very applicable to the Internet and have been echoed in the later writing of Newhagen and Rafaeli.

Other communication scholars assuming the importance of studying the Internet have suggested additional approaches to its study. December argued for the need to define specific units of analysis for Internet research that would act as guideposts for researchers, helping to facilitate cross study comparisons.

These four units were defined as media space, media class, media object, and media instance. He also proposed a definition of Internet-based computer-mediated communication as that which involves information exchange that takes place on the global, cooperative collection of networks using the TCP/IP protocol suite and the client-server model for data communication.

Messages may undergo a range of time and distribution manipulations and encode a variety of media types. The resulting information content exchanged can involve a wide range of symbols people use for communication. As such, he argued that the Internet is not a single medium but is instead made up of several media. Additionally, he cautioned that researchers studying on-line services such as Prodigy or America OnLine (AOL) should be aware that they were not actually conducting Internet-based research because these access providers offer proprietary services not available on the Internet. While this caveat is technically correct, it is perhaps overly restrictive. In addition to offering proprietary services to its users, on-line vendors such as AOL also function as Internet Service Providers (ISPs), allowing for communications to be exchanged via the global network.

In contrast to December, Morris and Ogan viewed the Internet as a single flexible mass medium capable of the synchronous and asynchronous transmission of text, audio, and video communication. They argued that the Internet provides the opportunity for communication researchers to rethink rather than abandon traditional views on mass media and to adopt a more flexible perspective on communication models. Additionally, they suggested that researchers study the Internet using a variety of existing frameworks, such as network analysis, and theories, such as social presence.

In summary, these scholars essentially argue that communication in relation to other disciplines should be a leader, if not the leader, in researching the Internet because it is a communication phenomenon. Communication scholars need to be proactive and creative in their research designs in order to reach this goal. To do this, they must possess a thorough understanding of how the technology works by taking an active role in the design and evaluation of future Internet applications.

RATIONALE

Knowledge of the extent to which Internet-related topics have been addressed and what methods of inquiry have been applied can assist communication researchers in placing their work within a broader range of studies. This information also identifies over- and under-emphasized topics and methods. Lastly, knowledge of the degree to which the Internet is represented within a discipline can provide researchers with a sense of the area's development and relative importance to the field as a whole.

It is not uncommon for communication researchers to analyse articles within an individual journal or a range of journals in order to assess the status of the discipline as a whole with respect to a particular issue. Examples of these studies include analyzing the frequency with which qualitative research is published, investigating the content and quality of published content analyses, and assessing the status of published mass communication articles by women across eight journals. Continuing this type of inquiry, this study examines the publication history of Internet research among five leading journals in the field.

JOURNAL SELECTION CRITERIA

While acknowledging the presence of newer electronic Internet and new technology-specific publications such as Internet Research and Journal of Computer-Mediated Communication, this study purposely focuses on mainstream, established communication journals. The reasons for this emphasis are threefold. First, and most obvious, the Internet is a channel for communication and as such it falls within the realm for study by communication researchers and, in turn, publication in our leading, established communication journals.

Second, established journals-those in existence for a period of decades-have the distinct advantage of having built both a reputation and a following over time. These journals are widely read within the discipline, contributing to scholars' perceptions of and currency with changes in the field. A third reason, closely related to the second, is that established journals can be viewed as historical records that document the field's evolution. Ideally, these journals reflect trends in the development of a discipline and the segments of society with which it deals as accurately as possible for the benefit of current and future scholars.

Selection of the five journals examined in this study employed two criteria: previous research identifying leading journals in the field and the reputation of Social Sciences Abstracts as a valid resource for communication research. In a content analysis of women's published research in mass communication, Dupagne, Potter, and Cooper identified eight leading communication journals, defined according to high circulation counts and low acceptance rates.

The journals identified in their study included: Communication Monographs, Communication Research, Critical Studies in Mass Communication, Human Communication Research, Journal of Broadcasting and Electronic Media, Journal of Communication, Journalism Quarterly, and Quarterly Journal of Speech. These journals functioned as a starting point for this study; however, application of the second criterion, communication research indexed in Social Sciences Abstracts, resulted in the omission of four titles from the original list.

The decision to further limit the journals examined was based on a twofold rationale. First, electronic databases are increasingly used by scholars to conduct literature searches because of their ease of use and convenience in comparison to print indexes. Within the vast realm of electronic indexes available for searching, Social Sciences Abstracts is a widely used leading index published by the highly reputable indexing service, H. W. Wilson Company. Second, subject-specific indexes, such as Social Sciences Abstracts, are typically more useful to and more likely to be used by scholars than general indexes, such as Expanded Academic Index, because they cover indexed journals in more detail, are more likely to index all articles in a journal rather than a chosen few, and they provide longer, more detailed abstracts. By restricting the focus to leading communication journals indexed in Social Sciences Abstracts, this study attempts to take into consideration a broader view concerning how scholars in other disciplines might perceive the role of our discipline in the area of Internet research based on the presence of communication journal articles contained in the index. With the application of this second criterion, the final list of journals examined in this study include: Communication Research, Human Communication Research, Journal of Broadcasting and Electronic Media, Journal of Communication, and Journalism and Mass Communication Quarterly.

MEASURES

This study uses December's definition of Internet-based communication but with a slightly more liberal view on what constituted Internet-based communication. An article was considered Internetbased if it focused on computer-mediated communication technologies requiring access to an ISP, including services such as AOL or Prodigy, or closely simulated an Internet-based communication environment (*e.g.*, intranets, e-mail exchange between AOL members). This definition broadly included the Internet in general, intranets, World Wide Web (WWW), e-mail, mailing lists, bulletin boards, newsgroups, chat, virtual reality games such as multi-user domains (MUDs), and video/audio/ text computer conferencing. From the interfaces specified above, it can be seen that in most instances Internet access was necessary for communication to occur.

As with any area of research, certain information is useful in providing scholars with an overall sense of an area's progress or current status. For the purpose of this study, the concept of current status is operationalized into nine measures-author name, authorship, author rank, affiliation, topic, interface, method, total number of Internet-based articles per issue, and total number of research articles per issue. Identification of an area's primary researchers provides scholars with a sense of which perspectives may be dominant in an area of study.

While quantity of publication by an author does not necessarily equate with quality of research, it can provide scholars, especially those new to an area, with a starting point in the literature. The same can be said for the order of authorship on an article. Distinguishing between primary and secondary authors can indicate, but not necessarily guarantee, which researchers are initiating studies, taking primary responsibility for the studies, and acting as primary contacts or "experts" in an area. Knowledge of which universities or organizations are conducting research in a particular area is beneficial for those interested in matters such as networking, educational, and employment opportunities. The rank (*e.g.*, faculty, staff, student) of an author provides information on the diversity or homogeneity of the contributors to an area of research.

RESEARCH QUESTIONS

This study attempts to answer two basic questions. First, what is the frequency and pattern, if any, of published Internet-based research articles in five of the leading communication journals? Second, what do the contents of these articles reveal about the status of Internet research within and outside of the communication discipline?

THE INTERNET AS A MASS MEDIUM

As of November 2000, the number of Internet users worldwide was estimated to total more than 407 million, up 242 million from January of that same year. CommerceNet projections estimate 490 million users by the end of 2002 and 765 million users by year-end 2005, which may be conservative estimates, considering it projected only 349 million users by the end of year 2000. Because of this rapid growth, the Internet provides an increasing opportunity to not only reach large numbers of people, but also the potential to mobilize immediate responses from those people regarding their needs and wants.

Such Internet availability has become a concern for government and corporate agencies alike, primarily because the rift between those with access to the Internet and those without has been growing as rapidly as the Internet itself. A number of corporations' have been leading efforts to help narrow this gap through special funding and grants used to provide computer and Internet access to low-income neighborhoods and minority populations. In addition, for fiscal year 2000 the Clinton administration sought $65 million in funding for community Internet centers. That figure is a $55 million increase from the previous year's budget request.

In light of these efforts, the Internet is evolving into a medium with the potential to engage a large segment of the general public in ways that were not possible in the past. Like mass media, the Internet has the capacity and the resources to send a tremendous amount of information to large numbers of receivers simultaneously; however, unlike traditional mass communication, it often gives the receiver the ability to respond immediately and directly to the information's source (or alleged source), as well as discuss the information with many other receivers, offering the opportunity to be both receiver and sender concurrently. In continuing efforts Towards development and accessibility, the Internet has the potential to eventually become the first global interactive mass medium.

INTERACTIVITY AND THE INTERNET

The potential for interactivity has been among the more heavily discussed characteristics of the Internet. It is important to avoid making the assumption, however, that the Internet is synonymous with interactivity. Studies of on-line journalism and business web sites have indicated that despite the interactive capabilities of the Internet, designers do not often implement interactive designs into their web sites.

Rafaeli and Sudweeks acknowledge that interactivity is not necessarily a characteristic of the Internet since definitions of interactivity are contingent upon the context to which they are applied. For the purposes of interpersonal communication, they define interactivity as the extent to which a set of messages are related to one another in a specific sequence, particularly regarding the relationship that later messages have to earlier ones.

In the context of commerce, it can be seen as a varying combination of content and communication that creates a powerful consumer encounter, as well as a person-to-person or personto-technology exchange of information designed to influence the behaviour or knowledge of at least one person. In many cases these definitions are subject to individual interpretation, however, limiting their applicability to varying contexts.

Heeter suggests that a range of meanings has emerged in the study of interactivity as it has evolved into a multidimensional concept. She examined a range of areas that covered many of the different ways in which the term interactivity is employed. Her dimension effort users must exert is considered one of two general categories of interactivity identified in this study. This dimension is defined as "the amount of effort a user of a media system must exert to access information."

In his mathematical definition of interactivity, Paisley identified a spectrum along which interactivity varies between the user of the system and the system itself. At one end users simply observe or read the information that is supplied to them by a media system. At the other, the users deliberate and choose what they access by sending messages to the system. The increase in the requirement of such effort is indicative of increased interactivity. Three of the seven dimensions of interactivity that are measured in this study fall within this category: complexity of choice, ease of adding information, and facilitation of interpersonal communication.

COMPLEXITY OF CHOICE

Indicated by the incorporation of various topics such as current events, advertisements, or entertainment, complexity concerns the extent to which an audience is exposed to a variety of choices. As an audience is provided with more choices, the level of interaction that is required in order for a viewer to make a choice increases.

EASE OF ADDING INFORMATION

The extent to which users can actually influence information content through interaction with a medium accessed by a mass audience also indicates potential for user effort. As technology has evolved, so has an increasing number of opportunities for users to become a source of information that can be communicated to a mass audience. This also increases the potential for users to expend energy interacting.

FACILITATION OF INTERPERSONAL COMMUNICATION

Although not synonymous with human face-to-face interaction, new media technology does provide the opportunity for users to send and receive messages directly, such as teleconferences, on-line discussions, instant messaging, and Internet chat rooms. Such interactivity via technology varies in its synchronicity, however. In some situations, messages are sent, received, and responded to at different points in time, or in an asynchronous manner. Synchronous interaction, on the other hand, involves immediate, concurrent participation. Both, however, potentially increase the attention and effort users must give to a medium during periods of interaction.

Although the opportunity for interactivity on the Internet is certainly available, whether that opportunity is utilized is also determined by the designer of the web site, not solely its visitors. The second general category of interactivity, effort producers must exert, will identify four dimensions in which web producers strive to decrease the effort required of the user, yet must devote an increased amount of attention to design and interaction with the users of the site in order for interactivity to take place.

For example, efforts to increase the navigability of a site may result in a reduction in effort exerted by the user. Less effort in this case would not necessarily indicate a lower level of interactivity, but rather an increase in the web site producer's share of the effort expended. Dimensions in this category include: monitoring information use, responsiveness to users, facilitation of site navigation, and immediacy of information.

Monitoring Information Use" is the extent to which a media system can monitor its use. On the Internet, the use of cookies and on-line user surveys provide examples of attempts to trace audience usage patterns of the World Wide Web. The use of such design considerations requires increased effort on the part of the web producers if they wish to effectively analyse, interpret, and utilize the data that is gathered.

RESPONSIVENESS TO USERS

This dimension is based on Rafaeli's19 concept of how "actively responsive" a medium is to its users. Active response refers to the degree to which communication between a media system and its users can resemble the highly sophisticated processes of human interaction.

Rafaeli positions this level of sophistication at the far end of a continuum of communication involving varying degrees of speaking and listening. A declarative, one-way model lies at one end of the spectrum, while a reactive two-way model lies at the other end. Interactivity also exists on different levels, including non-interactive, quasi-interactive, and fully interactive. For example, it takes little effort for a web designer to place an e-mail link on a site's home page to allow for one-way messaging; however, actually responding to users who contact the site's organization through that link can require much more time and effort. To respond in a timely manner requires more still, particularly for a site with many users.

Facilitation of Site Navigation

In the context of the World Wide Web, menu bars, search engines, and site maps all contribute to the clarity of a web site's structure and design. The use of such design approaches often means that making a site navigable for users takes increased effort and expertise on the part of the web designer.

Immediacy of Information

Massey and Levy2 added the dimension immediacy of information to Heeter's conceptualization of interactivity. This dimension indicates the amount of effort the web site producer has put forth in keeping the page current, in addition to saving the user effort spent trying to establish how current the information is.

This could be one of several ways to amend and organize the conceptualization of Internet interactivity provided by Heeter and interpreted by Massey and Levy. New media technologies, however, will continue to call for perpetual redefinition and interpretation of this concept. As models of interactivity continue to undergo evaluation through theoretical examination, so must the contexts to which they are applied.

THE INTERNET AND DISASTER COMMUNICATION

Voluntary disaster organizations perform any number of services to assist survivors with disaster response, providing food, water, shelter, counseling, advocacy, clean-up, education, training, repair, reconstruction, and consultation for community organizations. However, these organizations have now begun using the Internet in order to relay large volumes of information more effectively. For example, the National Organizations Active in Disasters includes a link that leads to more than 400 other natural disaster resources. As these fields of communication have progressed, attention has begun to shift from "what" the Internet can be used for to "how" it can be used as an interactive medium.

Having been described as a "lifesaver" in the flooding of Grand Forks, North Dakota, during the spring of 1996, Northscape News, the web version of the Grand Forks Herald, provided e-mail through which disaster victims could contact each other, bulletin boards for messages, and online video clips of damaged areas. Within a span of three weeks, site traffic skyrocketed from 4,000 to more than 75,000 page views a day.

This is but one indication of the powerful reach the Internet can have in disaster situations. To assist in flood mitigation efforts after a heavy rainfall in February of 2000, Palo Alto, California's city web site was used to provide frequent updates about rising creek levels.

In May of that same year, the Red Cross raised $340,000 in donations for disaster relief and other humanitarian services in its first national "virtual auction," believed to be the most successful Web charity auction to date. U.S. relatives of India's massive earthquake in January of 2001 used the Internet to follow updates and developments in their home country, as well as to search photographs posted on the Internet for familiar scenes.

RESEARCH QUESTIONS

Trends in disaster communication, coupled with the alleged potential for interactivity that is so prevalent on the World Wide Web, may lead one to expect that disaster communication on the Internet provides a predominantly interactive approach of communication among disaster victims, experts, volunteers, and agencies.

UNIT OF ANALYSIS

Disaster relief organization home pages, as well as charity organizations' disaster relief front doors were chosen" as the unit of analysis for this study.

A home page serves as the front door to a web site, is usually the default page for the organization, and serves as the common link among all inner web pages. Most web site visitors base their decisions about browsing further into the site on the impressions they get of the home page, which often tends to offer an indication of the contents of internal pages. There is also more consistency in looking at only the home page, as the size of web sites can vary a great deal, anywhere from one to thousands of pages. Front doors are similar to home pages, serving as the front page to a sub-dimension of an organization with multiple interests.

In order for site lists to be generated at a later time, a check list was developed of minimum criteria for a web site to be considered a source of disaster relief information, adapted from criteria used in a similar web analysis of family life education web sites:

- The site must have the obvious purpose of providing disaster relief information. Disaster relief information can be defined as that which pertains to the preparedness, recovery, relief, or mitigation of natural disasters. Although a site may contain other forms of disaster information (such as news coverage), it must supply basic information useful to volunteers and victims involved with some form of disaster relief.

- The site must be informative, providing facts, research, or recommendations about disaster relief, not solely links to other web sites.
- The site must emphasize one or more of the key elements of disaster relief: coverage, preparedness, recovery, relief, or mitigation, rather than coverage of the events surrounding one particular disaster.

For this study, a universe of regional, national, and international web sites accessible through search engines and other web sites was determined, and none of the sixty-four that turned up in such searches and met the above criteria was excluded.

It must be recognized, however, that less prominent sites with more localized interests could have been missed using this approach.

Therefore, this list excludes local disaster relief organizations that may have web sites that are not heavily trafficked, and therefore do not appear in web searches and are not linked to other web pages.

Units of Measure. Total interactivity score was strictly tabulated for descriptive purposes, and reflects the total of all seven dimensions of interactivity, including complexity of choice.

Although the complexity scores consist of half of the total interactivity score, it serves to describe sites' integration of all components of interactivity; therefore, a site that had a lot of content variety but none of the other six interactive design components, or vice versa, could not be considered as interactive as one that scored highly in all areas.

Effort users must exert is operationalized in three dimensions. Complexity of Choice Available is conceptualized as six content sub-dimensions: news, commercial, explanatory, agency, non-disaster, and commerce. Ease of Adding Information is conceptualized as the presence or absence of opportunities to submit information, such as electronic bulletin boards and on-line polls. Facilitation of Personal Interaction is conceptualized as the presence or absence of moderated and unmoderated chat rooms.

Effort producers must exert is operationalized in four dimensions. Responsiveness to User is divided into potential for responsiveness, based on the number of e-mail links to the agency or institution employees, and actual responsiveness to a standardized e-mail requesting information.Monitoring Information Use is conceptualized as the presence or absence of a site counter or user survey. Facilitation of site navigation is conceptualized as the presence or absence of a site map link or a search option on the home page. Immediacy of Information is conceptualized as the presence or absence of a web site publication date or "update ticker." Reliability coding of the interactivity dimensions, including all sub-dimensions of complexity of choice, was 83per cent.

COMPLEXITY OF CONTENT CHOICE AVAILABLE

The 64 disaster relief home pages scored very highly on both the "news" (mean =.94, SD =.24) and "explanatory" (mean =.97, SD =.18) sub-dimensions of complexity. There was also a moderate amount of "non-disaster" information present (mean =.56, SD =.5), as well as "agency" content (mean =.47, SD =.5).

Both "commerce" (mean =.11, SD =.32) and "commercial" (mean =.06, SD =.24) information was sparse. Of the 60 disaster relief home pages that contained news content, 82per cent contained agency information or reports; 45per cent contained international, national, or local news stories; and 12per cent contained weather-related information.

EASE OF ADDING INFORMATION

Only about 23per cent of disaster relief home pages allowed visitors to add or create content through their home pages (SD =.43). A majority of those sites used bulletin boards.

FACILITATION OF PERSONAL INTERACTION

The use of on-line chat rooms among disaster relief home pages was minuscule. Only four home pages39 provided links to chat rooms in which site visitors could meet to converse with one another.

RQ3: Extent of interactivity regarding effort producers must exert.

MONITORING INFORMATION USE

Only about 23per cent of disaster relief home pages used site counters or user surveys to monitor the visitors' access to their web site (SD =.43).

RESPONSIVENESS TO USER

Most home pages offered potential responsiveness to users (mean =.84, SD =.37); however, only 21 (33per cent) agencies responded to a request for more information, suggesting that this dimension of interactivity continues to serve more often as a function of appearance instead of opportunity for response to user input. The average response time was 17 hours and 50 minutes.

FACILITATION OF SITE NAVIGATION

Slightly under half of the disaster relief home pages contained site maps or search engines with which to assist visitors in navigating their sites (mean =.48, SD =.5).

IMMEDIACY OF INFORMATION

Slightly more than half of the 64 disaster relief home pages gave no indication of how recent the information on their web site was aside from a copyright date. Forty-eight per cent (SD =.5) of the home pages either provided an update ticker or a publication date.

RQ4: Correlations among dimensions of interactivity.

Each dimension used in the category effort users must exert, including facilitation of personal information, ease of adding information, and complexity of choice, were found to be correlated with one another.

Pearson Correlation Coefficients indicate that complexity of choice is highly correlated to ease of adding information, in addition to being correlated to facilitation of personal interaction.

Likewise, ease of adding information and facilitation of personal interaction were highly correlated. This indicates that sites with a greater variety of content were also more likely to employ the use of interactive tools such as chat rooms, bulletin boards, and polls.

Ease of adding information was also correlated to monitoring information use, indicating that pages using polls and bulletin boards could be more likely to use site counters and user surveys to monitor user activity.

In addition, complexity of choice was found to be correlated to facilitation of site navigation, indicating that site maps and search engines tend to accompany a larger variety of content.

Many dimensions of effort producers must exert, including monitoring information use, responsiveness to user, facilitation of site navigation, and immediacy of information, were also found to have correlations with one another. Monitoring information use was found to be correlated with immediacy of information, in addition to ease of adding information.

Therefore, not only may site counters and user surveys be related to the use of polls and bulletin boards, but such pages could be more likely to have the page dated as well.

Facilitation of site navigation was correlated with immediacy of information and responsiveness to user, in addition to complexity of choice.

This indicates that site maps and search engines are not only correlated with the use of e-mail addresses for contact information, but also with dated page material and variety of content.

DISCUSSION

Moderate would be the most appropriate way to describe the level of interactivity on these disaster relief home pages. The fact that roughly 84per cent of the home pages scored a 7 or below when design interactivity scores and content complexity scores are combined, and more than 30per cent scored a 4 or lower, indicates that there is still some room for increasing the level of interactivity in this area of web site development.

Although pages scored highly in news and explanatory content, all other sub-dimensions of complexity were moderate or low. The sparse presence of such tools as polls, bulletin boards, and chat rooms indicate, however, that the level of effort users must exert is often contingent upon complexity.

Site producers fared little better in their category. None of the four dimensions in effort producers must exert scored above a 50per cent, and only a quarter gave indication that there was interest in monitoring user activity on their home page.Although this may indicate a limited amount of interactivity for home page visitors, the elements used for measurement in this study only account for a tip of the iceberg when one considers the pace at which the Internet is continuing to evolve.

Software such as Flash(R) and Fireworks(R) continues to develop and contribute to the evolution of interactivity on the World Wide Web, in addition to features such as video conferencing and instant messaging that the Internet has to offer. Further, many sites now require free plug-in software, such as QuickTime(R), RealMedia(TM), or Shockwave(TM), to use video or audio clips featured on that page. Newsgroups, listservs, and other e-mail messaging systems, along with online billing, shopping, and banking, have also contributed to the breadth and depth of opportunities for interaction between individuals, discussion groups, organizations, and corporations.

Money and time constraints may require that a novice undertake the design process, which could subsequently lead to the exclusion of many design elements of which he or she does not have an understanding or awareness. Despite the opportunity for anyone to post a web page, one should not underestimate the amount of training, knowledge, and experience necessary to truly manage all of the components involved in web design.

Since the quality of interactive components was not a focus in this study, suggestions for improvement are limited to three recommendations:

- Acknowledge the im ant tat professional design can have on the utility and productivity of a web site, and perhaps appoint an individual within the organization to seek training for such endeavors, if hiring a professional web page designer is not feasible;
- Strive to more fully utilize the interactive features already in place; for example, responding to visitor e-mails in a timely and professional manner; and
- Increase the opportunities for web page interactivity with care and deliberation, and make a concerted effort to be mindful of design principles and user-friendliness when deciding which and how many interactive elements to implement into a web page or site.

It may be more beneficial to provide a greater variety of content and a more navigable site than to reformat current content in a flashy style.

LIMITATIONS

Several limitations to this study exist that must be considered. The fact that only home pages were used could provide veritable challenges to the application of this study to web sites in general. For example, a home page with a complexity score of one or two could be the doorway to vast amounts of varied information. Likewise, chat rooms and bulletin boards may be located on inner pages, which means that facilitation of personal interaction and ease of adding information scores would be higher for the site than measurements on the home page would indicate. In addition, conceptualizations used here may not be appropriate or applicable to all interactivity studies on the web.

For example, Heeter's complexity of choice was also conceptualized in a content analysis of health communication web sites. In McMillan's study, however, the number of links and presence of a search engine were used as indicators of complexity, which is vastly different from and even contrary to the conceptualization used in this study, since search engines were used here as an indication of navigability.

Furthermore, although the presence/absence coding enhances the feasibility of analyzing sixty-four web pages, it cannot adequately portray the depth or extent of each unit of measurement. For example, a site with one chat room was treated identically to one with seven. A study focused on the continued conceptualization of interactivity, coupled with a deeper look past home pages and into the interactive nature of entire web sites, is not only desirable but imperative to provide perspective for the results featured in this study.

FUTURE RESEARCH

One challenge for future research is a continued development of the conceptualization and typology of Internet interactivity. For example, complexity of choice can continue to be developed into a more consistent and applicable measure that more aptly reflects the variation of content within a fairly focused source of information, and studies could avoid employing different measurements for the same concept.

The number of bulletin boards and chat rooms within a site, along with the extent of their use, could be measured to get a richer idea about ease of adding information and facilitation of personal interaction. Follow-up e-mails could be sent to further test the actual responsiveness to user of web pages.

In addition, facilitation of site navigation could also be isolated and broadened. There are many elements besides menu bars, search engines, and site maps that contribute to the navigability of a web site, including the design of the site itself. Download options to accompany special interactive elements, the use of passwords, recent web accessibility issues and the use of frames in web page design, and e-mail update notifications for regular site visitors are all examples of navigation elements this study did not consider.Studies specific to the examination of monitoring information use could also be undertaken. For example, among the twenty-one agencies who responded to the e-mail requesting more information, nine reported using special tracking software or contractors that recorded things like search, visitor, and page traffic information.

Nine sites reportedly used only site counters, which indicate the alleged number of site visitors and provide no information about actual site visitor use. Five reported using information from e-mails, surveys, donations, and other submissions.

Two reported using no monitoring activities at all. Although this information was not acquired systematically and should not be treated as scientific data, it could lend itself to directing questions for future studies in this area.

In the application of an adapted conceptualization of Heeter's dimensions of interactivity and Massey and Levy's study of online journalism to disaster relief web sites, a more discriminate analysis of whether interactivity is becoming prevalent in online disaster communication can be provided. Although it perhaps presents as many questions as it attempts to answer, it also provides a useful framework that allows for examination of the development and utilization of the World Wide Web not only in disaster communication, but in areas such as business and health communication as well.

Analyses of how these web sites truly utilize the interactive potential of the medium, the funding and staffing constraints with which they are presented, and the economic utility of implementing interactive web page designs for nonprofit organizations are all areas in which more light needs to be shed upon the compelling, important topic of Internet interactivity.

Bibliography

Ajay Das: *Journalism : Editing and Reporting*, Omega Publication, Delhi, 2010.

Anurag Singh: *Journalism and Democracy*, Prateeksha Publications, Delhi, 2011.

Deepak Kumar: *Journalism and Information Technology*, Surendra Publications, Delhi, 2010.

Hari Mohan Agarwal: *Journalism in Practice*, Reference Press, Delhi, 2005.

Hari Mohan Aggarwal: *Journalism Administration*, Reference Press, Delhi, 2005.

J.K. Singh: *Journalism and Mass Communication*, A.P.H. Publication, Delhi, 2011.

James Glen Stovall: *Journalism : Who What When Where Why and How*, PHI Learning, Delhi, 2003.

Jaya Chakravarty: *Journalism : Concept, Approaches and Global Impact*, Sarup & Sons., Delhi, 2007.

K C Sharma: *Journalism in India : History, Growth, Development*, Regal Publication, Delhi, 2007.

Karun Shetty: *Journalism in Transition*, Pacific Publication, Delhi, 2011.

M H Syed: *Journalism : Editing and Reporting*, Anmol Publication, Delhi, 2006.

M H Syed: *Journalism : News and News Coverage*, Anmol Publication, Delhi, 2006.

M H Syed: *Journalism : Theory and Practice*, Anmol Publication, Delhi, 2006.

M H Syed: *Journalism and Information Technology*, Anmol Publication, Delhi, 2006.

Meenu: *Journalism and Mass Communication*, Murari Lal and Sons, Delhi, 2008.

Naval Prabhakar and Narendra Basu: *Journalism : Editing, Reporting and Feature Writing*, Commonwealth Publication, Delhi, 2007.

Naval Prabhakar and Narendra Basu: *Journalism and Mass Communication*, Commonwealth Publication, Delhi, 2007.

Pawan Kumar Saxena: *Journalism Ethics*, Random Publications, Delhi, 2012.

R P Yadav: *Journalism and Mass Media in Twenty First Century*, Omega Publications, Delhi, 2006.

R. Choudhary: *Journalism Ethics*, Centrum Press, Delhi, 2010.

Rahul Mudgal: *Journalism and Law*, Sarup & Sons, Delhi, 2009.

Rajesh Kumar: *Journalism and Democracy*, Sumit Enterprises, Delhi, 2011.

Rajiv Saxena: *Journalism : The Evolving Perspective*, Centrum Press, Delhi, 2010.

S N Das Gupta: *Journalism : A Digital Literacy Guide*, ALP Books, Delhi, 2009.

S N Das Gupta: *Journalism Innovation and Research*, ALP Books, Delhi, 2009.

S.K. Bansal: *Journalism and Electronic Media*, APH Publication, Delhi, 2007.

S.N. Dixit: *Journalism Development*, Pearl Books, Delhi, 2011.

Shekhar Verma: *Journalism and Mass Communication*, Sonali Publications, Delhi, 2011.

Stuart Allan: *Journalism : Critical Issues*, Rawat Publication, Delhi, 2008.

Suraj Singh: *Journalism in the New Millennium*, Centrum Press, Delhi, 2010.

T. Rajsekhar: *Journalism : Ethics and Objectives*, Sonali Publication, Delhi, 2007.

T. Rajsekhar: *Journalism Administration*, Sonali Publication, Delhi, 2008.

Tony Harcup: *Journalism : Principles and Practice*, Sage Publication, Delhi, 2009.

Index